STRATEGIC RENEWAL:

Becoming a High-Performance Organization

Michael A. Mische
University of Southern California

Prentice
Hall

Upper Saddle River, New Jersey

Mische, Michael.
 Strategic renewal: becoming a high-performance organization/by Michael A. Mische.
 p. cm.
 Includes bibliographical references and index.
 ISBN 0-13-021919-3
 1. Strategic planning. 2. Organizational change. 3. Organizational effectiveness. 4.
Industrial management. I. Title.

HD30.28.M567 2000
658.41012-dc21   99-058142

VP/Editorial Director: James C. Boyd
Acquisitions Editor: Melissa Steffens
Editorial Assistant: Samantha Steel
Assistant Editor: Jessica Sabloff
Executive Marketing Manager: Michael Campbell
Director of Production: Michael Weinstein
Production Manager: Gail Steier de Acevedo
Production Coordinator: Kelly Warsak
Permissions Coordinator: Suzanne Grappi
Media Project Manager: Michele Faranda
Manufacturing Buyer: Natacha St. Hill Moore
Senior Manufacturing and Prepress Manager: Vincent Scelta
Cover Design: Bruce Kenselaar
Cover Photo: Marty Honig/Photodisc
Full Service Composition: Carlisle Communications, Ltd.

10 9 8 7 6 5 4 3 2 1
ISBN 0-13-021919-3

To my son Michael:
Think differently and you will see the possibilities.
Act boldly and you will gain the advantage.

Contents

Preface

What makes a company great? Is there a formula or a standard model for creating a high-performance organization? What separates the high-performance companies from the also-rans? Can high-performance be acquired, or is it developed, and if acquired or developed, what are the best ways of doing so? These are some of the ageless questions that managers and leaders must always try to answer.

There is something both substantive and elusive about extraordinary business performance that transcends ordinary measurements such as financial results. Great companies such as Merck, DaimlerChrysler, Disney, Federal Express, Southwest Airlines, General Electric, Intel, Microsoft, and NEC did not become the dominant forces in business by just having good products and using slick marketing campaigns. Obviously, products and marketing are essential to success; one cannot be in business without a product or the ability to sell it. But products can be and are easily imitated by competitors. Similarly, there is nothing strategic about pricing or quality that cannot be matched and bettered by a competitor. No, the great performing companies have something more in common; they have qualities and behaviors that distinguish them from the others.

Visit any Disney theme park and you will find it to be an immaculately clean and safe place: it's the Magic Kingdom. Buy a GE product and you will find it impeccably built. Call GE for service and be prepared for a rapid response and high-quality work, the first time. The next time you are flying at 0.7 times the speed of sound at 35,000 feet on a Boeing aircraft, chances are GE made the engines or a large percentage of the componentry. Ask Federal Express where your parcel is, and they will tell you where it is, who has it, when it was delivered, and who received the package. Finally, how is it that Mercedes-Benz and BMW were able to come roaring back and put the Japanese on their heels in the luxury car market, and what did Chrysler and Harley-Davidson do that enabled them to beat the long odds of surviving?

The hunt for the secret to high performance has been on for many years. In *Built to Last,* authors James Collins and Jerry Porras construct a persuasive argument for core values. According to them, core values are pervasive prerequisites for enduring success. It is clear that they are. No high-performance organization, winning sports team, or extraordinary individual can achieve that status without conviction and dedication to a set of values along with the competencies and resources to advance them. Nichols Imparato and Oren Harai in *Jumping the Curve* argue that it is innovation that can make a company great. History proves that innovation is essential to survival. A company must be in a constant state of innovating its process and products and reinventing itself as well as its markets if it is to remain competitive.

In *Value Migration,* Adrian Slywotzky argues that it is the anticipation and recognition of where the "value" of an industry is migrating that can lead to greatness. Dr. Slywotzky is correct, but as the "Great One," NHL Hall of Fame member Wayne Gretzky is fond of saying about hockey, *"It's not where the puck has been, it is where the puck is going to be."* Foreseeing or anticipating where the value is going is fundamental to high performance. Nor does it matter how many products or SKUs a company may have or sell, or whether it has won the Baldrige or Deming Awards and is ISO certified. Those are interesting factors and, under certain conditions, prerequisites for doing certain types of transactions and business, but they are not the decisive elements of high performance and strategic dominance. A small company in a slow- or low-performing industry can be a high performer in the same significant way as, for example, a huge company such as Intel is in the fast and wild high-technology industry.

The focus of this work is on the critical aspects and qualities that great performing companies share *irrespective* of their industries. The following chapters will explore how those common qualities can be used as a basis for strategic renewal, revitalization, and high performance. In developing this work, over 40 different companies in very different industries were studied, and over 24 senior leaders and CEOs were interviewed and surveyed. In a sense, these great companies helped to define the term *high performance* and contributed to five significant conclusions about the relationship between high performance, strategy formulation, and strategic renewal:

1. The high performers share five common strategic traits and qualities, regardless of industry, age, or size. These attributes, or *strategic pillars,* include information technology, innovation, leadership, knowledge, and operational excellence and agility. If a company has integrated strategies for these five pillars, great products, profits, and market position will follow.

2. The great performers understand that enormous leverage comes from the selective integration of the five pillars of strategic renewal and high performance. All five pillars are important and are continuously cultivated by the high performers.

3. The high performers deliberately architect their strategies and organizations for leverage, high performance, and success. They strive for organizational and operational integration and collaboration with selected partners and, at times, competitors.

4. The dynamics of competing is changing at unpredictable and unprecedented rates. The high performers understand that the traditional methods of strategic planning that stress industry structural analysis are no longer as effective as they once were. Today, suppliers are partners, competitors are collaborators, customers are vocal and engaged, and employees have options.

5. The high performers recognize that size and presence are important but that the sources of competitive advantage, which have traditionally included size, industry positioning, leverage with suppliers and customers, and geographical location, have yielded to new sources driven by agility and the convergence of innovation, knowledge, and technology.

In the subsequent chapters of this book, we explore these in greater detail and also examine three major forces that are shaping the competitive arena of the future: globalization, information technology, and workforce diversification and mobility.

OPTIMIZING YOUR USE OF *STRATEGIC RENEWAL*

The objective of *Strategic Renewal* is to explore the dynamics of strategy formulation and organizational change with the goal of creating high performance and revitalizing the organization. Unlike more traditional approaches, the intent of *Strategic Renewal* is not to provide a formula for strategy or prescriptive process for strategy development. The reality is that there is nothing strategic about prescriptive frameworks or the canned strategy models that are offered by management consultants. Rather, *Strategic Renewal* presents a "point of view" and a general blueprint with deep and contemplative insights into the process and thinking of what it means to craft a strategy for high performance and strategic revitalization.

The structure and design of this book has been developed to serve as either primary or supplemental reading material in advanced elective courses on strategy, reengineering, and organizational change. *Strategic Renewal* can be used not only in the academic study of strategy, but it has practical applications in the business world in leading organizations to higher levels of performance. Additionally, it can serve as a reference manual, a general management guide, as well as a primary book on crafting strategy and organizational change for high performance. The resulting product is a book that will help leaders, researchers, and students of strategy in understanding what it takes to be a high-performing company and how to craft strategies for high performance, economic dominance, and a successful strategic change.

Strategic Renewal is written for the student and professional practitioner of strategic planning and organizational performance and change. Let's consider some of the ways that you might optimize your use of this work. Specifically:

- If you are a student or a teacher of management and strategy, you will find this work to be a different type of a textbook. The ideas and observations presented in *Strategic Renewal* are offered as an alternative and in contrast to the traditional academic thinking and approach to strategy. *Strategic Renewal* seeks to establish a broader, more complete treatment of strategy and change based on the experiences of high-performing companies. Ultimately, the emphasis is on the common characteristics of high performance as shared by different companies, irrespective of their industries. The result is a pragmatic and effective contrast designed to stimulate thought and discussion in the classroom. If you are a student of management and strategy, this work will advance and complement your understanding of strategy formulation and change.
- If you are an executive running a business or a manager aspiring to lofty positions of leadership in a business organization, you can use this book to enhance your own thinking, test your own organization, and apply its insights and lessons to elevate your organization's performance. The concepts and principles described in this text present valuable insights for interpreting market forces, assessing opportunities, forming strategic policy, and establishing a

renewal strategy for your organization. If you are responsible for a governmental service or a not-for-profit organization, you will benefit from adapting the key thoughts and concepts in this book for your own uses and constituents.

There are many other applications and uses for *Strategic Renewal.* I invite you to experiment, learn, and adapt it for use in the classroom, for formal training in private and public sectors, and for formulating innovative and effective ways of generating and sustaining high performance and strategic renewal.

Strategic Renewal includes 10 chapters, exhibits, an Acknowledgment, and References. Each chapter provides a comprehensive discussion of the subject matter, numerous quotes from business and thought leaders, case examples, extensive anecdotal matter, critical thinking and discussion questions, and a summary of key points. In this work, you will find over 40 criteria to use in assessing organizational behavior for high performance. The critical thinking and discussion questions are designed to help guide and stimulate your own thoughts and debate on these fascinating and important subjects. The Reference section contains a comprehensive bibliography with citations not only from books and periodicals but also selected URL addresses.

The challenge of understanding what it takes to be a high-performing company and to establish high performance and strategic renewal as strategic doctrines has been addressed. Companies that continually identify and understand such imperatives and how the five pillars of strategy can be used will achieve superior performance and outstanding competitive advantage; those that do not are destined to become footnotes in business cases.

Michael A. Mische
Los Angeles, California
2000

Acknowledgments

Very few things in life are singularly the result of individual effort, and so it is with *Strategic Renewal: Becoming a High-Performance Organization*. The participants in this work are wonderfully gifted and unique leaders whom I wish to thank for their contributions. Specifically to David Coulter, former CEO of Bank of America; Thomas Sidlik, EVP of DaimlerChrysler; Judy Rosener, author and educator; Jay Stark, Director of Knowledge Integration of General Motors; Susan Greenbaum, Managing Director of the Mahoney Group; Larry Olson, former CIO of the state of Pennsylvania; Ron Miskie, CEO of KTI; Warren Bennis, Distinguished Professor of Business at the University of Southern California; Gregg Schmidtetter, Director, Deloitte & Touche; Linda Chevez-Thompson, EVP of the AFL-CIO; A. Barry Patmore, retired managing partner of Andersen Consulting; Bob Guns, author and CEO of Probe Consulting; Thomas Cummings, Chair, Department of Management and Organization, University of Southern California; Robert Marshall, former CEO of Marshall-Qualtec Corporation; and Frederick Smith, CEO of Federal Express, please accept my sincere appreciation and gratitude for your time and interest. Special acknowledgment is due to the following reviewers: James L. Hall, Santa Clara University; Andy Klein, Keller Graduate School of Management; Tara Martin-Milius, University of California-Extension; and Richard L. McCline, San Francisco State University. In addition, to my good friends and colleagues, Stephen Todd Rudman, Alec Meyer, Hilliard Eure, Carl Voigt, Jack Dittrick, Samuel Lanza, and Vincent Trapani, thanks for the friendship and support. Your interest made a very challenging project enjoyable and achievable.

In developing this work, I was in a unique position to draw upon the research and energy of the University of Southern California (USC) and my faculty colleagues. The combination of USC, southern California, and the students and faculty added excitement and energy to the process. To them I say, "Fight On!" Special acknowledgment goes to two extraordinary researchers, Neil DeCarlo and Karolina Bakalarova, and my manuscript editor, Ms. Terry Routley. These three people are passionate about their work, professional, and very gifted. Thank you for all of your hard work, constant drive, and professionalism.

My wife Lynn and son Michael were great sources of inspiration to me. Their confidence and patience were exceeded only by the seemingly countless hours Lynn spent reading the draft manuscript. To my wife Lynn and son Michael, I can only express my love and infinite appreciation. Lastly, to my parents ... thank you for always believing in me.

Michael A. Mische
Los Angeles, California

CHAPTER

1

COMPETING AT THE SPEED OF LIFE

"The questions may be same, but the answers will be different."
—ALBERT EINSTEIN

INTRODUCTION

The genesis for this work dates to the late 1970s. It began with a personal journey to understand the complex relationship between organizational performance, financial results, leadership, and strategy formulation. As time progressed, the basic notions of the effort required that the research go above and beyond the obvious tactics of industry analysis, least-cost-provider themes, the quality movement of the 1980s, customer value and supply chains of the early 1990s, and academic pedagogy. Not to diminish the importance and validity of these vital tools and frameworks, but they are also the obvious ones. The real keys to great performance and competitive advantage are far more subtle and discrete.

Sitting in a reflective moment and thinking about how great companies compete and what makes them so successful, many questions come to mind, but six questions stand out as important:

1. What makes an organization great and what factors are influencing new competitive dynamics?
2. Why and how do certain companies consistently outperform their peers, the business community at large, and Wall Street's "whisper number" expectations?
3. Why is it that having great high-quality products and competitive prices no longer guarantees competitive advantage, breakthrough performance, and extraordinary financial results?
4. How did once-dominant companies such as Apple, Sears, Kellogg's, Sperry, RCA, Quaker Oats, Westinghouse, U.S. Steel (USX), Zenith, and General Motors (GM) fall from their lofty positions of industry dominance and investor infatuation?
5. What do high-performance organizations, irrespective of industry and as different as Dell, Federal Express, Charles Schwab, Southwest Airlines, the U.S. Marine Corps, and DaimlerChrysler, have in common?

6. What are the warning signals of strategic and performance decline, and can these declines be predicted and avoided?

Obviously, there are many more questions and lots of books and cases with ideas and examples, but these six seem to withstand the test of time and rigorous intellectual as well as practical examination. Theoretically, if you had the "answers" to these six questions, then you could probably formulate and execute highly successful business strategies; well, at least in theory. Thus, these are the questions that are addressed in *Strategic Renewal: Becoming a High-Performance Organization*.

Strategic Renewal began with and offers a simple and fundamentally important value proposition:

The objectives of strategy and strategic change are to create and sustain long-term high-performance and competitive and economic dominance.

This proposition entails several key aspects. First, it concentrates on the long-term time horizon that is defined and measured in years, even decades—not quarters. Second, it requires that the strategy be sustainable over the long term. Sustainability in this sense has dimensions of renewal, adaptability, and change to it. Third, it establishes an ascending trajectory that extends beyond simply doing well and beating industry benchmarks. Realization of this trajectory demands that the focus of the strategy be to create economic and competitive dominance. Competitive and economic dominance implies that, at some point, the strategy is so successful that it forces all other competitors to make adjustments in their strategies and operations or abandon the marketspace; thus, creating ever-changing entry and mobility barriers that present a perplexing challenge to rivals.

In considering the challenges confronting organizations, *Strategic Renewal* presents a direct premise:

To be a great company takes something more than just products, location, financial performance, quality, prices, and size.

Irrespective of industry dynamics and the level or strength of competition, great products and superior financial performance are the *results* of how a company operates and how well it is led. Sales growth and profitability are manifestations of how a company is managed, formulates its strategies, and utilizes its resources. More importantly, they are the end products of extraordinarily complex interactions among a number of different variables occurring within organizations and between them and their external environments on a continuous basis.

Winning the competitive battles of today is not just about competing better, or having strategies, or using continuous quality- and performance-improvement programs. It is about competing to be the best and, most importantly, competing differently.

WHERE ARE THEY NOW?

"Change is the law of life. And those who look only to the past or the present are certain to miss the future," stated President John F. Kennedy while visiting Frankfurt, Germany, in 1963. Indeed, change is the constant defining force of life, and those organizations that do not understand that change is ever-present are doomed to a secondary role in industry or society, and perhaps even extinction. Two thousand years earlier, the Chinese philosopher-general Sun-tzu noted that change was the inevitable part of the ebb and flow of human progression. For Sun-tzu, the key wasn't necessarily accepting change; such recognition was a fundamental given. Rather, it was the ability to understand and *anticipate* five essential conditions: (1) what is changing, (2) how it is changing, (3) how fast it is changing, (4) what will be the depth and breadth of change, and (5) why it is changing. Armed with this "foreknowledge," Sun-tzu believed that leaders could compete more effectively by influencing the factors driving change and the outcomes by more efficiently managing their resources for optimal performance.

The ability to anticipate change does not necessarily imply that the key to strategic leadership is to consistently predict the future. Such soothsaying is better left to others, and as Peter Drucker noted " . . . it's pointless to try to predict the future." That is because for many organizations, much of the future has already happened and they simply haven't realized it, or it is happening at such speed that it is impossible to predict. In the hunt for competitive advantage and strategic positioning, the challenge is not necessarily the ability to predict the future, but to create it. At the threshold of the new century, there are four certainties of competing:

1. The velocity at which change occurs is at the highest level that it has ever been and continues to accelerate at higher rates every day.
2. The level, scope, and breadth of change are increasingly unpredictable and more systemic, affecting more and more people, organizations and societies, and processes and technologies.
3. The classic boundaries that once demarcated industries, economies, markets, and countries are becoming increasingly blurred, porous, and transparent.
4. The historical sources of competitive advantage and methods of forming strategy that most organizations have used and rely upon have been largely neutralized or significantly mitigated by global political and economic changes, rapidly developing technologies, and changing demographics.

The well-documented statistics supporting the dynamics of the new competitive landscape and the need for strategic change are compelling. For example:

- In 1911, USX was one of the largest companies in the world. Where is it today?
- Approximately 70 percent of the largest firms in 1955 no longer existed in 1996.
- About a third of the Fortune 500 companies in 1970 no longer listed in 1983.
- Forty percent of the companies in the 1980 Fortune 500 disappeared by 1996.
- Only 3 of the top 10 companies in the world in 1972 remain in the top 10 today.
- The average life expectancy of a large industrial company is around 40 years, or the equivalent of the lifespan of Neanderthal man.

Exhibit 1.1 summarizes the movement of some of the top companies of the Fortune 500 for 1972 to 1999 based on the market rate of capitalization.

In the early 1980s, Microsoft, Compaq, Dell, and Gateway, four of the five leading computer technology companies in the world today, either didn't exist or were so small that only a few people and certainly only a handful of the industry stalwarts even noticed them. Rather, the information technology (IT) world revolved around

Company Position and Year			
1972	**1982**	**1992**	**1999**
1. IBM	IBM	Exxon	Microsoft
2. AT&T	AT&T	GE	GE
3. Kodak	Exxon	Wal-Mart	Cisco
4. GM	GE	Shell	Wal-Mart
5. Exxon	GM	Nippon	Exxon Mobil
6. Sears	Shell	Phillip Morris	Intel

Change in Relative Ranking		
	1972	**2000**
IBM	1	10
AT&T	2	20
Kodak	3	206
GM	4	80
Exxon	5	13
Sears	6	338
Microsoft	–	1

EXHIBIT 1.1 Movement among the Top 6 Companies in the World (Based on Market Capitalization)

Sources: Fortune, Business Week, Hoover's Online.

the product offerings of the Big 4: IBM, Digital Equipment Corporation (DEC), Burroughs, and Data General. These were four of the largest manufacturers in the computer business. In office automation, Wang Computers and Lanier dominated the commercial word-processing and document-management landscape in the 1970s and into the mid-1980s. Today, Intel, Microsoft, Dell, Compaq, and Gateway have all supplanted the industry stalwarts. Although only IBM remains as a significant force from the original Big 4, it is no longer the driving force in the industry. As a "first-mover" who was in that market long before Intel, SAP, Compaq, Gateway, and Dell, IBM is no longer the trendsetter, nor is it the dominator that defines the rules by which other technology companies must compete. It has become a descending power and a commodity provider of services and products competing for precious marketspace with EDS, Andersen Consulting, TSC, and several others. Although Wang and Lanier still exist, they are but skeletons of their former selves, far from being the trendsetters with established brands that they once enjoyed.

For generations, Sears and Roebuck represented the epitome of retailing in the United States. With its stores, comprehensive catalogues, sophisticated distribution systems, and captive financing capabilities (credit cards), Sears became the model for retailing taught in U.S. business schools for over 50 years. With a merchandising mix spanning the spectrum from ready-to-assemble package homes and automobiles to fashion, tools, garden tractors, and insurance, Sears was a benchmark that all other retailers emulated or envied. For a time, one could purchase through the Sears catalog all of the parts and supplies, together with the floor plans, necessary to construct a complete home. Such products were very popular in remote areas where labor was scarce and materials expensive to import. So dominant was Sears' position that its catalog was frequently used as a standard reference in researching products, determining freight and shipping costs, and establishing fair market value or prices for insurance claims and litigation cases.

Basking in its glory as the number one retailer in the world, Sears was secure and confident in its market and customer positions. But lurking in the background and beneath the radar coverage of Sears was a company named Kmart. With the advent of super-sized stores and new off-pricing formats, well-timed with the growth of Visa, American Express, and MasterCard as third-party credit card alternatives to Sears credit and financing, Kmart gradually penetrated Sears' traditional customer base. Soon, Kmart overtook Sears as the top performer in retailing. Its growth was faster, its sales per square foot higher, and its return to shareholders greater. By 1980, Kmart had sales of over $14 billion annually, and by the mid-1980s it effectively displaced Sears as America's retailing leader.

The retailing industry is marked by perpetual turmoil, a constant stream of new concepts, ever-changing formats, and endless merchandising ideas. Quietly evolving and growing in the obscurity of Bentonville, Arkansas, was yet another retailing company with a "new and different" concept. While fixating on Sears, Kmart failed to notice—or refused to acknowledge—that Sam Walton was opening stores at a rate of 7 to 1 compared to Kmart. Wal-Mart's sales per square foot were growing at a rate of 4.25 to 1.0 over Kmart. In a few years, Kmart itself was overtaken by Wal-Mart, which ultimately replaced Sears, Kmart, and J.C. Penney as the king of the retailing marketspace. By the late 1990s, Wal-Mart became the world's most successful and largest retailer. Based on 1999 market values, Wal-Mart is currently the seventh largest company in the world.

The growth of Wal-Mart has been well documented in the business press and in academic research. On its way to making retailing history, Wal-Mart essentially used a three-pronged strategy to create market dominance:

- Technology that linked point-of-sale and item-movement data at the individual item (SKU) level with merchandising and replenishment decision making and supported a hub design for product distribution and logistics.
- A store networking design that concentrated on less developed and saturated markets. Initially Wal-Mart concentrated on locating stores in rural areas and near military installations. It also employed a cooperative profit center concept that created a network of stores and stressed functioning as a unit within an area, as opposed to competing against one another as individual locations.
- Extraordinary leadership in the form and persona of Sam Walton, who expressed a vision with the passion and conviction to make the vision a reality.

In film and photography, Eastman Kodak, the owner of one of the most recognized brand names in the world, once ruled the United States as well as global markets. Today, after years of letting Japanese competitors such as Canon, Fuji, and Minolta consistently outperform them with new products and innovations, the company is fighting for its future. Caught in a heated battle with Fuji, Eastman Kodak has been forced to cut almost 17,000 employees and expects 10,000 more as it attempts to defend itself from a series of internal blunders, missed opportunities, and strategic miscalculations. Apparently, Kodak had all but forgotten about Fuji as a competitor. Relying on its reputation and perceived brand exclusivity, Kodak's leadership evidently elected not to compete with Fuji on price in the color print film segment. By doing so, Kodak literally created the opportunity for Fuji to offer itself as an economically competitive alternative to the consumer. As a result, Fuji captured substantial marketspace, giving Kodak more competition than it could handle. Unfortunately for Kodak and its shareholders, its leadership didn't look to history to assess its strategic options. There is ample precedent for this type of strategy, and it is relatively predictable, especially when Japanese companies are involved.

Strategically, Kodak's failure to neutralize Fuji represents a significant miscalculation as it caused Kodak to yield marketshare in its most important, core product offering: film. In just a few short years, Kodak's marketshare in the United States fell 26 percent from 95 percent to around 70 percent. Inevitably, this loss reduced highly coveted shelf space, customer loyalty, and the cash flows that were necessary to finance Kodak's other strategy, its foray into digital photography. But more importantly, customers discovered alternatives that were just as good and yet less expensive. As a result, Kodak has compromised its brand value and degraded its customer loyalty.

As a company, Kodak has all but bet its future on digital cameras, arguably a suspect strategy given the competitive dynamics of this marketplace and the product's value proposition to the customer. Its outgoing CEO, George Fisher, who masterminded the strategy, compared Kodak to Motorola and dismissed substantive challenges to his strategy by saying that he has "Been there, done that." Unfortunately for the shareholders of Kodak, Mr. Fisher was misguided in his strategic thinking. As a CEO, he hasn't "been there" and hasn't "done that." He was successful at Motorola, but he was also there at the right time and with the right product; when the forces of having the product and market demands converged, competition was still in its formative stages and prices were falling due to advances in technology. More importantly, the commercialization of the cellular telephone offered distinct and significant value propositions to the consumer in the form of convenience, safety, mobility, and business that is lacking in digital cameras. Collectively, these represented compelling commercial and personal reasons for consumers to adopt the technology. Undoubtedly, digital convergence is the trend and future direction for many products. However, the strategy for Kodak may be flawed and may fail in the long run unless Kodak partners with a more technology-oriented company. Watch Kodak closely—its best moments may have already occurred.

What is happening to Kodak can happen to any company. For many organizations, survival in the coming years will become more difficult, as the competitive pressures are exceedingly more intensive and complex than at any period before. This is because the strategic and operational mistakes made by an organization today carry greater ferocity and create greater consequences. They are amplified repeatedly in the press and among consumers and investors and magnified throughout an increasingly integrated network of vendors, suppliers, and business partners.

The experience of companies such as Kodak and the new dynamics of competing at the speed of life and on "Internet-time" lead us to several interesting questions about strategy and the ebb and flow of performance:

- What did Chrysler do to resurrect and catapult itself from the brink of collapse to a preeminent position of leadership?
- How did tiny Dell and Gateway grow from the obscurities of a cottage operation in a dormitory room and cornfield to outperform mighty IBM, NEC, and Toshiba as the leading PC technology providers in the world?

- How did unknown Cisco Systems outmaneuver the great AT&T to assert itself as the premier provider of routing technology in the communication age?
- What happened to the industry stalwarts (e.g., Sears, Quaker Oats, GM, DEC, Data General, and Unisys) that led to their demise?
- Why didn't Xerox, the company that developed the basic designs and concepts for personal computers, local area networks, and graphical user interfaces (Windows), bring those incredibly revolutionary products to market?
- Why and how did some of the great companies of the post-World War II period, such as RCA and USX, fail to sustain their positions of dominance?

The histories and operating results of these companies as well as hundreds of others provide us with a rich texture and an extensive empirical context for exploring the dynamics of business strategy and organizational change. Most importantly, they provide insights into the actions to be avoided, and amplify the importance of strategic renewal and revitalization to attain and sustain high performance.

THE TRADITIONAL SOURCES OF COMPETITIVE ADVANTAGE

Business strategy and strategic change have long been subjects that come in and out of management vogue. Sometimes, strategy will be at the forefront of management thinking; at other times, it is relegated to a backseat or falls victim to the latest management fad or trend du jour. Most often, it is mistaken for the annual budgeting process or confused with operational tactics designed to cure a tactical problem. The problems with strategy can be, in part, attributed to the fact that many managers and executives think of themselves as strategists, when in reality they do not or cannot address strategic issues. Thus, we have some measures, many fads and methods, and things like "Balanced Scorecards" that attempt to translate and bridge the gaps surrounding strategy but that can potentially impair the ability to think creatively and strategically.

Percy Barnevik, CEO of ABB (Asea Brown Boveri Ltd.) noted, "In business, success is 5% strategy and 95% execution." To some, Mr. Barnevik may exaggerate the proportionality a bit, but he is also fundamentally correct. Strategies are essential to business and are wonderfully exciting; nevertheless, they are only as good as their objectives and, more importantly, only as effective as their execution. Unfortunately, the business landscape is littered with lofty strategies developed by management consultants and CEOs that have produced little sustainable value. Working with a prominent management consulting firm, GM, for example, has been executing a series of "strategies" for the last five or six years only to see both its sales and marketspace decline and its profit per vehicle lag woefully behind that of Ford's and Chrysler's.

Today, and certainly in the future, simply being "competitive" by producing quality products and achieving adequate financial results will not be sufficient to sustain a company in an increasingly competitive world. Companies that continue to compete on the traditional basis of industry structure, good quality, multiple locations, streamlined supply chains, competitive prices, and satisfactory financials simply no longer hold the keys to competitive advantage or sustained performance leadership. They will not be successful against companies that *set* the prices, *establish* the pace of change, *create* the marketspace, and ultimately, *dictate* the rules that the others must follow. Invariably, companies that do not aspire to dominate their marketspace are forced to constantly react to the rules established by others; they are the followers who could and often do become the has-beens.

The term *marketspace* is used extensively throughout this work. For generations, managers and researchers have defined a company's environment in terms of geography, industry, and marketshare. But in the global and electronic economy, industry demarcations are now blurred and quickly disappearing, and geography and physical barriers have been bridged by technology. What industry is Microsoft in? Is Auto-by-Tele a car dealer, an Internet company, a broker, or information content provider? With links to entertainment, medical research, vacation destinations, personal advertisements, lifestyles, and a host of other services and products, what industry do Yahoo! and Excite reside in? Where are Amazon.com's and Buy.com's stores anyway? Today, organizations reside in a multidimensional space and construct that includes physical and virtual spaces and transcend traditional boundaries. They face an ever-changing variety of physical and virtual competitors. Thus, companies no longer compete in the traditional ways for marketshare or industry position, but rather for marketspace that either exists in multiple domains or is waiting to be created. The great companies—those companies that are identified and defined in this text as *high performers*—do both.

To fully appreciate the changes in the competitive landscape of today and the excitement of tomorrow, let's take a few moments to reminisce on the history of business. In the eighteenth and nineteenth centuries, industrialization occurred and humankind advanced faster and further in 150 years than in the previous millennium. Long-established monarchies and archaic economic systems began to succumb to more democratic forms of government. In search of employment and more dynamic social structures, people migrated from the fields to the cities. With this migration came the emergence of the middle classes, and ultimately, the working wealthy. This nouveau aristocracy had money to spend and the political and economic clout to demand access to better education and improved public services. Most importantly, they began amassing discretionary funds, which allowed them to invest in new ventures through participation in equity markets thus creating additional wealth. Finally, the founding and development of the United States provided what would ultimately become the greatest landscape of economic opportunity in history.

The industrialization of society helped to unleash the human potential and with it came a flurry of new ideas and inventions. In the United States and England, big companies grew out of the consolidation of cottage industries, the commercialization of innovative technologies such as the steam engine and vulcanization, and newfound political and economic freedoms. For a company operating in the early days of industrialization, the strategies for creating competitive advantage were fairly obvious. Those countries and businesses that had geographical and natural resource superiority, larger territory, and energetic populations generally enjoyed superior performance and growth.

As the industrial era progressed, organizations were beginning to learn how to optimize the use of their resources. They created efficiency by leveraging both labor and mechanization and specializing in the functional segmentation of processes, organizational design, and workforces. In the early years of U.S. industrialization, governmental intervention was minimal and relatively nonintrusive, at least until the dismantling of John Rockefeller's Standard Oil Company, the creation of antitrust legislation, and the birth of the Internal Revenue Service (IRS). In contrast, at the close of the twentieth century, there was an ever-growing list of state, local, and federal agencies, many dedicated to regulating some aspect of an organization's operations and competitive environment.

With the exceptions of war and economic depressions and recessions, the markets for most of the twentieth century were growing. Fueled by a continuous stream of immigrants who had strong work ethics and were highly motivated to pursue economic opportunities, discretionary income was increasing and markets were growing. Competition and technology were relatively predictable and stable. The combination of these factors supported the growth and the development of bastions of American industry such as Standard Oil, General Electric (GE), GM, E. I. DuPont, Pennsylvania Railroad, RCA, Union Pacific Railroad, USX, and Ford Motor Company.

It was in the smoke-stacked factories and great railroad companies of the U.S. industrial revolution that the fundamental theories of business strategy and management were forged. Early management luminaries such as Frederick Taylor, Andrew Carnegie, John D. Rockefeller, P. J. Harriman, Henry Ford, and Alfred P. Sloan created and perfected the classic strategic management doctrines of mass production, vertical integration, segregation of duties, and industry structure.

As provided in Exhibit 1.2, the traditional sources of competitive advantage largely came from location, size, price, product, and structure. Later, quality would become important. These elements, in turn, became some of the fundamental axioms for strategy formulation and strategic thinking, which were used by businesses and taught in business schools through most of the latter part of the twentieth century. Collectively, these concepts and frameworks provided the basic ingredients for success in the industrial period. Competing in this era was relatively straightforward: If a company had decent products, achieved repetition in form and function, was in a growing industry, had reasonable product quality, and organized itself for mass production with economies of scale, it would do well. Given these prevailing conditions, above-average performance and financial results were virtually guaranteed.

Today, physical size, location, marketshare, product, price, cost controls, and quality are no longer the great differentiators or drivers of strategic advantage that organizations can rely on to create and sustain leading positions. The environment and known and emerging competitors are too dynamic, too fast, and too unpredictable. All companies need products, services, good quality, and competitive prices to simply remain in the game of business. Having these prerequisites does not guarantee that a company will enjoy superior financial performance or competitive position. Sears, J.C. Penney, Nissan, Daewoo, General Mills, Kellogg's, and Quaker Oats are all excellent examples of companies with good products, large size, relatively efficient supply chains, established track records, and good locations. They are also examples of companies that are on descending trajectories and not high performers. The increase in venture capital as a source of financing has also changed the dynamics of competing. Financing start-ups and entrepreneurial ideas is much easier, and access to capital is far less restricted than in the days when banks were the only sources of capital. This has reduced the reliance on traditional banking services.

For most organizations, an analysis of its industry and competitors is necessary and helpful, but it does not directly lead to high performance or strategic thinking. The popular and widely taught strategic planning methods that stress industry dynamics and relative positioning that were developed many years ago have proven to be useful, even insightful. However, the current environment of rapid technological innovation, knowledge formation, and mobile workforces, as well as globalization, radically alters the basis of competition and quickly challenges historical business thinking and strategy

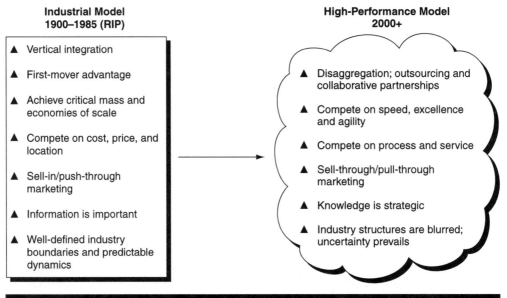

Industrial Model
1900–1985 (RIP)

▲ Vertical integration

▲ First-mover advantage

▲ Achieve critical mass and economies of scale

▲ Compete on cost, price, and location

▲ Sell-in/push-through marketing

▲ Information is important

▲ Well-defined industry boundaries and predictable dynamics

High-Performance Model
2000+

▲ Disaggregation; outsourcing and collaborative partnerships

▲ Compete on speed, excellence and agility

▲ Compete on process and service

▲ Sell-through/pull-through marketing

▲ Knowledge is strategic

▲ Industry structures are blurred; uncertainty prevails

EXHIBIT 1.2 Fundamental Changes Are Driving New Business Dynamics

formulation. The once well-defined industry boundaries that demarcated customers, competitors, and suppliers are now becoming increasingly porous and blended. Thus, much of the traditional thinking behind the established strategic planning methods has been compromised and negated by the velocity of innovation, ferocity of change, a convergence of technology with knowledge and process design, and a profound change in the political and social systems that emerged in the post–Cold War period. Ultimately, all of these factors led to new forms of competing.

In competing today, the primary issue is not so much on what basis a company should compete. That's a historical antecedent. Rather, the issue now centers on what makes a company great and the quest to achieve and sustain higher levels of competitiveness. Thus, the objective of contemporary strategy should not simply target improvements and be content to "do well," but rather aim to turn organizations into *high performers* and the dominant leaders in their marketspace.

Log onto www.amazon.com and search the titles or stroll through a well-stocked bookstore to confirm the popularity of strategy. With book and seminar titles ranging from the serious to the entertaining, some are extremely valuable, offering keen insights into how to create and sustain competitive advantage. In contrast, many others are superficial and devoid of fact and substance. When researchers or authors have nothing new to add or explore, they produce eclectic compilations of various other works and publish them under new wrappers and packages. The business books are full of theories and case examples about strategy, especially those that emphasize the dynamics of the industry, its competitive structure, and its composition. Most business students have studied the "cola wars" case, Wal-Mart versus Kmart and Sears cases, and Apple Computer. Understanding industry structure and competition are important, but in an environment of discontinuous innovation, globalization, and technology convergence, the key to significant competitive advantage lies in creating a new industry or dramatically altering the environment that others must compete in. Just look at a long list of has-been industry leaders with well-known names including Sears, Encyclopedia Britannica, Commodore Computers, DEC, Union Pacific Railroad, RCA, and USX and think about the impact of these new dynamics on their industry structures. Such is the ebb and flow of strategic doctrine in the *real* world of business.

The classical strategic planning methods, which stress industry analysis, go a long way in helping to visualize and develop strategy, but the truth is that great performance and business dominance know no secret sauces and no fad du jour. At the heart of the matter, indicators such as great products, impeccable quality, least costs, best prices, great process and product designs, energized and dedicated workforces, and industry position that management consultants and academicians advance are all *manifestations* of deeper, more unique characteristics and complex strategic thinking. They are the *results* of something other than analyzing the dynamics of an industry, assessing competitive threats, or streamlining the supply chain. Today, suppliers are collaborators, not adversaries; hence, the dynamics of bargaining are very different. Competitors can be co-optitioneers and alliance partners; thus, leverage and the definition of who the competitors are assume new and different meanings. Customers are now "guests" and "clients," not faceless members of the masses. Knowing the customer has been supplanted by having deep knowledge and intimacy with the customer. Prices are important, but it is the product's perceived and actual value to the consumer and the "buying experience" that are the essential differentiators.

Exhibit 1.3 summarizes some of the major changes occurring that are redefining and defining the rules of strategic thinking.

One of the problems with most traditional strategic planning methods and classical doctrines is their failure to account for the impact of information technology and change and innovation taking place in the world. Simply thinking metaphorically in classical competitor, customer, and industry terms is not enough to ensure the competitiveness and long-term viability of a company. Most likely, if the classic strategic planning methodologies based on industry structure, supplier leverage, bargaining power of buyers, and rivalries had been applied to Steve Jobs' Apple, Michael Dell's computer company, Steve Bezo's Amazon.com, or Charles Schwab's electronic brokerage firm in their formative stages, many would have concluded that those were not viable business concepts. After all, IBM, Barnes & Noble, and Merrill Lynch ruled those industries, had established brand names, had locked up suppliers, owned the supply channels, achieved economies of scale, and had created first-mover advantages. Undoubtedly, weren't those companies comfortable and secure with the barriers to entry and market position that they had created? Why would anyone want to compete against them? The traditional methods of strategy simply do not adequately consider the speed of change, impact of innovation on strategy, or uncertainty in their formulation of strategy. Furthermore, they discount or entirely miss the role of the entrepreneur and venture capitalist. In contrast to the realities of competing at the speed of life, they are stochastic and stalled in time and space.

One has only to take a casual but enlightened walk through the business landscape to see that it is littered with lofty objectives and elegant strategies. Conceived by aspiring Jack Welch and Peter Drucker "wanna-bes," there are countless numbers of business strategies that have achieved little. Look to companies like Acer Computers, Bendix, Morrison Knudsen, Kodak, Xerox, Quaker Oats, RCA, Levi Strauss, Sears, Dell,

Traditional Strategic Planning	High-Performance Strategy Formulation
▲ Imitate, substitute	▲ Innovate, collaborate, complement
▲ Competitors are rivals.	▲ Competitors can be partners and co-opetitor
▲ Leverage suppliers for concessions and lower prices	▲ Engage suppliers as collaborators
▲ Create vertically integrated structures	▲ Disaggregate and focus on core competencies and selectively outsource
▲ Organize for size and efficiency	▲ Optimize agility and adaptability
▲ Compete for industry position/rely on size and barriers to entry	▲ Create a new industry/define new rules of competing
▲ Reduce bargaining power of customers	▲ Engage the customer, delight the customer
▲ Compete on price and least cost	▲ Compete on value and offer a compelling value proposition; create a pleasant experience
▲ Create functional specialization and separation within the organization	▲ Emphasize selective organizational integration of functions and processes
▲ Compete for maximum marketshare within a well-defined industry	▲ Create virtual marketspace across industries and optimize profit pools

EXHIBIT 1.3 Changes Define New Rules for Strategic Thinking

Sony, Ford, and The Home Depot for contrasts between strategies that failed and strategies that succeeded. The result is that companies are either ascending in performance and market power or are descending in stature. Students of strategy and leaders of organizational change must ask two important questions about the plight of these companies: *Was it the strategy, or was it how the company executed the strategy* that contributed to its ultimate ascent or descent? Or perhaps there is something else? If you are an entrepreneur, a CEO of a publicly traded company, or a political leader, these are the important questions. As Einstein noted, the questions may be the same, but the answers today are very different from those of only a few years ago.

Unfortunately, when confronted with radical changes or challenges in their internal or external environments, many organizations either fail to recognize them or cumbersomely react by invoking traditional industry strategies and situational "intervention" tactics such as downsizing, price cutting, marginally extending product lines, and streamlining supply chains. In the process, rather than competing differently, many companies continue to compete in the same way, using the same tried and exhausted strategies, operating tactics, and strategy formulation methods—only they call them something different. They create a false sense of confidence in the precedent and logic of, "If it worked before, it'll work again."

There is comfort and perceived credibility in using legacy methods that were successful to address new problems. However, companies that adopt such a strategic posture often find themselves victims of their own inertia and quickly left behind by their competition. A study of 27 companies in 8 different industries performed by researchers Simold Cooper and Clayton Smith confirmed that established companies were more likely to link new initiatives and processes using old methods to support change efforts, thus diminishing their effectiveness. The authors found that only 7 of 27 companies were successful in their change efforts. A similar statistic is found in studies on reengineering and large-scale IT projects. Results such as these remind one of Einstein's definition of *insanity,* which went something like, "Insanity is a sane person repeating the same things time after time and hoping for a different result." There are many companies that fit that description. They keep repeating themselves and recycling their career managers, hoping for different results.

Traditionally, when forming strategy or implementing strategic change, organizations have often relied on size, quality, location, leveraging suppliers, and their bargaining power over customers as strategic themes. More recently, they have turned to quality and reengineering as strategic practices and ways of changing. Let's briefly discuss the role of size, quality, reengineering, and downsizing as sources of strategy formulation and competitive advantage.

Size

Size and marketshare are considered important strategic objectives and indicators of success for an organization. While undeniably important, they are not necessarily indicators of strategic dominance or high performance. In the 1950s, it was said that "What was good for General Motors was good for the country." With consolidated 1998 sales of $159 billion, GM is one of the largest industrial companies in the world. But size alone doesn't mean that GM is a high performer or the best at what it does. GM may be number one or two in global revenues, but it is only number 93 out of 100 in 1999 market value. Granted, GM has enormous market clout, but it isn't nearly the force that it once was in the industry or in the eyes of the consumer. Since the early 1980s and especially in the 1990s, GM has consistently ceded marketshare. It continues to underperform its rivals in several important measures. Despite the trend to disaggregate through collaborative partnerships and outsourcing set by leaders Toyota, Ford, and Chrysler, GM remains the most vertically integrated of all of the North American carmakers. Coincidentally, it is also the least productive and perhaps least innovative of the big auto-makers. Despite its massive investments in new IT systems and plant automation, GM's profit per car is the lowest of the domestic producers, its cycle time to market is apparently longer, and its quality, although significantly better, continues to lag behind Toyota. While Chrysler and Ford were sharing profits with employees that averaged $1,200 and $1,600 respectively, GM profit sharing for 1998 was an anemic $200 per employee. This condition is perpetuated, in part, through difficult relations with organized labor that has consistently rejected attempts by GM leadership to try to become more competitive and leaner through outsourcing more of its parts operations and disaggregating its vertical organizational structure.

Another example demonstrating that size no longer guarantees competitive advantage involves the high-technology sector. With a combination of product offerings, technical superiority, financing capabilities, and extraordinarily strong and loyal customer relationships, IBM set the standards and dominated the high-technology landscape for over 30 years. Most importantly, IBM held the keys to the corporate data center and maintained enormously strong relationships with its corporate customers, who became dependent on IBM for both services and products. From 1950 to 1960, IBM grew to be the largest provider of computers in the world, and it continued its dominance over the "Seven Dwarfs," including GE, Honeywell, Sperry Rand, and Data General, until the mid-1980s. Interestingly, although Honeywell, DEC, and later Japan's Hitachi made strategic inroads against IBM, none of the established leaders ever really challenged IBM's leadership or seriously threatened IBM's lead.

In a preemptive strike, DEC moved into IBM's weakest marketspace with the successful launch of its VAX midrange computer systems in the early 1980s, which were targeted against IBM's hopelessly archaic and simplistic Series 1 and System 38 computers. With its VAX product line, DEC would soon surpass Honeywell and, ultimately, ascend to the number two spot behind IBM in that industry. By the later part of the 1980s, IBM counterattacked with its enormously successful AS/400 series of midrange computing solutions. Code-named "Silver Lake," the integrated IBM product offering, together with IBM's Unix-based products, and the appearance of other Unix offerings by Hewlett-Packard would soon threaten and ultimately displace DEC's VAX line and its proprietary operating system.

With the introduction of more innovative products and the advent of greater competition, it was only a matter of time until DEC was surpassed and preempted by both IBM and Hewlett-Packard in the midrange and PC/workstation computing segments. DEC's decline and demise were cast long before its ill-fated emphasis on the alpha chip, seemingly inept senior leadership, and desperation lawsuit against Intel. Within 10 years, DEC ceased to exist as an independent company and was acquired by a younger company named Compaq. During this period, Data General, Sperry and Burroughs, and many other computer makers—both large and small—either abandoned the marketplace or succumbed to competitive pressures of upstarts Dell, Compaq, and others.

Like GM, IBM is still a colossus and a major force in high technology, but it no longer dictates the terms to either customers or competitors. A victim of the environment that it helped to create, IBM's share of the *total* computer industry, based on aggregate rates of market capitalization, actually fell from 46 percent in 1988 to a bit over 14 percent by 1997. Its growth is now more of a function of services than of technological leadership and customer loyalty. However, IBM has been successful at improving its market value from the number 13 position in 1998 to number three in 1999.

Quality

In the 1980s, quality became another popular initiative as a strategy for many companies. Quality is *essential* for any company wishing to compete. A company cannot be a high performer without quality. However, quality by itself will not guarantee high performance. Entering the U.S. market in the 1950s with smaller cars and consumer electronics of inferior quality, Japanese manufacturers deliberately began to engineer superior quality into their products. Using a calculated strategy of gaining market presence over maximum profits, the Japanese entrants quietly and methodically built marketshare one segment and one percentage point at a time. While U.S. companies were preoccupied with adding more options, making products "bigger," and offering a seemingly limitless combination of mass-produced models and products, the Japanese engineered quality and value-added into their products with a restricted combination of options and selections. Starting in the late 1960s, the American consumer began to discern significant quality and value gaps between U.S. products and services and those of their foreign competitors— in particular, the Japanese and Germans.

The differences in quality became strategic points of differentiation, especially during the oil embargos of the 1970s, which forced American consumers to consider more fuel-efficient alternatives. Using a strategy predicated on building marketshare through aggressive pricing, economy of operation, and better quality, the Japanese simply eclipsed the U.S. automotive, motorcycle, and consumer electronics manufacturers with higher quality and more innovative and exciting products. The Japanese presented U.S. consumers with a unique and unprecedented *value proposition* that focused on the relationship between features, quality, performance, and price. In the process, they not only redefined existing markets, but created new marketspace with innovative products such as the Sony Walkman and the compact disc player.

In consumer electronics, the Japanese offered alternatives to the large, monolithic-sized stereo/television combinations manufactured by U.S. companies such as RCA, Philco, Motorola, and Zenith. During the 1960s and through the early part of the 1970s, U.S. television manufacturers had virtually abandoned the smaller "portable" black and white television segment in pursuit of the large TV/stereo combinations. In the process, they allowed Japanese manufacturers (Sony and Panasonic, in particular) to enter unchallenged and unencumbered into this segment of the U.S. consumer electronics market. In effect, the U.S. manufacturers removed the barriers to entry by electing to abandon that particular market segment. Slowly, but progressively, the Japanese electronic makers built marketshare using a strategy of low prices, innovation, and quality, which, in turn, fueled growing sales and profits. Ultimately, those sales and profits were used to finance more innovation and automation in manufacturing, which ultimately drove costs lower and pushed quality and consumer choices higher. With this cycle, the Japanese electronic makers overtook the U.S. leaders such as RCA, Motorola, and Zenith as the innovation and quality leaders of the television, stereo, and VCR player industries.

In response to the Japanese quality threat and declining sales, the 1980s heralded in TQM (total quality management) and employee work teams as the great change levers and saviors of competitive advantage. TQM and work teams went a long way towards helping many organizations to become more competitive. In no way should the importance of quality in product, process, and customer interactions be diminished. However, as the quality of one company improved, so did the quality of the entire industry. Soon the competitive advantages and differentiating aspects of better quality were effectively minimized, if not neutralized, as all companies elevated their quality to a relative range that made differentiating based on quality very difficult. Today, for example, when one compares the quality between American and Japanese car companies, you have to look much harder and longer to detect the quality weaknesses in U.S. products. This brings us to a major conclusion regarding quality. For any company, quality is no longer a differentiating strategic weapon or source of competitive advantage. Unless an organization meets the essential quality standards established by its customers and achieved by its competitors, it cannot generate any sustainable competitive advantage or significant competitive leverage. Quality is a *necessity* and a *precondition* to becoming a high-performer and sustaining high performance. An organization simply must have it.

Reengineering

The 1990s were ushered in with the "R" word, which stands for *recession*. Rocked by a slowing economy and declining earnings, managers embraced the other "R" word—*reengineering*—with hopes of reincarnating themselves. Although the impetus behind reengineering was radical change, the concept was not new and was subject to much confusion and dilution. What followed was a plethora of activities ranging from downsizing to massive investments in new client-server systems and software packages, all under the reengineering banner. Although many organizations applied the reengineering label to their efforts, very few were actually reengineering. As researchers Barbara Blumenthal and Phillipe Haspeslagh note, "Many changes that are regularly referred to as transformation are not." The reality is that the majority of companies merely kept *managing* in the same conventional ways, using the same conventional measurement methods and the same conventional personnel practices, but they called it something else.

An example of such efforts can be found in one Fortune 500 company. This company used two of the largest consulting firms in the world to reengineer using new client-server enterprise-wide software solutions. They rationalized the use of multiple consulting firms on the same project in the belief that no one consulting firm had adequate skills to fully meet their needs. This company began its project as a $10 million investment, and ultimately ended it as a $90 million nightmare: overbudget, past due, and incomplete. By most measures, this company failed miserably in their efforts and in their leadership of the project. Summing up his experience, the company's project manager publicly stated, "We were a bit naive."

Naiveté is a poor excuse for an apparently questionable strategy and seemingly ineffective management, which may have cost shareholders millions of dollars in direct expenditures and tens of millions of dollars in forfeited opportunity costs. As Al Dunlap said, "It's a mortal sin to lose money," especially when one is warned ahead of time. The shareholders of this publicly traded company were lucky; it is a leader in a high-growth market segment. Although embarrassing, this type of management naiveté can be easily buried by double-digit growth, Wall Street euphoria, stock splits, and earning surprises. But, it is still money ill-spent, position forfeited, and momentum lost.

Reengineering can be enormously successful and can lead to significant benefits. But only when reengineering is married to systemic organizational change, new behaviors, and new measurements does it yield breakthrough results and new competitive advantages. High-performance change leaders understand this and approach their business from a holistic perspective in the management of their organizations and the designing of successful projects that drive competitive strategies.

Downsizing

As the last resort to chronic and systemic management problems, many companies and their boards turn to the slash-and-burn management tactics of downsizing. For example, since 1990, AT&T has terminated some 123,000 people. In 1996, after announcing plans to terminate 40,000 people, it gave former CEO Robert Allen a huge pay raise. Failing to achieve satisfactory results, a year later AT&T's new CEO Michael Armstrong announced a plan to terminate an additional 17,000 people by the end of 1999. But Mr. Armstrong has done something that Mr. Allen was either incapable of doing or resisted doing—Mr. Armstrong is moving AT&T in a different direction. He is repositioning the company and in the process leading its reinvention.

Known for his flamboyant methods, Al "Chainsaw" Dunlap, the former CEO of Scott Paper, author of *Mean Business,* self-proclaimed "superstar," and "fired" CEO of Sunbeam, terminated about a third of the employees of Scott Paper, sold the company, and pocketed $100 million in compensation and incentives for himself. Dunlap's leadership at Scott left a once-proud company as a skeleton of its former self, unable to compete on its own. But let's be practical. That may have been the only reasonable course of action for Chainsaw Al because it is questionable whether Scott could have survived on its own as a viable and vibrant competitive entity, irrespective of Chainsaw or his tactics. Scott was a tired company that was long known for its paternalistic style of management and lack of urgency. Its insistence on a highly vertical structure and mistimed capital investments in capacity when sales and demand were softening were merely indicators of a company long-dormant, poorly managed, and positioned for demise.

As a strategic option, downsizing and cost cutting have been proven to have only limited long-term positive effect on the economic performance and market value of the enterprise. A study of 52 corporate restructurings by the Wharton School of the University of Pennsylvania indicates that on the average, restructuring has only a limited effect on earnings or stock price performance. A survey of 1,000 companies performed by the American Management Association (AMA) found that less than 50 percent of those companies that had downsized managed to increase their operating profits. Those conclusions are corroborated by another study, which found that cost cutters and downsizers failed to achieve significant true long-term performance improvements. A follow-up study, also performed by the AMA, of 292 companies found that disability claims rose faster in the downsized organization than those that did not downsize. *The New York Times* cites another study that followed the financial performance of downsized companies. Those companies that sharply cut their payrolls averaged only a 4 percent increase in stock prices, whereas those that did not downsize gained 35 percent. It takes something far more creative than just cost cutting and chain sawing to renew an organization and position it for greatness.

Cost cutting and downsizing are not *always* bad. There are times and circumstances that warrant it. In fact, organizations like Unisys, Kodak, Bausch & Lomb, Xerox, and GM would benefit from the trauma of well-targeted cost cuts. For example, with less than 30 percent marketshare, GM is still configured as a company that once had over 45 percent of the market. Bausch & Lomb, at one time a Fortune 500 company, had somewhere between $80 to $120 million in unnecessary structural costs that it had to address. In these situations, deep cost- and employment-cutting tactics and shock therapists like Al Dunlap, Michael Price, and the late Sir James Goldsmith probably have a valid role. They serve as overhead eliminators and cultural transformers. But the lesson here, and it is a painful one for many organizations, is that companies do not become great by simply performing a situational reengineering project, downsizing, or cutting costs. At best, downsizing will buy an organization some time to reposition and recalibrate itself.

Exhibit 1.4 provides a summary of the strategic implications of downsizing.

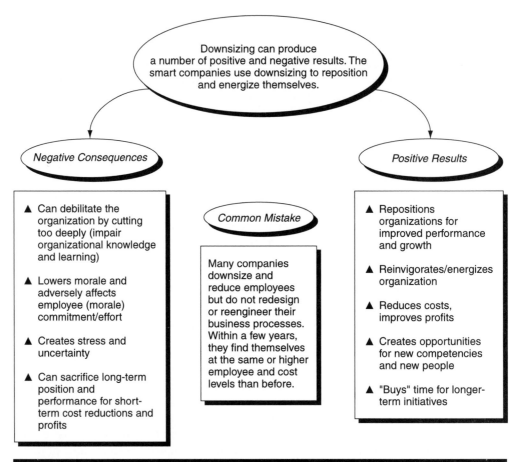

EXHIBIT 1.4 The Strategic Implications of Downsizing

SUMMARY

No single textbook or strategy development framework can provide all of the insights and tools necessary for developing a strategy for competing effectively in a world dominated by uncertainty. Such an endeavor is simply too formidable a task and unrealistic an expectation in a world in which change and the competitive balance of business and economic power shift with incredible speed and voracity. Strategy and strategic change are journeys, not necessarily destinations.

With the above in mind, *Strategic Renewal* has been designed to provide perspective and different contexts and insights into what it takes to create and sustain competitive advantage as a high-performance company.

Critical Thoughts and Discussion Questions

1. Thinking about the future, what factors and trends will help shape the business environment for the next 5 to 10 years? How will these factors influence

the behavior and performance of traditional companies such as Proctor & Gamble and GM and high performers such as Microsoft and Wal-Mart?

2. Discuss the sources of traditional competitive advantage and why these are no longer as valid and secure as they once were. In discussing this subject, consider how traditional strategic planning methods are affected.

3. Discuss the new sources of competitive advantage and how they can be used to stimulate organizational revitalization in traditional and established companies.

CHAPTER

2

DEFINING HIGH PERFORMANCE AND STRATEGIC RENEWAL

"Winning is not a sometime thing. It is an all time thing. You don't win once in awhile, you don't do things right once in awhile, you do them right all of the time. There is no room for second place."

—VINCE LOMBARDI

INTRODUCTION

The academic and general-management literature is replete with quotes, articles, and cases about being a high-performance company and how to lead strategic change. Occasionally, one of the popular business publications such as *Fortune* or *Business Week* will run a story about high performance. Yet despite this attention and popular rhetoric, high performance and strategic change remain elusive topics for all but a few select companies and leaders. In the absence of effective and pragmatic definitions, little substance exists supplying the necessary working framework and basis for meaningful management action. The need to develop a substantive definition for these terms is essential for both the formulation of strategies, as well as their practical application. Specifically:

- The failure to understand what it means to be a high-performance organization compromises the future of the organization. High performance should be an underlying theme and imperative of strategy formulation.
- The inability to change or successfully navigate change is a common characteristic of organizational failure and descending performance.
- The failure to understand that each change is a unique event and as such no two change situations are the same.
- Setting high performance as a standard and strategic objective without a definitional context and working construct is analogous to embarking on an expedition without a compass or a map; it is inefficient and generally leads an organization in a circular direction where much effort is expended, but little is accomplished.

- The inability or failure to understand that certain organizational dynamics affect change impedes the ability of an organization to successfully change.

Chapter 2 addresses these issues, defines the qualities of a high-performance organization, and describes the meaning of strategic renewal. In the process, it presents the relevant context and offers new insights and a fresh perspective with regard to the application and adaptation of such concepts, serving strategic development and renewal purposes, in particular. This chapter presents a number of questions:

- What is high performance, and what are the characteristics of companies that are high performers?
- What are the six strategic choices available to all companies?
- How is strategic change different from tactical and evolutionary change, and what are the various levels of change in an organization?
- What are some of the most important factors that influence an organization's ability to change?

Some readers may not fully agree with the terms and definitions presented in this chapter; nevertheless, the fact remains that the following research and the companies profiled in this work serve as examples for definitions of high performance. Essentially, the concepts presented and terms used reflect *their* definitions and are based on *their* behavior.

After reading this chapter, you should have developed a better perspective and a deeper understanding of some of the factors affecting strategic change and strategy formulation. Moreover, you will better comprehend and appreciate the essence of a high-performance organization. This understanding is critical for the subsequent discussions presented in chapters 3 through 10.

UNDERSTANDING STRATEGIC RENEWAL

"One thing is certain: things will change. How well you anticipate and how quickly you deal with change determines your success," notes Herb Kelleher, the entrepreneur CEO of Southwest Airlines. It is the independent and dependent interactions between the environment and the organization that make competing so uncertain and wonderfully challenging. Some of these interactions are planned and calculated; others are spontaneous, even surprises. The environment is, to a certain extent, like a living ecology. It is always in motion and always trying to find some form of equilibrium, albeit if only for a short period of time. As one introduces new factors into the ecology, be they new products, new competencies, new technologies, or new organizational designs, the ecology changes and balance shifts occur; as a result, some organizations ascend, others descend. Often these balance shifts are subtle; sometimes they can be discontinuous and extremely disruptive. When such events occur, new opportunities emerge and new competencies are born while others die or are rendered inconsequential. Inevitably, the basic rules of competing and survival change.

Great companies dictate the terms for other competitors by constantly introducing new factors into the marketspace, which the others must react and adjust to. The great organizations adapt, anticipate, overcome, or create many of these changes. In contrast, the wannabes and also-rans are constantly reacting to new conditions and situations and left guessing as to what to do next. Southwest Airlines, Chrysler, Intel, Dell, Citicorp, and Wal-Mart are just a few examples of companies that create or modify their environments. In the process, they develop an enormous competitive advantage by forcing others to use resources to try to anticipate, match, or catch up with their leads. The U.S. Marine Corps, arguably one of the most elite fighting forces on earth, calls it "Defining the battlescape"—a strategy that dictates the terms of battle to the enemy and generates a superior position.

There are six key issues with regard to change that all organizations must address:

1. How to change
2. When to change
3. At what velocity to change
4. How to effectively manage and successfully navigate change
5. Knowing what state and qualities to change to
6. Determining the organization's capability and requirements for change

To change merely for the sake of change is usually a self-defeating activity. Organizations that have done so have only caused more work for themselves, distracted their focus from more important issues, and, in most instances, achieved very little competitive advantage in the process. Knowing when to change is a matter of recognition and capability. Some organizations are slow to recognize the need to change; others—the high performers—are ahead of the pack. Additionally, not knowing how to change or the priorities of change is usually a prescription for disaster. However, some guiding principles emerge. Every form of change is a journey that should be driven by three objectives: (1) the need to create and sustain high performance, (2) the need to achieve a definable goal or correct a specific problem, and, (3) the need to advance and perpetuate the organization to a better, more competitive, position.

Companies that understand the implications of the competitive rules that work to create new environments and build high-performance capabilities will prosper. They will be in the spotlights of the business stage. Those that do not or fail in their efforts will most likely join companies like DEC, Banker's Trust, W. T. Grant, Woolworths, Commodore Computer, American Motors, and a long list of others as footnotes in the annals of business failures. To be a high-performance company, an organization must be realistic about, and anticipatory of, the influences that invalidate its sources of competitive advantage and degrade its management practices and traditional sources of competitive advantage and organizational change. It must not only be able to craft strategies designed to create or exploit change but also be able to develop the deep competencies and adaptable structures to successfully execute those strategies with extraordinary adroitness and precision.

An organization, irrespective of its market position, size, product line, and financial performance, cannot escape the inevitability of change. According to researchers Ansoff in 1965 and later Henry Mintzberg in 1990, as cited by University of Southern California faculty members Nandini Rajagopalan and Gretchen Spreitzer, "Strategic change is a sequential, planned search for optimal solutions for well-defined problems based on previously defined firm objectives." This is a valid conclusion based on the studies that those very accomplished scholars performed, but the realities of competing at the speed of life on Internet time is that strategic change and renewal are *not* sequential. In fact, they are anything but sequential—they are usually chaotic, discontinuous, and in a constant state of fluidity. Nandini Rajagopalan and Gretchen Spreitzer define *strategic change* as "a unitary concept measured through discrete changes in a firm's business, corporate, or collective strategies." That definition is closer to the contemporary realities of many companies, but it discounts the impact of discontinuous events. There is nothing discrete about new legislation, political instability (war), or a new technology that suddenly and violently changes the dynamics of competing in certain markets and with certain strategies. As noted by Peter Keen, once new technology was introduced within an industry, 50 percent of its members were gone within 10 years.

Researchers Barbara Blumenthal and Philippe Haspeslagh note that "The process of changing strategy seeks to regain a sustainable competitive advantage by redefining business objectives, creating new competencies, and harnessing these capabilities to meet market opportunities." Finally, author Gary Hamel defines *strategic change* and *innovation* as "The ability to reinvent the basis of competition within existing industries and to create entirely new industries." The reality is that strategic change can be sudden, discrete, planned, sequential, random, and chaotic. The fundamental management challenge is to recognize it, anticipate it, and successfully navigate it.

Change, in its simplest form, can be defined as the difference or the movement from one state or status to another. It can be operationally related, technologically oriented, organizationally related, or specific to collective or individual human behavior. Classic management textbooks on the subject tend to focus on behavior. In reality, however, most managers equate change with new process designs, new technologies, and new organizational structures or reporting relationships, while often regarding the human behavioral aspects as secondary elements.

Pragmatically, organizations plan and can experience many different types or states of change. These range from the very minor modifications of a process or change in a software program to those that are major, shocking, and systemic. For simplicity purposes, let's reduce the various states of change to three possibilities:

- Incremental change
- Tactical change
- Systemic transformation

Each of these states involve various levels and degrees of change.

Incremental Change

This type of change involves limited movement from one state to another. It presents a lower form of complexity, lower risk, and usually generates lower returns in the form of benefits. This type of change is generally restricted to performing minor modifications or incremental alterations to a part of a business process, the organizational structure of a limited number of departments, or routine software or technological upgrades. This state of change is being carried out daily in virtually every organization. Many continuous quality-improvement (CQI) programs (including TQM) can fall into this category of change.

Tactical Change

In contrast to incremental change, tactical change is more encompassing. This type of change is commonly referred to as reengineering. It is larger, more complex, presents greater risk, and offers the potential for a higher payback. Tactical changes require larger investments and typically involve the introduction of new performance measures, different organizational responsibilities, and new technologies and processes that are materially different from those that they replace.

Systemic Transformational Change

This level of change is the most dramatic, complex, and riskiest of the three states of change. Systemic change involves a wide-scale invention, reinvention, and redesign of business processes and organizational structures. It includes the creation of new performance measures and generally requires that new competencies, technologies, and leadership practices be developed and introduced. Acquisitions, mergers, major repositioning, and enterprisewide reengineering efforts, collaborative efforts with vendors and outsourcers, and the creation of global organizational structures represent typical examples of this form of change.

Strategic change assumes many different forms and variations of magnitude. Sometimes it is episodic; more often it is subtle and in a few cases, barely detectable in the immediate sense. In the strictest sense, anything that an organization or a person does differently from one moment to the next, technically, is change. Because employees will do even the most mundane and redundant things with minor variations, change is constant in all organizations. The issue centers on whether the change is systemically desirable or just related to individual behavior and mannerisms.

Essentially change occurs at five levels: (1) *enterprisewide,* (2) within a *business unit,* (3) within an *operational unit* and *business process,* (4) within an *organizational unit,* and (5) with respect to *individual human behavior.* As a strategic matter, any change is complex. The issue is one of relativity—that is, how large and complex the change should be. Enterprisewide change is the most complex simply because it involves the greatest number of people and is potentially the most disruptive. Business-unit change usually occurs within an operating business of a larger enterprise. This form of change can also be extremely complex and disruptive. Operational-unit and business-process changes are more analogous to the process reengineering efforts, which significantly redesign business functions, organizational structures, and performance measurements. Individual human behavior changes are specific to a person or a team. These changes can be either subtle or substantial.

Exhibit 2.1 provides a summary of the key characteristics and qualities of the states of change.

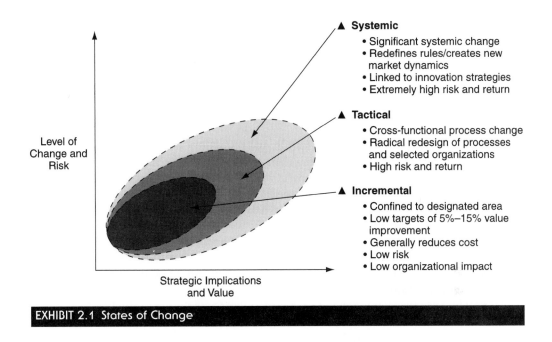

EXHIBIT 2.1 States of Change

TEN WARNING SIGNS OF STRATEGIC DECLINE

Ivonne Valdez, the former vice president of sales for the defunct Exponential Technology Company, observed that "People have to understand that it's all or nothing. You can make it big, you can die a slow death, or you can die a quick and violent death." When considering the rise and ultimate demise of any company, we are well justified in asking, "What happened to a once great-performing company that makes it today's has-been and tomorrow's footnote?"

In most cases, a company's decline is attributed to many factors. The academic literature provides an extensive treatment of the subject matter with an abundance of case and clinical studies. Unfortunately, scholarly research can be confusing and, at times, contradictory. Indeed, the work of Nandini Rajagopalan and Gretchen Spreitzer on strategic change demonstrates just how contradictory and confusing some of the academic treatment can be. Certainly, mergers and consolidations occur and constitute major factors. Technology changes accelerate competition and can significantly alter the natural dynamics of an industry or economy. Clearly, markets change, and in some industries, government intervention and deregulation constitute important elements contributing to the demise of companies. In other situations, innovation and new competitors such as Dell and Gateway overtake the established leaders, such as IBM. It's not just poor quality, lack of products, or high costs that contribute to a company's inevitable decline. Nor can new domestic competition, foreign competitors, and aggressive pricing fully explain such declines. For many organizations, including DEC, Kellogg's, and Kodak, their declines were gradual and not a result of some episodic event.

At this point, it is important to recognize that decreasing marketshare and declining profits are only the consequences of deeper causes of strategic deterioration. Indeed, while observing and studying such "symptoms" or "signals," we need to acknowledge and explore other, more fundamental aspects and issues that ultimately contribute to an organization's performance and its success or failure. Although there is an infinite number of factors that affect the performance and future of any organization, 10 behaviors *signal* strategic degradation and a descending trajectory:

1. The organization exhibits a lack in understanding the environmental and economic realities confronting it, or is in denial of such realities.
2. The management of the organization is arrogant with regard to its view of the world and assessment of its internal competencies.
3. The organization has lost perspective with respect to customers, products, suppliers, and competitors.
4. Management and employees have an insular focus or preoccupation with internal processes, internal measurements, and politics.
5. The organization has lost its sense of urgency and lacks an attitude of self-determination.
6. The organization is relying on historical and poorly conceptualized or inappropriate business strategies and traditional management methods to address new and different challenges.
7. The organization has a propensity to repeat mistakes and fails to learn from past experiences.
8. The organization has low or slow innovation practices and is late to market with new products and services.
9. The organization has a tendency to recycle marginally performing managers.
10. The organization relies exclusively on internal talent as a source for its leadership.

Exhibit 2.2 summaries these signals and their consequences. In addition, there are a number of other key factors that require consideration:

- **Age of the organization.** Generally, the "older" and more established the organization is, the more difficult it is to modify its behavior and reinvent its culture. Older organizations with established cultures have institutional memory, legacy practices, and long-learned behaviors that they must neutralize before they can change. Resistance to change is often high and well organized. Likewise, younger organizations that are experiencing hyper-growth are often unstable and unable to prioritize what change is needed. However, as a group, younger firms are "faster changers." In a MCI/Gallup poll of 550 CEOs reported in *Fortune,* 38 percent of the respondents said that the newcomers, not the traditional competitors, had taken the "best advantage" of change. Sixty-two percent indicated that the newcomers significantly changed the rules of competing.

    In a study of 87 companies, researchers Margarethe Wiersema and Karen Bantel found that the demographics of those organizations that exhibited the highest propensity for change shared six management attributes:

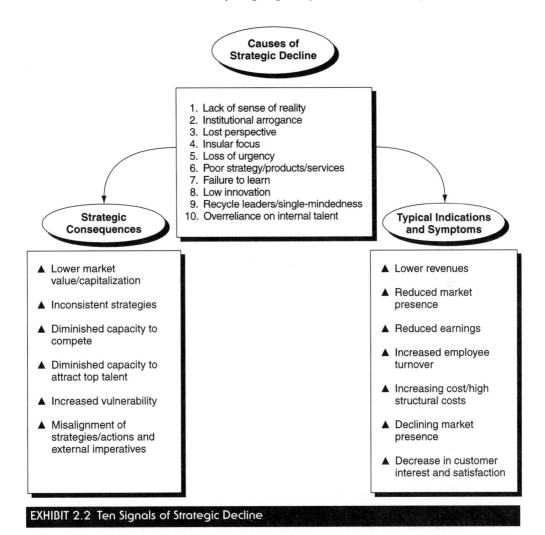

EXHIBIT 2.2 Ten Signals of Strategic Decline

1. Top management was relatively young.
2. Tenure in the organization among top managers was relatively short (under 11 years).
3. Tenure among team members was relatively long, suggesting high levels of teamwork trust and commitment.
4. Top managers had achieved higher levels of formal education, suggesting the ability to multitask and to assimilate complex and large amounts of data.
5. Top team members had academic training in sciences, suggesting analytical and logical prowess.
6. Top teams achieved heterogeneity in education, indicating diverse backgrounds, schools, and majors.

- **Size of the organization.** The size and structure of an organization play an important role in its ability to successfully navigate a change journey. Larger organizations, especially those that are highly vertically integrated, are inherently more difficult to change due to the number of people, embedded behaviors, and operations and processes involved. Global firms with operations distributed on a worldwide basis and encompassing many different cultures and work styles are also difficult to change. Although each part or segment of the organization is a member of a larger "whole" and community, each must be managed differently if change is to be successful. Each country and culture will have its unique preferences and reactions to change. However, smaller, entrepreneurial, and family-owned firms can also be difficult to change because of their unique characteristics and highly sensitive and concentrated power structures.

- **Financial success and past performance.** Past performance and financial success affect the ability of an organization to change. Often, organizations that have historically enjoyed significant financial and market success in stable industries may also engender the greatest resistance to change. They tend to regress and rely on legacy tactics and historical strategies, which are, for the most part, inappropriate for competing in today's real-time world. In contrast, companies that are experiencing poor financial performance and are the targets of investor pressure can institute many and sometimes divergent change initiatives that can dilute effort and distract the organization from its focus and purpose.

- **Ownership and equity structure.** The ownership and equity structure of the organization influence its ability to change in many ways. Public companies are vulnerable to takeover or merger as methods of change because their financial performance is reported and their equity is traded in the open markets. A drop in share price or a change in laws or organizational leadership may trigger an acquisition, as has been suggested in the case of Banker's Trust. The equity structure of an organization can also provide opportunities for participation from investment bankers, leveraged buyouts, private equity funding, and, in the case of growing companies, initial public offerings. All such actions can signal a change in ownership, operating status, and financial structure.

- **Environmental influences and pressures.** As noted, the environment plays a major role in change. The environment can define the need for change, establish the parameters for change, dictate the speed of change, and place limits on change. Organizations must constantly be mindful of the environment and the forces that affect their ability to compete. Moreover, they must be particularly sensitive to patterns and trends.

- **Ability to learn and discern patterns.** Learning is integral to competing successfully. If an organization has a low propensity to learn, its ability to successfully change is compromised. Those organizations that are higher and faster learning firms have a greater propensity for successfully recognizing the need for change, understanding the forces driving change, and navigating change.

- **Certainty/uncertainty.** The level of certainty and uncertainty surrounding change and change programs affect the ability of an organization to effectively manage its efforts. Those organizations that have a legacy of competing in relatively stable and predictable environments often face a more difficult challenge than those that have competed in highly fluid environments. A second consideration centers on certainty of change. Those organizations that have had successful experiences with change and have been successful at confronting uncertainty will have a higher propensity for success and a higher tolerance for uncertainty than those that have not succeeded in previous change initiatives.

- **Leadership.** Leadership is essential to any change journey and the ability of an organization to recognize and anticipate change. Leaders who fail to recognize the need for change, establish a vision, craft a path for change, or effectively manage the change effort place their organizations at significant risk and competitive disadvantage.

Most notably, the failure to change or change successfully can be directly traced to the failure on the part of management and leadership to recognize the need to change and their inability to successfully navigate their organizations through the complexities of change. For many organizations, it is their management teams that lack or fail to anticipate or acknowledge the factors influencing their organizations. Consequently, they are not able to craft responsive strategies and to effectively deploy their resources in the face of changing environmental conditions in a manner that allows them to become superior competitors and high performers.

It is worth noting that these symptoms, no matter how subtle they may appear at first, are precursors to declining sales, profits, and share-price performance that are so widely recognized and taught. Unfortunately, for some organizations, by the time these symptoms appear, it may be too late.

But just because a company is not doing well or is sustaining significant damage from competitors doesn't mean that it is necessarily dead. All companies experience such cycles. With diminishing marketshare, poor quality, and stiffening competition, Chrysler was on the brink of bankruptcy and corporate demise. In the 1970s and 1980s, it was the basket case of American business and required reading at the better graduate business schools of what not to do and how not to run a large company. The company had to receive a financial bailout from the federal government just to remain in business. With an unprecedented level of urgency and conviction, Chrysler worked hard to correct itself and, in the process, reinvented itself and the way it viewed the markets and manufactured and sold cars. Its breakthrough LH and truck products in the early 1990s launched the company on an ascending trajectory. By 1998, after several years of stellar performance and a constant stream of innovative and daring designs, Chrysler was the envy of North American automakers and the most profitable carmaker in the United States. In 1998, it was acquired by Germany's Daimler-Benz—another high performer—and is a now-critical operating unit of the premier automaker in the world.

On the very brink of the business abyss, the legendary American motorcycle maker Harley-Davidson almost succumbed to Japanese competition and its own misguided management efforts. Fortunately, Harley-Davidson had one thing that no other competitor—or for that matter, any other company—enjoyed: impassioned customer loyalty and brand affinity. Harley owners and lovers literally tattoo their bodies with the company logo and slogans. Tapping into perhaps the greatest brand loyalty in the world, together with U.S. governmental regulatory relief aimed at aggressive Japanese motorcycle manufacturers, Harley-Davidson roared back with a vengeance unrivaled in the history of American business. By 1992, it had completely recaptured its marketshare, profitability, and market dominance. By the late 1990s Harley-Davidson's waiting lists for its products exceeded on average a year, and prices for their motorcycles were in excess of $15,000. Harley once again rules the large motorcycle segment in the United States, and in 1999 it celebrated its 100 year anniversary with over 500,000 customers riding into Milwaukee to mark the centennial of an American icon. Imagine a half-million customers taking their precious vacation time and spending their own money by going to Detroit to celebrate GM's anniversary, or marching into Santa Clara to celebrate Intel's new chip!

THE SIX STRATEGIC CHOICES THAT ALL ORGANIZATIONS MUST MAKE

What did Chrysler and Harley-Davidson do that was so unique that it not only saved their companies but catapulted them to greatness? What did Dell, Microsoft, and Gateway do to assail and topple mighty IBM, DEC, and Apple? What does a company like The Home Depot have in common with companies such as Citigroup, Southwest Airlines, and Federal Express? Why did Xerox fail to revolutionize an industry? What can we learn from these companies? The answer is plenty. In all situations, the leaderships of these organizations had a great understanding of the realities in which they competed and a realistic sense of their organization's limitations and capabilities. Most importantly, they shared the urge to reinvent the rules by which others had to compete, and they made the right strategic choices.

As Matsushita Company CEO Konosuke Matsushita noted, "Today, the same day you put a new product on the market it's out of date." It's that instantaneous. Norman Rockwell's idyllic view of American business where the storekeeper waited for a customer to visit, gave the customer lots of personal attention, and shared the local gossip with them is long gone. Gone too are the post–World War II days of Andrew Wyatt's *The Organization Man* and the "employment covenant," implying that in return for conformance, loyalty, and reasonable performance, a person could expect long-term tenure with an employer, job security, and a pension. For graying baby boomers, those are but distant memories and mere recollections for a generation that has been downsized, reengineered, and right-sized. For most baby boomer managers, job security and performance are only as good as the latest transaction and this month's financial results. In the wake of the traditional "employment covenant" is a fast-paced, real-time world dominated by Generation Xers and Yers with here-and-now expectations and most importantly, unlimited options.

In a world of extended enterprises, virtual organizations, disappearing industry boundaries, and more integrated political systems and economies, the key to creating high performance and sustainable competitive advantage no longer comes from the traditional sources. In today's environment, streamlining the supply chain and leveraging procurement and vendor relationships are important, but every "good" company has already done those sorts of things. Any advantages gained from further improvement using those techniques are purely incremental and not strategically differentiating or sustainable.

To be successful, organizations must not only compete in this rapidly changing environment while servicing their existing markets, but they must simultaneously create global political systems, rapidly changing workforce demographics, and instantaneous information flows. Agility, unpredictability, uncertainty, and opportunity are the watch-words for competing today and creating marketspace. The high-performance companies, those that are the leaders of strategic change, work to anticipate change. More importantly, they work even harder to create the changes that others must anticipate and react to. The high performers are enormously sensitive to their environments, and they also have a highly refined sense of self-awareness and value. Most importantly, as in nature, they are driven by a strong sense of self-preservation, self-determinism, and self-perpetuation.

For any company, the strategic operating and planning horizons have been compressed. The time to recover from miscues and mistakes and the window to capitalize strategic opportunity to gain competitive advantage have collapsed. No longer are 3- to 5-year planning horizons appropriate. Rather, the planning time frame for many organizations has collapsed to 12 to 18 months, with an eye on longer trends and directions. In competing today, the time for reacting to competitors or recovering from mistakes and miscalculations is shorter and far less controllable, and the consequences are much more severe. The competitive advantages created and enjoyed by most companies are shorter-lived and easier to replicate. In this hyper-time environment, an organization that can think differently and anticipate changes in its environment correctly, while creating a new market and developing speed and agility as a competency, will develop extraordinary competitive advantage. Stay with the historical precedent, as did Rubbermaid, Kellogg's, Sears, and GM, or select the wrong course as did Quaker, W.T. Grant, and Apple, and the competition will simply outflank and outmaneuver the established industry leader as well as destroy the much-coveted advantages from being a first-mover. Caught in a shifting sea of change, the implications for many organizations are relatively clear. The choices, however, are not, and there lies the challenge and imperative of strategic renewal.

In formulating a strategy for change and competitive advantage, an organization has six basic strategic choices, which are summarized in Exhibit 2.3:

1. *Innovate* and reinvent itself and the rules by which others must compete.
2. *Substitute* itself in place of the competition.
3. *Imitate* the competition.
4. *Complement* the competition.
5. *Collaborate* with the competition.
6. *Withhold* from competing.

An organization may employ any one or *any combination* of these as a portfolio approach to creating strategic renewal and high performance. The selection and use of a strategy depend on a number of factors, including: the resources of the firm, customer needs and requirements, competencies of the organization, financial strength and market position of the firm relative to competitors, velocity required to support change, and the level of uncertainty confronting the organization. Let's discuss these strategic choices and their possible implications.

EXHIBIT 2.3 The Six Strategic Choices that Organizations Must Make

Most Aggressive   *Most Passive*

1	2	3	4	5	6
Innovate	Substitute	Imitate	Complement	Collaborate	Withhold
• High expense • High risk • Very high return • Create new rules • Force competitors to change • Set the pace • Create or sustain first mover advantage	• Create or capture market share within industry • Leverage existing assets and channels • Force competitors to make changes	• Lack innovation or low R&D • Perform better than leader • Content with being a follower • Lower risk • Unsure as to what to do	• Peaceful coexistence • Complement leaders, services and products • Backfill needs and requirements • Mitigate threat to leaders	• Create partnerships • Provides value-added content • Share risk • Requires trust • Requires commitment	• Preserve the right to compete • Fail to act • Unclear direction or need • Acquire necessary resources • Wait for clear signal

Key Themes

▲ Great companies use a portfolio approach of any one or a combination of strategies.

▲ At any one time, one or more choices will have priority over others.

▲ The choices are influenced by a number of factors, including industry dynamics, age, innovation and customers.

Imitate the Competition

When an organization is an imitator, it has signaled to the world that it is a follower, not a leader or innovator. Imitating the strategy of a competitor means that an organization is emulating the actions, processes, products, and capabilities of a competitor or a group of competitors. When any organization selects this strategy, it does so for a number of reasons, specifically:

- It may lack the ability to innovate, but it has the ability to copy.
- It may believe it can outperform the competitor and gain competitive advantage in cost, service, speed, or quality.
- It may be content to achieve parity with the competition.
- It may want to assume lower risk.
- It may be more convenient or expedient as a strategy.
- Like a deer caught in the headlights of an oncoming car, it may simply not know what to do.

One of the best ways of achieving imitation is through benchmarking and importing proven "best" processes and practices into the organization. However, as is discussed in chapter 9, because it is imitation, little, if any, differentiating advantage is achieved by using a "best" practice or common benchmark. At best, emulating a benchmark can only get an organization at parity with its competition. If the competitor is agile and innovative, such parity is very short-lived. Assuming that the costs of imitation and technology switchover expenses are tolerable, imitation has several advantages as a strategy. First, if another company is successfully using it, then the strategy is viable and proven. Second, as the majority of investment is incurred in development and experimentation, imitating a leader can be less expensive for the organization. Third, it takes relatively little insight or unique intellectual capacity to copy some other company's basis of competing. Fourth, imitation can be accomplished with relative expediency and with significantly lower investment costs, as compared to the initial development investments, risks, and efforts. Fifth, imitating a competitor can allow a company to invest in its processes, thereby creating advantage through process innovation and operational excellence.

Imitation is common strategy in the financial services industry, management consulting and accounting professions, and food services and grocery industries. Frequently this strategy is also used in the soft drink industry with the proverbial competition between Coca-Cola and Pepsi-Cola; beer manufacturers Anheuser-Busch, Miller, Coors, and the regional microbreweries; and the fast-food industry with McDonald's, Burger King, and Wendy's, as well as a host of others. When Phillip Morris acquired Miller Brewing Company, it immediately began to spend enormous amounts of money on advertising and promotion. As a consequence, overall industry expenditures for advertising and promotions escalated because other brewers were compelled to increase their spending on advertising. It is questionable whether more advertising led to proportionately higher, sustainable demand and greater operating earnings, yet because one large competitor was doing it, all had to imitate it.

Substitute Itself for the Competition

This strategy is direct, threatening, and confrontational. When an organization selects substitution as a strategy, it signals that it will compete on a broad front and usually head-on with the competition on such factors as price, quality, service, distribution, process, and the ability to change. Organizations that use this strategy are competing for existing portions of marketspace as defined by industry group, price points, products, quality, customers, and demographics, or are attempting to create new segments for products and services within an existing market or industry. The major advantages of this strategy are that it can:

- Create an entirely new segment within a market or industry.
- Leverage the overall resources of the organization.
- Force competitors to take compensating actions.
- Allow for selective substitution based on the company's strengths and capabilities.

The significant deterent to this tactic is that it draws the attention, and often the immediate reaction, of large competitors and market leaders. These countermeasures can be violent and lead to a protracted "war of attrition" based on pricing strategies, increased advertising expenditures, and relative trade-offs in marketshare positions. An organization adopting this form of strategy requires significant capital and terrific staying power to be successful.

This type of strategy formulation can easily be seen in the fast-food industry with competitors vying for consumer preferences and dollars between hamburgers, tacos, and pizza and in the soft drink industry between colas and noncolas. In the automotive industry, there is a constant battle of substitution among passenger cars, minivans, and sport utility vehicles (SUVs). In the early days of the computer industry, there was significant competitive substitution between suppliers such as IBM's DOS, Apple, and Microsoft's Windows. Ultimately, as is discussed in chapter 7, a dominant design emerges, which sets a de facto standard.

The difficulty with this strategy, as Kodak is learning with its digital cameras, is that it can require a complete re-education and re-orientation of consumers. In the case of Kodak, its digital camera strategy is attempting to substitute an expensive and relatively unique product for a time-proven, easy-to-use and inexpensive 35mm camera product. Unfortunately, this strategy has many deficiencies, and several problems have emerged. Notably, it cannibalizes existing products and reduces sales of both cameras and film. More importantly, both the product and strategy currently lack the compelling value proposition that would inspire consumers to move from traditional 35mm photography to digital cameras.

Innovate and Reinvent Itself

Researcher and author Gary Hamel noted, "While the stalwarts in the grocery industry have been focusing efforts on rationalizing the supply chain and turning out thousands of almost trivial product line extensions, the vanguard has been creating entirely new product categories and retailing concepts." The great companies that consistently outperform their rivals and create the new rules of competing place the greatest concentration of resources and energies on being innovative.

This is the most exciting and demanding of any strategic choice. It is risky and requires an entrepreneurial and high-learning culture. Organizations that select and practice this strategy have consciously declared themselves to be trendsetters who will redefine the rules for others. In the process, they will force competitors to imitate, substitute, withdraw, or complement them in their marketspace. This form of strategy involves systemic strategic change at the process, organizational, and cultural levels of the company. It also necessitates significant investment in technical infrastructure capabilities, new markets, and internal competencies. Thus, innovation as a strategy involves high development investments, switch-over costs, and risks, but potentially greater returns. The many advantages of innovation include:

- Can create entirely new markets, marketspaces, and new classes and categories of customers.
- Creates discontinuous shifts and radical changes in industry and economic dynamics.
- Forces competitors to take countermeasures and incur potentially high switch-over costs.
- Can neutralize traditional sources and methods of competitive advantage.
- Can generate significant financial returns.
- Energizes and invigorates the organization and its culture.

Organizations that adopt this strategy as a basis for competing have established the strategic objective to be performance leaders. As performance leaders, they generate higher proportions of their revenues from new products and services. They also generate higher efficiencies and returns from new process designs and a successful integration of IT with process and organizational design. As a result, they are capable of dominating their marketspace. For example, Senior Financial Editor Jim Jubak of *Worth Magazine* notes, ". . . it's easy to figure out the trends in the computer industry: it's headed exactly where Intel decides to drive it." It took just 15 years for Intel to outflank National Semiconductor and Texas Instruments to become an industry leader. It dictates the terms of business to its environment by constantly introducing new products, creating process innovations, and offering the value that others must react and adjust to. As former Intel CEO Andy Grove noted, "We push technology as far as we can and more is better." They accomplish this through innovation in the design of their products, standardization of designs, and the integration of selected business practices and processes.

Intel and high-performance leaders such as Microsoft, The Home Depot, Wal-Mart, Southwest Airlines, and Amazon.com create enormous competitive pressure and, ultimately, advantage by requiring others to expend resources to anticipate and match or catch up with their leads. In short, by innovating, they force others to use resources to imitate or substitute their leads rather than on becoming a leader. As a result, the others fall farther and farther behind.

Withhold from Competing

When an organization selects this withdrawal, or "turtle" strategy, it does so because it may:

- Be abandoning the market or business.
- Be unsure of itself.
- Be reserving or most likely preserving or reconstituting its resources to compete more effectively at a later time.
- Be waiting for other signals or stimuli.

- Have failed to read and acknowledge changes in the environment.
- Have failed to garner the proper balance and mix of resources and competencies necessary to compete effectively.
- Not have the financial or leadership resources necessary for competing.

Although there are times when this form of strategy is appropriate, it can be a dangerous tactic. Withdrawing or holding itself in abeyance from competing may cause an organization to atrophy and lose its focus. It may also lose valuable momentum if it does not try to constantly move forward or have high levels of urgency to it. When held in abeyance for long periods of time, assets—be they human, technical, or intellectual—are costly and can deteriorate. Windows of opportunity that were once open will close if one waits too long. Typically, when this occurs, the costs of "catching-up" are increased, as well as the effort and risks.

Complement the Competition

When an organization selects this strategy, it signals to its competition that it wishes for a "peaceful coexistence." In this strategic position, an organization can augment, extend, and complement the leader's core competencies, processes, markets, or product offerings. When an organization selects complementation as a strategy, it signals that:

- It is willing to coexist with the leaders.
- It will not directly challenge, compete, or move against the core competencies, products, customers, and markets of the leaders.
- It provides products and services that are complementary and value enhancing to the leaders.
- It is willing to function in a variety of positions, including upstream and downstream from the leader.
- It generally follows the initiatives and movements of the leader and "backfills" customer needs or leader inadequacies.

We often see this form of strategic competition among companies in the high-technology and software businesses, athletic industry (shoes, clothes, and equipment), and automotive/motorcycle after-markets. Complementing strategies can also include the selective or complete outsourcing of functions, such as product design, IT, shipping, inventory management, and customer care.

Collaborate

Collaboration occurs when two or more organizations come together for a specific purpose or project. Collaboration is complex and involves trust and coordination among all parties if it is to be successful. When an organization selects this strategy, it presents itself as a partner and a team member for a specified period of time, for a specified project, and generally, for specified responsibilities. Specifically, when an organization selects collaboration as a strategy, it signals that:

- It can be trusted and will assume co-ownership and responsibility for success and failure.
- It will dedicate the necessary resources and competencies to ensure the success of the collaborative effort.

- It can provide value-added subject-matter expertise and services that complement or replace those of the other party.
- It can perform complex processes and achieve the desired outcomes with greater precision, lower costs, and higher value, relative to the other party.
- It signals that it is willing to assume all or part of the risk for a particular aspect or portion of a process or function.

Like the complementary strategies, collaboration can include outsourcing and can also involve various forms of co-option. Collaboration has been a significant form of business organization in the entertainment (movies and music), automotive industry, and aviation industries.

One of the keys to understanding the intricacies of strategy formulation and strategic change is to acknowledge that once an organization has made a strategic choice and takes action to execute against it, it ceases to be the same and enters a new state. In this new state, it will do one of two things: *ascend* or *descend*. Successful strategic renewal requires time to learn and to adapt. The high-performance organizations recognize that there is an "uptake" period involved in those shifts, during which individuals and their organizations *learn* how to exploit the capabilities and opportunities created by the discontinuous shifts, or innovations. Thus, successful change requires not only direction, but also enormous commitment and "intestinal" fortitude. The importance of an organization's commitment to strategy has been an important topic discussed by many researchers, including Pankaj Ghemawat. Ghemawat defines *commitment* as "the tendency of strategies to persist over time." The issue of organizational commitment to a strategy centers on two very relevant considerations: (1) Is the strategy the correct one for creating high performance? and (2) What behaviors, competencies, and financial resources are necessary to sustain the organization's commitment to such a strategy?

The major lesson learned from the once-great companies is that strategic advantage is a fragile and fleeting asset. Commitment comes and goes. As a general rule: The higher the velocity of change, the greater the uncertainty and fluidity confronting an organization. The more fluid the environment, the more precarious strategic advantage becomes. In any organization competing globally, some markets are maturing, others are evolving, some are emerging, and an undetermined number of markets have yet to be created or discovered. Thus, to create and sustain high performance, an organization must have as its *core strategy* the commitment to *becoming* a high-performance organization.

THE HIGH-PERFORMANCE IMPERATIVE

What do you call an organization that over a period of time creates and sustains great financial, operational, and marketspace performance? How does one characterize the performance of an organization that year after year sets the standards that most others envy? The great companies, such as Amazon.com, Dell, Disney, Hewlett-Packard, Federal Express, Southwest Airlines, GE, Intel, Microsoft, The Home Depot, Citigroup, Wal-Mart, Ford, DaimlerChrysler, and Charles Schwab, didn't become the dominant forces on the business landscape just by offering good products, or by being in the right industry at the right time. Nor did they create and maintain their leadership positions by using slick marketing campaigns. These organizations may have a few "off years" of lower sales growth and slower earnings, but over the long term they enjoy ascending trajectories supported by a constant stream of new products and services. Why is it that these organizations consistently set the standards, irrespective of industry? When one thinks of excellent customer service, Hewlett-Packard comes to mind. When flawless execution is mentioned, Federal Express is usually thought of. When electronic commerce is referenced in the media, Amazon.com and Dell Computers are often the companies most prominently displayed. What makes these companies so special? How do they do it?

The business performance leaders didn't just wake up one day at the top of their industries, the darlings of Wall Street and the envy of their peers. Unique and compelling products and services clearly helped to propel them to those lofty levels, but something else—some other factor or combination of factors—came into play to keep them there. Surely, they had ideas and products, but lots of companies have ideas and products. Being first to market is important, but it isn't everything. There are abundant examples of companies that had first-mover advantage, then lost momentum. Being first to market with a concept is clearly beneficial, but it does not guarantee high performance or long-term viability. For example, Sony was first in the VCR market with its Betamax product, but VHS won out. Xerox beat everyone, including Apple, in the development of the PC, but failed to capitalize upon it. It was Apple that won the prize in the early days of the PC industry. Xerox apparently failed to recognize the personal computer as the greatest innovation since the telephone. Apple defined the PC market, but failed to successfully counter the IBM-compatible revolution. In the earlier part of this century, Ford mastered mass production and for a while dominated the U.S. automotive scene. But it was GM that mastered planned obsolescence and created market segmentation and model differentiation that displaced Ford to became the dominant force in the automotive industry for the next 40 years. International Harvester was first to introduce the SUV, but it ceded their leadership positions to GM, Jeep and Ford. Indeed, being first is no guarantee of high performance.

The great performers achieved their lofty places by creating synergy of purpose and design in their operations. Clearly, one aspect of their stellar rise has been their ability to create extraordinary leverage and competitive advantage through the integration of resources and competencies. They have the ability to leverage their resources and generate extraordinary energy out of them. In military terms, it is called a *force multiplier.* Organizations that can leverage and create synergies of purpose are high performers. They have a knack for making 2 plus 2 equal 5 or 6.

A key question regarding high performance and strategic change is, "What does it mean?" When a CEO stands before the shareholders and employees and announces that Acme Company will be a high-performance organization, what level or standard of performance is she or he advancing? Five challenging issues come to mind when considering high performance as a term, a strategic objective, and a behavioral profile:

1. What does high performance mean?
2. Can such a term and concept be realistically defined in a strategic context?
3. Relative to past performance, individual performance, an industry measure, or some other benchmark, how can high performance be measured?
4. What are the trademarks and the strategic, operating, and managerial characteristics of a high-performance organization?
5. How did the high-performance organizations become high performers?

The idea of high performance as a *strategic doctrine* is elusive and confusing; there are no easy answers and many opinions. Developing a definition without the clichés is difficult. There are so many variables and factors to consider that just separating the essential from the superficial and the fact from the fiction is a challenge. Although it's fashionable among executives to use the term, most business leaders, dictionaries, and popular management books do not define the term. A kindred definition can be found in the description of *high powered,* which, according to Scribner's, is "having great drive and energy." Management consultant Ken Blanchard advertises an equation that is: ROP = Productive Organizational Performance/Leadership & Employee Time and Energy Invested, where ROP is the return on performance and productivity. One could infer that high performance, either at the organizational or individual levels, can be derived through the manipulation of the denominators, numerators, and multipliers. If only high performance could be that easy, there would be many more high performers. There are no simple formulas or equations to follow or memorize and no shortcuts in creating and sustaining high performance.

The easiest tendency is to join the crowd and resort to the rhetoric and platitudes. Many of the popular business books and consultants describe high performance in grandiose and sensational terms using words like *hyper-growth, world-class, supercharged, turbocharged,* and *hyper-performance.* In a strategic setting, one cannot be sure what all those really mean, but they sound awfully good, especially at sales meetings and as titles for books and seminars. For all of their bravado, few consultants have actually ventured to try to define what a high-performance organization is with any deliberate definition, performance metrics, and meaningful context. That fact alone is interesting and somewhat disconcerting because if you can't define and describe it, you probably shouldn't be consulting on it or teaching it.

Ask any manager what high performance is and you'll likely get an initial response that centers on financial performance and comparisons to this year's (or this month's) budget and some comparison to the "industry." A moment of reflection usually leads to a discussion of other factors related to marketshare, quality, and operations. Some managers may even remember to mention something about customers and employees in their responses. But usually the first response centers on financial performance. So, to some, high performance is nothing more than financial performance.

One thought is that high performance simply means to do better. A French researcher defined it as "Continuously improving upon one's performance. That is, if a company or individual is performing better today than yesterday, then it or he or she is a high-performer." That's an interesting take on a Unitarian-like concept, but it falls far short of defining high performance, at least in any meaningful or useful way that explains why some companies dominate their marketspace. It fails to provide relevancy. For example, tiny Kingdom Computers in remote Mansfield, Pennsylvania, enjoys consistent growth, improving profits, and growing financial success. Nonetheless, it is not at the level or stature of Dell or Gateway and does not dominate its marketplace. It battles for life as an alternative and a substitute. As a basketball player, my friend Kevin was a star in high school and college. He constantly improved his skills and elevated his game, but when compared to Michael Jordan, he was not a high performer. In recovering from a stream of problems, Bausch & Lomb may have improved its financial performance and its stock price over the few last years, but in contrast to rival Johnson & Johnson, it is not the performance standard.

Another researcher claims that high performance cannot be defined because it "is different for each and every company and individual." That may also be somewhat true, but not entirely valid when considering the issue of high performance in the broader context of other companies that are leading their markets, dictating the rules to others, and successfully attracting investment funds. Another researcher explains it as "Doing the best a company or individual can do." That's okay but not very specific—many people will say that they are "doing their best," but they are not high performers.

Unfortunately, such definitions do little to advance the strategic thinking of business leaders or the competitive positions of their organizations. They lack clarity and depth in understanding and applying the realities of competing against both established and unknown competitors. But in the absence of any standard, benchmarks and definitions that draw on self-comparisons or invalid comparisons are relatively meaningless. Thus, the challenge for both the business leader and researcher is whether to develop a definition and work to support it, adopt one of the clichés, or wait to see what unfolds as one works his or her way through the subject matter. Rather than just selecting something that "sounded" like high performance and adding to the clichés or biasing the analysis by locking into a specific definition from the onset, the approach for this work was to let those organizations that outperform the others define the term for themselves. Hence, the definition that is offered has been cultivated from the behaviors of those companies that represent the high performers. A high-performance organization is defined as:

> One that consistently sets the performance standard in creating and
> sustaining competitive advantage, exemplary financial performance, and
> stakeholder value over a long period of time.

The term *competitive advantage* is a central and essential component to the definition. Establishing a competitive advantage extends far beyond focusing solely on the industry rivals to beat them. Of course, beating the competition is important, but if an organization exclusively focuses on beating the competition as an objective, it can distort its perceptions of reality, unnecessarily divert its resources, and dilute its long-term focus. High-performance organizations are cognizant of the competition and are enormously sensitive to the competitive landscape. They understand that the strongest competitive position is one in which *they* are the competition: the dominant force. That is, they *constructively compete* against themselves, they set the highest standards, they stay focused, and they mass and leverage their resources for their greatest success. In the process of constructively competing against their internal resources, they improve their internal competencies and skills, they build an organizational culture that probes, learns, and applies knowledge, and finally, they create a culture that knows how to effectively compete under conditions of continuous change and uncertainty.

To the high-performance organization, competitive advantage isn't about destroying the competition. Annihilation of the rivals may be a consequence of the competition not being as smart and as good as they should be. Rather, the high performers are always cognizant of the competition, but they are not fixated or preoccupied by what the competition is doing, or paralyzed by it. To the high performers, competitive advantage is about being significantly better than the competition by being the competitive standard that sets the rules. When they accomplish this, they have, as Sun-Tzu noted 2,000 years ago, "...subdue[d] the enemy's army without battle." A more contemporary battlefield commander, GE CEO Jack Welch, calls it "Finding a better way, every day." By defining the competitive environment, the high-performance companies, like Microsoft, Wal-Mart, and Charles Schwab, win before they even enter and are competing in it. They achieve this superior position by being different and continuously focusing on better ways of doing things.

For the high-performance organizations, two things are certain: High-performance is a strategic imperative, and it is a continuous and institutionalized process. The high performers are not just good at both, they are exceptional at them and better than all the others.

INDICATORS OF HIGH PERFORMANCE

What are the traits and visible signals of a high-performance organization? The most obvious answer is having outstanding products, achieving great financial results, and enjoying superior stock market performance. The most common indicators are financial performance as measured by stock price performance, sales growth, earnings, and return on equity. Yet, as a measure of high performance, financial results alone are not enough to indicate superior management or strategic posture. The list of financially driven companies that have demonstrated good financial performance but are not high performers or are no longer high performers is long and distinguished.

Driven by a leadership mandate for double-digit growth and decentralization, Bausch & Lomb enjoyed a stream of financial successes in the 1980s under CEO Dan Gill. Then, it all suddenly came to a very abrupt and painful stop, culminating with leadership changes and public disclosure of its corporate "dirty laundry" by *Business Week.* What followed was lackluster financial performance, situational cost-cutting initiatives, divestitures of well-known brands, massive inventory write-offs and adjustments, Securities and Exchange Commission (SEC) investigations, allegations of money laundering, and shareholder and customer lawsuits. Can Bausch & Lomb restore its lost luster and regain its once-dominant position? Perhaps—the jury is still out, but Bausch & Lomb is performing better. It has new leadership, a dedicated workforce, and great brand recognition built through years of impeccable quality, but the customer has changed and competitors have gained precious shelf space and earned customer loyalty forfeited earlier by Bausch & Lomb. The competition, especially Johnson & Johnson, enjoys competitive advantages and brand recognition that once belonged to Bausch & Lomb.

A distinct characteristic of all high performers is that they do not merely exist in business—that is, managing on a day-to-day basis, reacting to competition and customers, and taking what the market and competition provides. Rather, the high performers make business their primary focus, and they elevate it to a passion. Their organizational structures and cultures are *designed* for competing each and every day, and they come back the next day ready and lusting to play again. They have enormous staying power and confidence in themselves and their abilities. Although they abhor failure, they understand that failure is an inevitable part of the learning process. They have un-mitigated confidence and belief in what they are doing, and they are convinced that their goals are worthwhile and achievable. It is this conviction that drives many of the high performers to greater levels of performance and a never-ending process of learning, probing, adapting, and changing. In the process, they test and stress their limits and set newer and higher standards of performance. To them, high performance is a journey of continuous learning, change, and adaptation, not a fixed-point destination. Thus, their targets, expectations, and standards are always evolving, always changing, always rising higher and higher.

Craig Barrett, Intel CEO, summed it up nicely when he noted that Intel "... pictured themselves going down the road at 120 mile per hour. Somewhere there's going to be a brick wall to cross, but our view is it's better to run into the wall than to anticipate it and stop short." Mr. Barrett provides us a glimpse into the mind of a high-performance leader and soul of a high-performance company. Former Chrysler CEO Lee Iacocca set a cultural tone and a behavioral standard for the company when he said, "Lead, follow or get out of the way" in a national advertisement campaign. High-performance compa-nies make high performance a *busihdo*—a way of life. It is a credo and mantra. The very essence of their high performance and the need to constantly evolve and adapt are deeply ingrained in their culture and belief systems. Implicit in this is an advanced sense of organizational self-actualization, self-determinism, and self-perpetuation.

The high-performance leaders have a refined sense of the world and a real knowledge of their operating environments, and they use the power of new ideas, technologies, and human diversity to find new ways to create new strategies to com-pete by. Exhibit 2.4 summarizes some of the key criteria and behavioral dimensions of high-performance companies. While it is not necessary that a company satisfy each criterion, the high-performers typically meet a significant percentage of these per-formance indicators on a consistent basis.

With the foregoing criteria, the question becomes, what organizations best exem-plify the high performers?

EXHIBIT 2.4 Key Indicators of High-Performing Organizations

I. Financial Performance and Shareholder Value Creation
  A. Achieves and sustains 25% plus growth in revenue and/or profits and/or market value over a 5-year period.
  B. On the average, typically generates and sustains an annual return for shareholders of 1.5 times greater than the overall S&P 500 as a benchmark.
  C. Consistently meets official and Wall Street "whisper" revenue and earnings forecasts and estimates with minimal surprises and variances.
  D. Effectively manages investor relations, expectations, and communications.
  E. Assets are fully deployed in a manner that optimizes their use and return to shareholders.
  F. Consistently demonstrates that asset allocation and investment decisions are made with a clear purpose, with distinct economic value proposition, and with the best interests of shareholders in mind.

II. Strategic Positioning
  A. Demonstrates a commitment driven by a single or integrated set of strategic visions, directions, or imperatives.
  B. Achieves and sustains superior global market penetration and representation.

EXHIBIT 2.4 *(cont.)*

C. Extends and expands the enterprise through the selective and effective use of alliances.
D. Leverages information technology to increase market presence, customer reach, and vendor relations.
E. Consistently creates new "markets" and opportunities through new business venues, products, and organizational designs.
F. Consistently sets the standard and rules so other competitors must react, expend resources, and counter.

III. **Leadership and Innovativeness**
A. Actively demonstrates and exemplifies leadership characteristics (see chapter 8).
B. Aggressively cultivates pluralism as a source of leadership and competitive advantage.
C. Creates leadership development opportunities through job rotation and enrichment and investment programs.
D. Demonstrates and promotes a culture of customer/client focus and service.
E. Practices long-term succession planning and development for next generation leaders.
F. Consistently cultivates an environment of creativity and innovation.
G. Actively manages knowledge through the use of a knowledge architecture and Knowledge Management Process (KMP) (see chapter 6).
H. Fosters and encourages learning, probing, and discovery and is tolerant of mistakes and setbacks.
I. Hires and nurtures highly talented employees.
J. Generates 30% of revenues from new product introductions.
K. Creates and sustains a collaborative working environment.

IV. **Governance and Social Responsibility**
A. Cultivates active and engaged board involvement.
B. Board has a vested economic and moral interest in the financial and social behavior of the organization.
C. Board demonstrates a commitment to strategic positioning and long-term competitive advantage.

D. Board governance is relatively open; board members are accessible to shareholders.
E. CEO reports to the board, and board actively manages and evaluates CEO performance against strategic objectives and predefined operating results.
F. Board actively participates in setting the strategic direction of the organization.
G. Board aggressively acts on behalf of the shareholders as opposed to the CEO.
H. Demonstrates a significant financial commitment to the local economies and environments in which it does business.
I. Invests in the social structure of the local communities.
J. Actively manages its relationships with the local communities.
K. Sets and sustains a higher level of ethical and moral behavior.
L. Sets a standard for communicating with customers and the community on important matters.
M. Compensation practices and programs accurately reflect organizational performance and financial results.

V. **Brand Recognition and Quality of Products**
A. Has a preeminent brand name and image.
B. Has rationalized its brand identity and image at the enterprise level.
C. Generates high consumer confidence from the brand.
D. Generates high consumer interest in the brand.
E. Consistently sets the highest quality benchmarks and standards relative to its competitors.
F. Consistently creates/generates a high-value image and acceptance among consumers relative to price and performance.
G. Practices successful TQM methods designed to continuously improve value, quality, and performance.

THE HIGH PERFORMERS

On the quest for high performance and its definition, we went looking for organizations that exhibited, both implicitly and explicitly, the ability to keep the competition guessing and the consumer anticipating its next product. The result of our search is a composite of companies and organizations that have continuously set the pace for innovation, creativity, superior financial returns, attracted the best talent, and seemingly dictate and redefine the rules of competing. The following list depicts companies that have consistently established the standard for high performance:

AlliedSignal	Home Depot
Berkshire Hathaway	Intel Corporation
Citigroup	Johnson & Johnson
Charles Schwab	Merck
Cisco Corporation	Merrill Lynch
Coca-Cola Company	Microsoft Corporation
Dell Computer	Northwestern Mutual Life
Enron	Pfizer
Federal Express Corporation	Proctor & Gamble
General Electric Company	Southwest Airlines
Gillette	The Walt Disney Company
Hewlett-Packard	Wal-Mart Stores

By virtually any measure, these companies represent true high performers. Of course, a number of other organizations, including Asea Brown Boveri Ltd. ABB (Switzerland), U.S. Army Rangers, U.S. Navy Seals, Nikon (Japan), E. I. DuPont (United States), Vinten Group (United Kingdom), HFS (United States), Nucor (United States), Duke Energy (United States), Medtronic (United States), Ford Motor Company (United States), Exxon (United States), Amgen (United States), Amazon.com (United States), Lucent Technologies (United States), and Virgin (United Kingdom), qualify as, or nearly qualify as, high performers. The above group, however, exemplifies a long-term sustained greatness and best illustrates the key characteristics of high performance.

Interestingly but not surprisingly, the "all-industry" top 10 identified by *Fortune* as the "most admired" companies included all of our high performers. Moreover, 20 of them placed among the first 50 companies on the Fortune list, and most remarkably, the top 10 spots were virtually taken by 10 of the high-performance organizations.

Correspondingly, eight of the companies listed as high-performance examples also ranked in the *Business Week* top 25 for 1998 earnings. Noticeably, 10 of the companies were also listed by *Business Week* among the top 50 of the "new business elite" in terms of demonstrating the best performance in the S&P (Standard & Poor) 500 for 1998. Thirteen of the companies also ranked among *Fortune*'s top 50 companies generating the highest return to investors over the 1988 to 1998 time period. We have not researched the correlation between our list and those of *Fortune* and *Business Week,* but we do believe that the extent of resemblance is not coincidental. Intuitively, it makes a lot of sense that there would be commonality between *Fortune, Business Week,* and this work. After all, the research has been derived from the same population of businesses, using much of the same publicly available data.

In contrast, companies like Compaq/DEC, Westinghouse, Quaker Oats, Morrison Knudson, Apple Computer, Kodak, Kmart, Oxford Health Plans, Fruit of the Loom, Motorola, Xerox, Union Carbide, Bausch & Lomb, Kellogg's, Sears, GM, TWA, and Archer Daniels Midland did not make the list for high-performance companies. In some cases, the stock prices of these companies performed well, but so did the overall market. Other factors prevented them from elevating their status. It should be no surprise that some of these same companies also made *Fortune*'s "Least Admired List" and *Business Week*'s list of companies with the "Worst Boards of Directors."

Finally, it is no revelation that the high-performance companies are superior at financial management and at creating outstanding financial results. Indeed, the financial performance of the high performers has been extraordinary. For example, at the end of 1998, America Online outperformed almost all others. Between 1994 and 1998, its profits rocketed by an annual compound rate of 96 percent, and its sales during that 5-year period increased 123 percent by the same measure. In comparison, GM's net income had been declining at a 11.9 percent annual rate. Another outstanding high performer, Dell Computer, has returned a whopping 79.7 percent to shareholders—*annually.* In comparison, although IBM's earnings improved and its stock performed well, it has lost marketshare in the aggregate computer industry and has, according to Gary Hamel, diluted its market power. The high performers have consistently outperformed the S&P 500 with regard to revenue growth, stock price performance, earnings per share, and market capitalization (see Exhibit 2.5).

EXHIBIT 2.5 High-Performance Companies
Five-Year Annualized Growth Rates (1994–1998)

	High Performers[a]	*S&P 500*[b]	*Differential*
EPS	23.32%	13.56%	1.72×
Sales	28.30%	7.53%	3.76×
Stock price	37.75%	27.91%	1.35×
Market capitalization	54.64%	13.60%	2.09×
Dividend payout	21.37%	6.74%	11.80×
Total return on investment	33.8%	21.37%	1.58×

[a]Company data and records have been drawn from annual reports, based on either calendar or fiscal year periods between 1994 and 1998.
[b]S&P 500 statistics were current as of June 30, 1998.
Sources: Value Line, Inc., MSN Investor, Zacks.

The significant fact that stands out with respect to financial performance is that high-performance organizations tend to view financial performance in three important ways: as a process, as a result, and as an objective. Superior financial performance is both a *goal* and an *outcome:* a natural consequence of doing the right things and flawlessly executing its strategies and operations. High performers emphasize the *long term* through concentrating on value and positioning themselves for the future. To the high-performance company, the short term is important, but not at the expense of the long run. As GE demonstrates, high performers will tolerate short-term losses in exchange for a superior position and financial performance in the long run. The financial performance of the high performers reflects their internal management practices and standards for managing shareholder assets. For the most part, high-performance companies are conservative in the management of their finances. Being conservative does not necessarily imply that they are not risk takers or that they invest only in the 'sure things.' Rather, the high performers are conservative in the respect that they understand the value of money, not just in monetary terms but in strategic terms. They confirm that their investments are *aligned* with the strategies of the company, not just an isolated opportunity with little or no potential for broader synergies.

Given the foregoing context, there are two major questions that must be explored:

1. How did these companies become high performers?
2. What are the common qualities that they all share?

First, the high-performing companies possess certain behavioral attributes and operational qualities that set them apart from the pack. These characteristics allow them to create great products and strategies. The great performers share more than just great financial results, products, quality, and price. Having those things or achieving them are the results of deeper activities. Obviously, the products and services are central to their success; one cannot be in business without a product or a service to sell. Similarly, there is nothing strategic about pricing or quality that cannot be substituted for and bettered by the competitors.

The great-performing companies have something more in common—qualities and characteristics that are quite elusive to the wannabes. For the high-performance companies, market leadership is the result of a strategy based on five strategic pillars:

1. *Information technology,* which is used to extend and leverage the enterprise and neutralize many of the traditional sources of competitive advantage.
2. *Innovation,* as demonstrated through the successful introduction of new products, methods, processes, and management practices which contribute to revenue growth.
3. *Knowledge management,* as demonstrated through the creation of learning, dissemination, and transference of key knowledge necessary for strategic advantage.
4. *Leadership,* as exemplified by the ability to mobilize the organization and its people to accomplish extraordinary results.
5. *Operational agility and excellence,* as evidenced by flawless operations, exemplary financial performance, and the ability to constantly redeploy and reconfigure resources in an efficient manner.

Exhibit 2.6 illustrates the five pillars of strategic renewal and strategy formulation.

Much like the great architect Frank Lloyd Wright would design a building that achieved harmony with its environment and contributed to the beauty of its surroundings, the great companies of today are built through a vision and a commitment to a purposeful design incorporating these five pillars. In this book, chapters 5 through 9 discuss each of these pillars in greater detail and offer additional insights into how high-performance organizations use them to create competitive advantage and support strategic renewal. Still, to appreciate such companies and their influence on strategy formulation, it is beneficial to develop a more complete understanding of the role of change and the forces of change that are shaping a new and very different competitive marketspace.

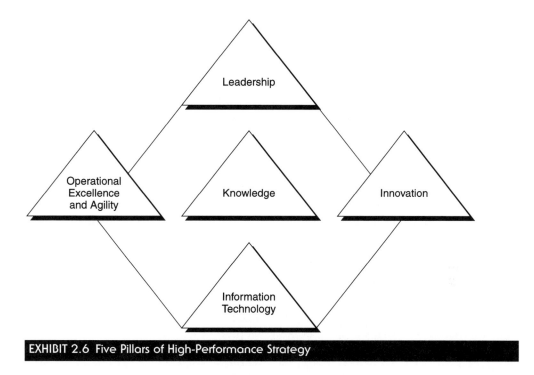

EXHIBIT 2.6 Five Pillars of High-Performance Strategy

With the context drawn and stage set, we now turn our attention towards those factors and influences that are affecting all major organizations. Two major themes are dominating the immediate and long term: globalization and changing demographics. Briefly:

1. Chapter 3 explores the strategic implications of globalization in greater detail.

2. Chapter 4 explores the influence of changing demographics, diversity, and multiculturalism.

SUMMARY

The foregoing brings us to one of the most important lessons about strategic change and about becoming a high-performance organization. To develop or sustain high performance requires that an organization constantly renew itself. Strategic renewal and becoming a high-performance organization force companies to anticipate, recognize, and constructively manage change. In doing so, the new fundamentals of strategy formulation require that an organization have, at the core of its strategy, the objective to become a high performer.

Becoming a high-performance organization requires a penchant for change, deliberate management design, specific competencies, and dedicated processes. In the following chapters, we attempt to define and describe the qualities that are common to all high-performance companies. These qualities provide the change levers and a change model for creating and sustaining high performance. In the subsequent chapters of this book, we explore these and discuss how an organization can create and sustain high-performance change strategies.

Critical Thoughts and Discussion Questions

1. Discuss the qualities of high performance and how they are the same across industries and companies.
2. Using external research on GM, Kellogg's, Microsoft, and The Home Depot as examples, apply the Ten Warning Signs of Strategic Decline to each of these organizations. Compare and contrast the results.
3. Using the results from the above exercise, apply the Six Strategic Choices to the organizations above to determine viable strategies for them.
4. Harley-Davidson and Chrysler Corporation represent two success stories of the later part of the twentieth century, yet they are very different companies. Compare how Harley-Davidson renewed itself to how Chrysler went about the process. What did these companies have in common? What did they have that was unique? How did these companies create new sources of competitive advantage, and what did they do to change the rules of competing in their industries?

ANNUALIZED COMPOUND GROWTH RATES: 1994–1998

Company	Market Capitalization	Sales	Net Income	EPS	Stock Price	Dividend Payout
AlliedSignal	46.69%	4.23%	15.08%	14.71%	21.12%	16.67%
America Online	135.99%	123.38%	96.19%	73.21%	96.78%	N/A
Berkshire Hathaway	44.97%	37.12%	54.65%	52.33%	27.97%	N/A
Charles Schwab	83.55%	26.62%	26.69%	25.74%	61.17%	28.01%
Cisco Systems	108.70%	61.51%	43.90%	34.07%	68.74%	N/A
Citicorp	74.61%	42.64%	44.67%	17.15%	35.72%	62.15%
Coca-Cola	25.58%	3.85%	8.45%	9.44%	21.08%	N/A
Dell Computer	187.91%	51.36%	76.87%	79.58%	137.19%	N/A
Enron	25.09%	36.88%	11.59%	4.41%	13.35%	N/A
Federal Express	22.31%	16.97%	25.25%	16.56%	10.89%	N/A
General Electric	40.40%	13.70%	18.43%	19.35%	31.95%	12.28%
Gillette	34.81%	13.45%	11.73%	4.72%	20.63%	26.28%
Hewlet-Packard	26.22%	17.14%	16.50%	16.00%	19.75%	22.23%
Home Depot	43.21%	24.75%	27.83%	24.58%	31.17%	25.47%
Intel	65.33%	22.89%	27.61%	27.73%	49.33%	23.93%
Johnson & Johnson	34.45%	10.73%	11.13%	9.34%	24.10%	15.75%
Merck	39.21%	15.78%	15.04%	15.94%	31.07%	11.96%
Merrill Lynch	37.59%	18.42%	5.49%	6.07%	30.15%	N/A
Microsoft	70.09%	32.86%	40.69%	37.83%	53.05%	N/A
Northwestern Mutual Life	24.50%	65.76%	18.45%	9.54%	14.60%	10.21%
Pfizer	61.85%	13.09%	26.75%	24.84%	45.28%	13.19%
Procter & Gamble	35.35%	5.23%	14.35%	15.27%	27.82%	11.41%
Southwest Airlines	34.24%	12.58%	24.69%	22.85%	24.97%	12.86%
Wal-Mart Stores	38.38%	13.66%	13.38%	14.30%	30.32%	21.40%
Walt Disney Company	25.07%	22.95%	13.61%	7.56%	14.46%	28.06%
H-P Average	54.64%	28.30%	27.56%	23.32%	37.75%	21.37%

Annualized Price Growth Rate—S&P 500 Index   27.91%

ANNUALIZED COMPOUND GROWTH RATES: 1994–1998, *continued*

Company	Market Capitalization	Sales	Net Income	EPS	Stock Price	Dividend Payout
Apple Computer	12.48%	−10.33%	−0.10%	−5.29%	2.51%	−100.00%
Bausch and Lomb	13.65%	6.30%	16.93%	18.27%	12.11%	1.30%
Compaq	58.62%	30.14%	N/A	N/A	39.68%	N/A
Eastman Chemicals	−4.05%	0.87%	−7.22%	−6.24%	−2.39%	8.66%
Eastman Kodak	9.80%	−0.52%	25.69%	27.00%	8.56%	0.13%
General Motors	5.50%	1.01%	−11.87%	−5.08%	11.18%	15.09%
Honeywell	23.89%	8.61%	19.67%	20.15%	19.05%	3.33%
K-Mart	12.38%	−0.26%	15.02%	12.52%	5.21%	−100.00%
Motorola	1.55%	7.22%	N/A	N/A	1.03%	17.91%
Sears & Roebuck	16.18%	5.76%	−7.86%	−7.50%	13.07%	−20.56%
L-P Average	15.00%	4.88%	6.28%	6.73%	11.00%	−19.35%

AMERICA'S MOST ADMIRED COMPANIES: 1998

		Total Return to Investors	
Rank	Company	1998	1993–98
1	*General Electric*	41.00%	34.20%
2	*Coca-Cola*	1.30%	26.10%
3	*Microsoft*	114.60%	68.90%
4	*Dell Computer*	248.50%	152.90%
5	*Berkshire Hathaway*	52.20%	33.80%
6	*Wal-Mart Stores*	107.60%	27.60%
7	*Southwest Airlines*	38.40%	6.60%
8	*Intel*	69.00%	50.60%
9	*Merck*	41.30%	37.00%
10	*Walt Disney*	−8.5%	16.90%
	Top ten average	**70.50%**	**45.40%**
	S&P 500	**27.10%**	**23.50%**
5	Pfizer	68.90%	
8	Home Depot	108.40%	
11	Enron	39.90%	
12	Procter & Gamble	15.90%	
21	Gillette	−3.80%	
32	Merrill Lynch	−7.50%	
40	Johnson & Johnson	28.90%	
45	Hewlett-Packard	10.70%	
48	Northwestern Mutual Life		
49	Citicorp		
65	AlliedSignal	15.90%	
71	Charles Schwab	101.80%	
118	America Online	585.60%	
165	Nike	5%	
	Amazon.com		

THE BOTTOM TEN: 1998

		Total Return to Investors	
Rank	Company	1998	1993–98
460	*Foundation Health Services*	−46.6%	N.A.
461	*Fruit of the Loom*	−46.1%	−10.6%
462	*Viad*	59.40%	27.00%
463	*Olsten*	−49.9%	−16.7%
464	*U.S. Industries*	−38.4%	N.A.
465	*Stone Container*	36.20%	5.80%
466	*Oxford Health Plans*	−4.4%	2.30%
467	*MedPartners*	−76.5%	N.A.
468	*Shoney's*	−57.7%	−43.1%
469	*Trump Hotels & Casinos*	−43.9%	N.A.
	Bottom ten average	**−26.8%**	**−5.9%**

THE BEST BOARDS OF DIRECTORS		THE WORST BOARDS OF DIRECTORS	
Rank	Company	Rank	Company
1	Campbell Soup	1	Disney
2	General Electric	2	AT&T
3	Compaq Computer	3	H.J. Heinz
4	Microsoft	4	Archer Daniels Midland
5	IBM	5	Dow Jones
6	Chrysler	6	Dillard's
7	General Motors	7	Rollins International
8	Intel	8	Occidental Petroleum
9	Colgate Palmolive	9	Ogden
10	Texas Instruments	10	Maxxam

OTHER HIGH-PERFORMANCE BOARDS
OF DIRECTORS

Rank	Company
11	Hewlett Packard
12	Johnson & Johnson
15	Coca-Cola
19	Pfizer
20	Merck

Scoring Criteria:
1   accountability to shareholders
2   quality of directors
3   independence
4   corporate performance

CHAPTER

3

GLOBALIZATION AND MEGAMERGERS: COMPETING IN A TRANSNATIONAL WORLD

"It was once sacrosanct to talk about our cars being 'Made in Germany.' We have to change that to 'Made by Mercedes,' never mind where they are assembled."
—JURGEN SCHREMPP, CEO, DAIMLERCHRYSLER CORPORATION

INTRODUCTION

The trend towards more open, interconnected, and interdependent economies and megasized organizations has redefined the ways strategies must be developed and how organizations manage their resources, develop their talent, and operate in their environments. As a result of globalization, the operating environment and strategy formulation efforts of virtually every major organization have been permanently altered.

Despite the fanfare with which many leaders speak of globalization and the visibility this term commands in their annual reports, only a few can really define it in any meaningful context. Defining *globalization* and its logical extension, *transnationalism* pose a challenge, but acting and being a global organization can be an even more difficult and daunting task. In the process, three key questions must be addressed:

1. What is an appropriate definition for globalization?
2. What are the factors driving globalization?
3. What is the impact of globalization on strategy?

Understanding the strategic implications of globalization is fundamental to high performance and strategic renewal for a number of reasons. Briefly:

- Globalization is defining completely new rules of competing. These new rules are negating traditional management and strategy formulation practices.
- Globalization is creating increasingly competitive and intensive environments.
- Globalization is creating significant investment and marketing opportunities.
- Globalization is driving new forms of business and global scales through megamergers and acquisitions on an unprecedented scale. With these mergers

also come increases in the number and complexity of global alliances and partnerships.
- Globalization is destroying the physical confines and geographic limitations of companies and industries.
- Globalization is forcing the need for new types of leaders and leadership styles.
- Finally, globalization is defining new ethics and morals for competing and leading.

This chapter will discuss the implications and importance of globalization and transnationalism and their impact on strategy and high performance. It begins by establishing the context for globalization by offering definitions, continues through a brief history of globalization, then explores the pertinent strategic, operational, and organizational implications of globalization and concludes with a series of discussion questions.

DEFINING GLOBALIZATION

"We are a global company," proclaimed the CEO of a Fortune 500 company in January 1997. When asked what that meant and what organizational competencies and behaviors were required to ensure the realization of the strategy, he responded, "You know, it means having customers and operations all over the world, reducing our costs and streamlining our supply chain." Not surprisingly, of the 30 senior executives and managers that were interviewed in this company, not one could interpret or define what it meant to be a global organization or how to successfully operate and compete as a global organization. More alarmingly, moving deeper into the company's structure, the disconnections in understanding globalization became fractures between senior leadership's intentions and the interpretations of middle management and the rank-and-file employees. One employee defined *globalization* as "Losing jobs to foreigners."

There are lots of platitudes but little substance surrounding the notion of globalization. In its 1999 publication, *The Evolving Role of Executive Leadership,* Andersen Consulting defines *global leadership* as "an extraordinary capability to unify a global workforce around a single purposeful vision, . . . thinking globally." Unfortunately, Andersen Consulting does not define what they mean by *global, thinking globally,* or *globalization.* Is the capability of "thinking globally" unique to an individual, or is it something that permeates the culture of an organization? The foregoing brings us to a very tough and common question that confronts many organizations and is the most logical starting point for discussion: "What exactly does it mean to be global?"

"Globalization is a hollow word. There is no generally accepted understanding of what it means," observed Deloitte Touche Tomatsu's European Chairman Jacques Manardo at the February 1999 World Economic Forum. Let's address some of the common definitions and misconceptions at the onset. First, just because a company has plants, customers, and employees in countries other than where it is headquartered or founded does not make it a global organization. Second, even if a majority of a company's revenues comes from sources outside of its country of origin or headquarters, it is not necessarily a global company. Finally, the mere fact that most of a country's revenues and trade come from sources outside of its natural borders doesn't make it a global leader. Denmark, Sweden, and the Netherlands are all countries that generate a disproportionate share of their national incomes from the sale and production of products beyond their borders, but they do not necessarily define *globalization* in a broader working context as world economic super powers.

As evidenced by its popularity in annual reports, advertisements, and organizational vision statements, there is a certain romance and panache to calling oneself or one's organization "global." We even see bumper stickers that compel us to "Think globally and act locally." Ted Childs, a vice president at IBM, contends that the new catchwords are "Think global, think local; act global, act local." That perspective is interesting, but it does little to define what it means to be a global enterprise. Moreover, it isn't very helpful in formulating high-performance strategies for competing in the global arena.

Let's begin to answer what being global means with a review of some of the definitions. Early leadership and management thinking on globalization tended to concentrate on understanding the differences and interactions between markets, the relationship between subsidiary and international operations to the parent, the importance of product branding, and the role of national identity or affiliation in competing globally. More recent thinking on globalization has expanded to include services, intellectual property rights, knowledge transfer, multiculturalism and diversity, and, most importantly, uniformity of enterprise identity. Ultimately, there has been an evolution in the concept to include the notion of transnationalism.

Global, multinational and transnational organizations are not new, but the interest and attention that they currently command have reached unprecedented levels, with companies such as BMW, GM, IBM, Alcoa, Toyota, and Honda providing precedence. Although these companies are global players, they have competed with distinct nationalistic identities. In contrast, companies such as Shell, Amazon.com, Nestlé, Ford, British Petroleum and DaimlerChrysler represent the first major wave and prototypes for transnational forms of business. Both globalization and transnationalism represent an inevitable evolution in organizational form and multi-national strategy. This evolution has been precipitated by a number of factors, such as advances in technology, domestic and global economic dynamics, and profound societal and political changes associated with the demise of the Soviet state, the end of the cold war and proliferation of technology. International and multinational companies can and often do retain a distinct country of origin, connotation, and identity. Transnationalism, on the other hand, represents forms of organization and strategy that have no particular country identity or nationalistic centering. A key to understanding globalization and its strategic and operational implications is that it is a point of view, a mentality; it is a way of thinking, leading, and viewing the world differently.

Professor Noel Tichy of the University of Michigan defines *globalization* as "The capacity to treat the world as one market while paradoxically dealing with the many culturally diverse merchants." Another perspective is offered by researcher Ray Reilly, who provides that globalization is the "... integration of business activities across geographical and organizational boundaries." Author Frederick Seppard defines *globalization* as "... the process of corporate structuring that focuses a company's core competency on a single, worldwide market, creating growth and profit opportunities through synergies and efficiencies in engineering, sales, purchasing, and distribution." Strategist Robert Grant offers the following perspective: "Globalization does not necessarily mean that companies became multinationals—that is, establish operations in different countries. The key is ... that they view national markets as simply segments of a broader world market." Finally, Barry Patmore, former Worldwide Managing Partner for Andersen Consulting's Telecommunication Practice, says, "Being global means that we are able to bring the best resources and the firm's knowledge to any client, anywhere and at anytime, irrespective of location." Thus, a common element among researchers and practitioners is to view the world as a single unit while recognizing the uniqueness of each operating context.

In 1983, Theodore Levitt defined *globalization* as a *systemic shift* in markets and commerce. To Levitt, globalization is driven by: (1) a convergence of consumer sentiment, (2) a massive and rapid proliferation of technologies and unprecedented access to knowledge, (3) global brand perceptions, and (4) the economies of scale afforded by standardization, which reduces cost and increases return on investments. Under Levitt's global model, products and services become increasingly *standardized* until individual product brand recognition begins to converge with the enterprise image. Convergence of brand identity implies that the identity exists at a higher, overall entity level and not at the individual product level or specific country level. Global brands such as Intel, Sony, Mercedes-Benz, Applied Materials, Coca-Cola, Airbus, GE, and Ericsson are examples of this type of standardization and the convergence of product, brand, and enterprise identity. A common attribute shared among companies that have achieved this level of global integration is that their products and operations have a similar look, feel, taste, and quality standard, irrespective of country or point of origin; in short, a common identity.

John Quelch and Edward Hoff advance the concept of globalization not as an "either-or" strategy but rather as one that can exist in various forms and degrees. Quelch and Hoff offer that globalization is situational and that different business functions allow for different degrees of globalization; thus, different levels of standardization can exist along a continuum of options ranging from full adaptation (custom and unique) to full standardization (homogeneous and common). In this respect, globalization can and is often highly situational, opportunistic, and variable. This is an important distinction and concept that influences strategy formulation and behavior because it can direct us to cultural frameworks as a basis for globalization, not just to technology, products, and organizational structures.

Another perspective, presented by Kenichi Ohmae, advances strategic thinking on globalization through what he calls "equidistant thinking." Equidistant thinking requires that organizations consider their customers, resources, and markets from a holistic and equidistant perspective, rather than as special domestic territories or different and unique operating units. For the global leader, this requires a high level of personal objectivity, awareness, sensitivity, and unbiased behavior. Thus, a key requirement for global strategy development is the ability to scan the global environment, correctly interpret and prioritize issues, and make the decisions that best optimize and leverage the entire resources of the organization on a long-term global basis.

The foregoing discussion provides us with a backdrop for defining *globalization* and *transnationalism* in the context of high-performance organizations:

> The process of viewing customers and markets on a geographically indiscriminate and culturally inclusive basis, in a manner that best leverages the organization's capabilities, optimizes its world-wide identity, and deemphasizes geographical uniqueness and national identity or origin."

Central to the above definition are six themes:

1. Competing on a geographically indiscriminate basis.
2. Leveraging cultural uniqueness and inclusiveness for strategic advantage.
3. Providing for the standardization of product and process using "cross-platform" designs.
4. Adapting the product and process to a wide variety of uses based on common platform designs, highly configurable designs, and standardized assessment measurements.
5. Adopting a consistent view of the market in its totality with the ability to "move" and reallocate resources and assets in a manner that optimizes strategic value.
6. Acknowledging the realization that an organization can exist in multiple states of "globalization" and while achieving and maintaining standardization.

UNDERSTANDING THE FORCES DRIVING GLOBALIZATION

The inevitable progression and forces driving globalization are complex; however, we can simplify them by conceptualizing the history and evolution of globalization in three basic stages: informal trading, formal agreement, and interconnectivity. The first phase of globalization was brought about through trading and bartering between villages, communities, and countries. This form of globalization was largely driven by geographical characteristics, natural resources, and individual consumer needs. It dates to the earliest days of societal interactions, long before we concerned ourselves with GAAT (General Agreement on Tariffs and Trade), tariffs, and transborder economy theory. The second stage of globalization is best described as one created by the political arrangements between countries. This type of globalization involves formal trade agreements and contracts between countries and, ultimately, companies. In this state, globalization is subject to legal interruptions and the discontinuities attributed to economic cycles, political accord, and wars, as well as changes in the internal political structures of countries. This form of globalization has been the dominant model for the last 100 years. Finally, the third stage is one that is based on interconnectivity and *synergies of purpose.* Driven by technology and economic and strategic needs rather than political incentives, this is the type of globalization that we see rapidly evolving today.

The concept of synergies of purpose is central to globalization. The most successful and effective global strategies create synergies of purpose through the integration of vision, consistent purposes, and strategies that are designed to create high levels of organizational competency and operational and organizational leverage. Synergy of purpose is best attained by:

- Focusing on the realization of long-term business and social benefits.
- Integrating social responsibility with business strategies, policies, and governance.
- Implementing financial, cultural, educational, and social commitments in the communities in which they are doing business, plan to do business, sell products, or draw resources.
- Working to develop effective levels of social affiliation between the organization and the local communities in which it does business through the areas of health care, environmental awareness, and quality of life (education, parks, and recreation).

High-performance organizations realize and acknowledge that the ability to understand the dynamics driving and defining globalization constitute an essential prerequisite to competing on a global scale. Although there are many factors that are propelling globalization, five emerge as significant engines of global growth and therefore new dimensions of strategic thinking:

1. The democratization of politically and economically repressed countries and societies is creating new markets and increasing the *mobility* of people in and among companies, careers, and countries.
2. The availability and convergence of information technology in the form of the Internet, Internet II, personal computers, wireless communications, and network computing is causing a *disintermediation* effect on organizations and in many industries, while *neutralizing* many of the traditional sources of competitive advantage.
3. The interconnectivity of economies and the emergence of borderless companies and markets are creating new interdependencies and interactions among people, nations, and companies. These interconnections are changing the basic equation of market and economic *equilibrium* and is forcing greater levels of *disequilibrium* between advanced and developing societies.
4. Increased consumer *knowledge* and choices are making it more difficult to grow through traditional domestic channels and markets, thus forcing companies to employ more innovative practices to create new products as well as new markets.
5. Megamergers and alliances among companies are creating new forms of organizations that have deep competencies, extensive financial resources, and the ability to redefine the rules of competing.

Most importantly, besides helping to define and shape globalization, these drivers necessitate new strategies for competing. They significantly influence an organization's perception of its environments and the way it deploys its assets, develops strategy, and makes decisions. The impact and influence of these factors on the overall strategic environment are especially important, so let's briefly discuss each of these in the context of globalization and their respective economic dynamics:

Democratization

Despite its apparent difficulties, democratization has created new societies, created new opportunities, and spawned new economies. It has also contributed to the mobility and transience of societies. The demise of the totalitarian regimes in Eastern Europe and Asia and the privatization movement in China have opened the human spirit to new economic opportunities and social interactions. As a result, completely new markets are emerging, and resources that were once unavailable, held captive, or underutilized are now being more fully developed and made available. Undoubtedly, when compared to the Western societies, these markets are immature, unstable, and highly fluid. But instability in many newly liberated countries is inevitable. Countries such as Russia, Bulgaria, Poland, and many others are moving forward with capitalism and democracy. China, a curious mix of communism and quasi-capitalism, grew its gross domestic product (GDP) at 10 percent annually for much of the 1990s. With a movement to privatization, China is a hotbed for foreign investment. For sophisticated global companies, these markets represent new and exciting long-term opportunities.

The key challenge in planning and operating as a global enterprise is developing the necessary sensitivity to changes in political, social, and economic balance of power. The changing balance of power and the constant shifts between *ascending* economies and *descending* ones represent some of the greatest challenges to strategic business planners. For example, China is an ascending power, while Russia is a descending one. China is supplanting Russia and is challenging Japan for political and economic supremacy in Asia. In Europe, Germany, Norway, the United Kingdom, and Sweden are ascending powers, while countries such as France, Spain, and Italy continue to descend at various rates. With the ascent and decline of some nations, four important conditions must be considered by the strategic planner:

1. Within certain areas, ascending and descending nations will collide, thus creating a very challenging strategic dilemma and fluid planning scenarios.
2. The role of government and governmental policy is redefined and significantly changed. This is especially the case in the European Union (EU), where one of the key questions will be whether certain governments will step up to the challenge and remove the regulatory limitations on employers such as those related to limiting the number of hours a person is allowed to work, vacation time, and the hiring and termination of employees which encumber mobility and agility.
3. Globalization and the acquisition of established organizations by nondomestic companies can create social backlashes and public objections, especially in the United States.
4. Corporate strategy must be redefined to include a higher awareness of governmental interaction and greater emphasis on local interests.

A key for developing a superior business strategy is to anticipate and to recognize these "pivot points" for ascent and decline and to create the strategies and necessary change competencies within the organization that can effectively capitalize upon them.

From the early 1990s and through the year 2000, the annual global workforce is estimated to grow at more than 25 percent, or 588 million people. Approximately 94 percent of new entrants into that workforce are coming from the less-developed nations. Consequently, the educational, business, and political acumen and the social skills of those new entrants will, in general, be lower than those who developed such skills in more-advanced economies. This creates challenges and opportunities for strategists charged with change and renewal.

Information Technology (IT)

The importance of IT is addressed separately and in greater detail in chapter 5. Speaking of the importance of IT, Larry Olson, former CIO (chief information officer) of the state of Pennsylvania noted, "Being connected means you now have a global marketplace. Not being connected means you can't compete with the competitors you have; whether you know it or not, they are out there." The key strategic point to recognize is that IT neutralizes the traditional sources of competitive advantage and significantly redefines and influences the strategic choices available for an organization.

Electronic commerce and extended enterprise agreements between organizations—irrespective of location—are, at least for the time being, relatively free from government intervention and interference, fees, and taxes. This "freedom" is contributing to the ease and speed of globalization and the creation of "virtual" global organizations. Successful global strategies leverage their technology investments to more effectively reach existing and emerging constituencies to communicate, transfer knowledge, share information, and leverage resources at any time and any place. In effect, they *extend* their enterprises to become borderless and boundaryless.

High-performance organizations understand that IT allows information, ideas, data, and institutional knowledge to be codified, embedded, and distributed in a manner that transcends traditional geographical boundaries and organizational borders. They use this ability to support collaboration and enable cross-cultural strategies. They understand that technology allows resources and competencies to work together more effectively to service customers and develop new ideas and products. The geographical source of the product or service, the location of people, and the placement of the "computer" all become inconsequential as a result of effectively leveraging IT to enable globalization as a form of strategy.

Interconnected/Integrated Economies

We exist in a world of increasingly interconnected economies, organizations, and countries. Anyone who may doubt that or challenges it needs only to look at the impact that Latin America, Asia, and Russia can have on the world's financial markets. Globalization drives more mobility among ethnic groups, diminishes market power of any one competitor, and opens up new venues for additional competition. The undeniable fact is that the momentum for globalization is growing. There will be setbacks, but it is inevitable that the commercial and political worlds will become increasingly integrated and interconnected. While the average growth rate for GDP tripled since 1950, global trade is up 16 times its 1950 levels. Part of this phenomenon is attributed to the increases in the trading community. For example, the World Trade Organization (WTO) estimates that it would have had 25 members in 1948. In 1998, it had 132 members with a waiting list of 30 more.

USA Today reports that the investment of U.S. mutual funds in global markets had grown from $1.2 billion in 1984 to $177 billion in 1996. *USA Today* also noted that one out of every eight dollars invested in the United States is subsequently placed in global markets and funds. By 1999, those numbers were all significantly greater. Further, the newspaper revealed that investments in Russia generated a 153 percent return, investments in Poland returned 77 percent, and the Philippines provided 30 percent, all for 1996. *Business Week* reports that Professor Tony Carter of Columbia University estimates that the United Kingdom, Japan, and the Netherlands each have at least $300 billion invested in the United States. Over 60 percent of U.S.-based IBM's revenues are derived from nondomestic sources. Mexico's $40 billion of imports to the United States represents 70 percent of the entire value of goods and services imported on an annual basis. The economic realities of globalization are significant.

Another dimension and measure of globalization is foreign direct investment (FDI). FDI represents the amount of capital invested in factories, inventories, land, capital goods, and other "hard assets" where the investor maintains control and usually management over the investment. Typically, the amount of investment is measured in historical, book, and market value. From 1950 to 1992, the U.S. Department of Commerce (DOC) reports that U.S. investment abroad grew from $11.8 billion to $486.7 billion at historical cost valuations. Market valuations for the 1950 to 1985 period were not provided, but from 1985 through 1992 market valuations of U.S. investments grew from $380.5 billion to $776.3 billion. Concurrently, for the 1950 to 1992 period, foreign investment in the United States grew from $3.4 billion to $419.5 billion, based on historical cost measures.

Given the level of FDI, a significant strategic issue arises concerning its allocation and use. According to data from the Survey of Current Business, over 90 percent of FDI in 1997 in the United States came in the form of mergers and acquisitions rather than through establishing new businesses or greenfield facilities. Thus, even though investment is increasing, the Survey of Current Business notes that employment levels have not. Ultimately, employment may indeed fall. For example, DaimlerChrysler has established a target of over $1.3 billion in cost reductions as a result of their acquisition of the former Chrysler Corporation. The bulk of that target will probably be accomplished through supply chain integration and by contributions from the former Chrysler company, the elimination of car models, and a consolidation of common functions into global shared service organizations.

The trend and its related implications are clear: Growth of U.S. FDI is another indicator of globalization. With significant capital flowing into emerging and growing markets, raising capital in the traditional U.S. markets will be exceedingly more competitive as overall performance improves. Any company wishing to compete for investment funds must now compete against and with global alternatives in mind. Those that are high performers will, of course, attract the greater number of investors.

Tariffs have always played a major role in the globalization of economies and trade. During the 1960s, for example, trade policies were liberalized. This liberation stimulated unprecedented rates of growth. World trade for the 1921 to 1938 period was largely affected by the Hawley Smoot Tariff of 1930 and the Trade Agreements Act of 1934, causing tariffs to rocket from under 20 percent to 59 percent in 1934. Following World War II, GATT was established in 1947 and was followed by a succession of acts and agreements such as the Torquay Round of 1950 and 1951, Geneva Tariff Cuts of 1956, the Kennedy Rounds of 1964 to 1967, and the Uruguay Round of 1986 to 1994. The 1970 to 1994 period witnessed greater protectionism and defensive moves designed to preserve selected domestic producers and markets. According to the WTO, tariffs in 1948 averaged 40 percent; by the year 2000, the WTO estimates that tariffs will be about 4 percent. According to U.S. government statistics, tariff rates have ranged from 50 percent in 1900 to a high of 59 percent in 1932 to an all-time low of 4 percent in 1994.

Designed to promote greater trade and cooperation among nations and ultimately producers, the WTO has an accelerating effect on global commerce and economic activity. Members of the WTO are required to open their markets and subscribe and adhere to the WTO's rules. The WTO has three primary objectives:

1. Establish procedures for the resolution of disputes and grievances among member nations.
2. Use multilateral agreements that are designed to reduce and/or eliminate trade barriers such as those related to the 1996 agreement on IT.
3. Increase overall trade between countries based on "nondiscriminatory and predictable" basis.

The end result of the tariff agreements and the WTO is a generally higher level of economic integration that, according to the WTO and *Financial Times,* represented an estimated $5,100 billion in goods and services in 1996.

From a strategic and competitive perspective, the EU represents a new set of global dynamics, different challenges for strategy formulation and new opportunities for strategic renewal. The arrival of the Euro signals the potential for a more unified European economic powerhouse. Economist Werner Schule observed, "Europe is going toward a true single market." With the EU and Euro currency (Economic and Monetary Union [EMU]), we are on the cusp of a more unified economic and monetary base. As Henning Schulte Noelle, CEO of Allianz AG noted, "The euro is going to change Europe more than anything since the second world war. The euro creates a common currency, which is a big step toward integration. We will see a convergence in our economic lives, fiscal policies and legal systems." In aggregate, the 11 nations that comprise the EU will represent the single largest market in the world. As of January 1, 1999, the EU had a population of some 300 million people, a collective GDP of $6.0 trillion, and a per capita GDP of $21,000. In 1997, according to J. P. Morgan, the EU would have represented about 19.8 percent of the world's GDP, as compared to the United States, which has 20.4 percent, adjusted for purchasing power parity.

According to the Bank of England, the transition to the EMU is progressive over the 1999 to 2002 "changeover period." The EMU became a standard for 11 members in 1999. For the 1999 to 2002 period, national currencies will continue to circulate and be legal tender. Single monetary policy will be formed, but no incentives or restrictions will be placed on the use of the Euro. Monetary policy, reserve requirements, and operating policies will be established by the ECB (European Central Bank). For 2002, the final year of the phase-in period:

- The Euro becomes the sole currency on July 1, 2002, with the issuance of currency and coin.
- All assets are converted and carried in Euros.
- National currencies are withdrawn from circulation.

Some of the competitive influences that the Euro and movement to a more unified economic and currency structure will create include:

- Increased competition due to selection and price transparency.
- Additional consolidation and integration of businesses and supply chains.
- Increased worker mobility due to the removal of currency conversion risk.
- Reduction in the complexity of managing organizational finances and treasury activities.

The administrative and operating challenges of the EU and EMU present strategy developers with many different demands and complex planning scenarios. New relationships and reporting requirements will have to be established, as well as developing working knowledge of new regulations and statutory requirements. However, revenue and profit strategies will also be affected. For example, if you are leader of a European bank, one of the major implications of the EMU will be the normalization of foreign exchange rates. As a result of the EMU, much of the revenue and profits for banks related to foreign exchange for "intra-European" trading will essentially go away. If you are a car dealer or a manufacturer, pricing will be affected, and differences between prices for the same model or product in and among nations will be more visible to consumers.

Increased Competition

For many organizations, globalization represents both a challenge and a significant opportunity that begs the question, "Should a company compete on a global scale and, if so, how?" With domestic economies becoming more saturated with products and competitors, global expansion is a viable and necessary strategy for any organization seeking rapid growth, greater profitability and opportunities for renewal. As the world's commercial transaction base continues to grow and global populations become more mobile, better networked through IT, and more affluent, competing using a traditional domestic or "international" strategy will not be as viable as it was in a world of fragmented and independent economies.

Does this mean that all organizations must be global? The answer is, not exactly. One could argue that for some of the advanced industries, such as semiconductors, consumer electronics, entertainment, transportation, and automotive, there is no longer an exclusively domestic competitive landscape—it is a highly dynamic global arena and will remain so. For other industries and products, including refrigerators, ovens, furniture, and housing, globalization is not an immediate factor or a significant determinant of performance. Domestic preferences will usually prevail but part sourcing will be a global activity. Globalization and more liberal trade agreements open up markets for new competitors and work to mitigate the power of any one company in these markets. Nevertheless, there is a general rule emerging that holds: Any company that has a global competitor working in a local or domestic market must consider itself a global company. In this situation, any organization that is confronting a global competitor is, by definition, competing globally.

Megamergers and Alliances

"At a stroke, the geography of the car industry will have been transformed," noted *The Economist* when commenting on the acquisition of U.S.-based Chrysler by Germany's Daimler-Benz. We are in the initial stages of a prolonged cycle of megasized, globally oriented acquisitions, mergers, and consolidations. Most notably, the $40 billion acquisition of Chrysler by German-based Daimler-Benz created the fourth-largest car company in the world. Despite the rhetoric from both companies, the transaction was an acquisition of one company by another and not a "marriage of equals." The Germans acquired and are managing the organization.

The acquisition of U.S. publisher Random House by German-based Bartlesman creates a publishing company larger than Viacom and Time Warner. The $55 billion acquisition of Amoco, one of the companies sired by John Rockefeller's Standard Oil, by U.K.-based British Petroleum (BP) signaled a consolidation in that industry followed by the merger of Exxon and Mobil. The $86 billion merger reunites two of the Rockefeller companies broken apart by antitrust rulings in 1911. The 2000 acquisition by BP-Amoco of California-based Arco, for $27 billion, created a company with $104 billion in revenues and a market capitalization of nearly $200 billion. The 1999 $10.1 billion acquisition of U.S.-based Banker's Trust by Deutsche Bank creates the world's largest bank. All of these indicate that globalization is gaining momentum and that we are in the midst of major megamergers and consolidations. In total, merger valuations represented an all-time high of $1.7 trillion in 1998.

The movement to more interconnected economies and more unified currency will further facilitate a consolidation of markets and companies. Annual mergers and acquisitions in Europe have grown from around $190 billion in U.S. dollars in 1990 to over $600 billion in 1999. As published by *The Economist,* British companies, according to the accounting firm KPMG, spent almost $128 billion in acquiring foreign firms. While the initial global consolidations were largely European-American based, the next big wave of mergers will be among European firms and European-Asian combinations as exemplified by the acquisition of Nissan Motors by Renault in 1999 and DaimlerChrysler acquisition of Mitsubishi in 2000. A strategist can easily expect more mergers and consolidations among the largest organizations as they continue to scramble for growth, try to reduce costs, and most importantly, seek strategic synergies of purpose. These mergers are driven by a combination of factors, including the:

- Need to create and secure new and additional markets.
- Obvious pressures to reduce costs and create greater economies of scale.
- Opportunities to collapse and compress supply chains and to leverage customers and part and material sources.
- Need to acquire new intellectual capital and knowledge.
- Opportunities to create organizational integration on a global scale.
- Availability of common equity shares of target companies on publicly traded stock exchanges.
- Availability of public information on organizational performance in the form of operating and financial statements and regulatory filings.
- Relatively open governance style of U.S. boards of directors.

With the increase in global mergers and consolidations as a strategy for competing comes an increase in the use of strategic business alliances (SBA). The concept of SBAs as a strategy is not new. The airline industry, entertainment industry, high-technology companies, and building and construction industry have all long used SBAs as strategies and organizational forms for deploying and managing resources. More recently, automotive and pharmaceutical companies are creating strategic alliances, especially in the areas of production and research and development. For example, the number of alliances among biotechnology firms increased from 152 between 1988 to 1990 to 375 for the two-year period of 1997 to 1998. According to the consulting firm of Booz Allen & Hamilton, over 20,000 SBAs were formed between 1996 and 1998, representing 21 percent of the total revenue of the Fortune 1000.

There are many reasons for moving into an alliance relationship with respect to strategy as well as sources of organizational renewal. For example, alliances create or provide the opportunity to:

- Extend and compliment the core competencies of the enterprises involved.
- Share structural costs.
- Mitigate risk by distributing it among the various parties.
- Facilitate the entry into new markets on a global and regional basis.
- Provide access to the knowledge of another organization.
- Create new market and customer opportunities for all parties.
- Reduce or circumvent barriers to entry in certain geographical locations and markets.
- Create significant synergies of purpose and scale.

- Diminish and destroy the physical boundaries that define the traditional corporation and classical industry structures.
- Quickly neutralize the strategic and operational advantages of a competitor.
- Accelerate the rate of innovation and strategic renewal.

The complexities of the world mandate that organizations look beyond their traditional boundaries, internal capabilities, and sources of competitive advantage to alliances as new forms of business and as a means of creating and sustaining strategic renewal.

GLOBAL STRATEGIES FOR HIGH PERFORMANCE

The issue of becoming a global organization has usually centered on customer, resource and market location. If a company had an operation and a market in a country different from its homeland, then it was considered international. In the realities of strategic change and strategy formulation, that is not globalization nor is it transnationalism.

There are many different ways and strategies for becoming a global concern. Some organizations naturally migrate to a global form of business. Others such as GE, Microsoft, DaimlerChrysler, and Ford followed more structured and deliberate paths, and yet another group, including BP and many airlines, used both structure and opportunism. Despite the strategy taken, three major attributes stand out as central to an organization successfully becoming a global high performer: (1) global management perspective, (2) global leadership, and (3) uniform global brand identity.

Global Management Perspective

"The new globality means a tremendous emphasis on speed, flexibility, versatility, and permanent change—in some respects, insecurity," noted Claude Smadja, the managing director of the World Economic Forum during its 1999 conference. At one time, having plants, employees, and customers located in countries other than one's national origin was the definition of being global. It was an international approach to commerce that treated each market as an independent entity and each facility as a separate subsidiary or strategic business unit. Under such an approach, little organizational integration and minimal operational leverage were achieved with respect to the resources and strategies of the organization, and companies often found themselves with duplicate capabilities, higher costs, and conflicting strategies.

Global high-performance companies act differently, are managed differently, and are measured differently compared to those that are domestic or international. In contrast to international organizations, global high-performance leaders view and manage resources as a worldwide single unit, their capacities as a single worldwide resource, and their markets as a complete, single entity. They recognize the power of entity-level branding and operational leverage and work to integrate their organizations along common process, organizational, supply, behavioral, and measurement lines. In contrast, organizations that assume a local market or traditional international perspective compete in the global market with operations, performance measurements, strategies, and brand identities that have not been rationalized across the enterprise.

Let's examine in a bit more detail the distinctions between international, transnational, and global organizations and how they influence strategy formulation and the ability of an organization to change.

International organizations are managed with high levels of local autonomy, specialized products, and dedicated markets. International components of a larger company tend to adapt the "parent" organization's knowledge, competencies, and capabilities to a local market. Once adapted, new and different strategies and "indigenous" competencies gradually emerge, and local autonomy and identity increase. This autonomy typically results in unique market offerings dedicated to a specific market, different forms of product offerings, and, usually, a different identity from that of the "parent." Along with this identity comes a form of "independence" from the parent, which is expressed by the creation of extensive infrastructures to support their operations. These infrastructures can include specialized accounting, legal, research and development (R&D), and human resources departments; unique marketing and distribution capabilities; and stand-alone ITs. The overall effect is a dilution in enterprisewide brand recognition and overall operational leverage and market synergy.

Some of the key differences between global, international, and transnational organizations are summarized in Exhibit 3.1.

A strategic fundamental of global high performance is the ability of the organization to view and manage itself as a *single, integrated unit.* Global organizations rationalize resources, leverage assets and capabilities, and view customers and markets from the perspective of equidistance. They understand that markets are interconnected microenvironments of a larger, increasingly integrated and infinitely more complex environment. They understand that some tailoring may be necessary and, indeed, desirable but that the standardization of brand identity, products, and services leads to synergies, greater brand leverage, and the ability to move and adapt products on a "cross-platform" basis from market to market.

EXHIBIT 3.1 Comparing International, Global, and Transnational Forms of Organization

	CHARACTERISTICS		
	International	*Global*	*Transnational*
Operations	Autonomous/specialized	Integrated/specialized	Integrated/interchangeable
Products	Fragmented/specialized	Configurable/custom	Common platform/adaptable
Sourcing	Local	Global/regional	Global/regional
Logistics	Fragmented/local	Integrated supply chains	Integrated supply chains
Organization	Autonomous/fragmented	Consolidated/centralized control	Consolidated/networked
Customers	Mass	Mass/segmented	Focused/targeted
Employees	Homogeneous	Diverse	Multicultural
Brand	Unique/specific	Somewhat uniform	Uniform/convergent
Governance	Homogeneous	Heterogeneous	Highly heterogeneous

Global Leadership

The advancement of civilization and technology make economic globalization inevitable. Economic globalization invalidates much of the traditional methods of strategic thinking and the old rules of competing in well-defined markets and traditional industries using size, location, price, and quality as strategies. The emergence of a more integrated global economy and a more fluid and uncertain operating arena is forcing new levels of organizational agility, operational excellence, and knowledge transfer—all of which necessitate changes in strategic thinking and leadership.

As discussed in chapter 2, the days of industry-based, geo-based political strategies, geo-based business strategies, and geo-based economies used so successfully by many organizations and governments are coming to a speedy close. This does not imply that industries, politics, and geography no longer matter in strategy. They do. But they are simply not as defining and stable as they once were. The competitive delineation that once clearly distinguished industries, nations, companies, and economies is still very much there and, in some respects, has deepened. But in the new economy of a real-time global environment where customers, competitors, and opportunities transcend historical boundaries and borders, stoic thinking in terms of antecedent industry theory and old economy rules doesn't work anymore. Under new global conditions and imperatives, one is likely to find traditional competitors and industry rivals collaborating on special projects, funding joint-venture initiatives and acting, as Intel and Microsoft do, as venture capitalists for emerging businesses.

While customers and suppliers were once localized and key organizational resources and competencies centralized, today talent and material are sourced and dispersed globally, and customers are located all over the world. Geographical placement of assets is secondary to access to technology and knowledge that, in turn, provides access to markets, talent, suppliers, and customers. Thus, it only stands to reason that competing globally requires different strategic competencies than those associated with domestic, international, and regional forms of organization, leadership methods, and strategy models. With globalization come new challenges that clearly point to different behaviors, strategies, and organizational management practices. The traditional ways of strategic thinking about operating in different parts of the world, cultivating each market as a stand-alone entity and forcing interdivisional competition and rivalries, are proving costly and ineffective in a world that is becoming more integrated and interdependent.

As DaimlerChrysler Co-CEO Robert Eaton noted in *Motor Trend,* "We're striving to be the first transnational industrial company in the world—one that people don't identify as located in any one country." Global and transnational organizations are, by definition, multicultural and highly diversified. They have to be; otherwise, they would not be global. Global organizations understand that one of the great sources of strategic advantage is the rich perspectives and experiences that many different people can bring to a problem, project, or opportunity. The most effective global strategies draw on an eclectic mix of carefully balanced and highly focused talent. Driven by a passionate vision and compelling value proposition, the senior leadership of high-performance global leaders is usually a diverse mix of individuals, each bringing a unique set of technical, professional, and life skills and blend of nationalities. Such a team will develop more exciting and innovative solutions than those groups that are predominantly homogeneous in composition. The dynamics of this type of group creates new knowledge and innovative ways to use that knowledge. An organization cannot compete effectively as a global entity if it does not have a strategy to operate using multiculturalism and diversity as core competencies and core values.

Although many organizations contend that globalization is important, Allen Morrison, Hal Gregersen, and J. Stewart Black report in *Global Explorers: The Next Generation of Leaders* that only 2 percent of 108 executives believed that they had adequate numbers of global leaders. Sixty-seven percent believed that their existing leaders needed additional global skills and competencies, as compared to 3 percent reporting having global leader capabilities of the "highest quality." Only about 8 percent of the reporting companies indicated that they had designed and delivered comprehensive development programs to compete globally, whereas almost 44 percent said they developed global leaders on an "ad hoc" basis. The above statistics, if they are to be accepted, point to a potential decline in the ability of many organizations to develop effective global strategies and, ultimately, to compete successfully as a global company.

The strategic challenges in the global arena are more complex and difficult because they are based on the need for cross-cultural interactions. These interactions require a different set of leadership analytical, communication, interpersonal and learning skills, and, most notably, life experiences. The basis of knowledge interpretation and application is different. Communication styles are different, and cultural norms and mannerisms vary. Global and transnational strategy is concerned with optimizing resources, competencies, and knowledge among many different factions, in many different locations, in many different cultures, using consistent methods, messages, and measures without regard to any particular national identity. The challenge for most companies is to figure out how to do those things in a relatively simultaneous manner. This means that leaders responsible for strategy formulation and execution must develop deep knowledge and working sensitivities to the unique aspects of each culture and environment in which they function and from which they draw talent and resources and do business.

Perhaps the most important aspect of strategic formulation in the global arena is recognizing that the leaders of these organizations work to embellish their cultures through multiculturalism and diversity. They do this through the deliberate human integration of their organizations, irrespective of nationality, gender, or ethnic background. The global high-performance leaders understand that multiculturalism is a source of tremendous operational leverage, innovation, and competitive value. The leaders of the global enterprise ensure that their organizations are culturally rich and highly integrated at all levels. Some of the leading organizations, such as Daimler-Chrysler, Applied Materials, CitiGroup, and Proctor & Gamble, understand that moving personnel to give them the broadest experiences with different cultures and nationalities is integral to developing a global perspective and, ultimately, developing and sustaining high performance.

For example, when Mercedes-Benz opened its first U.S. plant in Alabama, it moved U.S.-based employees to Germany for training and cultural immersion. The U.S. employees soon found themselves thinking in German but, more importantly, thinking like long-time Mercedes employees. The process accelerated the transfer of both explicit and tacit knowledge. Once their German-based training was completed, Mercedes then moved its German trainers to Alabama. The movement of German nationals who were long-term Mercedes employees to Alabama provided a "reverse" process of cultural immersion. The result is much more than just training and sensitivity to others. It represents the *fusion* of diverse backgrounds, different perspectives, and different life experiences that forms new cultural models. As noted by Robert Eaton, "To merge cultures requires exchanging people. It's the best way to transfer technology." "Made by Mercedes" is more than just a slogan—it is a cultural mantra. The great global leaders understand the strategic value of cultural integration and work to create opportunities for it.

Global high performers are dedicated to specific strategic objectives. The high-performance global leaders strategically align their enterprisewide resources to a uniform set of goals and plans through a process of *logical consolidation and physical distribution*. From a leadership perspective, this is an important concept because it provides a unique basis from which to view the operations and resources of the organization. Rather than viewing each component of their organization as a distinct and independent entity with its own unique set of problems, goals, and measurements, the global leader recognizes that the inherent competition and rivalry of such a structure can be destructive to the overall performance of the enterprise. Companies such as GM appear to be suffering from this type of embedded structure and legacy leadership style, complicated by a lack of rationalized business strategies and an anticipatory view of the operating environment.

Logical consolidation in global leadership implies the use of a uniform set of brand images, policies, value propositions, and strategies to compete. It also implies that standard methods of performance and contribution measurements as well as consistent recognition and reward systems are used throughout the organization, irrespective of geographical location. The concept of logical consolidation and physical distribution allows the global leader to use a networked structure of organization and management. This type of structure is highly adaptive to changing conditions and emerging opportunities.

Within the concept of local markets, nothing is more fundamental to the success of globalization than understanding and leveraging end-consumer/user demand. Global leaders understand that their environments and their customers create the demand for their products and services. They employ, therefore, demand-pull strategies to generate marketshare and new sources of revenue at the end-consumer levels, rather than the simple supply-push strategies that many companies fall victim to. Implicit in their understanding of the demand-pull environment is that they anticipate the needs of their markets, and they have enormous agility to satisfy demand at any time and any place.

Finally, global organizations employ a global governance structure. Their leaderships, as in the case of DaimlerChrysler and ABB, are composed of executives from various countries who possess complementary and cross-competency skills and personalities. Governance is focused on long-term strategic positions and social responsibility as well as profits and growth.

Uniform Global Brand Identity

The importance of branding has been well established. However, how branding is accomplished and its level of importance in the global arena have significantly changed. Traditionally, organizations built their brand identity from the products that they developed and marketed. Often, the result was a portfolio of independent product brands accompanied by little entity-level or enterprisewide operational synergies. The synergies that were created came in the form of operational and logistical benefits. To the high-performance companies, branding is more than a name or affinity. A company's brand conveys what it stands for and what values it has, and it is its signature on the world's stage. As Susan Greenbaum, managing director of The Maloney Group, notes, "A brand is not an abstract concept handed down from corporate Olympus, but a reflection of the company's true identity, which necessarily includes its employees." High-performance companies build their global enterprisewide brand identity first, then the products that will support the image and identity.

The high-performance organizations form and implement strategies that rationalize their images, messages, operations, and brands on *both* a worldwide and enterprisewide basis. Coca-Cola, IBM, Andersen Consulting, Nestlé, Microsoft, Intel, Applied Materials, Nike, DaimlerChrysler (Mercedes-Benz), Shell, and Sony, provide some of the better examples of companies that project a single global identity, uniform brand identities, and worldwide name recognition.

From a brand perspective, the high performers see the world essentially as one market, adjusted as necessary for individual nuances and emerging opportunities, but one market nonetheless. High-performance global leaders understand the importance of brand mobility and transferability. For example, Häagen-Dazs' dulce de leche ice cream, which was originally designed and targeted for Brazil, is now second only to vanilla-flavored ice cream in sales in the United States. Heavier denim jeans developed for the Japanese market by Levi Strauss are now being sold in the United States. And Nike running shoes designed with input from runners in Kenya are being marketed as "Air Streaks" in the United States.

"A brand is the most important asset that a company has," notes Robert Eaton. Global high performers understand and emphasize the importance of enterprisewide identity on a global basis without regard to any nationalistic identity and country. Thus, although individual brands are still enormously important, global leaders recognize that the strength of the brand is found at the *enterprise level*. When people buy a Mercedes-Benz, they buy a Mercedes—the specific product or model and where it is made are secondary. As a consequence, consumers see a single identity and entity. Thus, a strategic theme of the global leaders is that they face the world market with a single purpose and focus using consistent identities, measurements, and, most importantly, practices. Global strategies may use specialized "market zones" with segmented and semitailored (adapted/configured) offerings to generate local interest and appeal to colloquial or indigenous consumer values, but the core product and its image and value proposition to the customer remain consistent. It's a *common-platform* approach to strategic positioning and branding.

Exhibit 3.2 summarizes the impact of globalization on leaders and brand management.

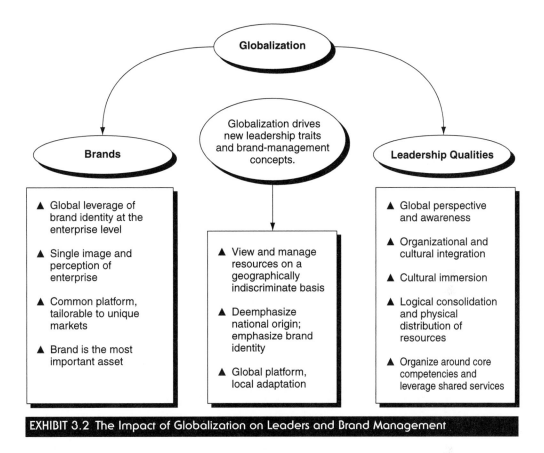

EXHIBIT 3.2 The Impact of Globalization on Leaders and Brand Management

SUMMARY

This chapter discussed the very difficult and complex subject of globalization and its effect on strategy and high performance. The global high performers have inherently different characteristics and qualities than those who behave in a more traditional domestic or international profile. Understanding and developing global strategy requires an integrated program that stresses not only professional development but also personal development. This includes developing extensive cultural sensitivities, knowledge of different political and social systems, and competency and fluency in global business ethics and protocols, as well as knowledge of local employee motivations and reward systems. Above all, it requires organizations to be extraordinarily flexible, be unafraid of the new and different, and have a passion for learning and changing.

Here are six key lessons for formulating a global strategy:

1. Globalization has permanently changed the competitive dynamics of virtually all organizations. In the process, it has created new strategic realities and the need to compete more creatively and effectively.

2. In the absence of governmental intervention and protection, globalization neutralizes many of the traditional industry theories of creating competitive advantage.

3. IT is a significant enabler of globalization. IT allows a small company, which only a few years ago would have been geographically constrained, to compete with big companies in the world market.

4. Strategy formulation for globalization requires different types of competencies and leadership qualities.

    a. As individuals and collectively as an organization, the high-performance global leaders are consummate learners and synthesizers. They are naturally inquisitive and seek both qualitative and quantitative insights to problems and new challenges.

    b. They are enormously adaptive in their views of the world, personal lives, working styles, and leadership behaviors. That is, they demonstrate a natural ability to assimilate their environments and adapt to them in a manner that optimizes their participation in that environment.

    c. Individually, the high-performance global companies have leaders who aggressively seek ways of "fitting in" and, in the process, work to build relationships and trust among those who they come in contact with. In the global arena, leaders also work to build credible and comprehensive understandings of local value systems, political processes, and communication styles—the lexicon of verbal, nonverbal, and physical ways people use to communicate and interact.

    d. Global companies and their leaders are explorers and pioneers. They understand uncertainty and accept it as both a matter of fact and challenge. Global leaders take on unknown challenges with high degrees of confidence and a certain personal elan. This confidence allows them to constructively confront uncertainty and new situations and approach them as a learning and developmental experience, which they both welcome and enjoy.

5. Global companies have agility, adaptability, and flexibility as a strategy. These allow them to embrace new ways of thinking and cultures with a passion and, most importantly, with an absence of elitism with respect to their own culture, education, and country of origin.

6. High-performance global leaders recognize the changes and contrasts in the environment. They understand the need to constantly monitor, learn, and anticipate their environments. As Universal Studio President Frank Stanek notes, "We are living in a global society. You have to know politics and what's happening around the world." In developing global strategies, the high-performance leaders use a number of tactics and processes, including hiring managers from other countries, building multicultural collaborative management teams and work groups, rotating key personnel throughout the organization and its locations, and accessing external sources as both thought leaders and sources of information.

Critical Thoughts and Discussion Questions

1. What makes a company a truly global competitor? What are the distinguishing qualities and characteristics of a global company, and how are they developed?
2. What major dynamics drive globalization, and what are the subsequent effects on the competitive environment? In particular, consider:
   a. General evolution of the external environment
   b. Emerging critical success factors and new strategic imperatives
   c. Implications on organizational structures and competitive/cooperative relationships
   d. Causes, reasons, and strategic purposes behind the growing instances of international mergers and acquisitions
3. How does globalization relate to the previously discussed concept of creating and competing in a marketspace, and why is the relationship between globalization and marketspace important?
4. What are the implications of globalization on change and organizational transformation?
5. How can you best describe the term *synergies of purpose,* and why is this concept central to understanding globalization and to successfully executing global competitive efforts?

CHAPTER
4

COMPETING IN THE CHANGING WORKPLACE: STRATEGY IN AN AGE OF PLURALISM

"The question is this: Is there a black, a Hispanic, or a woman in your company who, if all things are equal, can expect to become chairman within the next ten years?"
—REVEREND JESSE JACKSON, SR., IN *FORTUNE* MAGAZINE

INTRODUCTION

At no point in the history of humankind have people been more mobile, more connected via communication methods, and more entrepreneurial and untethered to traditional sources of income and employment. Driven by changes in political systems, new economics, and IT, these forces combine to create more diverse and multicultural societies and the subsequent need for more culturally centered and sensitive strategies.

This chapter explores the implications, strategic challenges, and opportunities of multiculturalism and diversity. We discuss nine drivers of multiculturalism that provide sources of strategic renewal and change, and ask:

- How do changing work patterns and worker mobility drive strategic renewal?
- What differentiating and new competitive advantages can be created by multicultural workforces and organizations?
- What new and different management challenges are presented by multiculturalism?
- What are the new and/or emerging work patterns and individual choices that are driving change and strategic renewal?
- How do changing work patterns and demographics neutralize the traditional sources of competitive advantage and strategy formulation?

This chapter pursues a number of learning objectives. First and most important, it focuses on the need to place multiculturalism in a strategic and operational context. Second, the chapter is designed to help stimulate your thinking. Third, it explores the linkages and drivers for multiculturalism. Fourth, it should help you to understand more completely how to use multiculturalism for strategic renewal. Last, it aims to leave you with a working knowledge of the subject and its possibilities.

UNDERSTANDING MULTICULTURALISM AND DIVERSITY

Multiculturalism presents highly unique and exciting challenges for strategic renewal and strategy formulation. Specifically, how does diversity differ from the definition of multiculturalism? How do leaders leverage multiculturalism for competitive advantage? What factors are changing the work lives, styles, and employment proposition, and how do they impact strategy? These questions are explored from a number of different perspectives, including income levels, taxation, changing workplace practices, and lifestyles, while considering some of the key topics related to the rich multicultural considerations of African Americans, Hispanic Americans, women, and Asian Americans.

The United States has the most heterogeneous and multicultural population of all advanced nations. In contrast, nations such as France, Spain, Denmark, Japan, China, and Norway are far more homogeneous in the compositions of their populations. As an indication of just how heterogeneous the U.S. society has become, there are some 275 different recognized ethnic groups and over 220 different languages spoken in the United States. Although English is the official language, bilingual education is taught in many parts of the country. This compares to China, the largest nation in the world with 1.7 billion people, which has 55 officially recognized languages; France, with just 56 million people, has one language; and the United Kingdom, with 57 million people, has English as its recognized language.

According to *The Economist,* from 1990 to 1995 the number of immigrants who were granted U.S. citizenship averaged approximately 350,000 annually. By 1996, that number jumped to 1.2 million. In 1997, the majority of newly hired workers in the United States were Latino/Hispanic American. For 1997, the U.S. Immigration and Naturalization Service (INS) estimates that naturalization of new citizens increased to over 1.8 million people. Some sources attribute this acceleration to changes in welfare and subsidy laws, others cite economic and social opportunity, and some point to the uncanny timing of an increase in new citizens with the 1996 presidential election.

To fully appreciate changes in U.S. culture, let's take a brief look at how multiculturalism is influencing workforce mobility in America:

- Prior to the year 1500, North America was populated by indigenous people, the Native Americans. However, after 1500 the U.S. population was predominantly English in the north and mid-Atlantic and was Spanish in what would become Florida, Texas, and California. By 1790 the U.S. Census Bureau estimates that the population of the United States was 19 percent African American, 50 percent English, 7 percent German, and 7 percent Scottish. The remainder of the population was composed of people who were Swedish, Dutch, French, Irish, and Native American. Today the United States has an estimated population of around 300 million people. Of this amount, slightly over 50 percent are female. The U.S. Census Bureau and Chisholm-Mingo Group estimate that there are 34.3 million people who are African Americans, 10.3 million who are Asian Americans and

Pacific Islanders. A significant majority of the remaining balance of the total U.S. population is of European origin.

- The composition of the United States is a wonderfully interesting mix of cultural pluralism. In the United States, when we attempt to define a cultural group—say for instance, Hispanic—the challenge becomes what groups best represent the Hispanic/Latin-American community. The U.S. Census Bureau estimates that around 11 percent, or 30 million people in the U.S., are Hispanic. Of this amount, 63 percent are Mexican, 12 percent are Puerto Rican, 8 percent are Cuban, and the balance consists of "Central Americans" and Dominicans. If all of the Spanish-speaking people in the United States were considered an individual nation, the United States would be the fifth-largest Spanish-speaking nation on earth. For the near future, 10-year growth forecasts place the total U.S. population at 350 million, with the greatest growth coming from the Hispanic/Latin-American community.

- Although the buying power of the Latino/Hispanic-American community is about $348 million, the poverty rate in this community of Americans is higher than that of African Americans. A factor contributing to this condition is education. Only about two-thirds of Latino/Hispanic Americans graduate from high school as compared to about 85 percent of African Americans and over 95 percent of Asian Americans. However, that is changing. According to the U.S. DOC, the "proportion of the Hispanic population ages 25 and over with a high school degree or higher increased from 51 percent in 1987 to 55 percent in 1997. During that same period, the proportion of Hispanics who had some college training increased about seven percentage points to 29 percent, and those with a bachelor degree increased to 10 percent."

- In 1997, the U.S. Census Bureau estimated that about 10 million people were of Asian descent or ancestry. Asian cultures are represented by individuals who are of Japanese, Chinese, Korean, Thai, Indonesian, and other Asian/Pacific Island origins. In California alone, there are 30 different recognized cultures and ethnic groups that comprise the Asian-American community.

Multiculturalism and diversity are key strategic themes for leaders of contemporary organizations and societies. Although the terms share similar qualities and conceptual foundations, there are important differences, which distinguish them as strategic themes. Diversity is usually thought of and presented as *gender, ethnic, and racial proportionality and representation relative to a population*. To many, it has become statutorily defined. An unfortunate aspect of this notion of diversity is that it is often associated with quotas, preferential treatment, and the hiring and promoting of people into positions of responsibility for which they may or may not be best qualified. Notwithstanding those distractions, these valuable programs generate numerous benefits in creating opportunities for minorities and fostering awareness, sensitivity, and an appreciation of the possibilities of multiculturalism.

Multiculturalism encompasses much more than ethnic, gender, and racial diversity. Although those qualities are included in any definition of multiculturalism, they are merely the starting point for a more inclusive and pluralistic context. Multiculturalism, as George Mason University Professor Howard Chu notes, "is a philosophical position and movement that assumes that the gender, ethnic, racial, and cultural diversity of a pluralistic society should be reflected in all of its institutions." To be multicultural means to be *pluralistic*. Thus, multiculturalism includes diversity *plus* different life experiences, religion, age, income, customs, sexual preferences, physical and intellectual capabilities, and personal choices that are reflected in society as a whole. These qualities are, in turn, influenced by a number of factors such as geographical origins, personal background, social affinities, education, economic status, and the personal commitments of the individual to his/her culture and customs.

From a strategic perspective, multiculturalism represents segments, micromarkets, and rich sources of talent. The high-performance organizations constantly "mine" those segments for new talent, trends, and ideas. They also understand that multiculturalism leads to more creative and innovative breakthroughs as well as critical thinking, all of which are essential for strategic renewal. Exhibit 4.1 compares diversity to multiculturalism.

EXHIBIT 4.1 Comparing Diversity and Multiculturalism

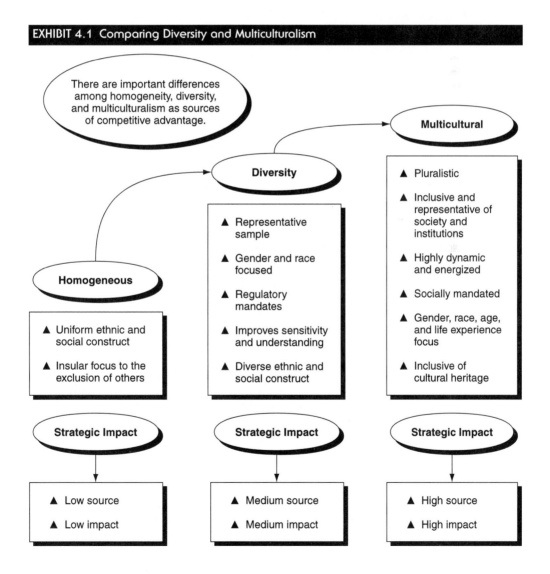

High-performance organizations understand that it is the convergence of these very dynamic and different cultural perspectives that contributes to great performance and breakthrough strategic thinking. According to *Fortune* magazine, the 50 organizations that compose the Diversity Elite outperformed the S&P 500 for the past 3- and 5-year periods, respectively. The top 50 companies for diversity and multiculturalism averaged returns of 125.4 percent versus 112.2 percent, and 200.8 percent versus 174.2 percent for the 3- and 5-year periods, respectively, as compared to the S&P 500. Similarly, in a 1992–1994 survey of over 3,200 companies that studied the impact of affirmative action programs on operational performance, Michigan State University economists Harry Holzer and David Neumark found that affirmative-action programs had little or no negative impact on productivity. According to *Fortune* magazine, the "best practice" diversity company has the following profile:

- Minority individuals represent 11.7 percent of their boards of directors.
- Minorities compose 24.9 percent of its total workforce.
- 23.8 percent of new hires are minorities.
- 7.2 percent of minorities are among the highest paid employees.

The importance of diversity and multiculturalism with respect to organizational performance, at least in the United States, is demonstrated by the level of attention and number of programs that companies are dedicating to these two issues. According to a survey of 175 members of the Fortune 500 performed by the Society for Human Resource Management (SHRM), 75 percent have formal diversity programs. However, only 54 percent measure the results of their programs. Over 80 percent of the top executives at those companies reported that diversity is important. Of those executives, 26 percent indicate that it is very important; 34 percent report it as important. The SHRM survey indicated that 32 percent of the executives believed their programs to be effective or somewhat effective (35 percent). The SHRM report also revealed that 93 percent are focusing their development efforts on African Americans, 92 percent are concentrating on women, and 85 percent target Latino/Hispanic Americans. Among the Fortune 500, SHRM reports that diversity programs typically include: diversity training (93 percent reporting), employee affinity groups (37 percent reporting), mentoring (30 percent reporting), and career development (24 percent reporting). Middle management, the level that has the greatest impact and interactions among constituents, receives approximately 8.6 hours of training annually, which is less than 1 percent of total available annual work time.

Unfortunately, many organizations are lured into a false sense of multiculturalism based on statistical representation and a statutorily prescribed definition of diversity, often to the exclusion of the most essential factors of cultural, life, professional, and geographical diversification. Simply concentrating on affirmative action and Equal Economic Opportunity Commission (EEOC) guidelines and regulations might achieve "statutory" diversification but not necessarily multiculturalism and usually not pluralism. Strategies that mistakenly rely on statistical diversity alone run the risk of missing greater opportunities.

A case in point is the diversity program of one very well known company that was highly regarded and held up as a stellar example of statutory diversity. Although the program achieved superior statistical results, it failed to achieve breakthrough performance and significant results in several key companywide initiatives. Thus, it was a parody for a management team that expected higher performance and more creative solutions. Upon investigation, researchers noted that a high-profile project team's diagnosis of issues, analysis of problems, strategic assessments, and proposed solutions lacked the "energy" and creativity usually found in high-performance groups. Research consultants who attended several sessions with two different teams confirmed that the correct competencies were provided and that group dynamics and interpersonal interactions were adequate and that there were no debilitating or dysfunctional behaviors or individual conflicts inhibiting group performance. According to researchers, team meetings were professional and productive and also demonstrated trust and significant levels of knowledge sharing and learning. Although diversity and proportionality were achieved, the researchers concluded that for this company the lack of progress in innovation and breakthrough thinking had to reside elsewhere. The results simply didn't match expectations and did not justify the effort and exercise.

When researchers interviewed the members of the various teams, a very discernible pattern emerged. Researchers learned that the majority of team members were long-term employees with an average tenure of 12 years with the company, a few having 25 and more years of service. Most of the team had grown up within a 75-mile radius of the company's headquarters. All of the team members had at least 8 years of service in the same operating unit/division of the company. The extensive tenure of the team indicated that they should have had no problems with the company lexicon or with communicating or functioning in their culture.

A review of the backgrounds of the team members indicated that virtually every member had gone to local high schools, ranged in age from 32 to 45, had relatively similar personal life and professional experiences, and had attended one of the several local colleges or the state university about 200 miles away. Most of the team members grew up in families whose head of household had worked for one of the other two major companies in the area. The researchers concluded that although this company had achieved statistical diversity, it lacked cultural diversification of opinion, perspective, and life experiences. Although it had satisfied statutory guidelines for gender and race representation, it did not achieve diversity with regard to the collective wisdom of the team. Because of this homogeneity, team members continued to use the same analytical techniques, draw on a common background, defer judgment to the same people, behave in an established manner, and look to known patterns and proven solutions in trying to solve new and very different challenges. Thus, the researchers concluded that although diversity was achieved, it was the lack of multiculturalism that contributed to the team's lower performance and inability to generate innovative results.

Clearly, multiple factors influence group performance and team success. For example, studies performed by researchers G. Stasser and W. Titus indicate that group members tend "to focus on information that they hold in common . . . and thereby fail to exchange effectively the potentially valuable information." As author Professor Peter Kim notes, if that occurs, "Groups become overly influenced by their common knowledge and may be more *susceptible* to overestimating the knowledge of others when the situation is familiar." Additional studies suggest that homogeneous groups tend to "exhibit conformity and a lack of openness to information."

High-performance organizations understand that multiculturalism and diversity are sources of significant competitive and strategic advantage. A great source of competitive advantage and a core capacity for strategic change is found not so much in the percentages and numbers that represent diversity, but in the diversity of the collective *wisdom* created through multiculturalism. As discussed, an organization can achieve arithmetic and statutory diversification based on affirmative action and EEOC guidelines and the numbers and percentages of gender, ethnic background, and race and still *not* achieve cultural inclusiveness and plurality. Clinical studies indicate "Diversity in information sources and perspectives suggests differentiation in an organization's belief structure that in turn leads to a perception of the feasibility of change and a momentum toward change." Thus, a key to leveraging multiculturalism for strategic renewal is to ensure that a diversity of cultures, life experience, and backgrounds is achieved. Collectively, these elements constitute the wisdoms of an organization that must be captured and cultivated.

CHANGING WORKFORCE DEMOGRAPHICS: A SOURCE OF STRATEGIC RENEWAL

The implications of competing globally and leveraging multiculturalism are relatively clear: Those organizations that aggressively embrace diversity and multiculturalism are better positioned for successfully competing in global environments and interconnected economies than those that do not. The high-performance organizations cultivate in their cultures an appreciation and awareness of the values and the political, religious, cognitive, and communication practices of the unique cultures and markets in which they compete. Organizations that develop and elevate their strategic positioning skills to this level and understanding are able to develop the foreknowledge and demeanor to recognize trends and lead globally. Three forces are driving significant shifts in the workforce and, therefore, set imperatives for organizations to develop their strategies and organize for change:

1. There is a systemic change in the working arrangements of most Americans. These changes will ultimately affect the workforces and organizations in Europe, Asia, and Latin America. Four major factors must be considered:
   a. Free agency of employees
   b. Women as leaders
   c. Position tenure
   d. Technology
2. There is a significant shift in individual expectations with regard to working, careers, and leadership. Two factors must be considered in the context of these expectations:
   a. Lifestyle and living
   b. Longevity
3. Education, earnings, and income influence strategic choices and the available tactics that any organization or individual has. Three factors play a critical role:
   a. Income and earning power
   b. Executive compensation, organizational performance, and income equity
   c. Education and earnings

The following discussion focuses on each of these aspects and further explores their impact on strategic renewal.

Working Arrangements

Despite the forecasts from the 1960s and 1970s for more leisure time, technology, organizational expectations, and competitive pressures have combined to increase the average workweek. Exclusive of commuting time, the average workweek for Americans has increased from 40 hours in the 1960s to over 53 hours in 1996 and estimates project a 60-hour workweek, on average. In his 1999 commencement address at Grambling State University President Bill Clinton noted that the increase in the number of hours Americans are working is creating other challenges, especially in family and personal lives. As a result, people have less time for personal intimacy, recreation, and self-improvement. Interpersonal and marital relationships are placed at greater risk, and stress-related illness and employment claims are on the rise. Not surprisingly, job satisfaction is declining. Among U.S. workers, senior managers apparently suffer the highest levels of stress. In contrast to other countries, the United States provides high levels of individual productivity. According to the Organization for Economic Cooperation and Development (OECD), given the average per capita GDP at 138 percent, the United States has the highest rate of productivity per person of the advanced countries. This compares to 77 percent for Spain, 106 percent for France, and 116 percent for Japan. In the United States, the average productivity per worker has, according to Charles Schwab, climbed 20 percent faster than growth in the overall workforce. One study on productivity performed by the consulting firm McKinsey & Co. indicates that the United States averages close to 40 percent above the U.K. output per hour per worker, whereas France and Germany outperform the United Kingdom in this respect by 25 percent.

The unemployment rate of many EU countries is comparably high by U.S. standards. According to information supplied by the National Statistics Offices, as reproduced in *The Economist,* the national average rate of unemployment for Germany is 10.7 percent, 11.8 percent for France, 12.3 percent in Italy, and 18.8 percent in Spain for 1997–1998. In France, the OECD estimates that 28 percent of the working population below the age of 25 is unemployed. The low unemployment of the United States, together with its political and economic systems, has long been a magnet for labor, immigrants, and aspiring entrepreneurs.

Free Agency

At the beginning of the twentieth century, approximately 50 percent of the population of the United States was involved in agricultural production. Today, that number is around 3 percent. With the industrialization of America, there was a permanent migration of workers from rural areas to industrial cities. Since the early 1980s, there has been a continuous structural shift and a change in the workforce and the working habits of Americans. The increase in the mobility of the labor force is a natural consequence of demographic, political, economic, technological, and lifestyle changes as well as individual choices.

A systemic shift is occurring in how people work, where they work, and how they are employed, and a new and different working arrangement is being defined. According to the Bureau of Census, somewhere between 6 to 7 percent of the U.S. workforce are now independent contractors and/or temporary workers. Microsoft Corporation alone has some 6,000 temporary workers. Although considered "temporary" for regulatory reporting purposes and calculation of benefit costs, the U.S. Bureau of Labor Statistics reports that in 1997 around 29 percent of temporary workers stayed on the same job for a year or more as contract workers. That is up from slightly less than 24 percent in 1996. Wages and salaries for independent contractors exceeded $30 billion in 1996. Since 1986, wages and salaries for temporary workers have increased over 360 percent, a testament to the growth in the industry. Although the largest component of the temporary workforce is clerical, the number of professionals is increasing, especially in the areas of high-technology and professional-management services.

The use of contract or temporary workers has many appealing aspects for organizations. First, by using a contract worker, organizations provide themselves with great flexibility. They can engage contract workers based on immediate needs and job requirements without incurring the expense of insurance, pension, and administrative costs associated with full-time employees. Second, they can utilize contract workers on a just-in-time basis, thereby maximizing benefits relative to need and cost. Third, organizations can secure the best resources for the task, relative to their needs, the complexity of the task, and financial limitations. Finally, contract workers can be terminated with relative ease and immunity from litigation arising out of gender, age, or race discrimination.

Another reflection of this trend is in the growth of employment created by smaller business concerns. Studies by the Small Business Administration (SBA) indicate that between 1989 and 1995 2.9 million new companies were created and 2.6 million "died." Thus, a positive net change occurred in the absolute number of going concerns. According to the SBA, companies with fewer than 500 employees generated 76.5 percent of the total number of new jobs added to the private sector between 1990 and 1995. On a comparative basis, those employed by companies with less than 500 people represented 52.5 percent of the total private-sector workforce.

The number of people working as independent contractors and/or under alternative (defined as "nonstandard working arrangements" by the Economic Policy Institute and Women's Research & Education Institute) is growing. According to their research, 31 percent of professional women and 25 percent of professional men had a nonstandard working arrangement in 1995. In total, *Fast Company* magazine estimates that independent contractors, "free agents," and alternative workers comprise about 16 percent of the total U.S. workforce, or 25 million people.

For individuals competing for jobs and recognition, regardless of generation, the ascent of temporary workers signals a distinct shift in emphasis from employment to *employability*. Workers—irrespective of organizational title, skill level, or age—must manage their careers as a *portfolio* of talents and experiences that are constantly adjusted in anticipation of the needs of the marketplace. For companies, this means that they must compete more creatively and furiously for quality personnel. Money paid to those who have the highest employability will be important, but probably not the deciding factor for attraction, longevity, and loyalty. There are dimensions of lifestyles, life enrichments, and social responsibility that will represent important variable factors for prospective employees to consider. These become even more significant as one progresses through his/her career and life.

Women as Leaders

Since 1966 the percentage of married women entering and working in the labor force has increased from 35 percent to 65 percent in 1997. According to the U.S. Bureau of Labor Statistics, women accounted for about 46 percent of the total U.S. labor force in 1997, or about 60 million working women. Of this total, 44 million worked full-time, while 16 million were part-time workers. For women between the ages of 15 and 64, about 70 percent are working. In comparison, Sweden has about 48 percent of its labor force as women; in Germany, women constitute about 40 percent of the country's workforce, but only 50 percent is employed full-time. France checks in with approximately 45 percent and Italy with about 38 percent. In general, women work less hours per week in Europe than they do in the United States, Latin America, and certain parts of Asia. Some of this is due to the labor laws, such as in France; part of the reason is attributable to culture, and some is undoubtedly due to lack of opportunities and closed doors.

Despite the apparent progress, women's earnings continue to lag behind those of men for comparable positions. The U.S. Department of Labor reports that women, in general, earn only about 74 percent of the salaries and wages of men. The Catalyst Group found that, among the highest compensated levels of executive pay, women earned only 68 percent of the amounts paid to their male counterparts in the most senior positions of their organizations. According to the Catalyst Group, of the 2,458 top-paid executives of the Fortune 500, only 61, or 2.5 percent, are women.

The "glass ceiling" continues to be a leadership issue. There is only a handful of women (notably Ms. Jill Barad former CEO of Mattel, Ms. Carley Fiorina of Hewlett-Packard, and Ms. Marion O. Sandler of Golden West Financial Corporation) who are CEOs of Fortune 500 companies. As compared to men, only about 5.3 percent of women hold the "line" management jobs that typically lead to the CEO, chief operating officer (COO), or executive vice president (EVP) positions. This represents just 3 percent of the 1,728 positions of the Fortune 500 that have the titles of CEO, COO, or EVP. According to the Catalyst Group, only 10.6 percent of all corporate officers of the Fortune 500 are women. In addition, only 11.2 percent, or 444 women, are board members of Fortune 500 companies. That's about one person in nine. Of this amount, 12.2 percent are women of color. In contrast to the United States, women represent only about 5 percent of board seats in the 200 largest U.K. companies. In the United States, women represent about 40 percent of all managerial positions, as compared to only about 30 to 40 percent in Europe.

As marginal as the percentages may be, the United States is significantly ahead of the rest of the world with respect to female representation in key business leadership roles. This is attributed, in part, to affirmative action and EEOC initiatives, a growing, albeit slow, recognition and acceptance of women as leaders by the corporate establishment, a generation shift, and active feminism. For example, 84 percent of the Fortune 500 have one or more women as directors, and 81 companies, or about 16 percent, have no women directors on their boards. Catalyst Group research indicates that GE, Amoco, Intel, and Compaq did not have female participation or representation as officers in their organizations in recent years. Politically, *The Economist* reports UN statistics that indicate that women hold about 12 percent of elected seats in the U.S. Congress.

This compares to Sweden, with about 41 percent women representatives, versus less than 5 percent for Turkey. Collectively, women comprise about 22 percent of elected positions in the United States and, according to researcher Nancy Adler, over half of all women political leaders have come into office since 1990.

Gender plays a big role in how each leader views her/his world and, therefore, her/his personal interpretations and approaches to strategic renewal will be different. The list of societal, economic, demographic, geographical, and educational differences that contribute to differences in the human condition and affect the way people view and interpret the world is endless. For example, Nancy Adler notes that "Most American male executives suddenly find themselves ill-suited to the wider world, trying to codify the uncodifiable, flanked by a huge surplus of lawyers using cumbersome rules where other nations enter trusting relationships with subtle communications." Additional research indicates that women managers are more participative, "interactional," and relational with respect to their styles of leading. Commenting about leadership, Carol Stephenson, CEO of Stentor Resources, Inc., noted, "The female model is a mix of old and new. Traditional virtues, such as self-confidence, a well-articulated vision, commitment to the company, and hard work, remain important. But the new strengths that women bring have become crucial for success. These include an ability to listen, to speak clearly and honestly. A skill in mediating between conflicting views. And an ability to brighten the workplace with a new sense of style."

Along with the increased presence of women in the workplace and in increasingly greater leadership roles has come scrutiny of the differences in the leadership qualities between men and women. According to a summary appearing in *HR* magazine, "Once again, women outscored the men," said Larry Pfaff of Lawrence A. Pfaff and Associates, a Michigan-based human resources consulting firm. He concluded that "Female managers—as rated by their bosses, themselves and the people who work for them—were rated significantly better than their male counterparts. The difference extends beyond the softer skills such as communication, feedback, and empowerment to such areas as decisiveness, planning, and setting standards." A second study performed by Pfaff suggested that managers and employees gave women managers higher evaluations for qualities such as goal setting, facilitating change, and technical expertise.

Women in the United States and other advanced societies such as Spain, Italy, France, and United Kingdom appear to be particularly and naturally qualified for major global leadership roles. Cases in fact: Sirkka Hamalainen, the former governor of the Bank of Finland, is on the executive board of the new ECB; Margaret Thatcher and Madeline Albright serve as two exemplary *global* leaders. According to research performed by Nancy Adler, "The new model of global leadership relies upon more traditional "feminine" qualities such as relational skills and team-oriented leadership, as these are the qualities and skills necessary to lead across cultures." Adler further notes that "American women display a relational style of communicating that is closer to the style of most non-American managers around the world than to that of most American male managers." Judy Rosener calls this the "paradox of gender" and notes that "Women do tend to lead differently from men ... they have an interactive style. It turns out that the very qualities for which women have been devalued are now considered very important traits: comfort with ambiguity and change, flexibility, sharing of power and information, collaboration. We are not promoting women because they don't act like men and at the same time we are training men to develop attributes that women have for which they have been devalued."

The perceptions regarding women and members of various minority communities as leaders notwithstanding, the "glass ceiling" and strong barriers to opportunities and advancement continue to persist. For women and certain cultural and ethnic communities such as Latino/Hispanic Americans, African Americans, and Asian Americans, stereotyping, exclusion from powerful personal networks, underappreciated skills and talents, the lack of sincere opportunities, and rigidity of the corporate culture continue to slow representation and participation at the highest levels of leadership. The Catalyst Group reports that 77 percent of women surveyed report that preconceptions and stereotyping are restraining them from achieving high levels of leadership. As Susan Greenbaum noted, "Not to diminish anyone's accomplishments, but it seems that women simply have to work harder to attain the same levels as their male counterparts." Almost 49 percent and 47 percent, respectively, report that exclusion from informal networks and lack of line-management experience are serious restraints to progress. Similar conclusions can be drawn for members of other minority groups.

With globalization and multiculturalism come additional issues and challenges for women as leaders. Certain cultures will not accept, or simply have formidable barriers to, accepting women as leaders. It is more difficult for women to achieve significant levels of leadership in Asia, Latin America, the Middle East, Pakistan, Australia, and Japan. Writing in the *New York Times,* Carol Steinberg relates a story of Kim Ainsley, an executive with U.S.-based Domino's Pizza. While traveling in Saudi Arabia on business, her visa was rejected; no one attended a meeting she initiated; she was asked to change her clothing from typical business attire to the traditional abaya; and she was not invited to the contract signing which was the culmination of a successful venture—all because of her gender. So, even though women may achieve significant levels of leadership in their domestic regions, they may be entirely omitted and treated poorly when competing globally in certain countries. Some of the difficulties are related to what the advanced societies would easily consider to be gender discrimination; other obstacles are formed by cultural norms and customs.

To be successful assimilating and working in a global arena, an organization and an individual must have developed "cultural dexterity." The issue of cultural dexterity is important from not only a gender perspective but also as a global competition factor. In certain cultures, establishing credibility and achieving gender acceptance require hard work and a combination of techniques. To be successful, one must first and foremost know the cultural rules and norms of the markets of concern. Second, one must be able to assimilate and appreciate the nuances of those cultures, without necessarily completely adopting them. That is, one does not become Japanese simply because he or she is doing business in Japan, but one must be knowledgeable and respectful of the local customs and mannerisms. Third, one has to learn and rely on signals, cues, and networks to establish informal and formal relationships. Fourth, one may simply have to double his or her efforts and work harder, in some cultures as opposed to others, irrespective of gender. Fifth, establishing strong presence and personal acceptance may take time and require lots of patience. Surely, realization and acceptance of these global and cultural imperatives/demands are important for anyone engaged in global business and competition; yet, they are even more critical for women and people of minority ethnic origins.

However, the deeper, more difficult issue is whether an individual should be knowingly placed in a position, where what would be considered gender or race discrimination by U.S. or, say, French standards, is a common and acceptable practice in the given culture. In the United States, it is illegal to show preference for assignment based on gender. Consequently, a natural conflict is created between what is legally required and morally right in one jurisdiction versus what is desirable, preferable, or practiced in another. The resolution can be a difficult one, especially for organizations that are aggressive in their advancement of women leaders and active in the global arena. One strategy is to let the customer dictate the terms. Another is to simply not put someone in a difficult situation. The resolution may be to select the person who will be the most effective and will derive the most professional and personal development from the assignment and experience.

Position Tenure

As New York University professor and author Richard Sennett notes, "Career originally meant a carriage road—and as applied to work, a clear path forward. We can no longer count on that. These days one is advised to anticipate 11 job changes during a typical working life." Job changing and "transitory tenure" have become facts of life. Some of this is the result of companies downsizing, outsourcing, and shifting employment to other parts of the country or the world (of working and organizing work). A portion is related to new processes and technologies that are supplanting the traditional methods of working. But a large part of the reason can be attributed to employees simply searching for a more desirable environment. It seems inevitable that the selection of lifestyles, together with technology, will continue to play a major role in the process.

The forecasts are supported, in part, by current sentiment. According to a survey of 2,221 MBA candidates conducted by *Fortune* magazine, 63 percent of those surveyed indicated that they planned to stay with their first employers for less than 4 years. That is a huge difference from only a generation ago when an employee might have only two, perhaps three, job changes in an entire career. During those days, if a person had more than three job changes, recruiters and human resource managers almost automatically concluded that something must have been wrong with her or him. There was a stigma attached to job changes, terminations, and job jumping. Today, there is no longer that type of stigma; shorter tenures and job displacement are realities in the new environment. In fact, many companies are attracted to employees who have that type of diversification, because it shows the ability to adapt, work under uncertainty, assume risks, and gain perspective.

Since the mid-1980s there has been a downward trend in tenure. Based on the survey results produced by the Heldrich Center for Workforce Development at Rutger's University and the University of Connecticut's Center for Survey Research & Analysis, 59 percent of respondents indicated that they were very concerned about their job security. Fifty-five percent indicated that they were satisfied with their job security, and 31 percent said they were somewhat satisfied. Although the AMA reports that downsizings slowed from a high of 40 percent of companies reporting downsizings in 1991 to about 18 percent in 1997, job security and tenure at any one company continue to be considerations for many workers. This is especially the case in mergers and acquisitions that provide companies with opportunities to consolidate redundant operations and eliminate duplicate administrative and overhead functions.

Business Week reports that research by the Employee Benefit Research Institute (EBRI) shows that between 1983 and 1996 the average tenure for a male worker over the age of 55 declined by 6 years from almost 18 years to 12 years, or by 29 percent. For males between the ages of 25 and 64, the average tenure fell by 19 percent from 1991 to

1996. Today, a 35-year-old male has an average job tenure expectancy of around 6 years. For the overall male population, the U.S. Department of Labor reports that the median tenure with the same employer is about 4 years. This trend is not an anomaly of the reengineering and downsizing fads initiated by so many companies but rather a systemic shift in how the employee and employer covenant is now structured. For example:

- Among all men, median tenure was 4 years in 1996, virtually identical to the figures obtained in January of 1983, 1987, and 1991, but in stark contrast to only a decade earlier.
- Since 1983, nearly all age groups of adult men experienced a decline in median tenure, with particularly sharp drops occurring among men ages 45 to 54 and 55 to 64.
- Tenure for adult women from 1983 to 1991 changed little but was up slightly in 1996 to 3.5 years, according to data released by the Bureau of Labor Statistics of the U.S. Department of Labor.
- The overall median tenure for adult women rose between 1983 and 1996, with nearly all of these gains taking place from 1991 to 1996.
- According to Challenger, Gray, & Christmas, the average tenure of a terminated manager was approximately 10 years as of March 31, 1998, with severance packages ranging between 13 to 25 weeks.
- A poll by Exec-U-Net in *Fortune* magazine indicates that among managers ages 35 to 45, it takes about 9 months (36 weeks) to find equivalent or better employment. The search time increases by about 12 percent to 13 months if the job searcher is over 45.

Race, gender, and age bias tenure. The federal laws on age discrimination notwithstanding, 77 percent of the Exec-U-Net respondents indicated that they experienced some type of age discrimination. The executive search firm Korn/Ferry International indicates that 55 percent of minority executives report leaving their jobs because of racism. The consequences of layoffs and prolonged searches can be devastating, with retirement savings, home equity, and credit card lending limits all used to support daily family needs. *Business Week* reports that less than 50 percent of all lump-sum retirement plans, which are usually paid out when a worker loses or changes jobs, are rolled over to IRAs or similar programs. That may indicate that the money saved towards retirement is being used to finance the present, which is a high-risk gamble but one that many people who confront prolonged unemployment are forced to make. And there are no offsetting tax benefits or relief for terminated or displaced workers.

Understanding the dynamics and influences of these trends is important, as they affect the operating environments of all organizations and, ultimately, the formulation of their strategies. The fluidity associated with changing demographics and workforce composition suggests that organizational change may be easier rather than harder in the future. That's because the workforce is younger and more acclimated to change and those baby boomers who remain active are more adept at change. But the decline in tenure presents two major strategic challenges for organizations: (1) Limited tenure usually means lower benefit relative to cost, especially for less experienced personnel, and (2) relative to experienced personnel, when they leave, they take their knowledge with them. This depletion of knowledge is an important issue, as knowledge costs both time and money to develop and perpetuate.

Technology

The convergence of technology, communications, and knowledge has enabled people to work in ways and in locations that only were fantasy and science fiction a generation ago. IT links nations, people, corporations, and institutions together into a web of instantaneous information and communications, making the world a much smaller place and rendering the traditional ways of managing people and resources obsolete. As a result, there is an emerging workforce comprised of individuals who are increasingly independent of the traditional structures of control and centralized support. These workers are far more knowledgeable, agile, and capable as decision makers than their counterparts of the previous generation. They aren't anchored to the bricks and mortar of the physical company. They work at home, with clients and customers located in distant places. For example, approximately 10.0 million people or 4.5 percent of U.S. working adults "telecommuted" in 1998. By 2001, that figure is expected to grow to 8.0 percent. Clearly, the business leadership skills that will be required to manage such resources are very different than those in the traditional hierarchy.

One other interesting trend as noted by the *Wall Street Journal* is that 70 percent of those under 30 do not read a daily newspaper. As an alternative to print media, many are accessing electronic sources that are more real-time and offer greater variety and greater mobility. One has only to check the Web sites www.thestreet.com or www.ibd.com for examples of real-time news sources as alternatives to the *Wall Street Journal* and day-old financial summaries found in daily newspapers. Chapter 5 provides a more complete discussion of the impact of IT and strategy formulation.

Expectations

It is clear that today the employment covenant has been changed from one of security and loyalty to one of individual satisfaction, employability, and "free agency." With this change, or perhaps as a consequence of it, comes a redirection and redefinition of many of the traditional attitudes, expectations, and measurements for working. In advanced societies and economies, people are seeking more meaningful and rewarding working relationships and arrangements. In today's climate, people demand empowerment, seek recognition, expect respect, and enjoy learning opportunities. They seek employment environments that encourage collaboration, express appreciation for individual and team contribution, listen to employees, and provide exciting and different assignments. They are also seeking a greater balance between personal time and professional requirements.

Lifestyles and Living

The increase in dual-household income means that the earners have more disposable income but also greater costs, greater mobility, and less free time for family and leisure activities. According to the Bureau of Labor Statistics and the Catalyst Group, in 1950 only 20 percent of U.S. households had dual incomes. By 1996 that percentage had doubled, with an increasing percentage of single-income households represented by women. The percentage of households with incomes over $100,000 has grown to over 7 percent of total U.S. households in 1995, as compared to 3.4 percent in 1976. That is a 109 percent increase over a 19-year period. From a strategic planning and renewal perspective, organizations must recognize that households with high-levels of dual incomes are generally economically more secure. Therefore, people are more confident and more likely to change jobs and/or become entrepreneurs. For many dual-income households, schedules are chaotic and must be carefully choreographed to include child care, work, personal time, household responsibilities, and, of course, more work and less leisure time. One way organizations are trying to address this is through flexible time programs. According to the consulting firm of William M. Mercer, from 1996 to 1998 the percentage of U.S. workplaces with "flextime" programs increased by 50 percent from 40 percent to 61 percent.

In general, U.S. companies lag behind their European counterparts in ancillary benefits and work-life enrichment programs. For example:

NORWAY
- Provides paid child leave at 80 percent of the employee salary after a new birth.
- Provides a cash payment to stay-at-home parents.
- Legislatively mandates that men take time off after birth of children.

GERMANY
- Provides free day care for 3- to 6-year-olds.
- Provides tax breaks for single-income families.

With increasing mobility and a shift in employment values, the big challenge for any organization, and certainly those aspiring to be high-performance ones, is creating an exciting work environment that also achieves a realistic balance with personal lives. *Fortune* magazine reported an Eli Lilly & Co. survey that indicated that only 36 percent of the company's workforce believed that it was possible to get ahead in the company while devoting adequate time to their families. While median income rose 6.7 percent from 1979 to 1994, costs for child care have climbed over 200 percent since 1990. New car prices are up almost 66 percent, while the price for new houses increased by 31 percent (four times that amount in California), and college costs jumped 67 percent. Thus, for many people, dual-household income or a second and even a third job are a necessity.

Additional indications of changes in workforce values and mentality can be seen in a survey conducted by Universum of 1,792 MBA students at 20 top U.S. business schools and in a study by *Fortune* magazine:

- 71 percent said building a family was important.
- 4 percent said that their careers would come before their families.
- 5 percent believe that the income gaps between the rich and the poor will become smaller.
- 78 percent of MBAs wanted their employers to provide a "good reference for my future career," thus further indicating the change in employment and career sentiments.
- 64 percent indicated that competitive compensation was important in considering companies.
- 62 percent indicated that they wanted to work for companies that had exciting products.
- 59 percent listed the variety of tasks as important career considerations.
- Not surprisingly, and in somewhat of an acknowledgement of the change in the employment contract and free agency, job security did not register above the 39 percent level.

Another indication of the shifts in employment patterns and sources of employment in the United States can be found in areas such as the Rocky Mountain region, Arizona, and New Mexico. These regions experienced rapid growth in jobs and populations throughout the 1990s. Dun & Bradstreet and *Business Week* report that business start-ups increased 10 percent in 1996 in the Rocky Mountain states. Collectively, this region created over 847,000 new jobs over a 3-year period. For some time now, there has been a trend of moving away from the traditional industrial regions and urban areas to the newer, less congested regions. Although 80 percent of the U.S. population continues to live in urban areas, the trend toward "newer" urban areas will continue because people desire to live in newer, cleaner, safer areas that have lower income taxes, lower housing prices and property taxes, better schools, and better climates. Technology, dual incomes and employee mobility combine to enable these choices.

Compensation alone does not create or sustain employee satisfaction or loyalty. It never has, because by human nature most people are not satisfied with their compensation, especially with CEOs earning huge amounts from stock options. According to a survey of over 405,000 employees of U.S. firms, International Survey Research found that only 43 percent were satisfied with their compensation. For example, a Towers Perrin survey of 700 U.S. companies indicated that the least "effective" means of recognition was the traditional cash reward. In contrast, the most effective was dinner with the boss followed by a gift certificate and recognition in the organization's newsletter. To address this situation, organizations must implement new and innovative recognition and reward systems. Considering the matter of compensation and recognition in a strategic sense, organizations must look to nontraditional means as a source for change. Simply paying a person isn't enough to guarantee high performance or loyalty. Rather, it seems that people are looking for more of a "human touch" in an age of borderless organizations.

Longevity

Another factor is the increasing life span of humans. People in advanced societies simply live longer and lead economically more productive lives. The United States and the EU have an aging population with an average life expectancy of about 76 years. Today, in the United States a person turns 50 at the rate of 1 every 8 seconds. America's workforce is composed of some 75 million baby boomers between the ages of 37 and 51. Although baby boomers represent an anomaly as far as proportionality to the total population is concerned, it is very likely that many will out-live historical mortality tables and longevity estimates due to healthier lifestyles and medical breakthroughs. For the year 2000, the Hudson Institute estimates that approximately 27 percent of the U.S. workforce will be age 55 or older. By the years 2020 and 2050, that percent is expected to grow to be about 37 percent and 38 percent, respectively. Even Hallmark, the greeting card company, notes the changes in aging. For 1997 the company estimated that it sold 20 percent more "Happy 50th Birthday!" cards than it did in 1995.

New actuary estimates confirm this trend, and many researchers think that we are at the precipice of medical breakthroughs that will extend life and the working years well beyond those of historical trends and traditional actuarial tables. Stanley Kranczer of Metropolitan Life Insurance estimates that life expectancy of a 65-year-old male increased by 5 months to 80.5 years. The broader strategic issue today is that although people once retired and made room for the younger generation, that is no longer the case. The U.S. workforce is older, healthier, and more active. As a result, they will, in all probability, want to work longer. For many people, financial security is also a consideration in wanting to work longer. The declining lack of confidence in government programs such as Social Security and Medicare is causing many to rethink their careers and retirement plans. The EBRI and the American Savings Council report that only 26 percent of nonretired Americans believe that Social Security will be an important factor and a source of their retirement income. This eroding level of confidence and lower expectations in government programs are not without justifiable argument. According to the Social Security Advisory Board, by the year 2013, program spending will exceed receipts as represented by payroll taxes, notwithstanding the "surplus." Unless adjusted, by 2021, spending will exceed receipts plus interest. Finally, by 2032, the Social Security Trust Fund is projected to be depleted to a point where it will be able to pay only about 72 percent of projected benefits.

The strategic implications are clear: It is very likely that an organization's payroll, pension, and health care costs will continue to rapidly escalate because retirement age will be extended, the workforce will grow, and overall health care and social administration costs will increase. An older workforce brings many advantages to an organization, but it also raises the overall costs per employee. For example, *Business Week* reports that the average health care costs for men 50 to 54 are 3 times higher than for men 30 to 34. That means that a company will have to be extraordinarily adroit at managing costs and encouraging healthy lifestyles. Secondly, extending the retirement age also presents some very significant challenges for attracting and retaining high-performance employees. More creative management and job-enrichment programs will be required to keep younger workers motivated and committed to the organization. These could involve additional education and ancillary benefits such as on-site day care, private school tuition reimbursement, college scholarship funding programs, and other such socially and family responsive programs to attract and retain younger employees.

Education, Earnings, and Income

Income and Purchasing Power

The Great Depression and Roaring Twenties notwithstanding, the gap between wealthy and the near wealthy and the poor and middle class is growing. The Gini Index, which is an indicator used for measuring income inequality, has consistently increased from around 0.36 in 1973 to about 0.46 in 1997, according to the U.S. Census Bureau. (1.0 represents perfect inequity, and 0 is a perfect equity.) For the 1965 to 1995 period, the Gini Index was 12.8 percent above its 1967 level and is widening for the 1998 to 2000 period. According to *The Economist*, in 1979 the differential between the top 10 percent of income earners was about 3.6 times the bottom 10 percent. By 1996 that gap had widened to 5 times. According to the Federal Reserve, the earnings of the top 10 percent of U.S. workers increased by 0.6 percent annually (based on real terms), while the earnings for the bottom 10 percent actually fell by almost 8 percent. On a comparative basis the U.S. remains the highest per capita income nation of industrialized societies. However, the dynamics during the disparities have changed. For example, in 1970, the U.S. per capita income was 31% higher than the average of industrial nations. Reflecting a systematic shift in the economy, that differential dropped to 10 percent in 1990. By 1999, it had increased to 22 percent, reflecting the impact of information technology on national productivity and per capita earnings. Thus, the income and wealth gap is becoming wider.

Depending on the source and the method of calculation, the average household income in the United States ranged between $34,089 to $43,250. For 1995, the U.S. DOC estimates that the median household income in the United States was $34,076, up only 4.7 percent from 1976, when adjusted for the consumer price index (CPI), while GDP per capita was $25,860. Correspondingly, the percentage of those households earning less than $34,999 declined from 53.7 percent in 1976 to 51.1 percent in 1995, attributed in most part to inflation. The number of households earning between $35,000 to $99,999 declined as a percentage of total households from 42.9 percent in 1976 to 41.7 percent in 1996. Using *Worth* magazine and the Bureau of Census data for 1995, the disparity between what is called median income ($32,420) and rich ($486,306) is 15 times. The "super" middle-class incomes, which averaged $81,051, are 2.5 times greater than the median household income. For Caucasians, the average income was around $40,000. In contrast, the average household incomes for the Latino/Hispanic-American and African-American communities were about $28,000 and $27,000, respectively. The aggregate purchasing power for these communities, as estimated by the U.S. Census Bureau and Chisholm-Mingo Group, is around $300 million for Hispanic/Latino Americans, $450 million for African Americans, $150 million for Asians and Pacific Americans, and $175 million for disabled Americans.

The key point about the foregoing is that although the incomes for these communities of interest remain below the levels of where most people believe they should be, they are, in fact, increasing. From a strategy standpoint, these communities represent growing and increasingly more sophisticated and dynamic resource pools and markets that present sources of new revenue, new growth, and, ultimately, organizational renewal. Any organization that has an objective of high performance simply must understand and cultivate and develop these communities as sources of talent, growth, and opportunity as part of its strategy.

Executive Compensation

An additional consideration with respect to performance, incomes, and equity revolves around the issue of executive compensation. Executive compensation, the amount of money paid to leaders of major companies, has been increasing faster than the wages and earnings for the general working population since the mid-1980s. In 1980 the differential between CEO and worker pay was only 42 percent. *Business Week* reports that in 1997 CEO pay was 326 times greater than the average salary for U.S. factory workers. Placing the disparities in a different context, the average household worker has to work somewhere between 220 to 300 years to earn what a top Fortune 500 CEO earns in 1 year.

According to *Time* magazine, the typical annual compensation for a Fortune 500 CEO is $7.8 million, including stock options, bonuses, incentives, and the like. Craig Barrett, CEO of Intel, earned $114 million in 1998. A significant portion of U.S. CEO pay comes in the form of stock options. According to the Investor Responsibility Research Center, the average stock option cash-in by U.S. executives in 1998 was $4 million. The gap between top executive and worker pay continues to grow. For 1996, executive base salaries increased about 39 percent. Add in stock options, benefits, and incentives, and the total percentage increase hits 54 percent. According to Brian Hall of Harvard Business School, the value of the stock option moved 53 times compared to that of the underlying change in the company's share price. Thus, even if companies are laggards or underachievers but the overall market is rising, CEOs will generally benefit from an upward market. Correlating CEO pay and organizational performance to stock options and compensation provides some interesting insights. According to a study performed by Smithers & Co., a London-based economics firm, 11 percent of America's largest companies would move from a profit to loss position, and 13 percent would have sustained a 50 percent reduction in profit, if the financial performance of these companies were restated for the cost of CEO stock options. In contrast, wage increases for factory workers inched up only 3 percent.

The differences between total CEO compensation and the average pay for working individuals presents an interesting and challenging dilemma for strategy formulation, especially when different societies and customs are involved. For example, according to Towers Perrin, in contrast to U.S. CEO pay, the average base pay for a CEO is $645,000 in the United Kingdom, $420,855 in Japan, and $398,430 in Germany. Factor in bonuses, incentives/awards, and stock options, and the differentials widen. For the United States, the average CEO compensation exceeds $1.5 million, followed by Argentina and the United Kingdom at slightly less than $700,000, and France at $600,000. Germany is number 8 of the top 10 at around $500,000. When the former U.S. company Chrysler Corporation was acquired by Germany's Daimler-Benz, Robert Eaton, CEO of Chrysler, earned eight times more than Jurgen Schrempp, the CEO of the acquiring and dominant company.

Organizational performance and the apparent misalignment between CEO performance and compensation represent another challenge to strategy and change. Companies such as DEC under Robert Palmer; Apple Computer under Gil Amelio; Scott Paper and later Sunbeam under Albert Dunlap; Disney under Michael Ovitz; GM under a succession of leaders including Roger Smith, Jack Stemple, and Jack Smith; Morrison Knudson under Bill Agee; Bausch & Lomb under Dan Gill; and Levi Strass under Bill Haas all provide case histories in compensation practices, which are in apparent misalignment with actual financial performance and stakeholder interests of those companies. All of these companies sustained marketshare declines, decreasing profits, and overall lower competitive value while their CEOs were highly compensated.

In the well-documented case of Al Dunlap and Scott Paper, thousands of people lost their jobs while he raked in $100 million in compensation. Similarly, while Bausch & Lomb experienced its free fall, CEO Dan Gill pocketed several million dollars in severance pay. Some allege that Bill Agee single-handedly contributed to the demise of Morrison Knudson through the implementation of faulty and misdirected strategy. It was rumored that when he and his wife Mary left the company and town, people lined the streets and cheered. While CEO of Apple Computer, Gil Amelio presided over ceaseless changes in strategic direction, numerous downsizings, continuous chaos, and an accelerated decline in sales and stock prices. During Amelio's tenure, Apple's stock price fell over 40 percent while its marketshare reached all-time lows. In the process, Amelio collected $23 million in compensation. With less than a year of employment at Disney, Michael Ovitz reportedly pocketed $100 million. The $100 million alone for either Mr. Dunlap or Mr. Ovitz represents the annual average income for almost 3,000 U.S. households. The list can go on, but the point has been made. To be a high-performance organization, leaders and boards of directors must do a better job of designing and aligning compensation practices with effective strategy formulation, contribution, and organizational performance.

From an organizational performance and change perspective, such compensation practices for underperforming and poorly performing companies are destructive, divisive, and dilutive. In fact, one could argue that these types of compensation practices could even serve as a disincentive for high performance. An organization cannot hope to achieve high performance with this type of disparity in performance measures, results, and compensation. Leaders must and should be compensated for making organizations great, expanding employment, and adding to the wealth of the stakeholders. With the income disparities growing between CEOs and workers, it is little wonder that the AFL-CIO, Teamsters, and other major unions are reacting negatively with Web sites discussing the relationship between executive pay, employee pay, company performance, and CEO accountability. (See www.aflcio.org/paywatch/index.htm for examples.)

Education and Earning Power

For the general population, there has always been a high correlation between income, earning potential, and education. This correlation has been somewhat changed in recent years due to the significant growth in self-employment and immigration increases. As a result, new wealth has been created; however, the gap between the top earners and wealth holders and the lower earners and wealth holders has widened.

Education, income, and earning power have always been interrelated. Calvin Coolidge once said that the "world is full of educated derelicts." That may still be the case—we all know bright and talented people who seem to be lost in life or lack direction. But education remains a significant factor in determining income potential and in the growth of economic and social disparities in society. It should come as no revelation that a number of studies point to an increasing gap in the earning power of those with and those without college degrees. In 1980, a person with a college degree could expect to earn about 45 percent more over his or her lifetime than a person who did not have a degree. By 1996, the differential had grown to 85 percent. Those with advanced degrees in business, science, engineering, and medicine can expect to enjoy an even greater differential.

In the United States, the number of people over the age of 25 with 4 years of college education as a percentage of its total population was 23 percent in 1995, as compared to only 14 percent in 1976. From 1965 to 1995, the average number of years of education increased from 11.8 to 12.7 years. That increase should come as no surprise because two factors contribute to it: increasing volume and complexity of knowledge, and a gradual decline in the quality of public education. Globally, the OECD countries report that the percentage of 18- to 21-year-olds enrolled in higher education curricula increased from 14.4 percent in 1985 to 22.4 percent in 1995. In the United States, the Department of Labor and Census Bureau reports that the number of people between the ages of 25 and 29 who have college degrees increased from 23.2 percent to 27.3 percent.

According to *The Economist,* higher education in the OECD represents 1.6 percent of the aggregate GDP. *The Economist* further reports that, among 25- to 64-year-olds, the relative earnings of a college graduate are, on average, about 60 percent higher than for those who do not have a college degree. Additionally, while the mean unemployment rate was 4 percent for college graduates, it was 7 percent for noncollege graduates. Another consideration with respect to education is the college/university the person attended. There is a correlation between where and what type of degree was earned and the earnings of the individual. As noted in a *Business Week* report on graduate business schools in the United States, graduates from the top 25 business schools command starting salaries averaging $20,000 per year higher than those who graduate from "second-tier schools," and they generally earn more throughout their lifetimes. Thus, education and the providing institution continue to be an important determinant of earning potential and "market power."

High-performance organizations recognize the strategic value of education, learning, and knowledge. They implement aggressive human capital development programs designed to advance, capture, and manage knowledge, and then make that knowledge accessible to employees. They are also committed to lifelong learning and to making learning opportunities available in their organizations. These learning opportunities are linked to the strategic needs of their organizations and with the needs of the personnel and, ultimately, are related to strategic change.

SUMMARY

In this chapter, we discussed a complex and very broad topic: multiculturalism. High-performing organizations practice five strategic axioms:

1. Developing an effective strategy in an increasingly diverse environment requires a working knowledge and commitment to enterprisewide coalition and collaboration.
2. High-performance organizations know that multiculturalism is a source of competitive and operational advantage.
3. Income, education, compensation, personal choices, and technology are driving new challenges for strategic thinking and formulation.
4. Understanding strategic change requires an understanding that transitory tenure is defining a new free-agency workforce, which provides just-in-time talent and expertise.
5. Leaders recognize that transitory tenure is defining a new employment contract.

Let's elaborate further because each of these items is an important guidepost for strategists.

1. High-performance organizations recognize that multiculturalism is a source of competitive advantage and a critical element in strategic renewal. They understand that diversity alone does not guarantee multiculturalism. Multiculturalism requires pluralism (the ability to endorse cultural and ethnic uniqueness) while maintaining an overall construct and context and enlightened appreciation for the differences that exist between genders and cultures as sources of innovation and creative thinking.
2. Income, compensation, and education are driving new challenges and themes for leadership. These themes allow new ways of strategic thinking, elevating organizational performance, compensating leaders, and sharing wealth with others. High-performance organizations explore new ways of compensating people that extend beyond traditional benefits and into recognition and reward programs.

One potentially promising strategy is to implement a variable benefits program that is linked to the "life stages" of employees. As an employee travels through life, her or his needs change, and so do the benefits. These benefits can include a wide variety of initiatives such as child care, stock options, tuition reimbursement, and health care benefits provided to younger adults. As an individual ages, the benefits could be tailored to include such items as vacation packages for high performance, financing college tuition for dependents, dental and eye care, supplementary health, life and accident insurance, financial planning, and mortgage financing. As an individual approaches retirement, the compensation and benefits package could be further customized to include items such as defined benefit plans, cash-value life insurance, long-term supplementary health care, and alternative savings and life-care programs.

3. High-performance organizations recognize that transitory tenure is defining a new employment contract and provides a means of engaging workers on a just-in-time and just-needed basis. They recognize that their workforces are more mobile, more confident in changing jobs, and more likely to change jobs. To help retain employees and improve loyalty, the high performers implement a number of creative programs. Recognizing that talent deserves compensation and equal treatment, irrespective of personal preferences and lifestyles, Bank of America, McKinsey, IBM, Levi Strauss, and Disney extend health insurance to domestic partners of employees in same-gender relationships. Another example of changing demographics and workforces influencing the ways companies attract and retain employees can be found at United Technologies (UT). UT offers its employees 100 percent paid tuition and 100 percent book reimbursement for undergraduate and graduate courses. The company provides paid time off to attend classes and study. Upon graduating, UT provides each employee with 100 shares of stock, which represents an investment in both the company and the person.

The impact and importance of multiculturalism on an organization points to some very obvious demands. First, if a company is to be a high performer, it has to understand that it *must* generate tremendous competitive advantage through multiculturalism and diversity. The high performers make a conscious and aggressive effort to find the best talent with varied cultural, gender, life experiences, geographical backgrounds, ethnic backgrounds, and *wisdoms*. There is enormous excitement, synergy, and spontaneity in diversity.

Second, multiculturalism requires that leaders manage and lead differently. Autocratic leadership styles in a multicultural workplace are out and will not work. Any manager continuing to behave in such a manner cannot expect to generate and motivate a multicultural workforce. Multicultural workforces are too sophisticated and intelligent to allow themselves to be exploited by those "chainsaw" tactics. In the place of administrator and checker, the manager must be a composer and a conductor. Given the broad perspectives of a diverse and enlightened workforce, the manager and executive must be able to influence and *choreograph* the talents that she or he is entrusted with, so that they operate at their highest levels and cultivate their fullest potential. This means creating and sustaining an environment where people are learning, contributing, and growing as opposed to just doing their jobs. That value will be measured by how quickly they learn and adapt to new things and, most importantly, by the *portfolio of perspectives* that they can bring and apply to new challenges and different situations.

Third, a strategic imperative for the high-performance organization is to help others to achieve a balance between work and personal lifestyles. The ancillary benefits that the organizations provide will help garner the loyalty of the employee and also the commitment of the employee to the organization. Companies that institute on-site day care programs, private school tuition assistance, college-bound savings programs, health and wellness programs, make corporate discounts from vendors available to employees, extend benefits to same-sex life partners, and institute "personal-enrichment" programs are the ones that will be the most competitive in attracting and retaining the best talent.

Finally, the high-performance organizations that exhibit a commitment to the dignity of each individual and are socially responsible will be the ones that distinguish themselves in the marketplace and garner customer loyalty and esteem. Society and individual workers are holding companies to higher standards of behavior and accountability. They *demand* that their organizations and leaders do the right things. Those organizations that set the highest standards for social and individual accountability and respect will be the highest performers. An organization cannot reach, and certainly cannot sustain, high performance without being socially responsible.

Critical Thoughts and Discussion Questions

1. To what extent can an organization leverage cultural diversity as a catalyst for high performance and innovative thinking? How can it leverage these talents?
2. What are the current major trends in working and employment patterns, and how do these factors influence career choices, "career behavior" (union worker/employee/independent contractor/free agent) job hopping, and organizational strategy?
3. What are the key differences between pluralism, diversity, and multiculturalism? What are the common mistakes and strategic "traps" organizations often fall into with respect to creating a "diverse" and resourceful workforce?
4. To what extent does managing in a multicultural environment require different skills sets and competencies than managing a homogeneous workforce?
5. What are some of the exemplary organizations that successfully create, use, maintain, and continuously renew/refresh their workforce to achieve a distinct and sustainable competitive advantage? How have they developed their competencies for this capability?

5

INFORMATION TECHNOLOGY: STRATEGY AND CHANGE IN AN INTERNET WORLD

"One of the tools which shows the greatest immediate promise is the computer, when it can be harnessed for direct, on-line assistance, and integrated with new concepts and methods."

—DOUGLAS ENGLEBART, SRI, 1962

INTRODUCTION

Information technology (IT) has taken the center stage not only in most companies but also in government, education, health care, and, for many of us, in our private and professional lives. The emergence and rapid propagation of inexpensive and "user-friendly" IT capabilities have created an entirely new environment in which we all must compete, live, and operate. This chapter explores the role of IT as a strategic pillar.

With an ever-expanding universe of IT capabilities and products, managing the strategic implications of IT is a difficult and challenging process, even for the most accomplished high-performance organizations. Historically, organizations have spent increasingly greater amounts of money on IT without necessarily realizing the benefit of comparable increases in productivity or return on investment. This condition, which has come to be known as the "productivity paradox," is attributed to many factors ranging from the technology used to the methods used to measure the return on IT. Nonetheless, in recent years the productivity and financial returns for IT have increased dramatically. IT has had a profound effect on the way organizations form strategy, view their environments, evaluate investments, arrange their structures, and assess opportunities and challenges. Undeniably, IT has played an important part in changing the basic dynamics and assumptions about strategy and in leading organizational renewal.

In the study of business strategy, the influence and effect (impact) of IT are often overlooked or addressed in only a cursory manner. This is due, to a certain extent, to the fact that because as a strategic imperative IT is relatively new and an extremely complex subject, it does not lend itself to easy discussion among academics and general business managers. That is because many people are uncomfortable with the technical aspects of IT and its related jargon. When IT has been addressed, it has been approached from either a technical or experiential perspective, using lots of examples and cases but offering few meaningful insights for the strategist.

In this chapter we address IT as one of the critical pillars of strategic change. We approach IT from a strategist's perspective by considering and discussing the economics of IT, the impact of IT on the economy, and how IT is changing the dynamics of leadership and competition in an increasingly interconnected, real-time world. We also discuss the major themes that are important in providing insights into how IT can be effectively leveraged and optimize the performance of an organization.

THE STRATEGIC IMPORTANCE OF IT

In the 1940s and early 1950s, IT was viewed almost exclusively as the domain of the scientific, military, and academic communities. It was only during the latter part of the 1950s that commercial applications for computers began to emerge, and an entirely new industry was launched. The 1960s saw the rapid proliferation of commercial IT applications, which was precipitated, in part, by the introduction of the IBM 360 family of computers. The 1980s ushered in the personal computer (PC), and the 1990s became the era of interconnectivity, the Internet, and the emergence of pervasive computing. The twenty-first century will be a time of digital convergence and anytime/anyplace computing and communications. Exhibit 5.1 illustrates the evolution of computing.

In the 1990s it is a strategic axiom that no organization can effectively compete or efficiently serve its customers or constituents without extensive IT capabilities. Today IT is a major financial, operational, and organizational component of any strategy. Hardly any major investment, acquisition, merger, reengineering project, plant expansion, or administrative function can be performed without considering the influence of IT. IT has become, in many instances, *infused* in the basic processes and management practices of the organization.

At the fingertips of today's typical knowledge worker is more computing power, greater access to data and information, and greater ability to reach out to customers and markets than could be found in the *entire* United States only a generation ago. Technology, which once took special rooms and legions of dedicated workers to support, now sits in the palms of executives on airplanes, on the desktops of elementary school students, in the home offices of over 50 million people in the United States alone and, very shortly, in our automobiles.

As a strategic pillar, there are five indisputable tenets about IT:

1. IT neutralizes many of the traditional sources of competitive advantage, including size, location, and leverage once enjoyed by industry giants; thus, IT is a strategic weapon.
2. IT extends the enterprise in multiple dimensions and into multiple markets. This extension further differentiates the performance and increases the strategic options of organizations, business units, and societies. As such, IT is a force multiplier for the organization.
3. IT has precipitated a permanent and systemic shift in the composition of the global economy, organizational dynamics, human interactions, and competing. Thus, IT has created a "new economy" and is both a catalyst and an enabler of strategic change.

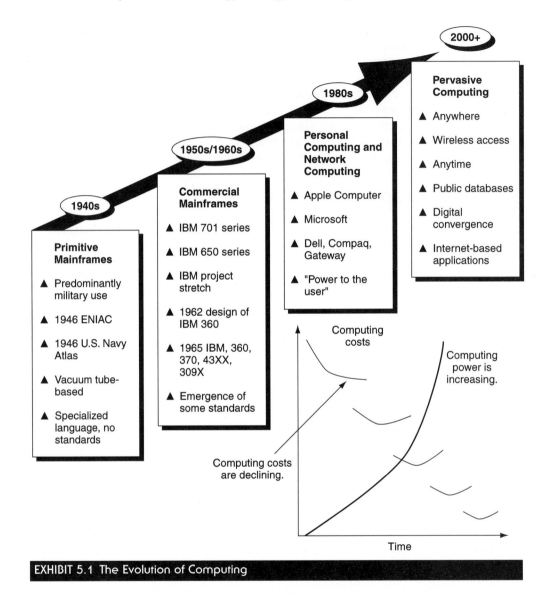

EXHIBIT 5.1 The Evolution of Computing

4. IT is a disintermediary that changes the historical models of customer contact, customer service, supply chains, and product distribution.
5. IT accelerates change and can disrupt the continuity and "balance of power" in any industry or economy, and is, therefore, a source of innovation.

Those companies that understand these five fundamentals and work to integrate technology with their strategic visions, organizational designs, and human performance will leverage their organizations to achieve superior performance and to position them to successfully compete in a rapidly changing world.

"You have to step back as you think about strategy and ask, 'Are there some crucial places where technology is going to play a key role in the evolution of the business?' " said David Coulter, the former CEO of Bank of America as he glanced out of his window overlooking the San Francisco Bay. This is an appropriate and vital strategic question. For many organizations competing in their traditional forms, IT has neutralized and/or systemically altered many of the traditional theories and methods of formulating strategy, including static industry planning models and legacy sources of competitive advantage such as organizational size, vertical integration, location, and geography. Where once building façade, location, and "presence" were differentiating factors and badges of distinction, today they can be nonearning assets on the organization's balance sheet. Physical location and size are now secondary to a company's Web site, databases, and communication technologies. Speaking of how Federal Express' use of technology affected the competitive position and dynamics of the rapid parcel delivery industry, Jim Barksdale, former CEO of Netscape, commented, "It [information technology] caused the whole industry to build similar systems." Point in fact, one of the initiatives that arch-rival United Parcel Service took to counter Federal Express was to invest $9 billion over 13 years to upgrade its IT capabilities. In the process, it also informed its customers and the public through aggressive advertising that highlighted the capabilities of their technology and its timing couldn't have been more fortuitous given the emergence of the Internet.

Historically, industries were clearly defined and demarcated by well-understood limits. Today, those boundaries are blurred, becoming increasingly indistinguishable and far more porous. As a result, the barriers to entry and mobility between organizations in many industries are less formidable and more assailable. IT transcends the economic and political boundaries that defined geopolitics and geoeconomic strategies as well as the physical and industry demarcations that, at one time, represented the clear limits for most organizations. IT allows for different types of business forms and multiple channels of customer contacts and distribution. This places greater pressure on the organization to explore more creative uses of IT that enable new organizational forms and operational designs.

Given the economics of IT and its importance to society and any organization, strategists can expect IT to play a larger role, while also continuing to command a larger share of their capital budgets. Thus, the strategic implications of IT cannot be overstated. This is especially the situation when new forms of business and extended enterprises are considered. The pace of spending and the level of expenditures for IT present new strategic and operational challenges for organizations. As summarized in Exhibit 5.2, IT presents three very distinct strategic options for an organization. Specially:

1. IT can act as a catalyst for strategic advantage and renewal.
2. IT can serve as an enabler for realizing strategic advantage and renewal.
3. IT can be an inhibitor to creating competitive advantage and strategic renewal.

Organizations must actively manage the investment in technology and its impact on overall financial and operational performance by establishing new measurements and standards. They must develop a working knowledge of how technology can interrelate and integrate with the organizational and operational strategies and structures of their firms, and how IT can impact productivity. In the process, there is a shift in managerial understanding and emphasis from the "cost control" mentality of IT to one that recognizes IT as an enterprisewide strategic resource and investment capable of changing the dynamics of an established firm or industry.

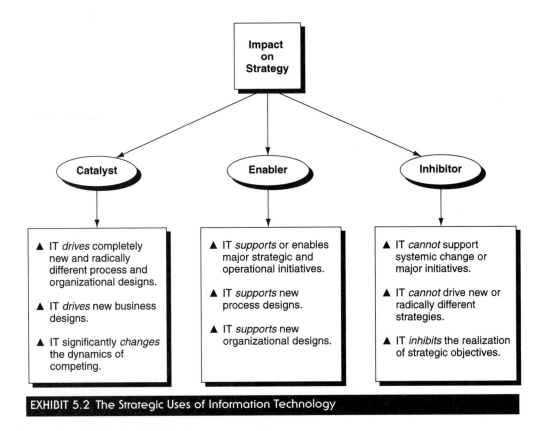

EXHIBIT 5.2 The Strategic Uses of Information Technology

To achieve and sustain high performance, organizations must embrace IT as a means of leveraging their resources and competencies and a means to transfer knowledge. Such an application of IT accelerates the communications flow and distribution of information in ways that present new management challenges and opportunities. IT enables organizations to develop highly focused and highly networked collaborative working groups and has allowed responsibilities and jobs to be distributed globally, while tapping into the diversity of nations, individual competencies, and life experiences, unique cultural perspectives and collective wisdom of the organization. Essentially, IT strategies for the technology, application systems, and data can assume one of four postures:

- Embedded intelligence in the technology used to support or drive a business process.
- Enable process transformation through its use and deployment.
- Provide management information for making decisions.
- Support the high-speed processing of transactions.

Exhibit 5.3 summarizes these capabilities and the strategic implications of IT.

IT has precipitated a permanent displacement and migration in the U.S. economy for workers, wealth, and valuation that were eclipsed only by what occurred when people moved from the farms and into the cities during the industrial revolution. This condition presents organizations with the need to plan for systemic shifts in how people

Strategic Themes

EI = Embedded intelligence. IT has knowledge embedded in it to facilitate process excellence, adaptation and organizational agility.

PT =
Process transformation. IT enables new process designs, consolidation of organizations and performance metrics.

MI = Management information. IT provides information and indicators from which to make decisions.

TP = Transaction processing. IT supports the processing of homogeneous transactions and volumes of data.

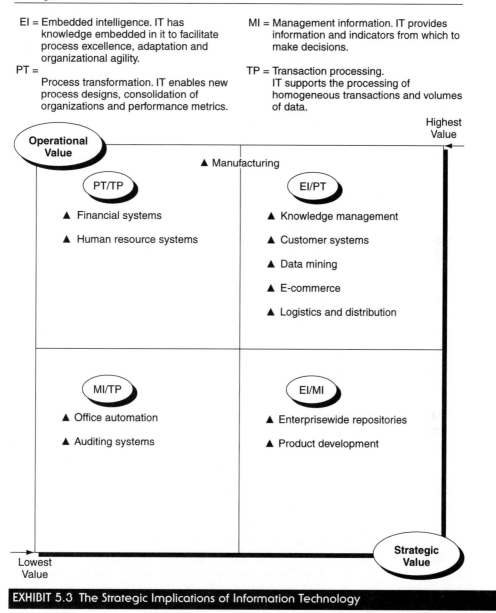

EXHIBIT 5.3 The Strategic Implications of Information Technology

work, live, think, and spend their income. There is, in effect, a value migration for skills and competencies from the very narrow and highly specialized to the very broad and highly competent. Emphasis is now placed on the ability to assimilate and learn new competencies and to play multiple roles in the organization. The implications are clear: Organizations must be positioned to present a different value proposition to their employees that is increasingly predicated on using IT not only for working but also for education, telecommuting, and job enrichment.

As a percentage of capital spending, IT now represents the single largest line item in most Fortune 500 companies. U.S. investment in IT has been estimated by some sources to be 34 percent of total equipment spending. In their *1997 Ninth Annual Survey of North American Chief Information Executives* survey of 488 companies, Deloitte Consulting found that overall IT spending represented 2.6 percent of revenues with an average IT budget of $5,800 per employee. According to their survey, the high spenders were the banking and financial services sector, which averaged 9.2 percent of revenue. Retailing continues to represent the lowest percentage of IT budget to revenue at 1.2 percent, which is considerably less than industry leaders Wal-Mart and The Home Depot.

When it comes to identifying the "right" level of investment in technology, "It's not what you spend, but how you spend it," advises Gregg Schmidtetter, co-author of the Deloitte Consulting study. "As a CIO, my primary focus should be on improving my business position. If I can do that with sexy new whiz-bang technology or through a more complex IT environment, then the investment may well be worth it." Rich Pople of Deloitte Consulting adds, "Today, more enterprises see the IT function as a business within the business. They expect results to match."

With budgets for IT approaching and surpassing 3 percent of revenues for most Fortune 500 companies and with expenditures for projects such as SAP R/3 implementations easily exceeding $100 million, organizations can ill afford not to understand the importance of IT and its impact on organizational performance. The reality for many organizations is that their investments in IT, sophisticated enterprise resource planning (ERP), and sales-force automation systems have not yielded the payback hoped for. For example, in a recent survey by the London School of Economics (LSE) conducted for Compass America, the LSE found that 80 percent of chief executives had been "disappointed" by the contribution of IT to the competitiveness of their companies, and only 25 percent believed that IT had made significant contributions to bottom-line financial performance. The Hackett Group, a consulting firm specializing in financial accounting operations, reports in *Business Week* that only 37 percent of large technology projects are completed on time, and only 42 percent are completed on budget. Read differently, that means that 63 percent of large IT projects can be considered unsuccessful. Imagine the implications to society if only 63 percent of all medical procedures were successful, or only 63 percent of all airline flights took off and landed safely. Less dramatically, it is safe to assume that any firm that had 63 percent of its manufacturing operations fail to produce an acceptable product or had 37 percent of its customer orders accurately processed would soon be out of business.

The implications of such "failures" can be potentially devastating to an organization. In October 1999 *The Wall Street Journal* reported that the net income of Hershey Foods Corporation fell by 19%. According to *The Wall Street Journal*, "Hershey said the problems stemmed from a nationwide order-taking and distribution system that had been disrupted by the introduction of systems intended to ease shipping." Hershey's $110 million systems project, which attempted to integrate three very sophisticated and complex applications on technologies which were not core strengths of Hershey, was apparently over-budget, past due and poorly implemented. As a result, Hershey sustained a decline in sales during a period when consumer demand surged, its market share declined, and its earnings fell short.

Despite the disappointments and project histories, the rapid increase in the use of technology has been propelled by a number of factors, including: advances in computers, software and communications, declining cost of technology, increasing availability of technology in the open market, the growing literacy and dependency among users for computers, and simply . . . *necessity.*

Almost 30 years ago, Intel cofounder Gordon Moore postulated that computing power would double every 18 months and quadruple every 30 months. Those lofty and aggressive predictions have now materialized and are on the verge of being shattered. The most significant performance gains and big cost breakthroughs in technology have come from workstations, client-servers, PCs, and networking, which move computing power to the point of execution with users. The convergence and integration of communications and multimedia capabilities with powerful networked computers have supplanted the mainframe as the mainstream standard for technology. It is in these convergent technologies where the most dramatic and exciting improvements in cost/performance, scalability, and modularity have occurred. Soundview Financial Group estimates that the "cost" of technology, as measured by the relationship between performance and cost, has declined from around $90 per MIPS in 1990 to about $10 per MIPS (millions of instructions per second) in 1996 for mainframe computing. Intel Corporation reports that the cost per PC MIPS has declined from $225 in 1991 to $7 in 1996, a factor of 32 times over 5 years. The performance and value advances in the personal and network computing environments do not necessarily signal the death of the mainframe or that the mainframe is no longer a key component in computing. Rather, the role and mission of the mainframe have changed. It is no longer the focal point of computing for many organizations, but it remains a valuable workhorse for enormous transaction volumes, data base management, and sophisticated communications.

Well into the future, we will continue to experience a *convergence* in computing, which will involve greater interconnectivity, more broadbanded network-based computing, and something that IBM and *The Economist* are calling "pervasive computing." Others refer to this emerging architecture as "ubiquitous" computing capabilities. Pervasive or ubiquitous computing is an anytime/anyplace computing capability. It provides for the convergent integration of many computing methods such as personal digital assistants (PDAs), thin client-servers, interactive video telephones, wireless communication, and multimedia service boxes; with technology delivered on the desktop, in palm-sized devices, automobiles, etc. Supported by extensive wireless and hardwired broadbanded networks and their applications, data and knowledge will be accessible on an anytime, anyplace worldwide basis. This evolution, which will continue to radically redefine the computing landscape and economics of computing, creates some very exciting strategic opportunities and challenges in the areas of data security, accessibility, and the use and management of IT. Pervasive computing is enabled through the use of the Internet and wireless communications as the definitive channels of distribution for computing resources and software. It also provides an alternative to the traditional client-server, PC-based, and legacy computing solutions. Forrester Research Inc. predicted that by 1999 a significant percentage (as much as 50 percent) of all software would be delivered through the Internet. Although the statistics did not materialize, there is significant growth in the use of the Internet as a media for delivering electronic products and services, including software. Microsoft, the dominant company in the software arena, estimates that 10 percent of its products will be delivered through the Internet within the next few years. Exhibit 5.4 illustrates the concept of pervasive computing.

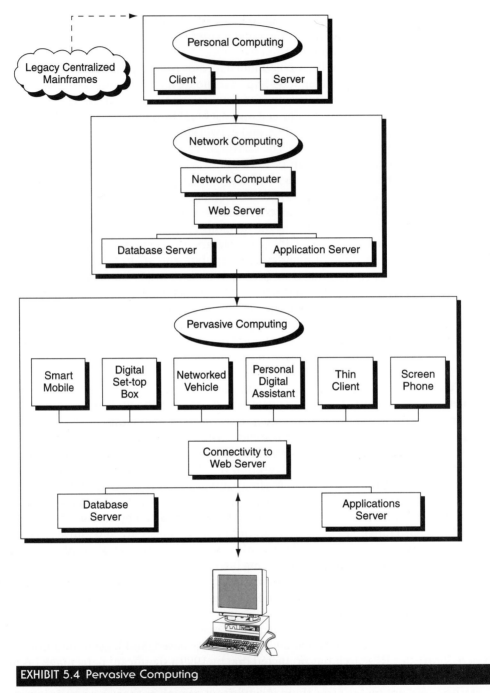

EXHIBIT 5.4 Pervasive Computing

Source: IBM and *The Economist.*

The web-centric configuration of computing and access to data and software provides a viable alternative to the client-server and PC-based solutions. The use of a Web-centric solution presents the potential for expanding access and reduced support and maintenance costs while allowing for the use of the most contemporary products, latest versions, and updated data. Oracle Corporation once estimated that Web-centric computing solutions could reduce costs by as much as 80 percent over traditional PC architecture. However, in light of Oracle's recent results with Web-centric computing solutions and canceled orders by companies such as Federal Express, that figure may be inflated at least in the foreseeable future. Nonetheless, the use of Web-based products is a significant trend and must be a factor in the technology strategies of virtually all companies.

THE IMPACT OF IT

Recognizing the impact of technology on the U.S. and world economies is fundamental to appreciating its influence on strategy and strategic change. IT is creating a new economy by changing the fundamental dynamics and measurements of "old" economic activity and vitality. As U.S. Michigan Senator Spencer Abraham noted, "Members [of Congress] increasingly recognize the connection between a strong high-technology sector and a strong recovery." For 1996, technology expenditures represented about 10 percent of total U.S. GDP. Since 1993, technology spending represented 27 percent of the growth for GDP. In contrast, the traditional housing and automotive sectors accounted for 14 and 4 percent, respectively.

In 1997, IT expenditures for computers, communications, video and voice data integration, and peripherals were estimated by *Business Week* to be approximately $420.3 billion. That represents a 77 percent increase in expenditures for IT since 1990. The $420 billion estimate excludes amounts spent on professional services or for payroll-related expenses to support technology. Add those components, and the technology sector represents at least a trillion-dollar industry. Investment and expenditures in technology continue to grow at double-digit rates. While the overall U.S. economy grew at 2.3 percent a year since 1991, the information technology segment grew well above that rate. Even Alan Greenspan, chairman of the Federal Reserve System, noted that "Information technology has doubtlessly enhanced the stability of business operations." From a strategic perspective, IT is a new and important determinant of economic activity.

According to a *Business Week* report, business spending on computers has increased by 86 percent since 1994, compared to other investments that increased 40 percent. Datastream estimates that in 1996 about 40 percent of U.S. business investment in capital equipment was represented by technology. This compares to estimates by other sources that project IT investment at as much as 50 percent of most budgets or approximately 4 percent of revenues. Other estimates put IT investment between 25 and 30 percent of the total capital budget. This spending pattern compares to slightly over 20 percent in the mid-1980s and less than 10 percent for the 1970s. Since 1993, consumer spending on technology has increased by 55 percent.

According to *The Economist,* about 80 percent of technology investment is incurred by business(es). As David Coulter noted about Bank of America (B of A) and its expenditures on IT, "B of A is a spender. B of A spends somewhere between a billion and a quarter and a billion and a half a year on running data centers, developing applications, supporting our customers and bankers, and ensuring that we are emphasizing being innovative." *The Economist* estimates that about three-fourths of technology spending is related to the traditional service industries such as communications and financial services. IT spending as a share of total investment spending by the financial services sector was close to 28 percent in 1998, up from 18 percent in 1985. In contrast, investment and expenditures in labor were up only 19 percent over the same period.

The impact of the new IT economy on the overall U.S. economy can be more fully appreciated by comparing IT and the automotive sectors. *The Economist* and Datastream noted that the 1996 combined sales of "New Big Three" technology leaders—Intel, Microsoft, and Cisco—were $33.6 billion or only 10 percent of the $372.5 billion generated by the "Big Three" automotive companies (GM, Ford, and Chrysler). The New Big Three technology companies employed only 7 percent of the total 1.1 million plus employees working for the Big Three automotive makers, but the total market capitalization of the New Big Three technology companies exceeded the Big Three automotive makers by a 2.6 to 1 ratio. Let's compare two of the companies:

Brains and Bricks

	Industry Position	*Number of Employees*	*Market Value*	*1999 Sales*
GM	1	388,000	$ 63.8 billion	$189.1 billion
Microsoft	1	31,400	$ 601 billion	$ 22.4 billion

Source: Compilation from various sources including: company annual reports and *Business Week* and *Fortune* magazines, 1999 and 2000.

The significance of this change in business models and their influence on the overall economy is reflected in the market capitalization of modern companies. For example, *Bloomberg News* reports that Microsoft Corporation, which became a public company in 1986, became in 1999 the first company in history to exceed $500 billion in market value. If Microsoft were a country, it would have the ninth-largest economy in the world and has 11 times the value of one-time leader General Motors. Of the top 12 companies with the highest market value, five are in the IT sector; the remainder are scattered among the "old economy" oil and gas, food, automotive, and consumer products industries.

The reality of the new economic environment is that knowledge, collaboration, and competition yield higher financial returns and greater productivity than traditional bricks and mortar. In this respect, there is what author Adrian Slywotzky calls a "value migration" away from traditional industrial forms of business to more knowledge-based forms of business that are IT intensive.

The U.S. Department of Labor, the Bureau of Economic Analysis, and *Business Week* estimate that approximately 9.1 million people are employed in the technology sector. On a comparative basis, the average salaries and wages earned by those employed in the technology sector are higher than those earned by employees in the traditional industries. This reflects, in part, the shift in emphasis to knowledge-based skill sets and the leverage created by IT-enabled process and organizational designs. *Business Week* estimates that wages for the overall economy, net of the technology sector, increased by only 0.3 percent for 1996, while wages in the technology sector went up by over 2 percent. Wage increases for the IT sector were 6.6 times the rate of wage increase for the general economy, and that does not consider stock options, bonus programs, and other environmental benefits of working in the technology sector.

A survey of "Silicon Valley" workers conducted by International Survey Research Corporation appearing in *Business Week* notes that "Valley" workers appear to be happier and have more favorable impressions and opinions of their employers "by a significant margin on 15 of 20 workplace issues over the national norm." Indicative of the growth and the shift in "value" towards technology is the number of new business ventures that were launched in the Silicon Valley. For 1997, the accounting firm PricewaterhouseCoopers (PwC) estimated that over 3,500 new businesses were launched in the Silicon Valley alone, with $3.7 billion of venture capital invested in them. That equates to a 60 percent increase over the prior year. Over 53,000 new jobs were created in 1997 in the Silicon Valley. For strategists, these statistics point to excitement, opportunity, and a clear indication of a shift in wealth and value from traditional industries to newer forms of organizational design with a higher dependence on intellectual capital and knowledge management.

To many it should come as no surprise that the United States enjoys a dominant position for the use and deployment of technology in the workforce and society. International Data Corporation (IDC) estimates that there are approximately 63 PCs for every 100 workers in the United States, and a Goldman Sachs study appearing in *The Economist* estimates that there are 174 computers per 100 public employees. This is an interesting statistic relative to issues of productivity and service levels in the public sector. Clearly, technology has permeated the U.S. workforce and is a major contributor to the significant productivity increases of the later 1990s. On a per capita basis, the International Institute for Management Development (IMD) and the World Economic Forum reports that there were 0.319 computers per person in the United States in 1994. This compares with only 0.118 and 0.151 computers per capita in Japan and Germany, respectively, which represent the second and third highest levels of penetration in the world. Since 1994, this gap has widened. This level of "penetration" brings up some interesting issues and questions with respect to government productivity, cost performance, and taxpayer value, but such issues are better left to others to debate. The International Telecommunications Union estimates in *The Economist* that slightly more than 42 percent of all U.S. households have personal computers. Australia follows the United States with about 37 percent. Germany, the United Kingdom, Japan, and France all have between 20 to 29 percent of their respective households with PCs.

By the year 2000, the U.S. Labor Department estimates that 60 percent of all U.S. households will have PCs. However, the U.S. Department of Commerce, together with the Federal Communications Commission (FCC) and The Strategis Group, forecast that 48 percent of all U.S. households will have at least one PC by 2001. The differences between these estimates notwithstanding, the implications are clear: The number of households with PCs, the number of PCs per household, and Internet connections will continue to grow. Much like televisions, automobiles, and telephones, most households will probably maintain multiple machines for use at work, in household management, for home office use, as well as for entertainment and education. Undoubtedly, we will experience a continued growth of households with multiple communication lines and increasing connectivity and transmission volume requirements.

The most significant differentiation occurs in aggregate computing power, the ability of the computer to process instructions. Based on their 1994 research findings, the IMD, World Economic Forum has estimated that 49 percent of the entire computing capacity of the world is resident in the United States. Other estimates are in excess of 50 percent. The next highest level of concentration is found in Japan with 7 percent and Germany with about 6 percent. Collectively, the EU will probably have about 30 percent to 35 percent of total computing on a consolidated basis. Clearly, by most counts the comparative advantage for technology deployment and use belongs to and will stay in the United States.

The above statistics are important because in a world that is becoming increasingly interconnected, those countries and companies that have the greatest computing capacities and best communication infrastructures inherently possess the greatest competitive advantage and ability to adapt to change. It is in those markets and among those companies employing highly sophisticated IT that the greatest potential for extended enterprise concepts, improved marketshare, and greater connectivity exists. The dynamics of these markets will continue to move at unprecedented rates of change and with increasing unpredictability.

A STRATEGIC VIEW OF THE INTERNET, INTRANETS, AND ELECTRONIC COMMERCE

"In five years' time, all companies will be Internet companies, or they won't be companies at all," according to Andy Grove, Chairman of the Board, Intel Corporation. In just a few short years, the Internet has completely rewritten much of how companies compete and view their marketspace. Since the introduction of the PC, nothing in technology is as exciting or as potentially explosive for an individual or organization as the Internet. The use of the Internet, Extranet, and Intranet has created the ability to communicate, conduct business, collaborate, and transfer knowledge anytime and anywhere in the world, regardless of geographical location and time zone. All one needs is access to the 'Net and a little bit of equipment.

There are three key characteristics that define the Internet and its relation to strategy: (1) it is a disintermediary, (2) it creates greater uncertainty, and (3) it accelerates change. The Internet changes the basic dynamics and structure of industries and how companies interact with customers, suppliers, and business partners. The Internet changes the fundamental (basic dynamics) of competing by enabling new and different organizational designs and alternative business designs. Several factors are worth noting. First, the economic barriers to create a Web-based business are low; the capital requirements are minimal. Second, Web-based businesses are gender-neutral, color-blind, and age-indiscriminate. These factors virtually eliminate the barriers associated with racism and other forms of discrimination. Third, although most Web-based businesses are unprofitable at first, they can achieve breakeven and profitability relatively quickly. Finally, the implementation of Web-based businesses can result in a "large" business with relatively low overhead and administrative burdens as compared to the traditional bricks and mortar business models. All of these are attractive features to entrepreneurs. Thus, the established organizations must be cognizant and more sensitive to the developments of new forms of business, which are constantly evolving on the Internet. Indeed, the potential affect of the Internet has not been lost on management. Even stoic GM has taken notice: "If we don't move with Internet speed, we could become extinct," said Mark T. Hogan, group vice president of GM in *Business Week*. According to the consulting firm Booz, Allen & Hamilton, 90 percent of managers responding to their survey believe that the Internet will transform the global market by 2001. Only a few years ago this percentage would have been below 20 percent and virtually indiscernible in the early part of the 1990s. Exhibit 5.5 summarizes some of the salient strategic implications of the Internet and e-business.

The emergence of the Internet and e-commerce has allowed organizations to communicate more effectively, work more closely and efficiently as collaborative teams, improve individual and collective productivity, reduce cycle times and logistical costs, and

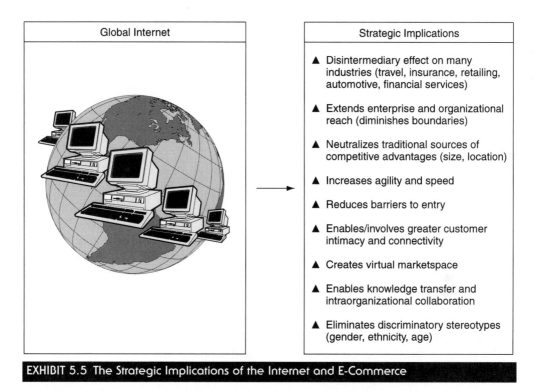

Global Internet	Strategic Implications
	▲ Disintermediary effect on many industries (travel, insurance, retailing, automotive, financial services)
	▲ Extends enterprise and organizational reach (diminishes boundaries)
	▲ Neutralizes traditional sources of competitive advantages (size, location)
	▲ Increases agility and speed
	▲ Reduces barriers to entry
	▲ Enables/involves greater customer intimacy and connectivity
	▲ Creates virtual marketspace
	▲ Enables knowledge transfer and intraorganizational collaboration
	▲ Eliminates discriminatory stereotypes (gender, ethnicity, age)

EXHIBIT 5.5 The Strategic Implications of the Internet and E-Commerce

extend the enterprise into new areas. According to ActivMedia, the number of commercial sites on the Internet increased from 2,000 in 1995 to over 414,000 in 1998. IDC estimates that the number of business Web-sites will increase from 700,000 in 1998 to 1 million in 2003. One of the factors contributing to the growth is the increase in the number of people exploring the Internet. Cyber Dialogue estimates that in 1995 14.3 million people surfed the Internet. By 1997, that number had increased to 41.5 million and to over 100 million in 1999. It is now estimated that anywhere from 240 million to 500 million people will surf the Internet by the early years of the twenty-first century. Implicit in this is the growth of E-commerce, which is estimated to increase from 53 million business users to 180 million users by Ovum.

E-commerce is defined as the exchange of information, goods, or services for value over the Internet and Extranet. There are two basic forms of e-commerce: business to business (b2b) and business to consumer (b2c). The rapid contagion of e-commerce and the Internet presents four very compelling and attractive value propositions for consumers:

1. It allows for unlimited (virtually) access to new, exotic, and geographically distant markets, services and an ever expanding universe of products.
2. It allows for limitless (virtually) variety and selection of products and services on an anytime, anywhere basis.
3. It provides for the ultimate convenience and ease of use on an anytime, anyplace basis, which is supported by pervasive/ubiquitous computing and wireless capabilities.

4. It provides for personal safety and security . . . no traffic, no shopping mall parking lots, and greater personal security.

For businesses, the Internet and e-commerce provide:

1. Direct contact with the end consumer, which, in turn, generates knowledge, rapport, and relationships.
2. Elimination and/or mitigation of intermediaries (brokers, dealers, middlemen) and direct contact with the manufacturer or service provider.
3. Ease of contact with the consumer for information collection and sharing.
4. Reduced business costs and accelerated cash flows. According to Ernst & Young, e-commerce can reduce the cost of doing business by 5 percent to 10 percent. The Giga Information Group estimates cost savings to business to increase from $17 billion in 1998 to $1.25 trillion in 2002.

Estimates as to the "size" of the e-commerce marketplace differ widely. The virtual reality created by the Internet is difficult to measure and estimate; thus, there is wide disparity and little consistency in measurements. What is consistent, however, is agreement as to the magnitude and growth of the Internet and potential for e-commerce. All estimates agree that the Internet and e-commerce are growing at terrific rates with an infinite capacity as to size. For example, for the 1996 to 1999 period, the value of consumer purchases grew 1,600%. Ernst & Young, in their 1999 Second Annual Internet Shopping Study, cites a study by the Boston Consulting Group and shop.org that estimates the 1999 value of goods sold directly to consumers via the Internet to be $13 billion and is forecasted to grow 200 percent per year over the "next few years." Other reports provide higher estimates, whereas some are lower. According to the Forrester Group, e-commerce is estimated to generate a $10 to $20 billion increase in U.S. GDP. The Department of Commerce estimates that 8 percent of GDP was generated through e-commerce in 1998. ActivMedia estimates that investment upgrades for e-commerce are expected to total $24 billion by 2002. For 1996, it was estimated that 14.7 million households were connected to the Internet. That is up from about 1 million at the end of 1994. By the year 2000, various sources such as the Forrester Group and Gartner Group project the number of users of the Internet could range between 300 million to 1 billion with 100 million host computers linked to it.

According to statistics compiled by the Computer Industry Alamac, North America represents the greatest concentration of computer users with 149 million in 2000, or 48 percent of total population. Western Europe is second with 87 million, or 22% of the population. Specifically:

Geographic Region	PC Users (in millions)	Per 1000 People	Penetration (%)
North America	148.7	479.1	48%
Western Europe	86.6	217.5	22%
Asia-Pacific	57.6	16.5	1.7%
South/Central America	10.8	21.1	2.1%
Eastern Europe	9.5	32.7	3.3%
Middle East & Africa	7.5	7.2	.7%

Source: Adapted from Computer Industry Almanac in *Business Week.*

According to Louis Harris & Associates and Baruch College, users of the Internet are better educated, more culturally and ethnically diverse, and wealthier than the general population. Forty-one percent of Internet users have a college or postgraduate degree, 45 percent are over the age of 40, 28 percent are self-employed, 67 percent are over the age of 30, 85 percent are Caucasian, and 41 percent are women. At $55,000, the average household income of the Internet user is about 1.5 times the national median of around $35,000 per year. Interestingly, Ernst & Young found that the majority of shoppers in their survey were male heads of households (49 percent) and 68 percent were over the age of 40. Finally, Jupiter Communications estimates that the number of children between the ages of 2 and 12 using the Internet will increase from 1.5 million in 1996 to over 21 million in the year 2002.

The U.S. numbers for e-commerce and the Internet are in contrast to those of Europe and Japan. The Forrester Research Group in *Business Week* estimates that European on-line business was $1.2 billion in 1998, but it is expected to grow to $64.4 billion by 2001. Internet use, based on the number of households, is 27 percent in the United States, 7 percent in Germany, 6 percent in the United Kingdom, and 2 percent in France. *Business Week* reports that the use of e-mail by the U.S. population has increased 650 percent, from around 2 percent in 1992 to over 15 percent in 1996, and it continues to grow. The growth prospects for e-commerce in the EU and Eastern Europe is reflected in a projected shift in the proportionality of business conducted via the Internet. For example, IDC estimates that in 1998, the U.S. accounted for 75% of total e-commerce sales. By 2003, that percentage is expected to decline to 50%. This shift presents new challenges and significant opportunities for strategic planners and organizations positioning themselves for high-performance.

Although significantly lagging the United States in the percentage of households with PCs and connectivity to the Internet, the EU is exerting leadership in how the Internet will be used and managed, especially in the area of data privacy and security. The EU has promulgated its Directive on Data Protection, which stipulates significant regulations regarding the privacy of data for individuals. In the United States, there is a lack of comprehensive privacy and ownership standards. The absence of such privacy and data standards allows companies to tag records with "cookies," configure custom sales sites for each customer, pitch cross-selling of other products and services to customers, and sell personal data such as address, income, age, family status, etc. Cookies are implanted on a client's (usually buyer's or user's) hard drive by the server (seller or Web site) to capture and build information about the buyer/user visitation habits. The information collected on these habits can be used to customize service and product offerings for the user or sold to third parties.

The EU Directive guarantees European citizens absolute privacy and *control* over their personal data. The Directive provides that if a company wants personal information on an individual, it must procure the approval and permission of the person. Article 29 of the Directive extends these conditions beyond the political and geographical borders of the EU by mandating other countries to provide similar provisions as a condition of continuing to do business with EU-based countries. This implies that cookies, which track and provide customer behavior, may be illegal, cross-marketing without customer permission will be illegal, and companies must disclose to individuals their data files on the person upon request.

Without question, the Internet is reinventing the traditional channels for consumer distribution and retailing functions. Examples of the impact of IT and the Internet on business abound. Cyber Dialogue reports that 19 percent of survey respondents indicate that they are shopping less in stores. Auto-by-Tel, an Internet-based auto-purchasing organization, which refers potential buyers to dealers, reports "selling" 1.5 million cars through Internet referrals in 1997. Dell Computer, the star of Wall Street, generates over $5 million a day in sales through its Web site. Cisco Systems will exceed $7 billion in sales generated through its Internet-based e-commerce. Other examples of the impact of the Internet and e-commerce include:

- Sixteen percent of new car buyers use the Web for shopping, up from 10 percent in 1995.
- Two percent of 15 million cars sold were the result of Web-based purchasing services. The 2 percent represents about $6 billion in revenue.
- Chrysler's Web site "Get a Quote" is attributed with selling 600 cars in its first 6 months of operation.
- Don-A-Vee Auto Group, a new car dealer in southern California, converts 50 percent of inquires into sales, 25 percent of which is new car sales, up from only 5 percent in 1997.
- Priceline.com, eToys.com, eBay.com and a host of other Internet-based companies are eliminating the intermediaries across a number of sectors with interactive, anytime, anyplace, and all-of-the-time services.*
  Sources: Various, including "Downloading Their Cars," *Business Week,* 3/9/98.

According to Booz Allen & Hamilton, 84 percent of insurance companies are "worried" that the Internet could displace and/or steal business. In the same study, 59 percent indicate that there is a "high risk" that the Internet could precipitate price competition and pressures. Another example of the potential disintermediary effect can be found in the new dynamics of the travel and touring industry. Phil Davidoff, founder of Belair/Empress Travel Company, estimates that commissions and fees from airline ticket bookings for travel agencies have dropped from approximately 62 percent of revenues to around 30 percent. Sales of airline tickets and books, as a percentage of total sales by product, through the Internet will run about 2.5 percent and 2.2 percent, respectively. Finally, Piper Jaffrey, the research firm, estimates that in 1999 37% of all retail stock trades were performed "on-line" and 50% will be expected via the Internet in 2000.

E-commerce on the Internet, on either the business-to-business level or retail level, is more ergonomically and economically appealing and less bureaucratic. Dell Computer maintains customer inquiry information for up to 2 weeks, so that when shopping electronically, buyers can refer to Dell and the products that they were most interested in without reinitiating the standard screens. Cisco Systems uses Internet-based e-commerce to respond to over 70 percent of all requests for technical help and assistance. An analysis of pricing for 'Net-based products reveals that prices can be "sticky." For example, studies by McGraw-Hill and IDC indicate the following comparison:

Pricing Comparison: Traditional versus E-Commerce

Source/Item	Pricing Traditional	Pricing E-Commerce
Gap jeans	$36.89	$41.84
BMW Z3	$32,470	$32,325
Toy at Toys "R" Us	$21.67	$34.94
Life insurance	$87/month	$87/month

Given the initial dynamics of e-commerce, which indicate an overall increase in the number of web-based businesses, price competition is inevitable.

The economics of prices and profits notwithstanding, the most exciting aspect of e-commerce and the Internet is that they provide organizations with new ways of structuring and competing. The emergence of e-commerce and the Internet has allowed for the formation of new and different forms of business. These new business designs are highly competitive and represent entirely different threats for established industry leaders. These threats force established leaders, such as Levi Straus and Merrill Lynch, to react to the leads provided by the new e-commerce business designs such as Charles Schwab and Guess.

Let's compare Barnes & Noble with Amazon.com:

Brains and Brown

	Barnes & Noble	Amazon.com
Date founded	1873	1995
1999 Sales	$3.49 billion	$1.64 billion
Titles offered	1.0+ million	13 million
Book returns	30%	2%
Market capitalization	$1.43 billion	$23.64 billion
Retail space	11 million square feet	—
Employees	15,200	7,600
Revenues per employee	$230,000	$216,000
Number of locations	1,011+	1 Web site +15 physical
Cash flow requirements	High	Medium

Source: Fast Company, Hummer Winbald, *Fortune* and *Business Week* magazines.

Amazon.com represents an interesting design and concept, which forces us to rethink how businesses are designed and organized. For example, with data and configurable "store fronts," companies such as Amazon.com can create a store for each customer. If they have 4 million customers, they ultimately will have 4 million virtual stores. Sales for Amazon.com were $610 million in 1998 with a market capitalization of $33 billion and average revenues of $392,000 per employee. Sales for 1999 are expected to exceed $1 billion. On a comparative basis, Amazon.com's market rate of capitalization in just 5 years exceeds those of 100-year-old Hershey Foods, giant retailers Kmart, Federated Department Stores, Toys "R" Us, and toy maker Mattel. The growth advantage and strategic positions have shifted to those companies that have successfully leveraged IT. The success of Amazon.com has launched other new concepts for selling toys, clothing, music, and groceries. The value of e-based businesses is reflected in the increase in value of their stocks. For the 1997 to 1999 period, the value of the stock of online commerce companies increased 477%.

Despite predictions for the retail market, much of the real impact of the Internet is obscured from the mainstream consumer and public. The business-to-business e-commerce market is estimated to make up about 78 percent of the total e-commerce marketplace. The Yankee Group projects that the business-to-business segment of the electronic marketplace will grow to over $134 billion by the year 2000 and to $1.3 trillion by 2003 according to Forrester Research. At this level, business-to-business e-commerce will represent about 2.6 percent of U.S. GDP.

"Intranets are the most important new computing platform since business computers were introduced into the business environment. Intranets are about corporate workforce connectivity. They connect people to people and people to information," notes Microsoft Corporation in a discussion paper. Technologies such as the Intranet enable companies to achieve higher and greater degrees of operational integration. This integration, in turn, creates greater operational leverage, better efficiencies, and improved performance on a global scale. For example, as an indication of Ford's use of IT for strategic advantage, the company announced in 2000 that virtually every employee will receive a company paid-for PC for their private use. Ford Motor Company implemented a proprietary Web site that links together over 120,000 employees into a working cyber-knowledge network. Ford's objective is to create an IT and knowledge infrastructure that provide it with a build-a-car "on-demand" capability and streamline its supply chains. This type of capability could potentially lower Ford's cycle time to fill a customer order for a new car from 50 days to 15 days. In the process, Ford will save billions of dollars in inventory costs, accelerate cash flows, move much closer to end customers, and establish a clear cost and time-to-market advantage over its rivals. If you are a leader of a competing car company, you better take Ford seriously and understand how technology can be used to create a distinct competitive advantage by building to demand and customer specifications.

Another example of Intranet use can be found at US West. Although much maligned for their protracted response times for customer services, US West has attempted to improve its customer service through a combination of operational changes, organizational initiatives, and technology. US West utilizes Netscape and Internet technology for its corporate Intranet. "Through the use of open Internet technology for its corporate Intranet, US West Communications has already realized benefits in the areas of better customer service, increased employee productivity, and a reduction in operating costs," notes Mike Homerm, senior vice president of marketing for Netscape. US West has used the Internet to integrate its operations by allowing its customer service representatives to check if telephone facilities are physically available before making installation commitments to customers. This has enabled US West to reduce missed commitments and has also lowered customer complaints.

According to a Louis Harris & Associates and Baruch College survey, 75 percent of the respondents reported that they used the Internet for education, with 82 percent reporting that they access the Internet for research services. At the college level, the Web abounds with sources for earning degrees or taking courses ranging from art appreciation to dream interpretation, notes *Information Week* magazine. Several universities, such as University of Phoenix, University of Maryland, Syracuse University, Washington International University, and Concord University offer undergraduate and graduate degree programs over the Internet. For example, Concord University offers a law degree with courses available on a 24-hour-a-day, 365-days-a-year schedule. Duke University has launched a virtual MBA. The $85,000 program uses a combination of study groups that link students together and several visits to campus for interactions with classmates and faculty. This type of "virtual" classroom is changing the dynamics of education by making knowledge and interactive learning available on a geographically indiscriminate basis and to those who have full-time professional commitments. It is also changing the basic cost structure of education. Concord's tuition is about $17,000 for a juris doctor degree that is recognized in California, pending the approval of the American Bar Association.

Clearly, the Internet is precipitating a dramatic shift in the accessibility and delivery of higher education. The combination of this accessibility with the technology and need for advanced education is driving increases in attendance in Internet delivery of higher education. For example, IDC estimates that 710,000 students or 4.8% of the total enrollment in higher education were using Internet-based delivery methods. By 2002, IDC estimates the percent to grow to 15.1 with 2.23 million students.

Interactive CD-ROM, compressed video, e-mail and other information-based technologies are other areas that are forging a new path to learning and knowledge dissemination. Companies such as General Electric Capital Corporation, Ford, Chrysler, and Boeing have created sophisticated knowledge-transfer programs using technologies. These technologies enable a "living" interactive learning environment for their employees. The advantage is that the knowledge is transferred consistently and on an anytime, anyplace basis. The University of Phoenix offers undergraduate and graduate degrees by using an interactive learning environment, which allows students to download lectures, interact with professors, communicate with other students, and take exams.

Organizations must appreciate some of the economic dynamics associated with e-commerce. For example, ActivMedia estimates that only about 46 percent of all Internet e-commerce sites are profitable from current sales. Twenty-nine percent of the 2,069 sites surveyed by ActivMedia indicate that they expect to be profitable within 2 years. For organizations, the route to profitability must be one of patience, selective investment, aided awareness, and good site design. Successful Web sites share several common characteristics. First, the public must have knowledge, access, and directions to the Web sites. Thus the road to the Web site must be clear and intuitive. Second, like any business, the products and services offered must be compelling. Finally, the design of the Web site must be inviting, easy to navigate, and intuitive. Perhaps most important is that they are designed from the outside in. That is, the sites are designed with the customers in mind. They portray the services and products and information that customers want to know about, not what a manager thinks is important. Specifically, the high performers share six distinct qualities with respect to the design and management of their Web sites:

1. **Products and services.** The high performers offer a variety of compelling products and services that have an immediate appeal and value to consumers.
2. **Brand identity.** The high performers stress enterprisewide brand identity and recognition, not just product identity. They recognize that the enterprise is the

attracting feature for consumers and stress brand recognition and affiliation at the entity level. Chapter 3 discussed the importance of branding in greater detail.

3. **Marketing.** To facilitate brand recognition, the high performers spend considerable amounts of resources on marketing and promoting their Web site. They recognize that aggressive marketing can build both brand identity and also consumer awareness of the URL coordinates. Knowledge of the coordinates is essential for marketing on the Internet.

4. **Design.** Navigating a Web site is an *experience,* not a process. Like physical shopping, successful Web site designs are those that present the consumer with a pleasurable experience. High-performance companies design their Web sites with an inviting and intuitive appeal. They are content-rich, easy to navigate, and inviting. They limit the number of clicks to a minimum, reduce paging, work to minimize download times, and provide easy-to-use hot links and page markers. They also limit advertising and promotional banners which, as most users of the Internet know, can be annoying. According to a study in the *San Francisco Chronicle,* successful Web designs have consistent presentation, minimize scrolling by placing the entire image on the screen, achieve download times of 15 seconds or less, and minimize "clicking." The use of customized Web site designs is providing a capability for IT to increase marketshare, expand into new markets, and enhance sales. A survey of 25 companies performed by the consulting firm of Booz Allen & Hamilton indicates that 40 percent offer personalized services; 93 percent say they will do the same within a year. For the survey population, participants reported that customized services boosted revenues by 52 percent and increased the number of customers by 47 percent. Companies such as Kraft Foods, Bristol-Myers Squibb, and Kellogg averaged a 27 percent increase in sales when they used targeted banners. The payback period for such custom sites occur in about 7 months, according to Jupiter Communications.

5. **Content.** High-performance companies provide content-rich Web sites. The information is more educational than advertising-related. They provide meaningful information about their products, often comparing them to the competition and cross-referencing them with other products and services.

6. **Strategy and governance.** High-performance organizations have established the Internet as a strategic priority. As a high imperative, they have aggressively funded development of e-commerce and e-business capabilities. They establish e-commerce as an enterprise priority, but usually delegate it to the operating units to implement and develop along the lines of consistent design. They may, as in the instances of Donaldson, Lufkin and Jennerett, and Barnes & Noble, establish an independent company for e-commerce or, as in the case of Dell, make e-commerce an integral and integrated part of their overall business architecture.

CREATING HIGH-PERFORMANCE IT CAPABILITIES

With an understanding of how IT influences the environment in which organizations must compete and how IT is creating new forms of business and organizational structures, let's summarize how IT affects the strategic dynamics of competing.

1. High-performance organizations use IT to selectively integrate important operational aspects of their organizations.
2. High-performance organizations extend their enterprises through IT to suppliers, vendors, and customers.
3. High-performance organizations leverage IT to increase marketshare, enhance revenues, support knowledge management, and improve customer relationships, attractiveness, retention, and loyalty.
4. High-performance organizations use IT to accelerate and enhance the product design and development process.
5. High-performance organizations create extraordinary speed and agility through IT.

Let's briefly discuss each of these.

High-performance organizations use IT to selectively integrate essential core processes of the organization. These processes include three critical activities: generating demand, supplying demand, and planning and managing the enterprise. Thus, integration is achieved at several levels including rationalizing certain operations, consolidation of specific organizational structures and tasks, accelerating volumes, and improving the value performance of the organization through the elimination of nonvalue-added tasks and activities.

High-performance organizations extend their enterprise beyond the physical boundaries of the organization through IT by creating interactive relationships with suppliers, business alliance partners, and customers. This form of extension allows them to outsource certain activities, tap the specialization of suppliers, and alliance partners to create alternative organizational relationships. Enterprises that extend their organizations through IT also create for themselves opportunities to enter new markets and create different relationships with customers. For example, Bugle Boy CEO Dr. William Mow, who has a Ph.D. in computer science from Purdue University, noted "Technology was a key to Bugle Boy creating competitive advantage. We had the technology that allowed us to predict sizes and supply our customers with the products that moved the fastest and had the best margins, for them and us. So what used to take us four weeks to pack, check, and ship is now done overnight."

High-performance organizations also use sophisticated data-mining techniques to improve their intimacy and knowledge of customers and discern trends. With these techniques, employees use elaborate data warehouses and inductive analytical mining methods to investigate and identify certain customer relationships, behaviors, and patterns. For example, US West selects customers based on 200 observations and criteria to scan for the most profitable and least profitable accounts. Using the information collected and patterns identified, US West provides tailored offerings for customers designed to enhance services, customer satisfaction, and account profitability. Bank of America calculates the profitability on each of its 70 million accounts on a monthly basis. The analysis is designed to develop targeted programs that are intended to cross-sell products, retain accounts, and enhance customer service. As a result, balances have grown by 10 percent.

Increasing sales is not the only strategic initiative. As Frederick Smith, CEO of Federal Express, noted about IT, "We decided years ago that the most important element of this business is IT and we have geared everything to that philosophy." Federal Express has used a combination of IT and outsourcing to help lower the logistics costs for its client National Semiconductor from approximately 3 percent of sales to about 1.9 percent of sales. Finally, as can be seen from our earlier discussion of Ford Motor Company's objective to build "on demand," the use of IT to improve and accelerate new-product cycle-development time can create significant competitive advantages.

How IT is viewed and managed in the organization plays an important role in how IT is leveraged for strategic value. High-performance organizations recognize that with technology, it is not so much an issue of what technology an organization is using or how much technology is represented as a percentage of revenues or budget. Rather, it is the way the organization is deploying and using its technology that influences its ability to create superior competitive advantage and performance. But the significant finding of a Deloitte Consulting study centers on the relationship between spending on IT and services delivered. Based on their data and analysis, Deloitte Consulting has concluded that the companies that are the highest spenders on IT spend almost as much as 10 times the lower-spending companies for the "same profile of IT services." "The data demonstrated what we knew anecdotally to be true: much time, energy, and money can be tied up in managing an overly complex IT environment, with very little gain," explains Rich Pople of Deloitte Consulting, one of the authors of the study. "Of course, if the high spend companies reap 10 times the investment return in IT, then they may have a case for the spending disparity—but that's not what we found," added co-author Gregg Schmidtetter. Indeed, Deloitte Consulting identified five fundamental behaviors that were directly linked to a company's propensity to overspend on IT. High-spending companies tend to have:

1. Greater investment in redundant, duplicative technologies (for example, several database platforms, scores of development tools).
2. Greater likelihood of custom-developed applications: In these days of quality packaged software, a CIO should be and is often hard-pressed to justify the cost and risks of a custom project for common functions such as general ledger and accounting.
3. Early and broader adoption of emerging technologies, such as voice recognition and expert systems—most often without a business justification.
4. Lower investment in human resources, particularly staff training and recruiting.
5. Greater degree of outsourced capabilities—a behavior that Rich Pople refers to as "convenience" outsourcing that effectively abdicates control over major parts of a company's technology environment.

Because the management of IT is enormously complex and becoming more intricate on a daily basis, let's try to streamline the thinking by concentrating on five fundamentals:

1. Leading integration
2. Managing IT as an enterprisewide resource
3. Creating organizational parity
4. Managing human capital
5. Measuring the contribution of IT

Each of these will be discussed in greater detail.

Integration

"We institutionalized strategic planning, relying on our systems for our business needs, and used IT first instead of later in the planning process," notes Robert F. McDermott, CEO emeritus of USAA, in an interview in *CIO* magazine. High-performance organizations understand that to create extraordinary return from IT requires an integration of process, organization, and strategic change. The key to leveraging IT is system integration. From a technology standpoint, system integration is simply the melding of divergent and often incompatible technologies, applications, and data. But that is a relatively pedestrian definition of *integration*. From a high-performance perspective, system integration encompasses the complete spectrum of business processes, managerial practices, organizational interactions, structural alignments, and knowledge management. High-performance organizations recognize that integration is a *state* in which an organization exists, and just because it has networked systems and sophisticated technologies does not mean that it is integrated. An overall business architecture is required to achieve systemic integration.

There are essentially four states of integration: (1) interconnectivity, (2) interoperability, (3) semantic consistency, and (4) convergence. Interconnectivity is the most elementary state of integration; it forms the foundation for all technical integration. Interconnectivity provides for the basic transfer of information between different technologies and components and little functional or knowledge integration at the process level. Interoperability refers to the ability to make one application and technology function with another in a manner that exploits the certain capabilities of both. Semantic consistency refers to the integration and rationalization of data. Finally, convergent integration involves the integration of technology with business processes. This level of integration provides capabilities for knowledge transfer and sophisticated extended enterprise concepts. To achieve an overall business architecture requires convergent integration.

High-performance organizations understand that it is the integration of business processes with human performance and technology, at a systemic level, that allows them to leverage technology for extraordinary gains. They acquire and deploy technologies that are synergistic to their strategies, organizational competencies, and operations. They strive to embed relevant knowledge in the process through technology. Most importantly, they recognize that IT is essential to leveraging strategic leadership.

Enterprisewide Resource

"You know, we had an organization that was more like a dinosaur that really couldn't provide the services that the governor felt were necessary to compete in the new economy. So we began an effort that was designed to make us an enterprise that could provide the governance and structure to take advantage of the technology," noted Larry Olson, former CIO of the state of Pennsylvania. To fully integrate and leverage the capabilities of IT requires that IT itself be approached as an enterprisewide resource. In addition to integration and organizational placement, significant leverage and return on IT can only be achieved by institutionalizing the strategies, priorities, and practices for delivering and deploying technology solutions. These practices include a uniform set of processes and heuristics for managing the important aspects of technology utilization, including systems development processes, and an effective introduction and deployment of those solutions throughout the organization.

Viewing IT as an integral and integrated part of the organization's social and business architecture requires that it use the concepts and principles of logical consolidation and physical distribution. These concepts provide a construct for managing IT as an enterprisewide asset on a consistent, flexible, and optimized basis. From a strategy perspective, the deployment of IT capabilities based on logical consolidation and physical distribution allows for the implementation of enterprisewide policies, strategies, practices, and measurements for managing the IT function on a rationalized basis.

Logical consolidation refers to the creation and implementation of a uniform construct for the management of all IT resources. Logical consolidation seeks to optimize the use and leverage of IT while minimizing and eliminating the redundancies that are so prevalent in the distributed and decentralized IT environments. Logical consolidation also works to eliminate the discontinuities in management styles, performance measures, and career development that are normally associated with decentralized and distributed IT organizations. Commenting on IT in state government, Larry Olson notes, "We felt that it was critical that we had a couple of areas standardized as part of our technology infrastructure."

The *physical distribution* of the IT resource refers to the actual location and deployment of IT assets and support structures within the enterprise and beyond to extended relationships. Under the concept of physical distribution, the IT resource is accessible at virtually all levels of the organization on an anytime, anyplace, as-needed basis. High-performance organizations understand that initiatives such as empowerment, employee discretion, and knowledge sharing are best achieved at the point of process execution and that IT can provide that capability.

The high-performance organizations use a number of methods to ensure the alignment of IT to the strategy of the organization. Three major criteria emerge as important determinants:

1. Existence of a clear *economic value proposition* for IT investments to the overall financial objectives of the organization.
2. Clear relationship between IT initiatives and projects to the strategic goals, purpose, and objective of the organization.
3. A direct cause-and-effect relationship between IT and results. They recognize that the presence of all three of these demonstrate an alignment of IT to the strategic and operational goals of an organization.

Additional considerations with respect to ensuring alignment include measuring the "success" of IT to deliver quality system solutions. Usually, success is measured in rather simplistic terms related to whether time commitments and budget targets were met and users were satisfied and "accepted" the system. However, measuring the effectiveness of the IT organization to deliver quality solutions using these important but rather basic measures can often be misleading. Admittedly, they are important *components* of a measurement process, but as single function points they prove little with respect to strategic alignment. High-performance organizations understand that the return generated by IT must be measured using a number of different criteria, including the overall economic *contribution* of IT to the enterprise and the ability of IT to support enterprisewide integration and collaboration.

High-performance organizations that leverage technology to its greatest extent use multiple vendors to provide not only the technology and products but also the knowledge, perspective, and information to best utilize it. Bob Martin, CEO of Wal-Mart Stores International, summed up the new relationship with vendors as, "Today at most of the industry-leading technology companies, the hard-nosed marketers are gone, replaced by engineers and account managers who want to solve business problems for us and are willing to be held accountable for whether or not the solutions deliver as promised."

Used effectively, the breadth of experience and industry perspective provided by external vendors can be invaluable to organizations attempting to renew or reposition themselves simply because they have experience with other organizations. External partners are also more independent of internal politics and provide perspective on how other organizations have used IT to support an integrated operational environment. Another consideration is that they tend to be better communicators than internally groomed personnel. External service providers tend to be more sensitized to many different personalities, management styles, and operational issues because they work for multiple organizations.

Finally, successfully creating enterprisewide IT capabilities and standards can be facilitated by organizing the IT function around core competencies and *Centers of Excellence* (COE). The COE provides for the concentration of human talent and resources and the creation of critical competencies necessary for sustaining common management practices, high efficiency, and productivity and for performing complex integration initiatives. The idea of a COE is not new but difficult to successfully implement. An article in *Computerworld* noted that 70 percent of all Fortune 1000 organizations have implemented some form of a COE. However, as indicated in the same article, 70 percent of companies claiming to have implemented COEs are experiencing difficulty in achieving the results expected from the initiative. We can probably trace the difficulty of implementing this concept to the competency and visions of the leadership involved, as well as the execution steps and definitions used.

Exhibit 5.6 provides a functional representation of how high-performance IT organizations are typically structured.

Organizational Parity

With the exception of the top leadership position, the responsibility of the chief information officer (CIO), chief technology officer (CTO), vice president of MIS (management information system), or chief resource officer (CRO) may be the single most difficult job in any organization. A 1995 *InformationWeek* survey indicated that the *average* tenure for an IT executive was only 14 months. Among senior IT leadership, Deloitte Consulting found that the average tenure of CIOs is around 5.4 years with a turnover rate approaching 18 percent. As if to indicate a strategic change by itself, the number of IT executives in the CIO role who have nontechnical IT backgrounds is increasing. Another survey, which appeared in the *Harvard Business Review,* reports that 42 percent of all Fortune 500 IT executives are non-IT professionals. This is a trend that is gaining momentum in the business community. As Gene Batchelder, CFO of GPM Gas Corporation, noted in an article appearing in the Harvard Business Review, "My advice to CEOs is this; 'Your IT function should be run by a great general manager, not by the traditional technology manager.' "

Creating the proper reporting relationship for the CIO is essential to leveraging IT as a strategic pillar. Leading and managing IT are challenges for even the most seasoned executive. Historically, because of the many complexities and the reliability of early IT

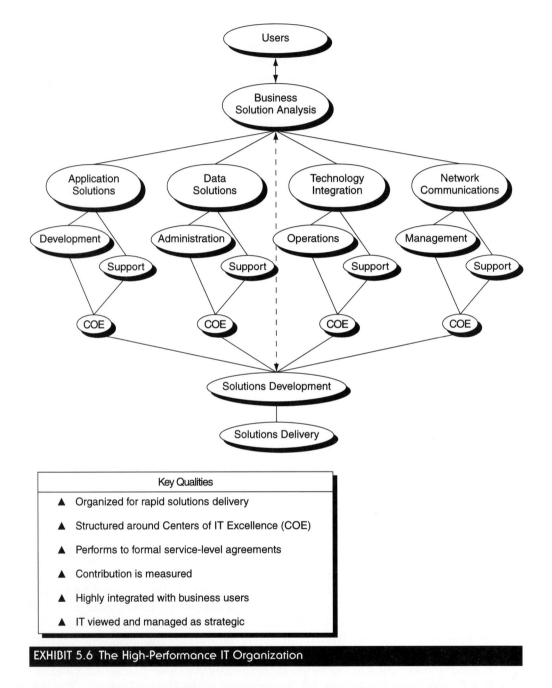

EXHIBIT 5.6 The High-Performance IT Organization

products and limited uses of IT, the logical placement for IT was in the finance function, and it became only natural that the IT function be organizationally placed as an overhead function. Tradition has it that the majority of IT leaders have deep technical skills and a history of reporting to overhead functions such as accounting. By nature and practice, overhead managers are administrators, are paid to be conservative and keep the score for those who manufacture and sell products, or create the intellectual capital behind the products. Managers of overhead functions such as accounting are not paid to be innovative in their approach to management or process design, customer interactions, and organizational relationships. They are paid to manage costs and ensure and enforce compliance to policies, standards, and rules. These qualities were once very much needed when IT was in its infancy, and the potential for making errors in IT investments and IT practices as a process enabler were high. Today, however, they are the antithesis of what is needed to creatively leverage IT.

No other position in the organization encompasses as broad a spectrum of activities and attention. Consequently, no other organizational function, other than that of the top leader, has as diverse and vocal a constituency, both internally and externally. As an enabler of strategy and change, IT must be led and managed as an innovative resource. In particular, high-performance organizations understand that to achieve operational leverage and organizational integration requires elevating the overall role and recognition of IT in the organization. Organizations that leverage their leadership through IT have elevated the IT reporting relationship by removing it from an overhead function. In the process, they elevate the reporting relationship of IT by creating organizational parity with business unit, financial, human resources, and legal leadership.

Human Capital

High-performance organizations recognize that human performance and the ability of the IT professional to bring integration services to business processes are fundamental to the success of the process-centric IT model. As Astra-Merck CEO Wayne Yetter stated, "Our IT people—we refer to them as solutions integrators—live and work in the process areas that make up our business. They are not isolated in a support department. They participate in business meetings and help identify ways in which technology can make the business more efficient or effective. They report both to business managers in the process area and the chief information officer." High-performance organizations understand that partnering and collaboration between those responsible for the technology and those who are chartered for using the systems is critical to leveraging IT and improving IT return.

Effective IT partnering and collaboration demands a different competency for the IT organization and the IT professional than those that were found among traditional IT professionals. In the traditional IT organization, premiums were paid for technical savvy but not necessarily for business acumen and interpersonal communication skills. As Tom Ross, vice president of IT for American Honda Motor Company, commented, "The hardest part is finding the right mix of technical competencies and business skills. It's getting more and more difficult." The IT professional must not only be technically competent, but she or he must also have the ability to quickly develop a thorough understanding of business issues, organizational processes, emerging needs, and new trends. This understanding must extend beyond traditional IT technical competencies and into actual *knowledge* of business processes, financial goals and economic value propositions, collaborative practices, and competitor initiatives.

To ensure effective business partnering and integration, high-performance organizations deploy an IT organizational structure, which provides for *strategic solutions integrator* (SSI). The SSI are IT professionals who function as the solutions provider and services integrator for the direct customer and user. The SSI is a "mission critical" position, which has a dual-reporting relationship that includes the IT leadership and the leadership of the organizational or process function, or client, that the SSI supports. This dual reporting requires that the SSI be formally evaluated by both areas, specifically the user and IT. The dual-reporting and evaluation process strengthens the commitment to the "customer" and facilitates the development of IT in understanding the requirements, operating environment, and political realities of the end-user's organization. Speaking of CIO John Cross' success of integrating and leveraging IT at BP, *CIO* magazine wrote, "To symbolize IS's new role within the company, he [Cross] eliminated all titles containing the words 'IT manager.' Those who held such titles are now called "business information consultants" or "partner relationship managers," reflecting a tighter alignment with business units."

Finally, it is equally important that IT leverages the personal presence and formal powers of the leader. Leaders recognize that they can leverage themselves and their organizations through the creative use of IT. IT provides leaders with extraordinary capabilities to reach new markets and constituents, organize and deploy their resources differently, and integrate various portions of their organizations. IT allows leaders to communicate their visions, strategies, goals, and aspirations to a broad audience, irrespective of the geographies and time zones. For example, the Intranet and Internet extend organizations, remove physical, ethnic, and racial barriers, and create opportunities for leaders to interact with constituents in many different ways and at many different levels. IT provides the leader with the ability to be a "virtual" leader, capable of responding to, reaching out, and communicating with others at any time and any place.

For high-performance leaders, this provides tremendous opportunities for leveraging their messages, communicating with their organizations, and making themselves more accessible to a wide range of employees and other interested parties. It also provides opportunities for leaders of organizations to become more "socially engaged" in ensuring that technology is available, people are trained, and the technology is disseminated at all levels of society, especially in schools.

Measuring IT Contribution

"We expect any proposed technology investment to reduce the complexity of our business, our processes, or our organization—not to add complexity," said Bob Martin, CEO of Wal-Mart Stores International Division. Leveraging IT for high return requires alignment with organizational strategies and objectives. For many organizations, IT is supplanting the physical and social architectures of the industrial era with new cyber-based designs. This makes the management of IT exceedingly more critical to the overall aspects of leadership.

The traditional measurements for IT investment have tended to rely on viewing IT as a cost or an asset capable of generating a return to shareholders. As a cost, IT investments were usually "budgeted" as a percentage of sales. Financial measures, such as return on investment (ROI), net present value (NPV), internal rate of return (IRR) and payback periods (PBP), became the de facto standards for assessing the financial desirability of an IT investment. Another traditional measure for IT is the concept of PBP. That is, given the investment outflow, how fast can the inflows recover the investment?

Over 75 percent of the responding CFOs expected paybacks from IT investments to materialize within a 36-month period.

In fact, many companies still use these measures in assessing the potential economic contribution of an IT investment, and herein lies one of the greatest problems for IT. ROI, IRR, NPV, and PBP are basic financial measurements and tools, developed long ago to assess the investments related to new buildings, machinery, and plants. They are good tools for finite-type investments that have a level of predictability with regard to cost outflows and returns. Build a widget machine, and its ROI is relatively easy to compute. Invest in a knowledge management system or worldwide communications network for collaboration, and its return is far more difficult to estimate and measure.

The ultimate benefit and value of any IT investment are whether they can help to make a company more competitive through revenue growth and provide a distinct, albeit often short-lived, competitive advantage. The concept of *contributed value* is important to organizations that are actively seeking to leverage IT for competitive advantage. Contributed value is defined as the real effect of IT and the IT resource on the organization. Contributed value also includes customer perceptions with respect to the experience that the customer has with the IT function. Speaking of Wal-Mart and its use of information technology, Bob Martin notes, "I want to see clearly how the capability that the technology supplies will simplify the way we make decisions or accomplish activities and processes." The key issue in assessing the viability of an IT investment is whether it can contribute to the generation of greater financial returns and growth for the company. Therefore, all IT investments, even those incurred by the public sector, should be guided by a clear and distinct *economic value proposition* (EVP). That proposition should be linked to revenue generation or major operational and organizational initiatives designed to create competitive advantage, which may come in the form of cycle-time reductions, cash flow accelerations, direct cost reductions, and higher collaboration among employees, customers, and suppliers.

SUMMARY

In this chapter, we discussed many issues and concepts related to IT and leveraging IT for strategic and operational use. Briefly:

1. High-performance organizations leverage leadership, strategy, and vision through IT and use IT as a means of reaching all segments of the organization and beyond.
2. High-performance organizations use IT to neutralize the traditional sources of competitive advantage by extending the enterprise beyond physical borders and industry boundaries.
3. High-performance organizations manage IT as an enterprisewide asset and resource and use data mining to discover new patterns, trends, and sources of customers and profits.
4. High-performance organizations use IT to selectively integrate portions of the enterprise, including customer services, new-product development, and order fulfillment.
5. High-performance organizations recognize that IT compresses time, space, and energy. IT accelerates velocity, so anything you do is faster. In leading IT, the

strategic choices are simple: Do the same things faster or do things differently and better.

High-performance organizations understand that IT is absolutely essential to operations and strategic positioning of their organizations. In this regard, they are actively involved in IT and the ways IT is deployed in their organizations. They understand that IT requires organizational parity with other "line functions" and that measuring IT using traditional accounting and data processing criteria does not provide a complete picture. Exemplary leaders are engaged and knowledgeable about IT and are passionate in their strategic views and use of IT.

Critical Thoughts and Discussion Questions

1. To what extent, if any, will pervasive computing and wireless communications affect the overall competitive dynamics of business?
2. What influence, if any, does e-commerce and sales through the Internet have on the brand identity and customer value expectations of a company? Specifically, does the influence contribute or have a dilution effect on brand exclusivity, recognition, and customer perceptions?
3. How does IT affect the strategic planning process for organizations?
4. What are the main competitive functions and applications of IT in creating a competitive advantage, and how can IT be best leveraged to best optimize organizational performance and competitive position?
5. What are the advantages of using a multifactoral approach to evaluating the contribution and performance of IT in the enterprise?
6. What are the main challenges with regard to managing IT and integrating IT for enterprisewide leverage?
7. How does the Internet change the traditional bases (i.e., location, size, price points, low-cost strategies, bargaining power and control, traditional business forms and cyber-based organizational structures, etc.) of competing?
8. What are the new, "virtual" sources of competitive advantage for Internet-based competitors?
9. What are the imperatives that an Internet competitor must successfully address to establish and sustain a competitive position in the virtual marketspace?
10. What is the *value proposition* Internet companies offer to their customers, vendors, partners, as well as themselves, and how are these values different from those of traditional businesses?

CHAPTER

INNOVATION: THE ENGINE OF CONTINUOUS RENEWAL

"You need to make creativity the norm and the lack of creativity the exception, as opposed to trying to take the company and say, 'Well, we're going to be creative this week.' "
—M. DOUGLAS IVESTER, CEO, COCA-COLA

INTRODUCTION

"There is no reason for any individual to have a computer in their home," proclaimed Kenneth Olsen, the CEO of DEC in 1977. From 1984 to 1994, while the computer industry rocketed in sales and changed the world, DEC lost $55 billion in market value and was subsequently acquired by a younger competitor. Innovation is the key to the survival of any organization. Those companies that are innovative and successfully bring those innovations to bear on their operations and markets outperform those that are not innovative.

Management thought leader Peter Drucker once commented that if a company had only one competency, it must be innovation. From a strategic perspective, the speed of innovation, the effectiveness of innovation, and the ability to innovate are, perhaps, the only truly *proprietary* competitive weapons that an organization has. Everything else that it does, including its products, processes, prices, and technologies, is all replicable, and any competitive advantage gained, particularly from price and quality, can be quickly matched and is, thus, short-lived and not sustainable over the long run.

According to a 1993 study of 150 companies performed by Jeff Mauzy of The Synectics Corporation, innovative companies "experienced growth rates that were twice as fast as those for non-innovative companies, with an even more significant difference in profit rates." Developing and sustaining the ability to innovate allows an organization to adapt to its environment or to change or create a new environment through new products, processes, knowledge, or structures.

This chapter discusses the second pillar of strategic renewal: *innovation*. The objectives of this chapter are to define innovation in the context of strategic renewal, discuss the dynamics of innovation, explore the strategic implications of innovation, and address how organizations go about the process of innovating. In this chapter, innovation is framed in both strategic and operational contexts, and insights are offered into how the high-performance organizations lead the process of being innovative to create and sustain long-term competitive advantage. Six important questions are addressed:

1. What are the unique aspects and characteristics that define innovation?
2. What are the sources of innovation, and how do innovation, creativity, and knowledge interact and interrelate?
3. Why is innovation important to the strategic renewal of any organization?
4. What are the cultural traits and behaviors that the high-performance companies have in common that set them apart from those that lack innovation?
5. What types of leadership practices and management techniques best position companies for innovation?
6. What types of human characteristics are necessary for creativity and innovation?

DEFINING INNOVATION

In 1899 Charles Duell, the commissioner of the U.S. Office of Patents, commented, "Everything that can be invented has been invented." Thankfully people like Walt Disney, Jonas Salk, Henry Ford, Bill Gates, Albert Einstein, Robert Oppenheimer, and a long list of others did not take him seriously. Imagine a world without PalmPilots, television, microchips in toasters, smart credit cards, the Internet, nuclear power, the PC, the NASDAQ, biotech medicine, e-commerce, the National Football League, and Disney World!

To his credit, Mr. Duell does proffer an interesting and fundamentally important aspect of innovation. Like so many other aspects of business and life, innovation is subject to individual interpretation and opinion. The difficulty for many managers in understanding the strategic role and value of innovation is that it leads to many different interpretations and conclusions. It is a subjective area, and what may be innovative for one company or individual may be common practice for another. Thus, for many companies and their leaderships, innovation is an enigma: They can recognize it when they see it, but they have great difficulty in understanding it, creating it, and, more importantly, visualizing how it will change the dynamics of their business.

Scribner's dictionary defines *innovation* as "changes in something, the introduction of new things." Tom Davenport, the author of *Process Innovation* and several other books, simply defines *innovation* as "something new." The great Viennese economist, Joseph Schumpeter, defined *innovation* as "combinations of new things and markets." Researcher and author James Higgins defines it as "the process of creating something new that has significant value to an individual, group, an organization, an industry, or a society." Others depict innovation in the context of creativity. Researcher Teresa M. Amabile in "Motivating Creativity in Organizations: On Doing What You Love and Loving What You Do" notes that "Innovation is implementation of creativity. Creativity is simply the production of novel, appropriate ideas in any realm of human activity and is the first step of innovation." Although different, creativity and innovation must be considered in the same context, at least when discussing it as a pillar of strategic renewal.

High-performance organizations define *innovation* with reference to creativity and the generation of new opportunities and things. Thus, a working definition for *innovation* is:

> The creation of new and different value-generating products, services, processes, markets, and designs.

In considering innovation, it is important to acknowledge that innovation is not just related to products. Innovation includes organizational design, process design, technology, compensation, knowledge management, human performance, product development, market development, or cultural advancement. The high-performing organizations are doing all of these activities. They approach innovation as a process and a portfolio of activities to be carefully nurtured and deliberately choreographed for higher performance and greater yields. An important observation about innovation and strategic change is that the most successful companies pursue product innovation, process innovation, and cultural innovation *simultaneously.*

Aside from the obvious competitive and financial benefits of innovation, other strategic advantages of innovation are more intrinsic and, arguably, far more important to the strategic position and capabilities of the organization. Specifically, five major advantages stand out:

1. Innovation is the way high-performance companies flourish. Innovation is one of many techniques that high performers use to reinvent their organizations and environments. It is a trademark, a signature, and a statement to the world and market about how it works, thinks, and operates.
2. Innovation is exciting, and excitement attracts, engages, and retains the best and brightest talent. The Silicon Valley is full of examples and stories of how bright people forego the high salaries of the tradition-bound companies to be associated with the next great technological breakthrough and the potential to be millionaires before they are 30 years old. It is not just the opportunity for a big payoff that attracts them; it's the excitement of being part of something new, something creative, and something completely unique.
3. Innovation stimulates learning and knowledge transfer, both of which are essential to strategic change. Innovative companies are always talking, always involved in the discovery and sharing of new ideas and information. They have a high propensity for probing and learning. Both of these qualities are absolutely essential to strategic change.
4. Innovative companies provide people with the personal latitude to grow, develop, and professionally diversify. Innovative companies encourage experimentation, foster and reward collaboration, and tolerate the inevitable failures associated with discovery, learning, personal growth, and strategic change.
5. Innovative companies seem to be the ones that also have the greatest levels of multicultural and cross-functional organizational and operational integration. They inherently have a high degree of collaboration within and beyond their formal operating boundaries and organizational structures. This collaboration is attractive to high-performance individuals and external business partners who have a passion for their work and creativity.

DISCONTINUOUS AND INCREMENTAL INNOVATION

To clarify our understanding of innovation as an essential characteristic of strategic change and high performance, it is useful to consider it in two dimensions: *discontinuous* and *incremental*. Understanding the distinctions between the two is important because they establish a strategic, as well as a behavioral, tone for the organization, and also determine, to an extent, how an organization manages itself with respect to innovation, creativity, and its investments.

Discontinuous

"Discontinuous history leads to the conclusion that in competitive, technology-intensive global markets, advantage is built and renewed through the more discontinuous form of innovation—through the creation of entirely new families of products and businesses," note authors Gary Lynn, Joseph Morone, and Albert Paulsen. Discontinuous innovation changes the basic structure and dynamics of the entire industry and economy. Discontinuous innovations are broad-based events that lead to significant breakthroughs and shifts in process, structure, product, behavior, and performance. They are the ones that can be episodic and revolutionary. These types of innovations can also be the most traumatic, are the most disruptive and threatening to the established members of an organization or industry, and can neutralize, destroy, or create first-mover advantages.

Discontinuous innovation represents a challenge for management responsible for strategic change because, as noted by researcher John Utterback, it "sweeps away much of a firm's existing investment in technical skills and knowledge, designs, production technique, plant and equipment." According to *The Economist,* there is some data that indicate that it takes a "little more than two years for such a start-up to formulate an innovative business idea, establish a Web presence and begin to dominate its chosen sector. By then it may be too late for slow-moving traditional businesses to respond." Although the size and critical mass of established industry leaders clearly provide many benefits, those same qualities can also serve as inhibitors to innovation and creativity. The industry establishment has embedded costs and long-established behaviors and legacy processes that can be difficult to change. John Utterback noted that "As firms grow larger, top managers function more as conservators than as creators," and change becomes more difficult. Researcher Donald Fry concluded that "Constant incremental innovation can create myopia in the ranks of top management."

As researcher Gary Lynn notes, discontinuous innovation relies less on formal analytical techniques and more on probing and learning. In many organizations, the discontinuous innovation process is one of discovery, iterative learning, unlearning, testing, and experimentation. It is represented by a process of successive approximation, probing and learning again and again, each time striving to take a step closer to a winning combination of product and market. In addition to breakthrough products and processes, discontinuous innovation can be stimulated by, or include, a wide variety of initiatives such as: IT, new governmental regulations, megamergers among global corporations such as Ford and Volvo and Glaxo Welcome and SmithKline Beecham, and rapidly changing political landscapes as exhibited by the emergence of the EU.

The foregoing brings us to a general observation offered by Richard N. Foster in his book, *The Attacker's Advantage,* "In competing for innovation, the nimble challenger will beat the muscle-bound industry leader about 70 percent of the time." Although they may lack the capital and resources of the industry stalwarts, smaller companies are, by design and often necessity, more agile, radical, and aggressive than those that are already established. Thus, through a combination of necessity and personality, they have a higher propensity for discontinuous innovation and rapid change. The upstarts are devoid of history and have no legacy management systems to rationalize, defend, and perpetuate. The major strategic and change lesson here is that the industry upstarts and outsiders with little or no vested interest in perpetuating the present or preserving the past have nothing to lose and have everything to gain by being different and embracing radical management practices and different operational strategies. Researcher Clayton Christensen observes that this condition exists, in part because "The leading, established competitors . . . had a difficult time reorienting their trajectories of product improvement, to excel in the new basis of competition. Most often the leading firms continued upward along their established trajectory of performance improvement while entrant firms or minor players in the industry were first to seize the opportunities created by the shifting bases of competition." In these instances, as we will discuss, performance improvement is usually achieved by incremental innovation, which by and of itself does not lead to breakthrough results.

Historical precedent can give us insights and a sense of what has happened to some organizations and what is continuing to happen today with regard to discontinuous innovation. In *Mastering the Dynamics of Innovation,* John Utterback traces the movements of the commercial ice business in the nineteenth century. Utterback found that while the dominant New England companies controlled the sources of ice (due to the weather and ocean shipping), southerners were developing refrigeration techniques to *make* ice. The trends were clear: The southerners were tired of being dependent on the north, cold weather, fast ships to get them their ice, and pricing that was beyond their control. If you had a warm winter or fewer ships, then you had less ice at much higher prices. As a consequence, while the New Englanders invested in better steam saws to cut ice out of frozen lakes faster and hoped for long, cold winters, the southerners made their own "weather" and ice through refrigeration. The rules of supply and demand were forever changed. That spelled the end of one industry and the beginning of a new one. So much for having cold weather, lots of pretty lakes, and fast steam saws. A new curve was created. The suppliers, the ice companies, failed to change, while the customers created an entirely new environment and new rules of competition in that industry.

Adopting an innovative strategy is critical to high performance; however, unless an organization sustains its ability to innovate, it will lose its leadership edge and position. For example, with its large volumes, colorful illustrations, and accurate and in-depth treatment of subject matter, the *Encyclopedia Britannica* became the research staple for many junior high and high school students. It was the industry standard, which dominated all other sources and the bookshelves of many homes. It was a formidable and impressive collection of books with rich and comprehensive content. But in the 1980s society's demands for how scholarly information should be packaged and delivered dramatically changed. With that change came the need for more elaborate content, faster updates, and more flexible and creative delivery methods. Unfortunately, Britannica either did not recognize or failed to acknowledge that the PC was about to sentence it to a slow deathwatch.

With the PC came a change in access patterns to information and the addition of new and exciting sources of information. As computing technology progressed the CD-ROM, the product and technology that ultimately displaced the record album and videotape, was about to eliminate the need for volumes of books and tons of paper. In an effort to embellish their product offering and make it more attractive to the owners of home-based PCs, PC makers and Microsoft began supplying diskette and CD-ROM versions of the *Encarta Encyclopedia.* Packaged with the basic Windows operating system product offering, a family could acquire a PC with a multimedia encyclopedia and access to the Internet and updates for less than the price of a traditional encyclopedia set.

Instead of sorting through page after page of the *Brittannica* for information that is, at best, several years old, a student can research the information and contents available through *Encarta* using multimedia CD-ROM products and now the Internet. The information is more elaborate, more timely, and more sophisticated than what Britannica could ever hope to provide in a hard-copy form. Additionally, multimedia formats also offer a more enjoyable and entertaining research and learning experience. The information was more timely, more comprehensive, and more easily accessible via the PC than through the traditionally published version of *Britannica.* Add those qualities to the fact that PCs are a necessity for work, and the *Britannica,* with its $1,500 price tag (updates additional), was a one-dimensional product, and it is easy to see why it was no longer competitive with the new delivery vehicle—the PC and the Internet. Although Britannica eventually launched a CD-ROM and Internet product offering, it was late and is a company in apparent decline. It is no longer a dominant player in scholarly information; it is now a competitor. Understanding the dynamics of the encyclopedia industry would not have led Britannica to a different strategy. The dynamics of its environment dramatically shifted, and a classic industry decomposition analysis and industry experience curves would not have revealed too much, other than the obvious.

The case of Britannica provides us with a contemporary example of an organization that failed to anticipate or acknowledge changes in its environment. Further, it depicts the forces that came to bear on it. The problem with Britannica was not its brand name or content. It had a great brand identity and an excellent content in its products. What Britannica apparently failed to realize was that there was a convergence in information sources, new delivery methods, and a major shift in buyer values, which was driving a shift in its operating environment. Buyers now had different values and more compelling alternatives, and the traditional products were no longer aligned with those new values. Britannica failed to anticipate them, failed to see them, and failed to capitalize upon them. Imagine the position Britannica would be in today if it had created with Microsoft a collaborative relationship? Chances are it would still be a dominant company without peer.

In another example, the U.S. tire industry was dominated by the "other" Big Three: Firestone, BFGoodrich, and Goodyear. For a generation, those three companies owned and parceled out the U.S. tire market, and that market was bias-belted tire technology. The capacity and consumer choices offered by the Big Three tire makers were supplemented by independent companies that had their own brands but not necessarily the lucrative and volume-oriented OEM (original equipment makers) contracts with The Big Three auto companies. In contrast, Michelin, Bridgestone, and Pirelli were the tire makers in Europe, Yokohama was one of the stalwarts in Japan, and the tires of choice in those markets were radial.

Since its debut in 1948, the superior performance and safety of radials over older, bias-belted tire technology were well documented among automotive enthusiasts and those who drove European performance cars. Notwithstanding the superior qualities of the radial tires over the bias-belted products, U.S. car manufacturers were slow to adopt the radial. Using the radial would have required Detroit to change not only their long-established and stable business model with the Big Three tire makers but also the suspension and drive train designs of their cars. Those types of changes meant an expensive retooling of their manufacturing capacities and the introduction of new engineering competencies. Apparently, U.S. tire manufacturers did not necessarily want to aggressively market the radial because their perceived customers, the automotive manufacturers, weren't pushing them, and they themselves possessed limited core competencies and production capabilities in that area. In fact, as recent as the early 1970s radial tires were usually special ordered, aftermarket items, which meant that the consumer always paid a premium for the product.

The oil crisis of the mid- and late-1970s, together with consumer awareness of the product superiority, was propelling major changes, unavoidable shifts in the industry, and changes in consumer demand. The Japanese and Europeans were equipping their cars with radial tires as standard equipment. Specialty auto and tire shops in the United States and the automotive publications were touting radials as *the* replacement for bias belts. The radial tires provided greater fuel economy and improved handling, had a better ride, and were longer wearing. As a result of the oil embargo and gasoline shortages, the U.S. government was implementing fleet mileage mandates, and radials could help. While all of this was going on, Michelin, a relatively unknown tire company in the United States at the time, began to quietly build a presence in the U.S. market. Soon its capacity and rich competency for radial technology came on-stream and were available to the driving public, at prices competitive with the Big Three bias-belted tire kings. What soon followed was a quantum, almost discontinuous, shift to radial tires. With a combined market share of 15 percent, Michelin now enjoys dominance over Firestone, owns Goodrich, and is locked in intense, neck-to-neck competition with Goodyear's 16 percent marketshare. One could argue that the U.S. tire market now has the Big Two: Goodyear and Michelin.

The foregoing discussion leads us to another important lesson regarding strategic renewal. For the industry establishment, the most dangerous competitors are the ones outside of the industry or the ones that are too small to be on anyone's immediate radar screen, or are beyond what I call OER (out of ego range). For example, the traditional brokerage houses such as Merrill Lynch didn't see Charles Schwab and E*Trade as viable alternatives to the full-service brokerage firms. The big banks and savings and loans did not see the brokerage houses and venture capitalists as alternative financial intermediaries. Founded in 1985 with $10,000 in capital, Gateway computer company was 57 years behind IBM, considerably younger than Compaq, and less than a fraction of the size of those companies. Yet Gateway and its rival Dell created new market dynamics for the sales and service of computers in and for which both Compaq and IBM must now compete.

The strategic innovations of Dell and Gateway were not necessarily in the design of the PC or its components, but rather in the way they sold directly to the consumer and in the sophisticated relationships they have with their suppliers and outsourcers, who supply subsystems and specialized services. The innovation of these companies was not in product but in process. Dell and Gateway, in particular, were more accessible to the customer, were faster in filling orders, provided customers with more current (fresher) technology, were easier to buy from, allowed for mass consumption of their products, and were more price competitive than either IBM or Compaq. Dell and Gateway changed the competitive rules of the PC market. More recently, the shift of both Dell and Gateway 2000 into business-computing, client-server, and work-station solutions threatens Sun and Silicon Graphics, whereas IBM's, Hewlett-Packard's and Compaq's recent moves to Web-based sales challenge Dell and Gateway.

Incremental

In contrast, incremental innovation leads to marginal changes and variations in theme and process. As author Gary Lynn notes, "Continuous, incremental product line extensions and improvements are essential for maintaining leadership, but only after it has first been established through the more discontinuous form of innovation." Incremental innovation is inherently more calculated, more controlled, and evolutionary in form and behavior. This type of innovation generally occurs with a natural rhythm that is less disruptive and threatening to legacy practices and the industry establishment.

According to researcher Clayton Christensen, "Incremental change refers to (1) improvements in component performance that build upon the established technological concept, or (2) refinements in system design that involve no significant changes in the technical relationships among components." Although incremental innovation is often easier and more comfortable for most organizations, it is not a great source of sustainable competitive advantage. The gains from incremental innovation are smaller and more easily duplicated. Simply improvising upon existing designs, products, and management practices is necessary, but those alone do not allow a firm to renew itself. Although the ability to successfully perform incremental innovation is important, relying on it alone can only lead a firm "closer to the inevitable end of its business with little preparation for the future."

The Home Depot did not invent the idea and concept of the hardware store. What this Atlanta-based company did was to elevate it to a new level and then perfect it. In doing so, The Home Depot changed the rules by which other home-product retailers must compete and created an entirely new shopping environment and retail segment. Cofounders Bernie Marcus and Arthur Blank elevated the concept to a new level: the super hardware store with on-site advice. The Home Depot defines the rules that Lowes, Scotty's, and the traditional hardware store must follow.

Similarly, Toyota didn't invent the automobile, but it did elevate the production and quality of the process to new levels. It used a continuous improvement process that included incremental innovation in manufacturing and design to offer differentiating products. It elevated the ownership experience to such a high level that, to stay competitive, other car manufacturers had to concentrate on quality and follow Toyota's lead. While the competition was spending time and money to catch up on quality, Toyota was spending more money on design and manufacturing automation.

SOURCES OF INNOVATION

"We are what we are because we push technology as fast as we can. Technology is good, and more is better," notes Andy Grove, former CEO of Intel. Innovation is driven by a number of factors, including the convergence of need, talent, technology, culture, process, and the perceived value that it creates. To be viable, innovation must have explicit monetary value in the commercial market as well as intrinsic and explicit value within the organization. Five basic criteria form filters or tests for innovation:

1. The effort results in the creation of *new* and *different* products, processes, organizational structures, services, and markets.
2. The process creates value, *stimulates markets,* and causes competitors and new entrants to engage in similar activities, creation of similar products, or presentation of rival concepts.
3. The drive to innovate reflects the recognition for *self-determinism* and self-direction of the organization.
4. The effort contributes, directly or indirectly, to the *advancement* of the organization.
5. The outcomes demonstrate direct commercial and *market value.* Many companies strive to generate 30% to 35% of their revenues from products that are less than 3 years old.

Irrespective of whether innovation is discontinuous or incremental, both share two common themes: (1) they have outcomes, and (2) there is some type of a process to them. Innovative outcomes can be spontaneous or the result of planned discovery, discipline, innovative processes, and creative thinking. Innovation processes involve the ways the organization goes about innovating, and include the individuals, tools, and techniques used to create innovative outcomes.

It is important to understand the sources of innovation because they translate into major implications as far as strategy formulation and leading strategic change. Literature and history indicate that *no* organization has an exclusive franchise for innovation. Innovation can come from anywhere, can occur anytime, and can be representative of individual or collective efforts. Some innovations require external events to stimulate their socialization and acceptance. For example, U.S.-based DuPont invented and introduced Neoprene as a synthetic rubber in 1931 in the midst of the Great Depression. At the time, Neoprene cost $1.05 a pound as compared to natural rubber, which cost $0.05 a pound. Clearly, the market favored natural rubber, and DuPont, owner of a product that was a significant disadvantage due to cost, could have discontinued its development processes. However, the advent of World War II changed the dynamics and economics of the rubber industry. The Japanese conquest of the Asian-Pacific nations thwarted the U.S. supply sources for natural rubber. This significant event served as a catalyst for the U.S. government to sponsor a consortium with $700 million in funding to develop alternatives to natural rubber, and Neoprene was central to the effort. Other innovation is the result of formal planning, management, and learning processes, whereas still other innovations have their origins in random experimentation and planned or accidental discovery. The important point to remember is that there is no single source for innovation or any universal method for "innovating" that is necessarily better than any other.

Essentially, there are three sources of innovation: autonomous, systemic, and collaborative, which can lead to either discontinuous or incremental innovation or some combination thereof.

Autonomous

Autonomous innovation can be either external or internal to the organization and the dominant industry players. It can be incremental or discontinuous. This type of innovation can come from anywhere, from anyone, and can occur at any time. Empirical evidence suggests that the most fertile sources of breakthrough innovation are generated beyond the known organizational boundaries of the enterprise and the industry. For example, in 1912 Joseph Schumpeter noted that "most innovation comes from outside the company and industry." In 1976, researchers Cooper and Schendel followed up with a similar conclusion.

Just looking to the recent past to Steve Jobs, cofounder of Apple Computer, Michael Dell of Dell Computers, and Bill Gates and Paul Allen, cofounders of Microsoft, provides us with examples of autonomous and discontinuous innovation that occur beyond the influence of the mainstream industry leaders. These companies and their products were clearly outside of the mainstream of computing industry as defined by then dominant giants like IBM, Hewlett-Packard, Data General, Burroughs, Sperry, and DEC. Yet, these companies were able to completely redefine the industry by inventing revolutionary ways of purchasing and producing PCs.

Autonomous innovation can occur in a number of forms. The Post-it product by 3M Company was born out of a project for adhesive glue and the need for a convenient method of bookmarking sheets of paper. The highly successful Glide dental floss product produced by W. L. Gore was originally developed as surgical suture material and was subsequently adapted for use in dental hygiene. In another example, Monorail Inc., a company that manufactures and delivers lower-priced PCs, reduced its order fulfillment time to two business days by using product design that fits into a standard Federal Express box. By the 1860s, refrigeration was used in railroad cars to transport food and other perishable items and in large "cold" facilities. Sometimes, however, innovation requires further innovation and discovery to become a viable product. For example, it wasn't until the discovery of Freon by GM and perfected by DuPont that refrigeration was commercialized to the point that it could be produced in sufficient quantities and at lower prices as to be viable for the consuming public. By the later part of the 1930s, over 50 percent of U.S. households had a refrigerator.

Chance and timing also play a role in innovation. For example, the discovery of the microwave as a source of heat and means of cooking was a random event, based on chance and timing. In 1945, Percy Spencer, the chief engineer for Raytheon Corporation, was standing near a radar transmitter when he noticed that the candy bar in his shirt pocket began to melt. According to the story, he then sent for popcorn and proceeded to watch the kernels ignite as popcorn. Hence, the idea of the microwave oven was launched, and in 1955 the Radarange was introduced to America as a commercial appliance, but it was the Japanese who perfected the product, reduced its costs, and made it a mainstay in residential kitchens. Image how long it might have taken to develop the microwave if Mr. Spencer did not have that candy bar in his pocket?

Systemic

Systemic innovation is indigenous to an organization. It is the result of a well-planned and formally managed process. Its outcomes are anticipated and monitored. Systemic innovation is often the result of complex organizational interactions between a number of factors, the formal systems used by the organization for fostering, and managing innovation and organizational cooperation. Systemic innovations generally will not yield radical or breakthrough results without organizational acceptance, interdepartmental cooperation, and formal management sanction. Rarely can systemic innovation be spontaneous or successful without the existence of preexisting acceptance or consent within the organization.

Unlike the industry stalwarts USX and Bethlehem Steel, which failed to see the Japanese as serious threats, tiny Nucor Corporation not only successfully competed against the Japanese but also recovered from the brink of bankruptcy. Under the direction of Ken Iverson, Nucor became a specialist in minimill steel production. To compete successfully against the Japanese, Nucor implemented innovative technology, management *and* operational processes to become the low-cost competitor in what was ultimately a commodity business. Nucor's strategic success is related to its innovative personnel practices and its ability to hire and retain personnel who want to share in the risks and returns of innovation in an extremely competitive marketplace. Central to Nucor's approach to innovation is the empowerment given to employees, a practice that was completely alien to the traditional steel companies. For example, some of Nucor's employees receive compensation that is linked to weekly production *and* cost performance. Manufacturing employees typically work in teams of 20 to 40 members. One group found that by using an ordinary garden hose, they could extend the life of certain equipment and reduce the cost of steel by about $25 per batch. Nucor provides an example of a company that used a portfolio approach to innovation to enable strategic change and create competitive advantage for itself.

Collaborative

Collaborative innovation is common and occurs when a group of individuals and/or organizations formally or informally come together with the single purpose in mind to innovate. Usually the collaboration is born out of a common interest and desire, the need to marshal specialized and often costly equipment and personnel, the need to share the risk, and the requirement for specialized subject matter expertise and competencies. Collaboration can occur between people, companies, and even industry rivals and competitors and can lead to discontinuous or incremental results.

By any measure, IBM's process for developing and launching its PC line was brilliant. In the late 1970s, in anticipation of its entrance into the PC marketplace, IBM turned to outside suppliers (and collaborators), including Microsoft and Intel, to develop key components of its PC. In 1982, IBM invested $250 million in Intel, which Intel used to change over its product-line capabilities to mass-produce the 30386 processor. Recognizing the emerging potential opportunities of desktop computing, IBM management established a special task force to develop a strategy to enter the infant PC market. One of the cornerstone suggestions of the task force was that IBM manufacture the product away from the politics and influences of New York. The task force recommended an autonomous unit that would operate outside the normal IBM construct and its bureaucratic practices. The theory was that such a strategy would allow it to be more creative, more innovative, and faster than the traditional IBM operations. Consequently, under the direction of Philip Estridge, IBM launched its PC in record time and quickly established itself as the dominant provider.

In a single move and by its sheer size and presence, IBM legitimized the PC as a tool and created the market. By 1988, IBM was the largest producer of PCs. Until the arrival of the IBM PC, the PC was a novelty. IBM's entrance and commitment to the PC legitimized the PC as a product and technology. IBM's funding of Microsoft and Intel created a franchise for those producers and ultimately contributed to the demise of IBM from its once lofty status as the industry technology leader. By collaborating with Intel and Microsoft, IBM provided the foundation that would ultimately contribute to greater competitive pressures and to a period of eroding performance and marketshare.

IMPEDIMENTS TO INNOVATION

There are many impediments to innovation and a multitude of factors that influence the ability of an organization to be innovative. Let's discuss three of the more common ones:

- Cultural and organizational learning impediments.
- Technology impediments.
- Measurement impediments.

Not surprisingly, elements of these factors are also present in the failure of many organizations to achieve strategic change. In addition, there are also process impediments that we will discuss in greater detail when we consider the models for innovation in the next section of this chapter. Exhibit 6.1 summarizes some of the more salient enablers and impediments to innovation. Let's explore the impact of each of these elements on innovation in greater detail.

Organizational Learning Impediments

Innovations, be they process, product, or managerial, will either enhance or destroy competencies, legacy processes, and long-practiced behaviors. Process and organizational innovations almost always require technology and competency changes. The combination of these factors mandate behavioral changes, which can be threatening to many executives, midlevel managers, and hourly employees. Learning methods and culture play important roles in the ability of an organization to plan, innovate, and navigate strategic change. For many organizations and their management teams, innovation is difficult because it requires them to unlearn long-held lessons and behavioral patterns. Jerry Hirshberg, founder and president of Nissan Design International, notes, "Innovation requires the capacity to disdain tradition and break with comfortable routines and mastered skills." Thus, institutionalizing innovation in practice can be much more difficult in older, established organizations than in younger ones. This brings us to a significant conclusion with respect to learning and culture: The stronger the culture, the deeper the vested interests and the greater the potential for pushback; hence, it is more difficult to introduce and successfully deploy new processes, technological, managerial, organizational, and cultural innovations.

Technology Impediments

Technology can present significant impediments to innovation. First, an organization may simply lack the proper technology to support innovation. Second, the technology may be so new that it is unreliable or difficult to maintain and learn, and thus it serves as an impediment to its use and ultimately innovation. Third, the technology may be er-

	Impediments	Enablers
Culture	▲ Strong commitment to past practices ▲ Inability to "unlearn" ▲ Lack of institutional priority or personnel deployment ▲ Lack of proper incentives ▲ Inappropriate people ▲ Poor physical environment	▲ Energized and diversified workforce ▲ Institutional passions ▲ Creative and conducive physical environment ▲ High learning and discovery environment ▲ Active knowledge sharing
Technology	▲ Lack of appropriate technology ▲ Technology is unproven or too difficult to use ▲ Technology can be too threatening to establishment	▲ High utility technology ▲ High ergonomics for technology ▲ Accessibility to technology ▲ Encourage experimentation
Measurements	▲ Inappropriate or nonexistent measurements ▲ Misplaced emphasis on measurements ▲ Overreliance on financial measurements	▲ Emphasize learning and adaptation ▲ Use multifactor measurements ▲ Emphasize long-term results

EXHIBIT 6.1 Enabling Innovation

gonomically challenging, requiring an enormous commitment to new learning and unlearning antiquated behaviors and knowledge. Fourth, the technology may be politically and culturally threatening. As noted by researcher Clayton Christensen, "The technological changes that damage established companies are usually not radically new or difficult from a technological point of view. They do, however, have two important characteristics: First, they typically present a different package of performance attributes. Second, the performance attributes that existing customers do value improve at such a rapid rate that the new technology can later invade those established markets." The most acceptable technology is that which can be most used by people. Thus, in innovation, the introduction and use of technology are fundamental to the acceptance and advancement of innovation. That is certainly the case with major process and organizational innovations.

Measurement Impediments

Measuring the impact and value of innovation on strategic change can be another impediment to innovation. The impact of innovation must be measured in ways different than the traditional financial accounting calculations. Applying the traditional financial measurements to innovation may simply be a bureaucratic exercise because they do not provide insights or accurate representations of innovation. Although there are financial accounting pronouncements from the American Institute of Certified Public Accountants (AICPA) related to R&D expenditures and the capitalization and expensing of certain costs, there is no accounting pronouncement instructing the auditor on how to value *innovation* or intellectual capital. There is no ratio for the CFO to use to distinguish between "good" innovation and "bad" innovation and no universal metric for predicting the financial success or failure of innovation efforts and investments. What we have are the results of innovation: breakthrough thoughts, processes, and outcomes. Had Bill Gates, Michael Dell, or Henry Ford relied exclusively on traditional ROI analysis and accounting forecasts, it is questionable whether these visionaries would have gone to market with their ideas.

For example, when he had only a rudimentary working model and a dream, Chester Carlson, the inventor of xerography and founder of Xerox Corporation, was turned down by the then industry leaders IBM, GE, RCA, and Remington Rand when he was seeking financial support. It took 15 years of development and patience for the product to be successfully launched as a commercially viable venture, which came 22 years after Carlson filed his patent for the concept. Years later, Peter McClough of Xerox commented on the product that launched the company ". . . whether xerography would today pass the test that we now put all new products or ideas through, such as financial analysis, including return on investment, return on sales . . . and so forth. I think there is really a good possibility that we would not have undertaken to do what we actually have done in the xerography field."

The accounting systems used today were established around the dynamics of the industrialization movement to control and value physical assets and capital such as machinery, labor cost, inventories, and the number of widgets produced. Ford Motor Company was famous for its "Blue Book," which had costs described to a finite level. Unlike machinery or cash, there is no balance sheet item for creativity and intellectual assets that go into innovation. Yet we know that companies such as Microsoft, Yahoo!, and Disney are very creative and highly intellectual capital companies. Why does the market rate of capitalization for these relatively new companies far exceed their accounting book values and the value of "old economy" stalwarts? It's because these companies have intrinsic value that is generated from their innovation, brand names, and intellectual capital. Without that intellectual capital and creativity, Disney would simply be another amusement park, not the Magic Kingdom. So in analyzing innovation, there is a leap of faith, an acceptance of the intellectual logic that innovation will result in the desired strategic changes and economic outcomes. As a general rule, high-performance companies generate around 30 percent of their growth and revenues from innovation, as expressed in the form of new products and services that are less than 3 years old.

UNDERSTANDING THE DYNAMICS OF INNOVATION

Many attempts have been made to try to illustrate how innovation actually occurs in the organization. One of the seminal questions related to innovation is whether or not it can be represented as a life cycle. That is, does innovation act or behave like a product or technology? One approach, offered by researcher John Utterback, characterizes innovation as a life cycle. Although the evolution of an innovation is far more complex than what can be realistically represented as a simple life cycle, the use of such concepts helps to build a context for understanding how innovation develops and evolves. It is especially helpful to understanding the importance and the role of a dominant design in innovation and how it affects subsequent behaviors and the dynamics of an industry. Furthermore, such concepts are convenient methods of representation that help us to intellectually relate to the dynamics, uncertainty, and fluidity of innovation, and the process of innovating. Thus, even though no one particular method can completely explain the behavior of innovation, developing an appreciation of a basic life cycle is important to understanding the larger, more complex structure.

Almost all innovations, even those that are discontinuous and revolutionary, eventually establish some type of rhythm, an ebb and flow to their processes. To this extent, they demonstrate elements and portions of a distinct life cycle where ideas and creativity are gestated, born, incubated, grow, and mature. Some reach the market; a majority of ideas and concepts do not. As a result, new products are developed, business processes are transformed, new markets are created, new businesses enter markets, existing businesses exit them, and new competencies and employment opportunities are created. It is an intricate choreography, combining technology, the number of entrants and extrants to markets, market demands, financial resources, human capital, and knowledge management, which all affect the timing and viscosity of the innovation life cycle. John Utterback, in *Mastering the Dynamics of Innovation,* describes the three phases of the classic innovation life cycle: (1) fluid phase, (2) transitional phase, and (3) specific phase. Exhibit 6.2 illustrates these phases.

Fluid Phase

This is the most turbulent phase of the innovation life cycle. During this initial period, there is a tremendous level of activity marked by many new designs, new competitors, false starts, and many sources and variations of products and themes. For example, the late

EXHIBIT 6.2 Innovation Life Cycle

Fluid Phase	Transitional Phase	Specific Phase
▲ Highly turbulent	▲ Emergence of a dominant design	▲ Switching costs become high; sometimes prohibitive
▲ Very uncertain		▲ Products become less differentiated
▲ Many competitors and concepts	▲ Entrance of more established firms	▲ Reduction in the number of competitors
▲ Switching costs are low	▲ Reduction in competing designs	▲ Branding becomes increasingly important
▲ Dominant design is developed but has not emerged	▲ Shift in emphasis from design to process efficiency	

Source: Adapted from John Utterback, *Mastering the Dynamics of Innovation.*

1970s and early 1980s marked the fluid phase for the PC industry. In the late 1970s, there were only a few PC makers, most notably Apple, Tandem, and Commodore. By the early part of the 1980s, there were over 100 different vendors, and by 1986 there were over 200 manufacturers of PCs. As the industry grew and matured, the number of producers continued to increase but ultimately settled on less than a dozen dominant sources including Dell, Hewlett-Packard, Compaq, Gateway, IBM, Toshiba, and NEC. Apple, with less than 4 percent of the total PC marketplace, is still in business but is no longer a driving force. Some of the key characteristics that distinguish this phase of innovation include:

- Turbulent industry and competitor changes.
- Outcomes are uncertain and speculative.
- Rate of product and process change is rapid.
- Early technology is usually: very expensive, relatively crude, often unreliable, overly complex, and difficult to maintain.
- Markets are created and grow around the innovations.
- The emergence, but usually not the recognition, of a dominant design or the significant and *defining* elements of it.
- Process innovation and sophisticated management practices lag behind product innovation.
- Usually, organizations are younger entrepreneurial in nature; informal and smaller-scaled organizations and channels of distributions.
- Switching costs for technologies and business models are low but once established become very high.

Although development efforts usually involve limited numbers of people within the organization, high-performing companies also invest and collaborate with external firms that are smaller, entrepreneurial, and specialty-based. High performers also experiment with alternative forms of organizational structure and use concepts such as "skunk works," "focused factories," "incubators," and "entrepreneurial areas" to facilitate innovation and stimulate creativity.

According to researcher and author Dorothy Leonard, as much as 46 percent of all resources devoted to product development during this phase are spent on efforts that are canceled. A Booz Allen Hamilton Study concluded that for 100 development projects, 63 percent are dropped, 12 percent are flops, and only 5 percent are successes. The balance apparently land in "inno-limbo." Another study, described by Amal Kumar Naj in the *Wall Street Journal*, found that "only one in ten [creations] developed in the laboratory ever gets to market." Even Sony's PlayStation discards upwards of 15 percent of their initial projects.

Thus, a major lesson of the foregoing is that innovation is risky, and the majority of innovations fail to reach market. This has significant implications for any organization that has adopted an innovator strategy or is relying on innovation to create the so-called first-mover advantage. Often what happens from a strategic perspective is that those companies aspiring to be first-movers expend significant resources on development but lack sufficient resources or organizational commitment for commercial follow-through. Thus, they become vulnerable to other companies that use an imitator strategy.

Transitional Phase

This second phase provides a shift in emphasis from product innovation to process refinement. During this phase, the number of competing products stabilize and the shift to innovate production and distribution processes are accelerated. Some of the major characteristics that signal the transitional phase include the emergence of a dominant design and increasing stability in design and process. Other signals include increasing consumer awareness and intelligence, greater emphasis on formal organizational structures, increasing scale and economies of operations, and greater market specialization.

The major characteristic of this period is the emergence of a *dominant design* for the product, organization, or process. A dominant design is one that has the "weight of many innovations that tilted the economic balance in favor of one approach" and is generally distinguished by a number of characteristics:

- It is the design that wins the acknowledgement and allegiance of the marketplace.
- It becomes the de-facto standard that other competitors and innovators emulate if they hope to generate a significant following.
- The design embodies the requirements of many different classes of users and segments of customers, even though it may not meet all of the needs of any particular class or segment.
- The design reduces the number of unique and specialized performance requirements (exceptions) by incorporating those requirements in the design, such as multiple temperature settings for refrigerators and variable speed for windshield wipers.
- The design is the result of the interplay between technical and market choices at a particular time.
- As demand and production grow and more uses are found, the number of firms entering the market with variations to the basic design and product offering *increases.* Over time, the number of firms ultimately declines due to competitive pressures.
- As production efficiencies increase and products become less expensive and more accessible, larger markets are usually created.

The emergence of a dominant design forces a reduction in the number of competing designs. It is during this phase that the largest or best financed members of the industry are both most vulnerable and best positioned to capitalize and incrementally improve upon a design—if they are inclined to recognize it as superior or marketable. Thus, the distinctions of the dominant design begin to become blurred as "clones," replacements, variations, and the like enter the market. More importantly, the emergence of a dominant design is usually recognized in retrospect; after it has been developed (PC format versus Apple). That is, it was created in the fluid phase, but not fully recognized or acknowledged by consumers and competitors as being dominant until the transitional phase.

Nowhere is the impact of a contemporary dominant design more prevalent than in the PC industry. Microsoft's ascendancy to its current status was facilitated through the failure of Gary Kildall to enter into a nondisclosure agreement with IBM, Steve Jobs' erroneous judgment on the importance of software, and the personal persistence of Bill Gates. Bill Gates used his acquisition and subsequent adaptation of Ron Brock's SCP-DOS software to secure the contract to write the DOS operating system for IBM's new line of PCs. That operating system soon became the dominant design, until MS-Windows was released a few years later. Windows then became the de-facto standard for the majority of PCs and graphical user interfaces (GUI).

In the transitional phase, the dominant design stabilizes and companies begin to compete more and more on operational efficiency, logistics, and prices rather than on design or process innovation. During this phase, product variations continue to appear but are directed more towards incremental change rather than radical redesign.

Specific Phase

This phase represents the most dangerous part of the innovation life cycle for an established industry leader. As authors and researchers Gary Hamel and C. K. Prahalad assert, "A company surrenders tomorrow's business when it gets better without getting different." Any company that remains and operates in this phase cannot sustain competitive advantage over the longer term. This is the point at which strategic renewal must be emphasized with a deliberate shift in strategy formulation to thinking differently and reviving the dynamics of the fluid phase.

During this phase, organizational barriers between processes and functional areas are erected, and internal defense mechanisms to change and innovation are often created. As a result, strategic renewal and change become more difficult and organizationally more complex. Some of the key qualities that define this phase include:

- The use of a "value ratio" concept appears, which is the measurement of quality to cost as a basis of competition.
- The convergence of product *and* process, which, ultimately, become indistinguishable or synonymous in the organization.
- A maturing of organizational structures, which become more formal and rigid.
- A reduction in the number of competitors, but those that remain have significant strength in operational leverage, buying power, and established customer relationships.
- Competing products become relatively undifferentiated in substance but not necessarily form (PCs, automobile styles, consumer electronics, etc.).
- An increasing importance of a common brand identity at the entity-level as a source of differentiation.

In this phase, product differentiation is usually achieved through price, service, brand recognition, and marketing. However, within the organization, especially those that are mature, the distinctions between a product and process become more transparent and less distinctive. The product becomes the process, and the process becomes the product. Achieving greater economies of scale, lowering costs, standardizing the process, and the constant attention to incremental quality improvement constitute the conventional management wisdoms. Maintaining this stage for any length of time will lead to certain demise. A company cannot perpetuate—let alone advance—itself in this state.

During this phase, organizations tend to become more inwardly focused and change becomes a slow process. Emphasis on radical innovation for product or process is low, and emphasis on incremental intervention programs such as TQM, CQI, and streamlining than on systemic process change or radical innovation increases. Many of the companies in the automotive, consumer products, retailing, and airline industries are in this phase of innovation. Although the companies in these industries are generating new products, the innovations in both product and process are not of the systemic breakthrough types. Their investment in research and development may appear to be growing, but it is usually earmarked for situational replacement or incremental improvement to existing practices. Undeniably, automotive makers are building better en-gines with greater power, better mileage, greater dependability, and lower maintenance, but they are still internal combustion engines. They use the same engineering principles and design concepts that were developed in the late nineteenth century. Those types of innovations are incremental and will not help a company if someone else perfects the fuel cell or other alternative fuel–powered (AFP) cars. Incremental innovation is im-portant, but it will not provide sustainable competitive advantage over the long run.

LEADING INNOVATION

Understanding what innovation is and how innovation behaves is important, but creat-ing innovation is essential to the survival of any organization. "Simply stated, our strat-egy is to discover new and better medicines through breakthrough research and then to demonstrate their value to physicians, payers and patients. Maximizing revenue growth in the long term depends on—more than anything else—the discovery of important new medicines," notes Raymond V. Gilmartin, CEO of Merck. Mr. Gilmartin's state-ment describing the strategy of Merck clearly implies that it is an innovator. Any com-pany that wants to compete against it must do so knowing that Merck wants to set the direction, tone, and rules for competing in its marketspace. A good strategy for com-peting with Merck would be one of complementor/collaborator.

Innovative companies such as Disney, Emerson, Motorola, 3M, Microsoft, Sony, Merck, and GE make innovation a way of life—it is a discipline. Although each company is very different and competes in different industries, they share five characteristics:

1. They have institutionalized innovation as a way of life.
2. They have leaderships that foster innovation and build creative and collaborative learning environments.
3. They hire, nurture, and, indeed, covet innovative people.
4. They recognize and reward creativity.
5. They are not predisposed or biased to preconceived outcomes, nor are they attached to a predetermined answer; rather, they let the answers and outcomes evolve toward a general target.

High-performance organizations are committed to embedding creative and dis-continuous thinking into their cultures and processes. That is because the discontinu-ance process is most effective in environments where traditional industry behaviors are no longer the standard. Three conditions appear to be essential to this type of innova-tion strategy and behavior:

1. Less emphasis is placed on analysis and more emphasis is placed on the interactive process of probing and learning from the experience gained through each subsequent probe.
2. The process becomes one of successive approximation, each time striving to take a step closer to a winning combination of product and market.
3. The effort must be strategically central to the needs and objectives of the organization or management will fail to muster the staying power to persist and learn from the years of twists and turns and unpleasant surprises.

Sadly, there are indications that, at least in the United States, managers appear to be slow to grasp the power and importance of innovation in creating competitive advantage. Authors Gary Hamel and C. K. Prahalad reference a study in their book *Competing for the Future,* which indicates that 80 percent of U.S. managers believe that quality will be a source of competitive advantage in the year 2000. In contrast, less than half of the Japanese managers in the same survey believe quality to be a fundamental component of competitive advantage. Many factors contribute to this sentiment; perhaps the most significant is that Japanese managers have considered quality to be a competitive imperative and intrinsic to the product, whereas quality only came to the forefront of U.S. management thinking in the 1980s and 1990s. For the Japanese, quality is important. However, an interpretation of the survey may also indicate that they recognize that quality can be matched and neutralized as a strategic and differentiating characteristic.

Another study notes that 50 percent of U.S. managers believe that the United States is losing the innovation edge to other countries. The same study also notes that less than 50 percent of U.S. managers believe that new profits are going to come from new products. This compares to 87 percent of managers polled in Japan. On a comparative basis, U.S. R&D expenditures are 3.7 percent of revenues versus 5.5 percent and 5.7 percent in Japan and Germany, respectively. According to the consulting firm A.D. Little, 82 percent and 71 percent of Japanese and European managers believed innovation to be important to securing long-term profitability, and only 51 percent of American managers indicated that innovation would be a material factor. Thus, for many U.S. companies, there may already be a crisis in innovation that will ultimately compromise their ability to successfully compete and renew themselves in the highly dynamic environment discussed earlier (see chapters 1 to 5).

Andy Grove, the chairman of Intel, said, "Ultimately, the speed of innovation is the only competitive weapon we have." The speed and persistence at which a company innovates are second only in criticality to what it innovates and how it innovates. However, innovation in formal organizations is rarely spontaneous. Rather, it requires process methods and a combination of personality qualities and environmental factors:

1. Creativity
2. Leadership
3. Human performance
4. Environment
5. Innovation models and processes.

Creativity

As John Young, the former CEO of Hewlett-Packard, noted, "Creativity is the only American competitive advantage left." Organizational and individual creativity are fundamental to innovation. Thus, the failure to cultivate creativity leads to the failure to innovate. However, creativity is difficult for many organizations and individuals because it requires the ability to think differently, to continuously learn, to discover and discern ambiguous patterns, to draw inferences and form conclusions in new and different ways and to take risks. Creativity requires the individual to have the capacity to visualize new and different products, processes, measurements, and organizations. Finally, creativity requires personal courage and conviction to be different and to constructively challenge the status quo, legacy practices, and established doctrines and known patterns.

Creativity drives innovative processes and outcomes. John Kao, in his book *Jamming,* notes, "Creativity becomes a process, not an event." Creativity can be entirely unique or it can come through adoption, adaptation, and repackaging of someone else's original idea. There are literally hundreds of methods for facilitating the creative thought process. As a result, innovation and the process of developing innovation through creativity can be highly formal and structured, such as that used by Xerox, or independent and entrepreneurial as in the case of Sony, 3M, and Rubbermaid. Some innovation may be driven by the need to create new products or markets. Others are driven by the need to develop extensions and complements to existing products and services. Other forms of innovation are the result of well-defined business needs and parameters.

We will now discuss some techniques that can support and stimulate innovative thinking.

Creative Imaging

This technique involves building alternative scenarios and images of a possible end result and/or the processes used to create the end result. The images can be reduced to graphic depictions and storyboards for thought stimulation, presentation, and communication purposes. The three basic steps of this technique include:

1. Describing the possible outcome, defining the context, creating the metrics.
2. Using the image(s) as a rallying point to work towards.
3. Creating a common understanding of the strengths, weaknesses, and benefits of the image(s).

Morphological Analysis

This technique involves:

1. Defining characteristics; defining change attributes; ask why, what, where, who, when, and how.
2. Identifying random relationships and develop analogies.
3. Exploring and evaluating possibilities.

Inverse Brainstorming

This technique involves conceptualizing a solution or outcome and working backwards, through a number of issues and steps, to arrive at a design for business integration. This goal-based approach forces individuals to focus on the outcomes and path of least resistance to that outcome. The major steps that support this process include:

1. Taking a satisfactory outcome, design, or situation and working to find problems with it.
2. Using destructive logic as the motivator for creativity.

Mitsubishi Technique

This is a variation of the famous Lotus Blossom technique in which each member of the creative design team provides individual input and personal perspective. For each issue or problem, individual team members develop eight ideas as possible solution sets. Once this process is completed, the entire team converges to identify the root causes and problems, attack the problems, and develop solutions as a collective group. The major steps that support this process include:

1. Identifying and defining the problem(s).
2. Developing eight ideas for each problem.
3. Developing an idea map that helps to describe ideas visually.
4. Iterating and extending ideas to develop other solutions.

Gordon Little Technique

This technique is a classic example of issue-tree analysis, decomposition, and root-cause analysis. It is designed to focus on the essence of a problem through an iterative approach that drives issues and problems to lower levels of detail with each iteration. The major steps that support this process include:

1. Decomposing the issue, problem, activity, or process one level at a time.
2. Developing relational issues and questions.
3. Defining the problem at its essential level using the relationships as thought guides.

Dupont Technique

This is a published technique used by E.I. Dupont & Company in their internal R&D efforts. The basic notions behind this method are that big ideas can come from anywhere and that one must always think in positive terms. Central to the process is the notion that positive thinking generally yields positive results. The major steps that support this process include:

1. Lateral thinking methods.
2. Metaphoric methods.
3. Positive thinking methods.
4. Association techniques.
5. Capturing and interpreting dreams.

Japanese Innovation Process: Five-Step Approach

This technique is more of a philosophical method to develop high-idea organizations. The major advantage of this approach over others is that it includes the capacity for continuous improvement and the renewal of proven products and processes. The major steps that support this process include:

1. **Tansakii** = search for new ideas
2. **Inysei** = nurture, protect, and incubate new ideas
3. **Hassoo** = generate breakthroughs
4. **Kaizen** = continuously improve
5. **Saitiyo** = recycle the old

INNOVATION TACTICS

1. Use self-organizing teams.
2. Learn across disciplines.
3. Use nonsequential development methods.
4. Use nonintrusive leadership; set direction.

Eastman Kodak Company

This method is similar to the "gating" techniques popular in the 1970s for R&D. The technique involves a formal evaluation and review process and the active "marketing" of the concepts in the organization for sponsorship and funding. The major steps that support this process include:

1. Idea generation
2. Initial screening
3. Group review
4. Sponsorship
5. Commitment
6. Commercialization

Xerox PARC Method

This method has its origins in the Palo Alto research facility of Xerox. The method is a relatively straightforward set of techniques that have been formalized and institutionalized into a process. The major steps that support this process include:

1. Problem identification
2. Problem analysis
3. Potential solutions
4. Select and plan solution
5. Implement solutions
6. Evaluate solutions

Prototyping and simulation testing

This is a proven process of trial and refinement from which learning occurs and new ideas are spawned. The major steps that support this process include:

1. Develop it.
2. Try it.
3. Fix it.
4. Use it.
5. Change it.

There are various techniques and methods for supporting innovative thinking and idea-generation techniques. Typically, these techniques are designed to help stimulate the creative thought processes of the individuals chartered with developing and deploying innovative solutions. They can also be used to help address problems, identify issues, and focus efforts. As in the selection of a technique, the use of thought "generators" is situational to the organization's needs, learning ability of a team, and objectives of the innovation effort. Some techniques to consider include:

Linear vs. conceptual thinking. Linear thinking is progressive, sequential, and can be relatively tedious. It is the type of thinking that is used in traditional functions, such as accounting, and transactions processing. Conceptual is based on abstracts and scenarios, visions, etc. This type of thinking is usually found in architecture, systems design, art, and music.

Continuous vs. discontinuous thinking. Continuous thinking usually results in sequential analysis, incremental gains, and linear solutions. Discontinuous thought processes are best represented as random patterns that are constantly configured to new concepts and ideas. Discontinuous thinking can result in major quantum shifts and leaps to new levels and new structures.

Lateral thinking. Lateral thinking explores new patterns and ways of learning, understanding, and developing ideas. The process involves looking beyond the normal construct to identify issues and patterns differently. It looks for solutions that do not fit normal patterns or known parameters.

Adoptive vs. initiating. These are very closely aligned with cultural "styles." Adoptive styles take proven designs and continuously improve upon them (such as the Japanese auto industry). Initiating styles are experimenters and leaders in breakthrough thinking and process design (such as Microsoft and 3M).

The ability of the organization to be creative is a reflection of the individual personalities, values, intellectual capabilities, and institutional values and its propensity to learn. Authors and researchers Robert J. Sternberg, Linda A. O'Hara, and Todd I. Lubart have identified six competencies necessary to fostering creativity in the enterprise: knowledge, intellectual abilities, thinking styles, motivation, personality, and environment. To this list I add personal conviction and leadership.

There is a distinct element and requirement of leadership for innovation to occur. In fostering an environment for innovation, high-performance organizations work with urgency and a sense of "controlled chaos," which represents the consequence of knowledge, process, human passion, and excitement. High-performance companies understand and place such issues as the organization's need to change its propensity to change, cultural inhibitors to change, the measurements for innovation, and the integration of technological innovation with human performance, in strategic context. Jerry Hirschberg, founder and president of Nissan Design International, refers to the process of creative abrasion as a method of stimulating and sustaining innovation. Hirshberg notes that it "Is an interpersonal process. It means harnessing the frictional energies released between distinct perspective and work styles to generate new directions and novel solutions." Arthur Koestler in *The Act of Creation* defined *creative abrasion* as "the sudden interlocking of two previously unrelated skills or matrices of thought."

Leadership

Chapter 8 provides a more comprehensive discussion of leadership, so only a brief summary of a few key points will be touched on here. A fundamental requisite for strategic change and innovation is leadership. High-performance creativity and innovation require the commitment of the leader to an almost relentless pursuit of thinking and working differently. Leading innovation requires the managing of highly capable and energized and impassioned people, people who have extreme personal conviction about what they are doing. It also requires that the leader function as a *protector,* learner, and advocate. Leaders must be proponents of innovation. In this capacity, they must be capable of directing and deploying resources, coordinating activities, and fostering the appropriate levels of collaboration to achieve the right balance of skills, personalities, and probable outcomes. The leader must also be capable of leveraging and successfully converging polarized positions and views that are so often associated with highly creative and emotionally charged environments. "Their work is a daily struggle to balance chaos and control, brilliance and budgets, experimentation and efficiency," notes Paul Roberts about the challenges of managing highly creative and energized individuals at Sony PlayStation. One aspect that effective leaders of innovation share is that they have a personal passion for and deep personal conviction for their projects. They convey this passion through being serious about innovation and displaying a sense of urgency and personal dedication to innovation and those chartered with being innovative.

Most importantly, leaders create a culture for innovation. The combination of organizational culture and personal behavior are significant determinants of the success of innovation in an organization. Researcher Charlan Jeanne Nemeth notes, "Creativity and innovation may require a culture that is very different and, in a sense, diametrically opposed to that which encourages cohesion, loyalty, and clear norms of appropriate attitudes and behavior." For example, consider the creativity and innovation that is expected by a high-performance leader such as Microsoft or Merck as compared to that found in an accounting firm. Thus, a primary task of a leader for innovation is to ensure that the "right people are in the right place," as noted by researcher B. Schneider. If culture change is necessary, then it should be performed with immediacy and conviction. Former Daimler-Benz CEO Helmut Werner said, "We had to understand that the world had changed, and that the philosophy Mercedes had pursued so successfully had to come to an end."

One of the keys to successfully leading innovation is "calibration." Calibration is the ability of the leader to exert personal influence and direction without adversely impacting individual creativity and freedoms. Too much emphasis on compliance, direction, and intervention can stifle innovation. Research by Charlan Jeanne Nemeth confirms what most exemplary leaders already know: "The directiveness and strength of the leader can actually thwart creative thought and the expression of divergent views." The influence of the leader on personal innovation is further supported through research offered by Robert J. Strenberg and Janet Davidson, who conclude, "Too much control can undermine self-determinism and a sense of self." Thus, when managing innovation, leaders strive for a balance between organizational compliance, personal expression, and creative freedom extended to those responsible for innovation. Finally, leaders work to ensure that innovation is supported by a distinct value proposition that is aligned with the business strategies and performance measurements of the organization and that the proper rewards and recognition systems are installed.

Human Performance

Innovation is impossible without human performance. Some individuals, as noted by researcher M. Csikszentmihalyi, are simply more inclined towards innovation than others. If an organization wants to be innovative and produce innovative outcomes, it needs an innovative leadership and workforce. That means selecting and providing opportunities for people who have a passion for their jobs, have a real zest for life, have balance in their personal and professional priorities, and are motivated by the goal, not necessarily the reward. High-performance companies seek people who have a wide range of interests and a broad perspective. For leadership positions they look for those who have lived in *many* environments, not just one, and demonstrate an appreciation for other cultures. They also seek people who have a higher propensity for creativity and learning.

Scholars and authors Anne Cummings and Greg R. Oldham define *employee creativity* as the "generation of novel and useful products, ideas, and procedures that are the raw material for innovation." But fostering and achieving creativity in the organization are, as noted, challenges. A key to creativity lays in achieving a balance between three critical success factors: leadership, people, and culture/environment. The most essential factor in creativity is the people. Individuals who are inclined towards creativity exhibit five distinct personality qualities:

1. Highly creative people are intrinsically motivated and are driven by a deep personal conviction and passion for innovating, not necessarily by compensation. Researcher Teresa Amabile has defined *intrinsic motivation* as the ability "to work on something because it is interesting, involving, exciting, satisfying, or personally challenging. A number of studies have demonstrated that a primarily intrinsic motivation will be more conducive to creativity than a primarily extrinsic motivation [coercion or money]." Robert Oppenheimer's Manhattan Project is a perfect example of individuals who were motivated by a cause and personal conviction.

2. According to researcher F. Barron, "Creative people are characterized as high on personal dominance and forcefulness of opinion and, in addition, they tend to have a distant or detached attitude in interpersonal relations, though they are not without sensitivity or insight." Creative individuals focus their energies and personalities on their projects and the discovery and learning associated with the process of innovation. As such, they may be detached and withdrawn from more common and casual forms of social interaction that occur in the workplace.

3. Creative people are typically experts in their fields. According to Dean Simonton, "Expertise is the foundation of all creative work. One needs knowledge in a relevant field to lead creativity." He notes that "substantial achievements occur, on average, after at least 10 years of involvement in a field." Creative people also draw on life experiences and multiple disciplines and use life metaphors to stimulate their creativity. They are able to draw from a wide range of personal and professional experiences and apply the learnings from them to new situations and challenges.

4. Creative individuals are adept at change. They understand that change is typical, not atypical, and that change stimulates and challenges creativity and the traditional practices of innovation. They are calculated risk takers and inherently are highly self-disciplined and focused. As individuals, they have a high tolerance for ambiguity and uncertainty. They keep working, even when the conventional wisdom says otherwise.

5. Researchers Robert J. Sternberg and Janet Davidson, editors of *The Nature of Insight,* note that creative individuals have a high propensity for perseverance in the face of uncertainty.

The roles of personality and learning are major determinants of how a person works and whether that individual is more inclined to be innovative and creative or adaptive. The research is rich with other studies on personality and creativity that indicate that creative people share a particular group of personality descriptors. As an example, auditing is a high-compliance profession, one that would be more inclined to hire and nurture more passive, conformist, and adaptive individuals. In contrast, the software business demands creativity, and any organization wanting to do well in that business would attract individuals with rebellious, probing, and innovative characteristics rather than adaptive personalities.

One means of determining a potential for creativity is to "inventory" certain personality and behavioral qualities. Studies performed by R.T. Keller and W.E. Holland on Kirton's Adaption-Innovation Inventory suggests that the Kirton inventory is a reasonably good predictor of employees' creativity at work. They conclude that adaptive styles work incrementally on problems using established rules and frameworks. In contrast, innovative styles are likely to ignore established frameworks, redefine and reframe the problem, and develop their own methods for creativity and problem solving. Some of the predictive criteria, as described by M.J. Kirton in *Adapters and Innovators: A Description and Measure,* include individuals who:

- Want to create more than improve.
- Have fresh perspectives on old problems.
- Cope with several new ideas at the same time (compartmentalize and multi-task).
- Are not methodical and systematic in their approaches to problems/projects.
- Do not impose strict order on matters within their own control.
- Do not like the protection of precise instructions.
- Seek to bend or break the rules.
- Often risk doing things differently.
- Can stand out in disagreement against the group.
- Act without proper authority.

Additional tools for measuring these characteristics include Gough's Creative Personality Scale (CPS). Developed by H.G. Gough and A.B. Heilbrun, the CPS is a list of 30 items empirically derived from a broader, 300-item personality test, called the Adjective Check List. Empirical data from those diagnostical assessments indicate that an employee with a generally creative personality is clever, humorous, informal, insightful, inventive, original, reflective, resourceful, self-confident, sexy, snobbish, and unconventional.

Organizations that place high premiums on innovation to create competitive advantage hire and engage employees who challenge established doctrine and power structures. This requires very different leadership skills than those that were so carefully cultivated by the traditional hierarchical management organizations. Perhaps reflecting on his years at GM, Jerry Hirschberg, of Nissan Design International, noted, "The least appealing kind of staff I could imagine for any business was a congregation of like-minded yea-sawyers, cozy, comfortable, mutually reinforcing, and nonthreatening to top management."

Environmental Factors

The cultural, physical, and emotional environments play a large role in the ability to produce innovative outcomes. "The first thing a visitor to PlayStation headquarters notices is how fresh everything looks. Cubicles and offices are spangled like dorm rooms with posters, plants, and sci-fi monsters," notes Paul Roberts in writing about the success of Sony's PlayStation, a company that went from zero revenues in 1994 to over $10 billion in 1998. In contrast, a visit to a well-known consulting firm that has its research and development facility in the Midwest found a dimly lit environment dominated by cubicles with a gray and black color scheme, carpeting that was gray and black, and concrete walls that were left in the natural color—gray. Devoid of personality, the environment seemed to be depressing, especially during the long winter months and even on sunny days of the short summer. It was hardly a place that one could define as conducive for spontaneous innovation and radical thinking.

The environment is an important determinant in planning and managing innovation. For example, when Ford Motor Company moved its Lincoln Mercury Division to southern California, General Manager Mark W. Hutchins said, "It wasn't a move to California. It was a move out of Detroit. We needed to break out." The inference is that Lincoln Mercury had to break out of a Detroit way of looking at and thinking about the world. It needed a fresh perspective and the eclectic energy that only a place like southern California can offer. That may explain, in part, why over 14 of the top automotive design studios in the world are located in that part of the world. The climatic and physical working environment is almost as important to innovation as are the people and the technologies.

The results of researcher Teresa Amabile's 12-year study involving 26 different companies and 12,000 employees indicate that the work environment significantly impacts the creativity of work that they produce. Three major factors emerge as important considerations in creating an environment conducive to innovation: (1) open, active, and direct communications, (2) rewards and recognition systems, and (3) fair performance evaluation. Several other factors that must be considered include:

- Value placed on innovation by the organization.
- Sense of pride in what is being performed and accomplished.
- Emphasis on self-determinism and self-directedness.
- Importance and complexity of work.

When Ford Motor Company set about building the new generation of its highly successful Mustang, it emulated the design practices of several industry leaders and also moved its design team to a new and different place. The new physical and emotional surroundings stimulated creativity and teamwork and a break from tradition and legacy practices. The result was a car that was built with 25 percent less time and 30 percent less cost than any before.

One could contrast the Mustang experience with the development of the new Taurus a few years later, which took place in the basement of a building and under a noisy heater. According to Mary Walton, in *Car,* the Taurus team had to fight for the simplest of resources, such as copy machines, and worked under severe stress in less-than-ideal conditions and under questionable leaderships. As a result, the debate continues as to whether Team Taurus built a car that outperforms its intended target, the Toyota Camry. Apparently, if it weren't for fleet sales to rental car companies and corporations, the Taurus would be a marginal sales performer at the individual consumer level. To many observers, the problems for the Taurus team were obvious from the start.

Innovation Processes and Models

Most innovation can be planned, directed, and anticipated. In all organizations, there is always some form of innovation occurring. Most organizations use some type of process or model to perform and manage their innovation efforts. Some of these models can be extraordinarily sophisticated in their structure and use; others can be

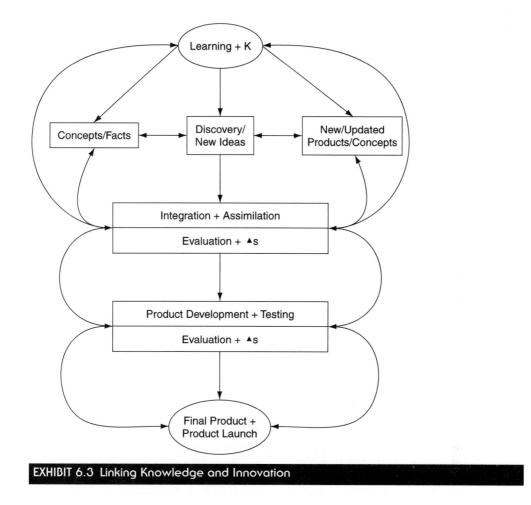

EXHIBIT 6.3 Linking Knowledge and Innovation

relatively simple. However, as illustrated in Exhibit 6.3, there is a correlation between learning, knowledge, the discovery and new ideas, and innovation; and therein
lies the key.

No single innovation process or model is appropriate for all organizations. The selection and successful use of a model is problematic to the organization, its strategic
needs, and other factors such as the financial and operational performance of the company, market and industry expectations, and the relative competencies and capabilities
of the organization. Intel, for example, uses a variety of different types of innovation
models that are selected based on the need, the strategic importance of the idea, level
of complexity, personnel involved, and financial requirements. 3M uses a process that
allows for significant latitude and empowerment at the individual employee level with
respect to innovation, while forcing competition for funding as the idea matures in its
life cycle. Pharmaceutical companies such as Merck and Johnson & Johnson have to use
more formal prescriptive processes for the development of their drug products simply
due to the regulatory considerations involved, the threat of litigation, and the need to
be socially and ethically responsible.

The popular literature is full of innovation models and ideas. With names like the "Toll-way," "FasTrak Innovation," "Results Directed Innovation," "Rapid Product Development and Management Process (RDM)," and "Innovation Magic," it is easy to understand how any organization and its management can be enticed into thinking, sometimes falsely, that it is innovative by simply using a popular scheme. For example, one well-known company (Company A) spent several hundred thousand dollars with a prominent consulting firm to create its new product development methodology. The objective was to accelerate the cycle time to market for new products. They christened it the "Turnpike Method," which was an appropriate title since it included many stopping points for checks, internal audit reviews, financial calculations, sign-offs, approvals, more checks, and more reviews. At any one point, a project could be subjected to more reviews, internal challenges and defenses, and changes and justifications, all of which added time, increased effort, and contributed additional expense to the process. Yet, the new process was justified on the basis that it would accelerate innovation, reduce costs, and compress time to market. In reality, it was driven by the accounting department and focused on cost control rather than accelerating time to market or emphasizing the needs and voice of the customer. The result was a process model that had many different points of authority for initiating change but no single construct or point of responsibility for those changes. As concepts and products moved through the model, responsibility was constantly shifted, and with those shifts came new and often conflicting priorities and objectives. Everyone had responsibility for the project, but no one had authority or accountability. The company experienced many manufacturing change orders, missed budget estimates, and missed product-launch targets. More importantly, customers felt that the "new" products were behind those offered by the competition.

In contrast, the company's leading competitor (Company B) used a single "program manager" who was responsible for the entire product development life cycle. The development life cycle included all appropriate aspects of the company, so that the personnel at different levels had shared authority and responsibility for the success of the product. Accountability for the project was centered on one person. Implicit in their approach was listening to the "voice of the customer," which included the participation of selected customers in virtually all aspects of product design, market planning, manufacturing, and even product rollout and launching. While Company A entangled itself in a web of internal politics and work and product change orders, the competitor was using QFD (quality function deployment) techniques and DFM (design for manufacture) methods to ensure that its new products addressed the needs of the customers and were designed to best leverage the planned manufacturing and distribution competencies of the organization and its supplier partners. Company B was twice as fast and 60 percent less expensive at getting new product and manufacturing designs implemented and to market as Company A.

Mark B. Myers and Richard S. Rosenbloom in *Engines of Innovation* summarize the many different models for innovation into three basic types: (1) linear, (2) chain-linked, and (3) total process. It is useful to review these types because they help to explain, at a basic conceptual level, how innovation might work in an organization.

Linear Model
As the name implies, the linear model of innovation stresses sequential processes and activities. This form of model is generally used in "tollway" and "turnpike" meth-

ods that provide for the sequence and ordering of tasks, approval processes, and "proofs" of concept viability. The linear model of innovation has four phases:

1. Research
2. Development
3. Production
4. Market distribution and service

Notably, the above stages are similar to those of the traditional product-development life cycle model. For example, researchers Gary Lynn, Gerald Fryxell, and Robert Dooley present a five-stage model: (1) idea generation, (2) screening, (3) development, (4) testing, and (5) product launch. Some of the key qualities of the linear model include:

- Highly sequential activities and decision-making
- Tends to separate departments and people; by design limits interaction
- Tends to have many formal steps, approval points, and formal authorities
- In mature companies, this approach generally requires lower cultural and individual changes
- Asynchronous and formal communication flows
- Can be a protracted process with slower decisions
- Low to minimal collaboration
- Low to minimal external party involvement
- Subject to "restarts" and resequencing when information or planning parameters change
- Tends to attract structured individuals who like certainty

Due to the sequential nature of this model, its major disadvantage is that it results in a lengthy process, which ultimately can adversely affect the ability of a company to achieve first-mover advantages, sustained leadership, and accelerated concept to market performance. Typically, the linear approach requires the restarting and resequencing of activities when new knowledge or facts are introduced into the process. Another disadvantage of this approach is that it can limit the participation of the market (customers) in the early phases of the development process. However, the major deficiency of this model is that it tends to "compartmentalize" the innovation process into many different fragments and isolated pieces. This lack of integration compromises the overall innovation process and ultimately its effectiveness.

The linear model is a classic and traditional approach to innovation. It is simple to use and relatively easy to manage. One would expect to find this approach still in use by companies with less creative cultures and dynamic leaderships, in relatively stable and highly predictable industries, that experience low process innovation and stable product designs, and that have known competitors.

Chain-linked Model

The chain-linked model, according to researchers Stephen Kline and Nathan Rosenberg, provides a close approximation to what actually occurs in many organizations where "innovation is a complex and often disorderly process with varied and diverse outcomes." It is an interlinked network between research, knowledge, and formal phases or stages for innovation. The five phases that compose the chain-linked model include the following actions:

1. Perceive potential market
2. Invent or create
3. Detailed design and testing
4. Redesign and production
5. Market and distribution

The chain-link approach to innovation is more representative with respect to how products, processes, and management practices can best be developed. Some of the salient characteristics of this model include:

- Beginning and ending linkage to markets
- Potential significant cultural and individual behavior changes
- Continuous feedback loops
- A network to internal and external knowledge and research sources
- Moderate to high collaboration
- External parties
- Relatively dynamic and fast decision making
- Multiple communication flows
- Minimal restarts

The chain-link approach is appropriate for companies that need relatively dynamic and progressive innovation tactics and fast capabilities. This approach is inherently more favorable than the sequential model because it provides for higher levels of cross-functional integration and communications. Although it has many advantages over the linear process, it may still "compartmentalize" decisions which could inhibit speed and efficiency.

Total Process

This model of innovation is a natural extension and expanded version of the chain-linked approach. The salient feature of this approach is that it incorporates learning cycles or loops into its basic architecture. These learning loops are important to the overall process of innovating. However, to be effective they require the organization to have knowledge-management capabilities that capture and disseminate both explicit and tacit knowledge. The total process model integrates general knowledge, R&D, firm-specific knowledge, and technology. There are several qualities that differentiate the total process model from other forms of innovation. Specifically, it:

- Is highly dynamic and fluid
- Initiates and ends with linkages to specific markets and *constituents*
- Provides for iterative learning and discovery
- Integrates internal and external knowledge sources and knowledge management through organizational relationships and "communities of practice"
- Provides for the looping of unfiltered and spontaneous feedback and information throughout the organization
- Considers the impact of emergent technology on innovation
- Integrates the effect of incremental and discontinuous innovation into the overall innovation management process

- Encourages collaborative work efforts within and internal to the enterprise; allows for the outsourcing of part or all of innovation
- Mitigates restarts and resequencing
- Tends to attract highly creative and less-structured individuals

Total process innovation is most appropriate for those companies that must compete in highly dynamic and uncertain environments. The total process model requires organizations and people who are sophisticated in their approach to innovation, emphasize collaboration and cooperation, and have advanced knowledge-management techniques. This form of innovation can extend and augment the capabilities of the firm through linkages and formal "outsourcing" agreements with external service providers such as specialized design studios, craftspeople, and suppliers. Due to its highly networked design, the total process model for innovation can also embellish innovation and decrease the time to market for new products or decrease the time required for organizational change. The network design allows for closer cooperation among individuals, the development of common knowledge practices necessary for collaboration, tighter integration among initiatives and strategies, and greater leverage of formal processes with human performance and IT.

HINTS FOR MANAGING INNOVATION

Innovation can be stimulated and managed. The high performers:

- Establish clear goals and objectives for innovation. Define the context, construct rationale, and expected benefits for innovations.

- Apply broad definitions to the problem and issue at hand first then systematically refine it to specific focus on areas(s) and "problem sets." They break down complex issues and problems into manageable segments, explore multiple dimensions of the problem, and map the various relationships among problems. Identify and prioritize common themes and elements.

- Develop questions and issues relative to each problem. As a starting point, for each problem identified above, define the central theme of the question, and work around the question to develop ancillary questions that are related to the central theme by exploring the impact on people, processes, technologies, and strategies.

- Commonly use metaphoric techniques to develop questions and visualize issues.

- Use key words for association and to stimulate thought processes.

- Identify three generations of relationships, such as manufacturing plant, supplier, and customer. Try to think one generation ahead.

- Establish priorities of questions and issues based on any number of criteria, such as interdependencies between questions, occurrences, timing, known constraints/solutions, goals and objectives, etc.

- Develop assumptions for each question and issue. For each assumption develop a set of three to five characteristics or statements that describe or are integral to the assumption. Perform a pattern match for all the assumptions and identify common themes. Map common themes to the questions.

- *Think Differently.*

SUMMARY

"Today's great companies live and breathe creativity," notes researcher John Kao. Innovation is fundamentally important to the survival and competitive position of any company. The high-performance organizations place a premium on innovation and innovative people. They understand that innovation can come from anywhere and anyone, and they nurture cultures and environments that cultivate innovation. The high-performance companies also understand that innovation is absolutely essential to any business strategy because innovative breakthroughs can render a traditional industry strategy and any competitive strength completely impotent.

A company knows when it is closing in on a high-performance innovation when it has:

- Attracted and retained creative people.
- Established methods for identifying different types and sources of innovations.
- An energized workforce that practices innovation in their approach to everyday problem solving.
- Formal and informal methods in place to sponsor, manage, and measure sources and levels of innovation.
- Generates at least 25 to 30 percent, or more, of its growth and sales from new products introduced within the preceding 30 to 36 months.
- Leadership that constantly extols and challenges the organization to be innovative.
- Formal methods for measuring innovation and its potential impact and actual contribution.
- Extensive external collaborations in place to stimulate and cultivate innovation.
- Recognizes that creativity is the essence of innovation and rewards those who are creative.
- The methods and means to commercialize innovation and translate it into growth, revenues, and a distinct competitive advantage.
- The appropriate technologies and methods in place to facilitate innovation and innovative thought processes.
- Extensive knowledge sharing and development.

The high-performance companies understand that innovation occurs in everything they do. It exists in process, management, culture, customer relationships, and products. They stress this in their selection of personnel and encourage personnel to seek better ways to do things. For those individuals whose job is to be innovative, the high-performance companies do more than pay them; they recognize them and provide environments that are conducive to innovation. Finally, high-performance companies use collaboration to help innovation, and they work hard to disdain organizational arrogance, which may inhibit or distract from the innovation process.

Critical Thoughts and Discussion Questions

1. The management of established products and the successful development and launching of new products are challenges for many organizations. What are the key management and strategic issues related to managing new-product development while simultaneously optimizing the life cycle of existing products? In your discussion, consider the implications of new products on marketshare, customer loyalty, pricing policy, channels of distribution, and manufacturing resources.

2. How can innovation be accelerated to support high-performance and strategic renewal? In your discussion, consider methods such as concurrent engineering, rapid prototyping, the use of third parties, collaborators, and co-opetition.

3. To what extent does IT affect the dynamics and process of innovation?

4. Given the six strategic options companies face (from Chapter 2: innovation, imitation, substitution, withholding, collaboration, and complementing), how would you assess the value of innovation, its risks, potential for marketspace dominance, and competitive leadership relative to each of these choices? Is innovation itself a guarantee of sustained high performance? How does innovation need to be managed/leveraged for high performance?

5. What are the sources of innovation and creativity, and how can organizations ensure that these are present and continuously nourished in the company? (Consider, for example, recognition/reward structures; open, creative environment; encouragement; establishment of appropriate organizational norms; and attraction, selection, and nourishment of necessary talent, etc.)

6. Describe, in context, the terms *discontinuous* and *incremental* innovation. What is the distinction and, consequently, the strategic implications of each (i.e., which promises a more aggressive and sustainable source of competitive advantage and why)?

7. What are the typical impediments to innovative efforts? What actions can a company take to reduce and eliminate these impediments?

7

KNOWLEDGE:
THE ESSENCE OF
COMPETITIVE ADVANTAGE

"Our behavior is driven by a fundamental core belief: the desire, and the ability, of an organization to continuously learn from any source, anywhere—and to rapidly convert this learning into action—is its ultimate competitive advantage."
—JACK WELCH, CEO, GE

INTRODUCTION

"A failure to create knowledge and manage it as a critical organizational asset may account for the declining performance of many well-established firms," notes researcher Andrew Inkpen. This chapter discusses the third pillar of strategic renewal and high performance: *knowledge.* High-performance organizations recognize that knowledge is the source of great competitive advantage and differentiation for competing more successfully and, most notably, differently. Knowledge is also a source of strategic change and renewal. However, for many organizations, knowledge is a confusing subject. This chapter focuses on some important questions and considerations about knowledge and explores such issues as:

1. What and where are the sources of relevant knowledge necessary for competing differently and more successfully?
2. What is the relevant knowledge necessary for the organization to successfully create and sustain competitive advantage?
3. What is the definition of knowledge?
4. What is "knowledge management"?
5. What are the most effective strategies for knowledge and knowledge management?

These questions emerge as critically important, especially if we are to understand how to use knowledge as a strategic pillar for competitive advantage and continuous renewal.

THE STATE OF KNOWLEDGE

"We are not in the product business. We are in the knowledge business," notes Johnson & Johnson CEO Ralph Larsen. That is a significantly powerful statement that emphasizes the point: *High-performance organizations rely on knowledge and intelligence to drive their strategies, products, and operations.* Knowledge is generated, used, and assimilated by people. At this point in human and business evolution, knowledge is being generated and is disseminated at unprecedented rates of speed and is accessible to an ever-expanding literate population. Knowledge is also becoming *embedded* in processes that are being delivered through technology. The result is extraordinary human and technological leverage, more responsive organizational and process designs, and higher performance through knowledge.

"Those companies that develop an edge in both creating knowledge, but more importantly, applying knowledge, whether they have created it themselves or borrowed it from someone else, will, in fact, create significantly more value for their shareholders," commented Jay Stark of GM. High-performance organizations recognize that knowledge is not static and that there are many sources for it, many ways of learning and changing knowledge, and many different ways of interpreting knowledge. Thus, the knowledge management process in any global or large organization is an extraordinarily challenging and complex task. Because knowledge is dynamic and constantly evolving and advancing, what was relevant today may be and often is extraneous and outdated tomorrow. The constancy of this condition presents a threefold problem for organizations trying to manage knowledge as a source of competitive advantage: (1) how to define the parameters for knowledge, (2) how to identify what is relevant knowledge given various time horizons and operating scenarios, and (3) how to best manage knowledge for competitive advantage.

There are five strategic tenets related to knowledge:

1. Knowledge is the only truly unique asset that any organization has. Virtually everything else that it does or has, including its products, suppliers, prices, customers and processes, are replicable by a competitor. But its knowledge is wholly unique; therefore, it can be strategic.
2. Knowledge enables an organization to anticipate changes and compete in many different ways and in many different venues; therefore, it can be a catalyst and sustaining element of strategic change. Thus, knowledge is strategic because it supports social, commercial, and functional differentiation.
3. Products, processes, services, and performance are the result of knowledge. Knowledge is a source of competitive advantage because it is a determinant of the quality, functionality, and success of these components and outcomes in the marketplace.
4. Knowledge allows an organization to structure itself differently, develop its people, attract new people, and perpetuate and reinvent itself.
5. Effectively using and adapting knowledge to the strategic intentions of the organization is one of the most important competencies that an organization can develop and possess. Thus, learning and knowledge are inextricably linked. An organization cannot leverage knowledge for its strategic betterment unless it can learn how to use it and create it, and it does an organization little good to learn knowledge if it is not relevant to its immediate needs and longer-term strategic objectives.

Understanding how to use knowledge for competitive value and leveraging organizational intelligence is gaining commercial momentum and is attracting the attention of strategic planners. Knowledge is important to the strategic health and future of an organization in many ways. Specifically:

- An organization's ability to compete and to successfully renew itself is contingent on the collective knowledge, skills, and learning abilities of its employees; its organizational intelligence. These factors, either considered individually or as a group, are unique qualities that are difficult to replicate.
- Knowledge can transform the behavior and performance of an organization.
- Knowledge creates a cost/benefit relationship that has greater intrinsic value than what traditional measurement practices are able to capture and quantify.

According to *Fortune* magazine, "One organization trying to capture and leverage this softer, often tacit knowledge is Hughes Space and Communications, a division of Hughes Aircraft that has $1.2 billion in annual sales and is the world's leading maker of commercial communications satellites. Customization characterizes knowledge work—whether it's tax auditing, writing scripts for situation comedy, or designing satellites—and satellites are not only made to order but are also enormously complex, expensive and unforgiving. Consequently, says Arian Ward, leader of business engineering, it's very, very important to leverage what we learn so we can do the job better and faster next time." The challenge, according to Ward, is in "losing the recipe," or in not having the capability to package and transfer knowledge from one user to another. Too often, organizations create "islands of knowledge" that become difficult to access and use. The answer is to keep maps, not encyclopedias of knowledge, as in knowing which people have the recipes in their heads. You tap into these people, who can then get to talking about what they know in story rather than factual format."

There are many examples of companies competing on knowledge-based strategies. BP Amaco has an active and aggressive knowledge management strategy and process. As a result of BP Amaco's integrated approach to knowledge management, the company has reportedly generated $400 million in savings and/or incremental revenue. Another company that is making significant progress in its management of knowledge and its valuation is the European-based insurer Skandia, a global company with operations in the United Kingdom, United States, Mexico, and other countries. Skandia has made a deliberate effort to capture its knowledge in what it calls its "Organizational Capital." As noted by CEO and President Bjorn Wolrath in the supplement to Skandia's Annual Report, the process of identifying and collecting organizational capital ". . . creates the conditions for the rapid sharing of knowledge and sustained collective knowledge growth. Greater clarity, multiplicative competence and rapid learning lead to a steeper knowledge growth curve. Lead times between learning and knowledge are shortened systematically. The dynamic human value can be further leveraged by linking it into systematized organizational capital."

High-performance organizations understand that knowledge is essential to their competitive survival and ability to create extraordinary intrinsic and explicit value for their stakeholders and customers. In the United States, Dow Chemical is trying to systematize its knowledge and intellectual capital-management processes. In 1993, Dow created the position of director of intellectual asset management. According to Gordon Petrash, the former director of the function, "The idea was to turn a passive function—central record keeping for Dow's 29,000 in-force patents—into active management of the opportunities patents represent." As a result, Dow Chemical estimates that through its active management of knowledge and patents, it will increase its licensing royalties from $20 million in 1997 to $125 million in 2000. Amoco Company (acquired by BP in 1998) is another organization that has an active program of knowledge management. Amoco's Progress Group is chartered with developing and implementing knowledge management techniques that will help the company with cultural changes.

Despite its importance and growing management attention, many organizations continue to grapple with the concept of knowledge and its role in creating competitive value and sustaining high performance. Not surprisingly, they grasp, in a general sense, the big concept of knowledge but are at a loss as to what it means to compete with knowledge. More importantly, they lack the necessary comprehension and/or competencies to fully manage and leverage knowledge for strategic and competitive advantage. For all of our familiarity and understanding of knowledge, it remains an enigma and knowledge management an elusive process and practice.

Several recent studies have indicated the interest and emphasis on knowledge as a strategic and operational imperative. For example, a 1998 survey performed by the accounting and consulting firm KPMG found that over 85 percent of respondents believed that knowledge led to better decision making. Three-quarters indicated that knowledge was a factor in reducing costs. Surprisingly, less than 25 percent viewed knowledge as an important factor for increasing the equity price and value of their firms. That would seem to contradict other studies and senior management indications that knowledge is important to overall organizational performance. Following are the results of the KPMG survey:

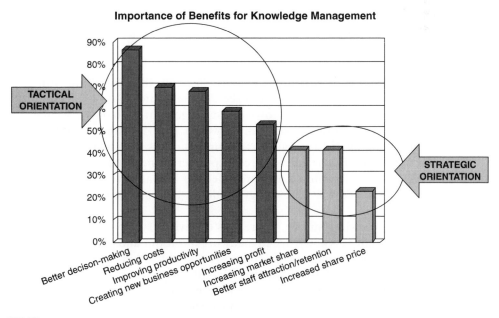

Source: KPMG

Interestingly, when asked to value what knowledge is most important, respondents to the KPMG study indicated that customer knowledge and market knowledge were of the highest value. Unfortunately, those subjects are very broad categories, and the specific attributes of customer and market knowledge were not elaborated upon with any significant detail.

Another, somewhat more extensive survey composed of 1,626 respondents was performed by Management Review and AMA Research in 1998. The AMA found that:

- 18 percent believed that their companies had an effective knowledge management process.
- 44 percent reported that their companies had no processes for managing knowledge.
- 78 percent reported that they had effective knowledge management programs designed to improve customer satisfaction.
- 60 percent reported that their companies had effective knowledge practices that improved employee satisfaction.
- 79 percent of 575 respondents indicated that they believed their companies were effective in creating databases and retrieval systems for knowledge.

An Arthur Andersen survey of 80 major companies concluded that:

- Although 74 percent of participants said that it was important or essential to identify knowledge gaps in their organizations and find ways to close them, only 12 percent rate themselves as good or excellent at doing so.
- Although 88 percent of participants said it was important or essential for the firm to encourage and facilitate sharing knowledge, only 47 percent rated themselves as good or excellent at it.
- Although 79 percent of participants said managing organizational knowledge should be important or essential to their business strategy, 59 percent said they were doing this poorly or not at all.
- 91 percent of participants said they have no way—or poor ways—to link knowledge management to financial results.

Another study of 870 companies performed by the consulting firm of Bain & Company and appearing in the *Wall Street Journal* found that only 27 percent of survey participants said they used knowledge management, with only 25 percent of those indicating that knowledge was substantially used. In a 1997 study of 431 U.S. firms, the accounting company of Ernst & Young found that less than 50 percent of executives believed that their organizations were adept at creating knowledge. Only 13 percent believed that their organizations were effective at transferring knowledge. Ninety-four percent believed that knowledge could be leveraged for better organizational performance.

The above notwithstanding, the results of several surveys and studies summarize the most likely state of knowledge in many organizations and provides insights into the status of knowledge management and knowledge utilization in many organizations today. At this point, it is relatively safe to conclude that although it is recognized as being important, knowledge management is in a formative state. For many organizations, the notion of "knowledge management" as a source of competitive advantage is still embryonic and unformed, and its management as a strategic asset unchartered.

DEFINING KNOWLEDGE: A HIGH-PERFORMANCE PERSPECTIVE

Not surprisingly, there are many competing and conflicting definitions for knowledge. Undoubtedly, the conflicts among these definitions are contributing to the confusion surrounding what knowledge is and how to use knowledge to create competitive advantage. The substance of these definitions tend to fall into one of three groups: (1) those that attempt to define what knowledge is; (2) those that seem to rely on delivery methods for knowledge; and (3) those that relate to individual and organizational learning. For example, a quick glance of the definitional landscape yields definitions such as: "Knowledge is data and information necessary for decision making," "Knowledge is enabled through IT and interconnectivity," "Knowledge is our most important asset," and "Knowledge is what a company or person learns." Finally, there is "Knowledge is what you know." Not a bad selection of definitions for entertaining or stimulating discussions, but they miss the mark badly as far as effective strategic definitions.

The definitions for *knowledge management* are even more interesting and confusing. For example, AMA Research and Management Review used the following definitions as multiple-choice selections in defining *knowledge management:*

- "Managing tangible intellectual capital, copyrights, patents, royalties, and licenses."
- "Gathering, organizing, and sharing the company's information and knowledge assets."
- "Creating work environments for sharing the company's information and knowledge assets."
- "Creating work environments for sharing and transferring knowledge among workers."
- "Leveraging knowledge from all stakeholders to build innovative corporate strategies."

Unfortunately, none of these definitions is entirely adequate because they have many deficiencies inherent in them. For example, one cannot define *knowledge* with the word *knowledge* in the definition. Using the word *innovative* implies that there is a uniform basis for evaluating what is and what is not innovative. Finally, the latter definition is restrictive because it limits itself to "corporate strategies."

In defining knowledge and its strategic implications, the distinctions between knowledge, data, and information must be delineated. As illustrated in Exhibit 7.1, there is a logical progression and iteration from (1) raw data to (2) formed data to (3) information to (4) knowledge to (5) applied relevant knowledge. Although each stage of this progression is clearly related to its successor and is interrelated, data by itself are not necessarily information, and information in the absence of referrential context is not knowledge. Data represent the "raw" facts. It is the first order of information and is also the most elemental form of information. Information represents the evolution of data into a logical and coherent presentation. Data are arranged so that they have particular substance and meaning, thus they become information. As researchers Tom Davenport and Larry Prusak note, information "gives shape to data." Knowledge is the final product of data and information. Knowledge has dimensions of relevancy, context, and insightfulness to it. It is the result of formal and informal learning, experience, institutionalization and ability, and incorporates tacit adaptation and extension. With the differences described, *knowledge* is defined as:

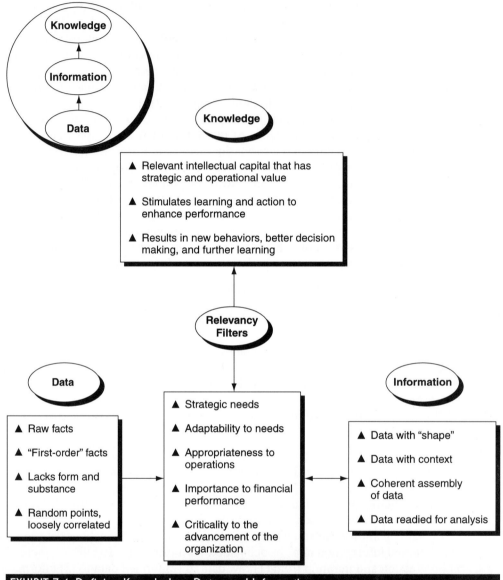

EXHIBIT 7.1 Defining Knowledge, Data, and Information

Any relevant intellectual capital, information, learning, and personal perspective that stimulates, contributes to, or results in greater understanding, deliberate action, new behaviors, better decision making, adaptation, and further learning.

Knowledge involves timing, an aspect of appropriateness, varying levels of comprehension, intelligence, various levels of adaptability, and further learning. From a strategic change and strategy formulation perspective, the most important consideration is that there must always be a dimension of *relevancy* to knowledge. That is, the knowledge developed, learned, and transferred must be meaningful to the individual and the organization as an institution and its strategic intentions. The knowledge must have clear alignment with the strategies and operational goals of the organization and the developmental and functional needs of the individual. It does little good to have extraordinary knowledge of American football if you are running a high-technology company or trying to compete in the soccer World Cup or the National Hockey League.

The relationship of relevancy to knowledge is not new, but it remains a unique and challenging concept. As Thomas Fuller noted in 1723, " 'Tis not knowing too much, but what is useful that makes a wise man." Thus, a key challenge for any organization is developing an understanding not only of what the role of knowledge is in the organization but also what knowledge is relevant today and, even more importantly, what will be relevant tomorrow. In trying to manage knowledge, many organizations have difficulty separating the relevant from the interesting and the absolutely required from the nice to have and from the superfluous. By defining *knowledge* as relevant intellectual capital, virtually all aspects of timing, value, need, and context are considered in an appropriate context. That appropriate context is usually linked and aligned with the strategic and operational needs of the organization.

The issue of intellectual capital offers another dimension of the definition: What is intellectual capital? University of Michigan Professor James Ulrich defines *intellectual capital* as "competency times commitment." That is interesting but far from a working definition for intellectual capital required for strategic renewal and high performance. *Intellectual capital,* at least in the high-performance sense, is any *relevant* data, knowledge, and wisdom that exhibit the following characteristics:

1. Has appropriate meaning for the enterprise.
2. Fulfills an immediate or long-term need or emerging need of the leader and the organization.
3. Contributes intrinsic and/or explicit financial and performance value to the organization.
4. Contributes to the advancement and perpetuation of the organization and to its ability to adapt to new and changing environments and stimuli through continuous learning.
5. Enables individuals and their organizations to leverage operations and interactions with stakeholders (employees, shareholders, and customers) through learning, better communications, more enlightened perspectives, and appropriate behaviors, actions, and decisions.

Central to the notion of knowledge management is the recognition that it is both individualized and institutionalized. The key for any organization is to acknowledge that there are specific sources, structures, and shapes for knowledge, which, in turn, affect its ability to be used by the organization to create and sustain high performance. In addition, there are formal aspects to knowledge as well as social dimensions that impact its usefulness, the ways it is created, managed, and shared, and how quickly it can be transferred and assimilated by the organization. The recognition of these factors brings us to an important aspect of knowledge and its components. Researchers Nonaka and Takeuchi (1995) conclude that the structure of knowledge has two distinct components: *tacit* and *explicit.* All organizations, individuals, and societies, regardless of sophistication, have a combination of both tacit and explicit knowledge, which they apply, adapt and advance every day. Specifically:

- Tacit knowledge is the information, experiences . . . the "knowledge" . . . that each of us as individual human beings learn, develop, and accumulate over our lifetimes. It can be acquired through formal training, but it is predominantly experientially oriented and learned through life's trials. Therefore, it almost always includes strong personal impressions, beliefs, biases, individual perspectives, and life's lessons and values. As such, this knowledge is generally unique and is difficult to extract.
- Explicit knowledge is the formal knowledge that is captured, codified, taught, and learned. This form of knowledge is the type that we learn in school, from others, or from company-sponsored training programs. Knowledge in this form is usually codified in many different ways, including books, curricula, training, software, multimedia, and readily available product offerings from manufacturers and retailers. Consequently, explicit knowledge is usually accessible.

The key to high performance is not necessarily the amount of explicit knowledge that an organization has. Of course, that is an important and essential consideration, and any organization that is trying to create or sustain high performance must have extensive explicit knowledge or it will find itself reinventing the obvious. Rather, it is the capture and transfer of the unique and relevant tacit knowledge and its ability to turn it into explicit knowledge that leads to the greatest levels of differentiation. For an institution trying to manage knowledge, tacit knowledge is the most difficult to capture, rationalize, and transfer.

Regardless of whether the organization is a business, a military unit, or a society, knowledge usually begins at the individual level and travels a journey involving many interactions and levels of personal interpretations. It passes through a multitude of personal, social, and collective organizational interpretations until finally it has become institutionalized at all the appropriate levels of the organization. However, unlike many organizations, once institutionalized, knowledge in the high performers does not stop its journey. Rather, it *continues* to develop and evolve at different rates and with different interpretations. Researchers Nonaka and Takeuchi envision the constant flow and exchange of knowledge as a "spiral" effect, which suggests that knowledge is discovered, validated, replicated, and embellished as it travels. This is an accurate description, but rather than a spiral, knowledge, as it travels through the organization, appears to be more of a cyclone, a funnel cloud in the form of a tornado. (See Exhibit 7.4). As knowledge travels through the organization, it is constantly being modified, gaining, or losing "power," changing directions, encountering barriers, and confronting challenges as well as identifying new knowledge sources and uses. As it is used and reused, its value moves in an exponential relationship to its use. The higher and more frequent its use, the more valuable the knowledge.

THE KNOWLEDGE ARCHITECTURE: THE BLUEPRINT FOR MANAGING KNOWLEDGE

Effective knowledge management and utilization requires an organization not only to develop a knowledge strategy but also an overarching *architecture* for its management, use, and renewal. The knowledge architecture is best described as an integrated plan and framework of how the organization arranges, manages, and uses knowledge for strategic advantage. The knowledge architecture must include a variety of components such as the definitions of *knowledge,* descriptions of the content of the knowledge, knowledge "maps" that direct users to the sources and custodians of knowledge and subject-matter experts, and guidelines for accessing, using, and updating the technologies that support the knowledge architecture. Four components are fundamental and must be included if the knowledge architecture is to be successful as a strategic pillar and source of renewal:

1. A strategy for the use of knowledge as a strategic asset and source of renewal.
2. A knowledge management process (KMP) that provides for the identification, extraction, and distribution of knowledge in the enterprise.
3. The proper relevancy filters used to identify, mine, and qualify knowledge for inclusion in the KMP and use in the organization.
4. Technology delivery and administrative standards for active and effective management of knowledge and access to knowledge assets.

Exhibit 7.2 provides a summary of the elements of the knowledge architecture. Let's address these in greater detail.

EXHIBIT 7.2 The Knowledge Architecture

Knowledge Architecture			
Knowledge Strategy	**Knowledge Filters**	**Knowledge Management Process**	**Knowledge Management Standards and Procedures**
▲ Deterministic	▲ Strategic	▲ Discovery/extraction	▲ Leadership
▲ Emergent	▲ Operational	▲ Development/codification	▲ Commitment
▲ Synergistic	▲ Financial	▲ Dissemination/accessibility	▲ Management
▲ Reservation	▲ Scenario	▲ Assimilation/embellishment	▲ Learning/adaptation
		▲ Application/learning	
		▲ Renewal/regeneration	

⟵ **Strategic Alignment** ⟶

▲ Cause-and-effect relationship

▲ Distinct value proposition

▲ Functional fit

▲ Relevancy to immediate and long-term goals

Knowledge Strategy

The development of a knowledge architecture is absolutely essential to the effective use and maintenance of knowledge as a strategic asset. A prerequisite in using knowledge as a strategic pillar of high performance requires the development of a strategy for knowledge. There are essentially four strategic options for knowledge:

1. Deterministic knowledge strategies.
2. Emergent knowledge strategies.
3. Synergistic knowledge strategies.
4. Reservation strategies.

Selecting and establishing a knowledge strategy is important because it influences how leaders design and implement the formal knowledge management practices in their organizations.

Deterministic

Deterministic strategies are formed around very specific and well-defined objectives and criteria. This approach generally has a shorter timeframe than that of emergent or synergistic approaches and, therefore, can have both predictability and a sense of urgency to it. Deterministic approaches typically involve such activities as data engineering, data mining, information engineering, measuring knowledge, and assessing various sources of new knowledge. Deterministic approaches also tend to stress the absolutes of knowledge as expressed by a definable cause-and-effect condition, trend analysis, and correlations among predefined variables. Although deterministic strategies can also be opportunistic, they may not lead to a *sustainable* competitive advantage. That is because they tend to be focused on the short term and are usually restricted by a narrowly defined set of relevancy filters. If the criteria are defective in form or definition or are incomplete, the knowledge management process and ultimately its use in the organization will be compromised.

Emergent

Extending on the work of Henry Mintzberg on general business strategy, emergent strategies of knowledge management are longer term in comparison to the deterministic approach and have far less predictability associated with them. Emergent strategies tend to rely on a variety of cultivation and development techniques that include experimentation, discovery, probing and learning, incubation, and scenario planning. Inherently, they are more evolutionary in form and use. In contrast to the deterministic approach, which uses well-defined and highly prescriptive relevancy filters, developing an effective knowledge management strategy based on emergent concepts requires the organization to develop a series of "loose relevancy filters" that are variable and adaptable. These filters function to screen and accept knowledge that satisfies predetermined and developing criteria. This knowledge can be used immediately or can be "incubated" for use at another time. Typically, the timing for using knowledge is linked to the longer-term strategies of the organization and alternative planning scenarios. Emergent strategies tend to better position the organization for sustained competitive advantage because they focus on the longer term and are better positioned to consider alternative scenarios.

Synergistic

Synergistic strategies represent a *combination* of both the deterministic and emergent frameworks. Synergistic approaches bridge multiple timeframes, usually involve both specific and variable filtering criteria, and use incubators of knowledge, which are linked to both the known long-term strategic needs of the organization as well as assumptions about emerging or possible needs. This approach to knowledge management works well in a variety of situations where long-term transformational strategies and challenges are involved. The synergistic approach to knowledge management best positions the organization for sustainable competitive advantage and growth.

Reservation

Using the reserved strategy approach for knowledge management is just as the term implies; the organization simply takes a "wait-and-see" posture. Typically, this strategy involves informal practices and/or ones that are associated with follower and late adapter approaches. In applying this strategy, organizations run the risk of signaling that knowledge is not a priority as a strategic initiative. Typically, there is little strategic advantage for an organization to select this course of action as a long-term strategic alternative, especially if it competes in a rapidly changing environment.

High-performance organizations use various combinations of these four options based on their strategies, financial resources, operating performance, and internal competencies to compete on knowledge but also place a greater emphasis on synergistic strategy formulation and implementation.

Knowledge Management Process

The second major component of the knowledge architecture involves the creation and implementation of a knowledge management process (KMP). The KMP "operationalizes" the knowledge strategy of an organization and is absolutely fundamental to the effective use of knowledge as a pillar of strategy and as a catalyst for strategic renewal and change. A key to understanding how knowledge is managed is to acknowledge that it is a continuous process, not an episodic or annual event. Thus, having a dynamic and adaptable KMP is critical to an effective knowledge management process.

In most organizations there is a significant debate about how to "best" manage knowledge as an asset. Some of the discussions center on such things as "knowledge audits" as the best approach; others advocate that computer software, data warehouses, and communication networks are knowledge management. However, neither approach will yield an effective KMP, at least in the sense and spirit of high-performance organizations. Similarly, technology and databases merely enable the accessibility and distribution of the knowledge, but by themselves they are not knowledge assets.

A quick review of those organizations that have some semblance of effective knowledge management practices indicates that knowledge usually falls into one of several classifications of repositories: third-party external, internal formal, and external public. These are supported by sophisticated databases, data extraction and mining techniques, and extensive networks and IT capabilities. But, as discussed, they are not knowledge processes or strategies. In fact, it is questionable whether they are really knowledge assets.

The reality is that managing knowledge and creating knowledge are two very different things. Managing knowledge requires an integrated system that is designed to excavate and institutionalize the appropriate aspects of knowledge for the organization. Implicit in the management of knowledge is the alignment of knowledge with the strategies and challenges confronting the organization. This alignment is best measured using a combination of criteria, including:

- Cause and effect of the knowledge with respect to the operational excellence and agility of the organization.
- Value proposition as defined by the economic and strategic potential of the knowledge for both the organization and individual.
- Functional fit between the knowledge and the immediate and anticipated needs of the organization and individual.
- Relevancy of the knowledge to the immediate and long-term needs of the organization.

Creating the appropriate relevant knowledge requires that the organization have a clear understanding of what the core knowledge requirements are or will be and possess a means and method for finding or developing that knowledge and its sources and converting it into something that has institutional meaning and accessibility. Such processes require a synergistic approach to KMP. This approach effectively spans the certainty of the deterministic approach and the evolving/developing aspects of emergent needs.

As illustrated in Exhibit 7.3, the KMP is composed of five stages:

1. Discovery/extraction
2. Development/codification
3. Dissemination/accessibility
4. Assimilation/embellishment
5. Renewal/regeneration

EXHIBIT 7.3 The Knowledge-Management Process Model

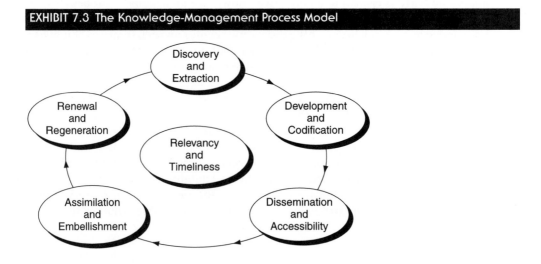

In form and application, the KMP is a circular looping of processes, composed of knowledge creation, discovery, codification and adaptation of knowledge, knowledge sources, and uses, learning, and extension. It stresses the updating and interrogation (review, questioning, analyzing) of knowledge that involves a number of key activities, which follow.

Discovery/Extraction

All organizations have abundant quantities of knowledge and knowledge sources. The issue centers on the quality and relevancy of the knowledge. Much of the newer knowledge is tacit and vested in the personal experiences of the people in the organizations. A significant percentage of knowledge is embedded in institutional practices and memorialized in things like standard operating procedures and in the massive collections of data and databases that are maintained by IT groups. So, having knowledge has never been a problem for any organization. The real challenge has and will continue to center on whether the knowledge is *relevant* and *appropriate* for the organization. Because the delivery and access of the knowledge are relatively easy through IT, *relevancy* of knowledge to the strategic needs of the organization is the central management issue that must be addressed.

Discovery and extraction is the process of finding, screening, selecting, and extracting or specifically identifying appropriate and relevant data and knowledge that meet or support the strategic intentions of the organization and the functional needs of the individual. The discovery process can be enabled through formal programs, outsourcing relationships, alliances, trial and error, "dumb luck," and very formal and deliberate development processes. The key in discovering and extracting knowledge is to develop and use the appropriate knowledge filters to determine the relevancy of knowledge, so that only the most relevant, appropriate, and meaningful knowledge is extracted.

High-performance organizations employ both formal and informal discovery and extraction techniques that constantly comb the organization and its environment in search of new and relevant knowledge. These techniques include structured knowledge exchange sessions, periodic baselining and benchmarking, 360-degree feedback sessions, the formalization of projects, knowledge mapping, and, most importantly, the active rotation and/or exchange of key personnel among areas and the interpretation of successful business processes. High-performance organizations understand that knowledge extraction is facilitated through the use of formal methods such as specific fact-finding criteria, technologies, critical questions, and human interaction.

The ability to transfer appropriate and relevant tacit knowledge into explicit knowledge represents the greatest competitive value for any organization. This form of knowledge is a truly unique asset and a significant source of competitive advantage for any organization. For example, during World War II, returning B-17 crews were extensively debriefed about their mission. It must have been very difficult for those young men to return to their bases in England and replay the drama of life and death again and again. But the interviews were necessary for capturing and institutionalizing knowledge. The debriefing sessions focused on the battle tactics and air defense systems of the German fighters. The information obtained was analyzed for common trends and any innovations and institutionalized for use by the B-17 crews on subsequent missions. Based on that information, the air wings and squadrons adjusted their formations and set their defensive strategies for the next mission. It was a continuous process of knowledge updating and transferring and learning using very specific and formal knowledge identification, extraction, and "mining" methods.

This *knowledge mining process* uses a number of techniques such as on-site visitations, knowledge agents, formal debriefings, structured write-ups, lessons learned in debriefing sessions, and very specific knowledge filters that are aligned with the strategic objectives of the organization to find and extract the appropriate knowledge. The process also involves decomposing and analyzing results of major initiatives to identify the relevant knowledge about the key components, structure, content, or form of a process, design, idea, or operation. Critical to the success of the extraction process is the convergence and calibration of tacit and explicit knowledge to the known and anticipated specifications and experiences of the organization. The results of the extraction are used to convert the tacit to the explicit for institutional use.

The effective discovery and extraction of knowledge requires that the appropriate filters for knowledge be developed and applied. Essentially there are three families or categories of filters: strategic, operational, and situational. Some of the key filters that can be found in these categories include:

1. Relevancy of the knowledge to the *strategic direction* and competency needs of the organization.
2. Adaptability of the knowledge to the strategic, operational, and situational needs of the organization.
3. Freshness (newness) of the knowledge as applied to a subject area and needs of the organization.
4. Relevancy of the knowledge to the *operational* needs, aspects, culture, strategies, and/or competitive position of the organization.
5. Importance of the knowledge to the financial performance and objectives of the organization.
6. The long-term strategic and economic relevancy of the knowledge to the advancement and perpetuation of the organization and its values and competencies, and to the individuals within the organization and its internal and external stakeholders.
7. Cause and effect of using the knowledge related to an operation, situation, or the strategy of the organization.
8. Adaptability and relevancy of the knowledge to a specific issue, tactical situation, or special situation of the organization.
9. Credibility of the source of the knowledge.

Without the appropriate filters, knowledge has no defining boundaries and no meaningful domain for the organization. In the absence of any boundaries and domain, knowledge cannot be managed or leveraged by the organization for strategic or competitive advantage. The filters are key to identifying the knowledge that will be institutionalized and carried forward through the learning and dissemination processes. This knowledge is resident in the company's employees, customers, business partners, culture, operational processes, or major products or deliverables. The multiplicity of sources complicates the identification of knowledge because it occurs in so many different forms, iterations, and locations. High-performance organizations recognize this and sensitize their followers and constituents to be on the lookout for new relevant knowledge. Thus, the extraction process must be highly efficient because protracted efforts reduce the utility of the knowledge as time marches on. Any organization involved in the process of finding and institutionalizing knowledge must have the appropriate filters and procedures in place to accelerate the mining process and ensure that the proper knowledge is extracted for institutionalization.

Development/Codification

Development and codification of knowledge involves arranging and organizing both tacit and explicit knowledge into a formal explicit format that is codified into some form for organizational use. Once knowledge is codified, it can be "packaged" into various formats for delivery and use throughout the organization. Intrinsic to the success of this aspect of the KMP is the unconditional requirement that knowledge be formatted in a manner that lends itself to use and further learning.

It is important to realize and keep in mind that discovery and codification do not necessarily mean that the knowledge has to be fully developed into some encyclopedic form. Such efforts are usually outdated before they can be fully completed. Rather, knowledge maps that point the way to primary, secondary, and external knowledge sources can be created. The maps can describe the content, clarify it, and provide guidance as to its best utilization. Knowledge maps illustrate where knowledge is generated, where it resides, and who is responsible for its quality and content accuracy. The use of maps can significantly increase collaboration in an organization, accelerate knowledge exchange and learning, and reduce the tendency to produce redundant knowledge.

To embellish and extend knowledge, high-performance organizations typically employ formal intelligence-gathering methods to develop knowledge about their external environments and competitors. These "Corporate Intelligence" units have several objectives, including developing insights and intelligence about the competition, processes, and customers. According to a *Business Week* report, the number of large companies with intelligence capabilities has tripled since 1988 based on estimates of David Harkeroad of the Futures Group, Inc. Companies such as Xerox, Kodak, Monsanto, and Johnson & Johnson have formal organizational units and efforts dedicated to the collection of competitive and consumer intelligence. These types of capabilities should allow their organizations to better understand competitor initiatives and to concentrate on the overall competitive landscape. Yet, given the competitive posture of both Kodak and Xerox, one must challenge their ability to effectively convert such intelligence into competitive advantage. In addition to internal programs, there are a number of external organizations that specialize in competitor intelligence services. One organization is the Society of Competitive Intelligence Professionals, which has 6,000 members located in 44 countries. Another example is CorpTech, which reportedly has information on some 170,000 executives. These external organizations provide supplementary and new perspective for leaders relative to their competition, personnel, and operating environments.

Codification is an important aspect of knowledge management. Codification places the knowledge in a rationalized format that is accessible to the organization. This accessibility is desirable from the perspective that it facilitates use and institutionalization, but its use is only as effective as the person's own knowledge and learning capabilities and it is subject to broad and variable interpretation. Therefore, not all knowledge can or should be codified. Certain types of knowledge, such as how to implement software products, design a human resource system, or implement a new chart of accounts for an accounting system, and describing the dynamics and tendencies of an industry, provide examples of knowledge that can be easily codified. These types of "knowledge events" can be easily codified because they can be captured and described. In the case of software, such as ERP solutions, the knowledge is prescriptive, predictable, and reuseable, and certain routines and things are done over and over again, irrespective of industry and type of business. In general, this form of institutional codification requires significant investment in IT and in the development of knowledge management and administrative practices.

In contrast, some approaches to codification rely on less formal methods. These "adaptive" approaches typically involve the creation of extensive personal networks that require humans to seek out one another for subject-matter expertise and direct personal experience and perspective. This type of codification is effective in transferring tacit as well as explicit knowledge in sophisticated areas such as new-product development, strategy formulation, and organizational change. These types of subjects are less formal and prescriptive in form and approach and demand critical thinking and evaluation. The significant deterrent to this approach is that it can fail to consistently capture knowledge and is susceptible to human emotions, lack of an appropriate network, and individual bias. There are no formal filters or institutional checks and balances to ensure that the proper knowledge is extracted and used. Typically, this form of knowledge codification is difficult to maintain and update and is less reliant on IT. As such, it is less efficient in transferring knowledge and making knowledge available to a large constituency.

Dissemination/Accessibility

The third stage of the KMP process involves the dissemination and distribution of knowledge in the organization. Assuming that the content of the knowledge is appropriate and suitable, it must be accessible on an as-needed and just-in-time basis. There are many different ways of enabling the dissemination and accessibility of knowledge. For example, accessibility is enabled through formal training and knowledge-transfer programs, mentoring, career pathing and developmental methods and, of course, IT. The key issue to be recognized by organizations is that there is no single "best" way of disseminating knowledge. High-performance organizations employ a number of different ways to distribute and share knowledge in their organizations to ensure that it is available to the widest possible group.

One way of ensuring that knowledge is extracted, disseminated, and accessible is to directly involve those who are responsible for creating and using it . . . employees. One of the more highly regarded "best practices" for knowledge leadership can be found at GE. Recognizing that it is the combination of explicit and tacit knowledge that serves as the nucleus for great performance, GE implemented what is known as the "Work-Out program." The foundation of this program is a series of "town meetings" attended by employees who suggest ideas for process improvements and changes in the design of a process. Rather than assuming the traditional bureaucratic process of an endless stream of reviews at the "head office," GE's approach is for managers to either approve or reject the suggestions and ideas "on the spot." This real-time process enables GE to discover ideas and mine knowledge from its ultimate source: those who possess it. It also demonstrates a commitment to employee involvement and works to build trust and communication among stakeholders. As CEO Jack Welch notes in "Brain Power," an article by Thomas Stewart that appeared in *Fortune* magazine, "The only ideas that count are the A ones. There is no second place. That means we have to get everybody in the organization involved. If you do that right, the best ideas will rise to the top."

Most organizations rely on IT to enable knowledge management in their operating environments. In the process, they often confuse knowledge management with managing the IT function. In knowledge, we are not simply considering training programs or the implementation of technology-based products such as Lotus Notes, the development of data warehouses, connecting to the Internet, Intranet, or Extranet, or some other groupware and enterprisewide applications as knowledge management. Most of this investment has been made in the IT necessary to support an effective knowledge management practice and not necessarily in the quality of the content of the "knowledge" captured.

For much of knowledge, investment is measured in IT expenditures. For example, Eric Woods, an analyst with Ovum Inc., estimates that expenditures for knowledge management software will triple from $285 million in 1998 to $1.6 billion by 2002 and $5 billion when services are considered. Similarly, Nextra Enterprises in *Knowledge Management Technologies: Perspectives on Recent Trends and Impacts,* indicates that:

- 55 percent of survey participants indicated that their companies are spending money on Intranets.
- 45 percent indicate expenditures for document management.
- 40 percent indicate investment in data warehouses.

The creation of "virtual" organizational capabilities as well as Intranets and Extranets are necessary infrastructure components of knowledge management, but by themselves are not KMPs.

The vast data warehouses and databases that so many companies proudly refer to or vendors offer as knowledge assets with names such as "best-practice knowledge repositories" do not satisfy the working definition of knowledge and generally fall far short of effective knowledge management processes, at least from the high-performance perspective. One of the problems with "best-practice" databases is that no definition or criteria has been proven to identify and designate a process or practice as "best". Consequently, lots of knowledge may, in fact, not be related to a best practice. Commonly, many organizations point to massive data warehouses as bastions of their knowledge. Notwithstanding the reality of these rather impressive collections of *data,* they do not represent knowledge. For many organizations, the huge data warehouses that they created are only different representations of the shelves and filing cabinets that once filled the floors of libraries and lined office walls. Granted, the data may and hopefully are more accessible and better organized, but in isolation the data and its supporting IT are not knowledge. Although technology-based products may provide the "skeletal structure" and a delivery construct for knowledge, they are not knowledge.

Assimilation/Embellishment

The assimilation and embellishment of knowledge occurs when individuals and the organization access knowledge, learn how to use it, apply the knowledge to what they are doing, and then, *extend* and embellish the knowledge based on their own experiences and circumstances. The extension of knowledge is demonstrated by its embellishment and further advancement. This embellishment (or advancement) is usually the result of a combination of personal learning, tacit application, the accomplishments achieved, and personal perspectives. The assimilation of knowledge, and ultimately its embellishment, can be facilitated through the use of knowledge maps as well as formal knowledge repositories.

Renewal/Regeneration

Finally, as knowledge is assimilated and embellished, it travels through a process that allows it to be proven relevant or obsolete. Simultaneously, it can be newly developed, replenished, renovated, and/or discovered. One of the key challenges is to understand the longevity of knowledge and recognize, or better yet, anticipate the point in time when it becomes obsolete.

MEASURING AND VALUING KNOWLEDGE

Measuring knowledge has been a keen subject of academicians and business people for many years. Much research effort has gone into measuring knowledge and how much knowledge a person has acquired. For most organizations, one of the most difficult and perplexing aspects of knowledge management is whether it can or should be measured. The question of whether the value and impact of knowledge can be quantified with any degree of precision and confidence is one of contention in many organizations. Some organizations, such as Scandia, have developed elaborate and somewhat exhaustive measurements for knowledge. Other organizations do not attempt to measure knowledge at all or use only a limited number of measurements. Measuring knowledge is difficult because knowledge itself is so intangible, almost impossible to quantify, and highly dynamic . . . it is always changing. Many valuation attempts center on the financial value of knowledge. These types of measurements often attempt to reduce the value of knowledge into traditional financial returns, using accounting measurements such as ROI or IRR. In reality, the value of knowledge is not so much a function of financial return; rather, its value is better measured by what it contributes to the overall strategic position, decision making, and performance of the organization and how and how often it is used. There is a multitude of processes that profess to measure and value knowledge. Some of the more common approaches include:

- Complexity theory
- Balanced Scorecard (variations)
- Calculated intangible value
- Indirect intangible valuation approach
- Knowledge bank calculation
- Skandia variable approach

Briefly, complexity theory has been used to describe, mathematically, the relationship of knowledge to a process and the effort required to learn the process and use the knowledge in performing the process. The approach is predicated on many assumptions including the use of equivalent unit costs, which by their very nature call to question its appropriateness. For example, it is difficult to intellectualize the economic value and relationship between learning how to do brain surgery and changing a bedpan. The units of measurement may be mathematically proven, but how a person learns and adapts the knowledge to a given situation cannot be fully described with high levels of confidence. The use of this approach, or any approach that places an emphasis on the "unit cost" of learning or knowledge, is dangerous for two reasons. First, it assumes that the units of learning and knowledge are defined correctly and are rationalized across all companies and organizations. Secondly, it assumes that organizations use all of the knowledge available to them to perform a process and/or compete in the marketplace, which is a highly unlikely situation. Still, such approaches are useful exercises because they require documentation and discipline.

The Balanced Scorecard has been popularized in the academic and business press as a means of evaluating all sorts of performance and contribution. Typically, the Scorecard includes four measurements: Financial, Customer, Knowledge, and Infrastructure. The deficiency with this approach is that one can get mired in the details and it can create a false sense of accuracy that is based on the subjective reasoning of others.

In contrast, the calculated intangible value approach attempts to quantify the firm's intangible assets. This approach is highly subjective and requires experienced judgment and business acumen to use. Implicit in its use is the assumption that the "market" recognizes the value of the assets as reflected in the overall market value of the firm. However, that is not often the case, especially when the share price of the company's common equity has a high beta and is subject to broad variations in market valuations.

The indirect intangible method holds that the intangible value of an organization's assets is equal to the market value of the firm less its working capital less its physical assets. Again, this approach makes some broad assumptions that the market recognizes the value of a firm in its capitalization, but it neglects to consider the impact of market fluctuations, timing, and the emotional effect of "irrational exuberance" on market capitalization values. Therefore, it is suspect as a valuation method.

Another approach that attempts to reconcile traditional accounting concepts to knowledge is the knowledge bank calculation. This method reformats the income statement of an organization by "moving" nonphysical plant capital expenditures to its own category as a capital item. The problem with this approach is that the items moved may not be related to knowledge.

Finally, Skandia, a company much-heralded for its use of knowledge management practices, uses an approach that attempts to link knowledge to strategy with a complex formula that includes human, structural, and financial criteria. The structural component is further delineated by customer focus, process focus, and renewal and development. The Skandia approach is cutting edge but difficult to manage and use because there are over 100 different indicators and variables that influence the value of knowledge.

It should be apparent that no single method can completely and accurately depict the near and long term quantifiable and intrinsic value of knowledge. Rather, when one values or attempts to value knowledge, a multifactoral approach should be used. This approach should reflect and be aligned with the value propositions presented by the pillars of strategy and strategic renewal: innovation, leadership, operational excellence and agility, and IT, and the various time horizons and operating scenarios that are relevant for the organization. Approaching the valuation of knowledge from this perspective allows an organization to qualitatively determine the value of knowledge and, if appropriate, use alternative methods to estimate its potential monetary value. For example, one method may be to assess the near-and long-term strategic value of knowledge and learning using four "life cycle" categories:

1. *Develop.* This valuation suggests that the knowledge be aggressively developed for either the near or long term. Typically, the knowledge will have a potential high value proposition and well-defined linkages to innovation, leadership, operational excellence, and/or IT.

2. *Incubate.* Knowledge that is valued for incubation purposes is usually knowledge that has been developed or is under development and that may have high value at some future time or under certain circumstances.

3. *Archive.* Typically this form of valuation indicates that the knowledge may or may not have some future use and value. Its value to the organization, for both the near and long term, is ambiguous, but there may be the potential for some future use and value.

4. *Discard.* Valuing knowledge on this basis may imply several things. First, the knowledge may not be good, may not be accurate, or may be incomplete. Second, it could mean that the knowledge simply is not relevant to the company and anything that it does. Third, it may signal that the knowledge is marketable and is sold by the company for its commercial value.

The consideration of whether knowledge can and should be measured brings us to two more important conclusions: (1) Like a language, the "value" of knowledge grows exponentially as its use increases; and (2) the need and importance of trying to measure knowledge diminishes the more rudely the knowledge is used. For our purposes, we define *value* to include such aspects as strategic, developmental, financial, and overall performance of the organization. There are situations where knowledge is absolutely essential to the performance of the organization but cannot necessarily be reduced to, or fully captured in terms of, financial measurement.

If knowledge is used, advances performance, and is reused then, implicitly, its value is high. For example, in organizations that place premiums on measuring the return on knowledge as a prerequisite for managing knowledge, the value of knowledge is stressed early in the decision-making process. It is, in fact, a deterministic criterion for selecting knowledge for "management and dissemination." Other organizations place the emphasis on the impact of knowledge and how knowledge improves the overall performance of the organization. The emphasis is more emergent and synergistic. As Jay Stark, director of Knowledge and Process Integration for GM, commented, "We believe that the value of knowledge is in its use . . . that knowledge is actually an asset that appreciates in proportion to its use." Thus, in many instances, attempts to measure knowledge as a prerequisite for knowledge management can be a futile and misdirected effort. Exhibit 7.4 illustrates the use of knowledge relative to its value.

Knowledge Administration

Providing for the effective administration and management of knowledge is a challenge for even the high-performing organizations. With multiple factions competing for dominion over knowledge, it is not unusual for many different functions of the organization to lay claim to knowledge management as part of their charter. In virtually every major organization, knowledge management is claimed by such diverse disciplines and competencies such as human resources, IT, training and development, and individual executives and employees. The existence of multiple factions all laying claim to knowledge complicates the leader's ability to effectively manage and, more importantly, leverage knowledge for competitive advantage.

The institutionalizing and administering of the knowledge created at the individual and collaborative group levels for use throughout the organization is one of the significant challenges for most organizations in managing knowledge. Many high performers

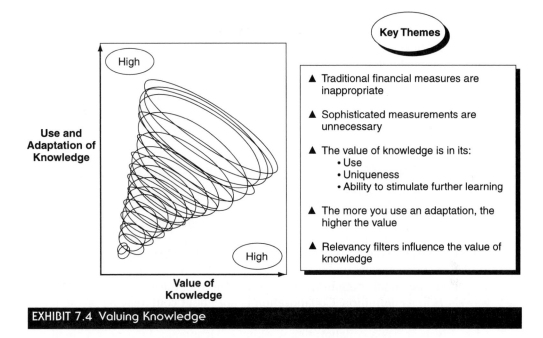

Key Themes

High

Use and
Adaptation of
Knowledge

High

Value of
Knowledge

▲ Traditional financial measures are
inappropriate

▲ Sophisticated measurements are
unnecessary

▲ The value of knowledge is in its:
  • Use
  • Uniqueness
  • Ability to stimulate further learning

▲ The more you use an adaptation, the
higher the value

▲ Relevancy filters influence the value of
knowledge

EXHIBIT 7.4 Valuing Knowledge

approach this process through the use of formal organizational structures and management positions such as that of the chief knowledge officer (CKO). The CKO has the responsibility for identifying, mining, rationalizing, and disseminating the knowledge, which are essential for organizational performance and perpetuation. The CKO is responsible for identifying and leveraging the intellectual assets of the organization that enhance productivity, collaboration, and networking. It is important to draw the distinction between the role of the CKO and that of the chief learning officer (CLO). In contrast, the role of the CLO is oriented towards individual training programs that are designed to deepen competencies or modify behavior.

Some organizations center the administration and management of knowledge on the CIO. The CIO is typically responsible for such activities as creating technology strategy, deploying technology, and delivering technology solutions to the organization. From the perspective of developing knowledge as a high-performance characteristic, this may be an unfortunate choice. The roles of the CKO and CIO could not be more different. Although one might argue that the CIO is in a good position to be the CKO because the "data is there," the two roles require very different personalities, competencies, and analytical skills. The CKO is responsible for what the organization considers to be knowledge, how the company and its employees learn, and how the company manages its knowledge capital. Ron Miskie, the founder and chairman of the Knowledge Transfer International, Inc., describes the role of the CKO as "One who sets strategic policy for an organization's acquisition and distribution of knowledge and learning, based on the premise that increasing the person(s) capacity to take action will enable them to respond more effectively and efficiently to their customers. Of all executives, the CKO can have the greatest impact on the productivity and motivation of people in an organization." In contrast, Miskie notes that "CIOs are still technology driven."

Setting titles aside, the key concepts and practices shared among high-performance organizations are their use of formal methods and structures to generate, filter, and disseminate knowledge throughout the organization. They have dedicated organizational competencies designed to ensure the effective management of knowledge. They also have formal methods in place to ensure learning. Finally, they recognize that knowledge and *continuous* learning are required for continuous renewal and the constant regeneration of growth.

COLLABORATION: THE CORNERSTONE OF HIGH-PERFORMANCE KNOWLEDGE MANAGEMENT

Collaboration, partnerships, and alliances are frequently cited concepts that have drawn attraction in management today. In a magazine advertisement a few years ago, GTE Corporation defined *collaboration* as "Sometimes termed dataconferencing, document conferencing, or applications sharing. [It] allows people to share information stored on a personal computer, server, or the Internet during a conference." GTE falls way short in its definition. Collaboration is not about conferencing or the technology used. Just because a company invests in the technology does not mean that it is knowledge driven or has a collaborative working environment. IT is only a small part of a much larger and complex human and social interaction process.

It does not matter what technologies an organization uses to support its collaborative efforts because collaboration is behavioral. It is a human and social process, not a technology-dependent event. The technology does not make collaboration possible; technology only makes it easier. For example, the members of the Manhattan Project did not have the benefit of the extraordinary advances of today's computing power, instantaneous access to data, or communications networks that are now commonplace on most desktops and in many homes. Yet, driven by passion, purpose, and vision, the team still collaborated to create the atomic bomb. Alternatively, consider the Disney animation teams of the 1930s and 1940s or the Boeing engineers who designed the great bombers of World War II and airliners of the 1950s and early 1960s. Neither of these groups had "dataconferencing," at least not in the way GTE advertises and pitches it, or Lotus Notes, Intranets, or Extranets. Despite the lack of technology, those organizations were enormously successful in their efforts to collaborate. The point is that technology can only support collaboration, but it does not make collaboration happen or guarantee its success.

In the context of high performance, *collaboration* is:

> A process in which a group of motivated and talented people come together for a specific purpose to produce results through individual and collective learning, knowledge sharing and solving.

Collaboration involves bringing individuals and teams together from all sorts of different sources into interactive learning and knowledge-sharing environments to attack complex problems and produce exciting results. The high-performers understand that collaboration is about discovering, sharing, and creating knowledge, and that occasional failure is inevitable and a necessary part of the process.

Bob Guns, the author of *Faster Learning Organizations,* notes, "High-performance leadership requires that organizations learn faster and better than the competition." The key challenge for any organization then is knowing what knowledge to capture, learning how to rationalize it for institutional use, how to disseminate it, and, most importantly, learning how to use and advance it. Thus, understanding the sources of knowledge is critical. There are two sources of knowledge: internal and external. Internally generated knowledge is created through the organization's own efforts (employees, contractors, consultants). External knowledge comes from sources outside of the organization, including alliance partners, customers, formal and informal education, governments, suppliers, and competitors. Understanding the source of knowledge is important because it establishes credibility and context. In general, the more credible and reputable the source of knowledge, the more significance it has in the organization. Secondly, the more referencable the knowledge and the more it can be confirmed and cited the more credible it is. One of the most effective means of knowledge creation is through a combination of internal idea generation and experiences, the importing of good ideas from across cultures, geographies, and industries, and the creative adaptation of the knowledge to a given business situation. In a sense, this is collaboration among a wide collection of different people with varied backgrounds and characteristics.

High-performance organizations understand that collaboration is a coming together of talented people, who often have *divergent* and sometimes conflicting academic and personal backgrounds, different life perspectives, and strong personalities, to attack a problem or a project. Under this concept of teamwork and collective problem solving, the most productive and dynamic teams are those that are populated with highly diverse individuals who have open minds, a passion for learning, and a profound appreciation for unlimited accomplishment possibilities. Although their team members have different perspectives, different academic skills, different life experiences, and different temperaments, they are driven by the same passions, personal commitments, the common belief in what they are doing, and a sense of trust in their fellow team member.

As a case in point, let's consider the Nissan Design International (NDI) studio in La Jolla, California. Founded and led by Jerry Hirshberg, NDI is responsible for automobiles such as the Infinity, Pathfinder, the extremely successful Xterra, and some 4 million cars on U.S. roads today. NDI goes about the process of design and collaboration by "pairing opposites"; that is, NDI seeks to hire and cultivate people in divergent pairs. It hires people who have dissimilar but complimentary skill sets and who possess quite different points of view and life experiences. NDI President Jerry Hirshberg says that the different points of view create better products. He noted, "I believe in creative abrasion. And I mean abrasion. We have titans in the field going at each other. That friction can produce wonderful results." Members of these teams have absolute confidence and belief in what they are doing and why they are doing it. They are committed, energized, and engaged. They are not afraid of failing; they understand that setbacks are inevitable but that they also present great opportunities for discovery and learning. Hirshberg adds, "You have to have a pretty secure sense of self when a person working on the same project has an entirely different set of priorities. The folks we're hiring share almost nothing, except a deep belief in their own way and passion. This place is not for the weak-kneed."

Collaboration extends beyond the borders of the organization to business partners, suppliers, and external thought leaders. A significant amount of external collaboration is found in the research and development of new drugs, computer software, computer and communications hardware, and consumer products such as cars and airplanes. Andersen Consulting, one of the world's largest professional services firms, has used external thought leaders and subject matter experts, including Warren Bennis, Tom Davenport, Charles Handy, and this author, to help them think through issues or inject a new and unique perspective into their strategies and client-service offerings.

Recognizing that labor represents a source of knowledge, the AFL-CIO has established a "corporate university" named the National Labor College (NLC) in the George Meany Center. The NLC offers tailored curricula to union members designed to improve their effectiveness, not only as representatives and members of organized labor but also as contributors to an organization. A unique example of collaboration and its possible impact on the competitive abilities of an organization is developing between organized labor and the employing organizations. The AFL-CIO also has a program called Center for Workplace Democracy. This program is designed to help union members to improve their collaborative and problem-solving skills by developing a greater knowledge and sensitivity to the management decision-making process and the issues managers confront. In this manner, according to Linda Chevez-Thompson, executive vice president, "The AFL-CIO provides its membership with a distinct value proposition and the capacity to perpetuate itself through collaborative problem solving and cooperation, rather than confrontation. For the companies we are involved with, the possible payoff is equally significant with the potential for increased revenues and enhancements in quality, performance, and morale."

The International Association of Machinists (IAM) has also established a program that brings union members and management together. The program is designed to create a collaborative problem-solving and idea-generation process that is designed to increase productivity, improve quality, or attack some other operational issues. Clearly the unions have an intrinsic motive—to protect union jobs and pay scales—but their overarching mission is to attract new members and make their memberships more valuable in the global economies.

A number of characteristics become obvious when an organization is closing in on successful collaboration:

1. Collaboration is occurring naturally and frequently.
2. Collaborative work teams are formally and informally formed.
3. The work groups demonstrate high levels of morale, the ability to constructively challenge one another, trust, esprit de corps, and a passion about their purpose.
4. The organization demonstrates a higher level of urgency and discovery.
5. The organization develops more open and unfiltered communications among departments, functions, and personnel.
6. The organization forms exciting and innovative solutions that create competitive advantage and enthusiasm.
7. Collaboration exhibits the appropriate mix of internal and external resources.

The major point to keep in mind is that the high performance leaders are using collaboration as a method of leveraging resources and creating competitive advantage. In turn, collaboration leads to greater, more effective learning and higher performance levels.

LEARNING AND KNOWLEDGE

"The important thing is not to stop questioning. Curiosity has its own reason for existing," stated Albert Einstein. One can hardly argue or take exception to that assertion. Einstein, the consummate thinker of the twentieth century and Time's "Person of the Century", gave us a wonderful insight into the human condition as it relates to learning and, ultimately, to knowledge. The high-performance organizations have a passion for learning and knowledge. In fact, one could argue that learning and knowledge are the centerpieces of their energy—their most valuable and essential core competencies. Any discussion of knowledge would be deficient without addressing the relationship between knowledge and learning. For organizations using knowledge as a strategic pillar, the issue of learning centers on two broad criteria: individual learning and organizational learning. As suggested in our discussion of the KMP, learning is endemic to knowledge. Authors Tom Cummings and William Snyder note that "Learning is organizational to the extent that: (1) it is done to achieve organizational purposes; (2) it is shared or distributed among members of the organization; and (3) learning outcomes are embedded in the organization's systems, structures, and cultures."

Learning and knowledge lead to higher performance and earnings for both individuals and organizations. Says Jay Stark, director of Knowledge Integration for GM, "Learning is about a company getting smarter over time, and getting smarter over time means that the enterprise actually finds a way to learn." Each organization and individual learns differently. These differences can be either significant or subtle; sometimes they can be both, depending on the subject matter and circumstances. Learning involves the application of existing knowledge *and* the discovery of new knowledge or how to adapt knowledge to new situations. What one learns and how one learns this morning can become the knowledge that provides the basis for further learning and additional or new knowledge in the afternoon. We know that one of the better ways to learn is through an interactive process that facilitates discovery, rewards success, and uses failure as a positive venue for learning. The great composer and conductor Igor Stravinsky noted about himself, "I have learned throughout my life as a composer chiefly through my mistakes and pursuits of false assumptions, not by my exposure to founts of wisdom and knowledge." The ability to translate failures into positive learning experiences is a trademark of high-performance KMP practices.

In learning, high-performance organizations use life's experience as references and match known patterns with new situations and emerging factors. Learning is the successful application of a four-part process that includes the recognition, assimilation, application, and extension/adaptation of knowledge to new challenges. The rate of knowledge transfer is affected by several factors including the speed at which an organization and a person can learn, wants to learn, and can apply the knowledge in a practical sense. This "learning rate" is influenced by a number of factors, including intellectual capacity, quality of the learning process, attitude, urgency, and environmental considerations. Thus, people and organizations learn differently and at different rates, and not all people or organizations necessarily want to learn new things. Author and Harvard University Professor Peter Senge notes that "people learn what they want to." As a result, there are those who are simply content with what they know and are not too concerned with what they do not know. For these people and their organizations, learning is usually more difficult and performance and prospects compromised.

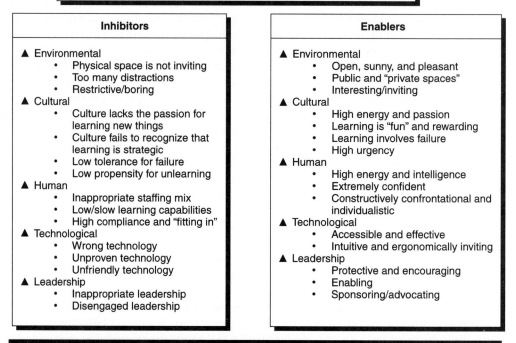

EXHIBIT 7.5 Inhibitors and Enablers to Knowledge Transfer and Learning

High-performance organizations covet learning and knowledge as sources of competitive advantage and energy. Recognizing that knowledge is the intellectual engine that they use to compete, they create atmospheres in which learning and experimentation are fostered, failure is understood and tolerated, and results are recognized and rewarded. High performers understand that failure is inevitable in learning, and although they do not like to fail, they understand that failing can offer valuable lessons. Exhibit 7.5 summarizes some of the key enablers and impediments to learning and knowledge sharing.

Effective knowledge transfer and learning requires breaking away from the traditional methods and organizational legacies. In considering knowledge, Peter Drucker once commented that the major challenge for many organizations is that they must be prepared to abandon knowledge that has become outdated or obsolete. Winston Churchill summed up his perceptions of learning as, "I'm always ready to learn, although I do not always like being taught." Thus, personality, individual perceptions, and organizational culture play pivotal and critical roles in learning effectiveness and knowledge transfer. As Jay Stark comments, "Organizations are reluctant to admit their failures. As a result of that reluctance, it's very, very difficult to, in fact, learn."

In using knowledge for creating strategic renewal and high performance, there is an "unlearning" process which must take place at both the individual and collectively at institutional levels. Abandonment or the unlearning of knowledge requires a process that is difficult for both the institution and the person. Peter Senge concludes, "Although members of the organization may be intelligent as measured by conventional tests, they can be alarmingly simpleminded when it comes to understanding organizational challenges and to developing systemic approaches to address them." Most mid-level managers are afraid that their competencies and long-practiced behavioral patterns will be invalidated by new knowledge. This inability to "unlearn" amplifies the organization's overall inability to learn. The inability of the organization to learn directly adversely affects the organization's ability to generate and manage knowledge as a source of competitive advantage and strategic renewal. For many companies trying to compete against the high performers, it is a vicious and never-ending syndrome.

Many inhibitors to learning and knowledge have been defined and studied by researchers. Peter Senge and others use a variety of metaphors such as "learning disabilities," or as J. G. March and J. P. Olson suggest as "incomplete learning cycles," to describe the malfunctions and breakdowns in learning experienced by many companies. For example, M. E. McGill and J. W. Slocum describe the inhibitors as "learning obstacles," and Dorothy Leonard calls failure to learn "knowledge-inhibiting activities." The labels or terms notwithstanding, all indicate a propensity for failing to learn and transfer knowledge. One method to stimulate unlearning and new behaviors is to change compensation and measurement methods. As GE CEO Jack Welch notes, "You can talk—you can preach—all you want about a "learning organization," but, from our experience, reinforcing management appraisal and compensation systems are the critical enablers that must be in place if rhetoric is to become reality."

There are many factors that contribute to the inability of an organization to learn and effectively manage and leverage knowledge for strategic advantage and change. One major barrier is the lack of organizational and operational integration. Organizations that are fragmented, highly bureaucratic, and compartmentalized are less likely to have effective knowledge management and learning programs than those that are more networked and integrated. So, organizational design and structure contribute, in varying degrees, to the effectiveness of learning and managing knowledge. Professor Morten Hansen, of the Harvard Business School, has concluded that one of the most important considerations affecting the use of knowledge in organizations revolves around the centrality of the knowledge relative to its sources and uses. Hansen's research indicates that the types of formal and informal relationships are significant influences on the formation, use, and relevancy of knowledge. The relationship of organizational design and personnel are directly related to the relevancy issue discussed earlier. For example, Hansen found that those people and operating units with the greatest levels of centrality tend to be more effective in the transfer and use of knowledge.

Other factors impacting learning and knowledge include the attitudes of the organization with respect to learning, the level of recognition given to learning by leaders, and the organization, overall quality of human resources, and the processes that organizations use to collect and disseminate knowledge and operationalize learning; its KMP. A deficiency in any of these areas will compromise learning. For example, the processes used may be faulty, and the transfer methods employed for training may be inefficient and ineffective. Finally, the practical application of transferring knowledge in business is more effectively achieved and learned using stories, metaphors, and actual examples, rather than complex theoretical and academic frameworks.

SUMMARY

Knowledge is a complex subject and one that requires much greater attention and research than this chapter can reasonably offer. There are, however, a number of important factors to consider, including:

1. High-performance organizations take responsibility for creating and managing knowledge as a source of competitive advantage and differentiation. They understand that to remain effective and maintain a competitive position, knowledge represents perhaps the single most important trait and competency. Knowledge is difficult to create and accurately replicate in highly dynamic organizations. They understand that knowledge is both explicit and tacit in form, and that in addition to the formal methods of knowledge capture and dissemination, there is a social aspect to knowledge that affects its transfer rate, organizational learning, and individual acceptance.

   With the high rate of workplace mobility that was discussed in chapter 4, capturing, institutionalizing, and disseminating knowledge are key competencies, which organizations must develop and sustain. High-performance organizations recognize that the decline in employee tenure together with increasing employee mobility are influencing how knowledge is created and managed. With higher mobility and less tenure, employees who leave their organizations can also take important knowledge with them. That does not imply that they are taking proprietary knowledge with them; most of that type of knowledge is explicit. Rather, they are attempting to extract the relevant long-learned tacit knowledge. This tacit knowledge, as we discussed, is the most difficult to learn and recapture. As a result, tacit knowledge about the nuances of the operation and job must be regenerated and relearned. In certain companies and for certain positions, this can be a costly proposition.

   High-performance organizations recognize the importance of trying to capture the tacit knowledge possessed by departing employees. For example, Debra Speight, CIO of Harvard Pilgrim Health Care, notes in *Fast Company* magazine, "I don't need to retain that person; I need to capture those answers." To capture the knowledge of departing employees, Speight has implemented a process where "With people on the way out, we ask the same questions and more: What knowledge do you need for your job? What secret code words and procedures do you use?" The responses to these questions by exiting employees are evaluated by a panel, and departing employees are paid anywhere from $1,000 to $5,000 depending on the quality of response. Although the direct results of these types of knowledge-capture programs have yet to be determined, implicitly, the capture of important tacit knowledge can minimize learning curves and regenerative costs.

Identifying what knowledge is important is critical to the effectiveness of the leader. Moreover, understanding how knowledge can support and aligns with the organization's objectives and strategies is crucial for both strategic positioning and organizational effectiveness. High-performance organizations accomplish knowledge transfer in a number of ways, including the use of predetermined filters that help to ensure that the appropriate knowledge is captured and developed.

2. Learning requires personal and organizational dedication and unlearning. Creating an environment conducive to learning and knowledge requires more than just technology and slogans; it requires structure and a formal management, measurement, and recognition system. More importantly, as former Herman Miller CEO Max DePree, notes, learning requires a personal commitment on the part of the employees. Those companies that are successful at knowledge management recognize and reward the effective creation and use of knowledge. In knowledge-creating environments, leaders encourage employees to challenge doctrine, experiment, make mistakes, and continue working with new and improved ideas. Thus, with knowledge comes greater empowerment and alignment to the strategies of the organization. DaimlerChrysler Corporation's Executive Vice President Tom Sidlik states, "Our employees must be increasingly informed, educated, trained, and empowered in order to provide the highest levels of quality service to the customers we serve." To do that requires knowledge and an environment that encourages learning, experimentation, adaptation, and knowledge extension.

3. Collaboration is the key to knowledge creation. Collaboration is the highest form of teamwork. Any organization that wishes to perpetuate and advance itself and its values understands that the single most important aspect of strategic renewal is getting people to work together and to get people focused, inspired, and concentrated on a single purpose. The keys to effective work groups are leadership and personal commitment. Leaders are responsible for institutionalizing collaboration and making it successful.

4. Managing knowledge for strategic advantage demands an overall architecture and a process. Effective knowledge management requires that an architecture be established for knowledge that has a clear alignment to the overall strategies of the organization. There are, essentially, four strategic approaches for choices: deterministic, emergent, synergistic, and reservation. High performers realize their knowledge strategies through defining and implementing a KMP with relevant filters. These filters are designed to actively preclude certain types of knowledge while reinforcing requirements.

5. Knowledge must be meaningful and relevant to the organization. This relevancy is best demonstrated through the alignment of strategic and operational needs of the organization as well as developmental needs of the individual with knowledge strategy and KMP. The one dominant guiding principle is that knowledge must lead to further learning and action. Such action is expressed in several ways, including behavior or better decision making.

Critical Thoughts and Discussion Questions

1. What makes knowledge so unique and difficult to copy as a source of competitive advantage?
2. Considering the definition of knowledge, what are the key aspects and attributes included in this term in relation to strategic renewal and competitive leadership?
3. What kinds of knowledge exist in an organization? For strategic purposes, what kind of knowledge entails the highest value? Describe the differences between tacit and explicit knowledge.
4. Discuss the differences between data, information, and knowledge as related to "intellectual capital."
5. Why is the assessment and management of knowledge so difficult, and how should organizational leaders effectively address these challenges?
6. What are the critical components in developing successful knowledge architecture? Specifically, discuss (1) the role of knowledge strategy, (2) the use of KPM, (3) the need for relevancy filters, and (4) the key for the successful administration and management of KPM.
7. Knowledge and learning are two closely interwoven concepts. Discuss the relationship between knowledge and learning.
   a. What are some of the impediments to KM and learning, inhibitors to the knowledge-transfer process?
   b. What are some of the critical success factors in learning and knowledge transfer?

CHAPTER

8

STRATEGIC LEADERSHIP: THE CORE COMPETENCY FOR HIGH PERFORMANCE

"Leadership is the art of getting someone else to do something you want done because he wants to do it."

—DWIGHT DAVID EISENHOWER, 34TH PRESIDENT OF THE UNITED STATES

"I learned that a great leader is a man who has the ability to get other people to do what they don't want to do."

—HARRY S. TRUMAN, 33RD PRESIDENT OF THE UNITED STATES

INTRODUCTION

This chapter discusses the fourth pillar for high performance and renewal: *strategic leadership*. The introductory quotes by two dominant figures of the twentieth century provide us with a glimpse into the thinking of a leader. In Eisenhower and Truman, we have two prominent *world* leaders whose lives intersected and overlapped and who were key players in many of the defining events of the twentieth century. Both men knew many of the same people and even came from similar parts of the United States, the heart of the Midwest. Although each agrees on the essential activity of the leader, their fundamental perspective regarding human behavior and leadership is so divergent that they demonstrate just how complicated and challenging leadership can be.

As a lifelong journey of learning, self-discovery, exploring new environments, and personal growth, leadership lends itself to new interpretations of known conditions and new revelations. Much of what we know about leadership is constant and enduring, whereas other aspects are always evolving, requiring leaders themselves to be in a constant state of self-renewal and reflection.

Crafting and sustaining high performance requires high-performance leadership practices. It is an all too common story of how once great and dominant organizations, such as RCA, Sears, Levi Strauss, Apple Computer, and Kellogg's, have relinquished their status due, in part, to leadership, or the lack thereof. This chapter discusses why leadership is a strategic pillar and what type of leadership best supports high performance and strategic renewal. In the process, we ask a number of questions:

- What is the role of leadership as a pillar of strategy and strategic renewal?
- What are the essential qualities of high-performance leadership?
- How do leaders lead for strategic change and high performance?

In this chapter, we present the five essential qualities of leadership and discuss how they are used in strategy formulation and as catalysts for strategic renewal.

STRATEGIC LEADERSHIP

We begin this chapter by establishing four fundamental tenets with respect to leadership and high performance as a pillar of strategy and strategic change:

1. The notion of a single, omnipotent or heroic leader who is able to right the world and solve everyone's problems is archaic in a global economy of rapid change. The world is too interconnected and too complex for any one individual to have all of the answers. In a 1999 article appearing in *Business Week,* John A. Byrne writes, "Success will belong to the companies that are leaderless . . ." That is an interesting and provocative statement. There will always be leaders and the need for leadership—society and business organizations demand leadership, but what is important to recognize is that the definition and expectations for leadership have changed.

   Today, and certainly in the twenty-first century, leadership will be shared and administered among a group of individuals. Leadership, as used in the context of strategic change and high performance in this book, refers to a person or a group of people who can influence, direct, and/or make the decisions that materially affect the allocation of an organization's human, technological, and financial resources. Researchers R. Cyert and J. March note that it is a top management team, or a "dominant coalition of individuals responsible for setting firm direction." Thus, when the terms *leadership* and *high-performance leadership* are used in this chapter, they refer to the leaders of an organization, interchangeably indicating either a team, group, or individual(s).

   Exhibit 8.1 compares some of the significant differences in leadership between high-performance leaders and traditional models.

2. A condition of leadership in strategic change is that leading and following form an interrelated and interdependent equation. One cannot lead without followers as much as one cannot follow without a leader or a group of leaders. They need one another and must constantly work to ensure that each is a part of a larger "synergistic" equation. High-performance leaders have the confidence and unselfish quality of being able to switch roles between leader and follower, depending on the situation and subject matter.

3. Perhaps most important, all strategic change requires a willing and committed group of followers who are energized and impassioned. Leaders may move the organization to change, but it is the rank-and-file followers who make the personal sacrifices, professional commitments, execute against the vision, and ultimately, determine the success of the leader.

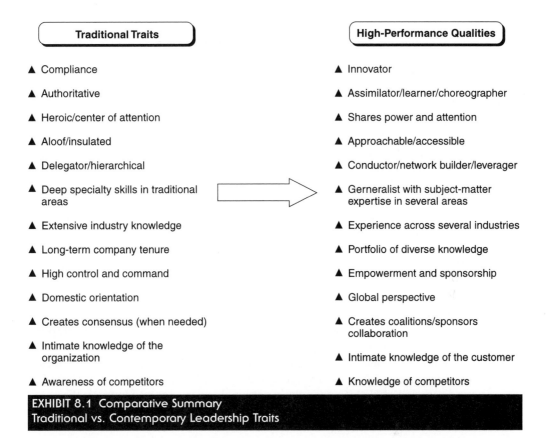

Traditional Traits	High-Performance Qualities
▲ Compliance	▲ Innovator
▲ Authoritative	▲ Assimilator/learner/choreographer
▲ Heroic/center of attention	▲ Shares power and attention
▲ Aloof/insulated	▲ Approachable/accessible
▲ Delegator/hierarchical	▲ Conductor/network builder/leverager
▲ Deep specialty skills in traditional areas	▲ Gerneralist with subject-matter expertise in several areas
▲ Extensive industry knowledge	▲ Experience across several industries
▲ Long-term company tenure	▲ Portfolio of diverse knowledge
▲ High control and command	▲ Empowerment and sponsorship
▲ Domestic orientation	▲ Global perspective
▲ Creates consensus (when needed)	▲ Creates coalitions/sponsors collaboration
▲ Intimate knowledge of the organization	▲ Intimate knowledge of the customer
▲ Awareness of competitors	▲ Knowledge of competitors

**EXHIBIT 8.1 Comparative Summary
Traditional vs. Contemporary Leadership Traits**

4. Leadership in some form or another is a core competency of strategy and strategic renewal. No strategic change or renewal process can be successful without highly effective and engaged leadership, at all levels of the organization or society. High-performance leadership is accountable, responsible, and approachable.

With that backdrop, let's begin our discussion of high-performance leadership with an anecdote that is sadly replayed, even today, in various forms and with various degrees of seriousness in organizations throughout the world.

In a 1990 meeting at KPMG Peat Marwick, Chairman Jon C. Madonna and Deputy Chairman James Brocksmith discussed the impending restructuring and downsizing of the firm's partnership. With much fanfare, Mr. Madonna and Mr. Brocksmith, both auditors by training, referred to the need for the firm to be more competitive, to have greater focus on clients, and to develop deep industry capabilities. Leading the way would be what they called the "partner of the 90's," which they believed to be the key to the competitive success of KPMG. As the partners sat listening intently to the words spoken, some were agreeing, others were not, but most seemed to be trying to figure out exactly what they meant by the phrase "partner of the 90's." Finally, a distinguished partner, with silver hair who was immaculately dressed, stood up and asked Mr. Madonna the all-important question, "What did 'the partner of the 90's' really mean? What are you looking for?" What he was asking for, of course, was some indication, a definition, insight, or a personal perspective on what Mr. Madonna was describing. Mr. Madonna seemed to be uncomfortable with the question and referred it to Mr. Brocksmith, who cleared his throat and said something along the lines, "It's like class, we'll know them when we see them."

In 1990, KPMG Peat Marwick, as it was known then, ranked first or second in the world in terms of total professional service revenues as compared to the other "Big Six accounting firms," depending on the measurement used. In 1996 the *Wall Street Journal* reported that "Mr. Madonna's six-year tenure was marked by major upheavals at the accounting firm, which a decade ago was No. 2 in the profession," and "morale plunged and the firm's revenue became lackluster." During the tenure of these two leaders, KPMG apparently experienced partner defections, a succession of organizational restructurings, and diminished marketshare relative to its peers. By 1996, the end of the Madonna/Brocksmith term, the *Wall Street Journal* reported that KPMG had fallen to the bottom spot in the Big Six based on revenues per partner and has been seeking a merger partner for the last several years.

There is something wonderfully perplexing and unique about leaders. Leaders are relatively easy to spot but incredibly difficult to define, and they present an even greater challenge to develop and evaluate. Leadership and our impressions of leaders run the spectrum of emotions, sometimes bordering on euphoria, other times on the fringe of despair and occasionally, embarrassment. That is, in part, because leadership involves the complex interactions between the intangible qualities of the human spirit, interpersonal communications, and a dynamically changing environment. Leadership, as noted by Judy Rosener, is both "an art and a science" and is, as one could conclude from the above discussion of KPMG, a uniquely personal experience and journey. We come to an important question for any leader, organization, or follower: "Can leaders lead effectively if they themselves cannot clearly articulate a meaningful and realistic definition and vision of leadership nor their expectations?" The answer is, "Probably not."

Let's define *leadership* from the onset as the:

Art or process of getting others to think, act, and do things through their own belief, and often at their own initiative, risk, and device.

Leadership is much more than formal power, organizational status, personal wealth, education, and training. Leadership involves getting others, either individually or collectively in some type of team or collaborative work group, to do things. Fundamental to this is the ability of the leader to effectively guide and influence human behavior. Few would dispute that business managers or ranking personnel in the military can compel people to do things through organizational rank and status or that organized labor must perform to their contractual obligations under collective bargaining agreements. Peer pressure, as we all know, can make people do things and perform at levels, good and bad, that they may have never contemplated or accomplished if left to their own volition or designs.

Given the foregoing, it is now appropriate to revisit the classic questions of leadership: What makes leaders great, and what makes a great leader? To find the answer, many researchers have concentrated on studying the lives of leaders in hopes of identifying common qualities, experiences, and traits. The rationale for this biographical approach is that by analyzing such things as their backgrounds, early childhood development, parental influences, education, and their personal lives and interests, we would glean precious insights into leadership and the process of becoming a leader. Other approaches have tried to look to genetics and environmental factors and influences to provide explanations to those questions.

To some clinical psychologists, leadership can be explained by behavioral diagnostics that reduce leadership to quantitative scores that are designed to identify leaders, predict leader behavior, and forecast leader potential with some semblance of statistical accuracy. Other researchers have taken an anthropological approach to studying leadership. Unfortunately, leading in sophisticated organizations and in an increasingly interconnected global arena is different than leading a communal tribe in the jungles and certainly varies from the ways primates interact in their natural setting. Academic literature is full of articles and clinical studies that describe how to statistically characterize and/or predict a leader's ability to perform under various conditions. Although these techniques might be useful tools and possible indicators for leaders, they are not absolute predictors of leadership talent or the potential success of the leader, especially against a backdrop of high uncertainty and rapidly changing environments. The clinical approaches require carefully constructed protocols and protracted periods of time to amass data and perform the analysis necessary to support accurate conclusions. By the time most of these studies are subsequently validated by second parties, the environment will have changed so radically that many of the assumptions used and conclusions reached may no longer be appropriate. In predicting leadership, there is no accounting for courage, character, or the strength of the human spirit when pressed into action.

The above approaches are all interesting exercises that tell us *something* about leaders, but they fall far short in giving us definitive direction into how to be a high-performance leader. Rarely do they provide any new significant revelations. Studying the life and times of leaders is entertaining, but leaders come from all walks of life and from all parts of the world. Hence, drawing conclusions about backgrounds and geographical origins makes for great reading but provides little insight into what constitutes a high-performing leader. As individuals, each leader has different life experiences and frames of personal reference. Because no two people are alike, it only makes sense that no two leaders are alike.

Attempting to draw conclusions about leaders based on educational background is also an interesting exercise, but it gives us little knowledge into leadership. As Calvin Coolidge observed, "The world is full of educated derelicts." In major corporations, education and technical knowledge are the "threshold" competencies. At the very least, individuals must have the appropriate education in certain disciplines to be even considered as potential employees, let alone as potential leaders. The reality is that leaders have different educational experiences and pedigree. Some, such as former Intel CEO Andy Grove and a former Bank of America CEO David Coulter, were gifted students earning doctoral degrees from prestigious institutions. Others, such as the legendary U.S. General George Patton, had to work extra hard to overcome natural learning disabilities and earn their grades. Some, including Abraham Lincoln, came from impoverished backgrounds and were self-educated. Some leaders, such as John F. Kennedy and Franklin Roosevelt, went to esteemed institutions of higher education, whereas others went to public colleges. The well-documented academic careers of Michael Dell and Bill Gates provide more contemporary profiles of leaders and education. As a group, leaders studied all sorts of subjects, including liberal arts, classics, music, art, architecture, business, science, and engineering. In business, an MBA is indispensable but simply having an MBA does not develop leaders or guarantee high performance. In fact, many business schools do not address leadership in their curricula with any serious rigor. Clearly, it does not make a difference what and where leaders study.

Understanding the family environment that leaders came from satisfies our curiosity, but not in a very meaningful way. Some leaders come from complete family units, others from broken families. Some leaders come from wealthy families, others from poor ones. Some point to intense sibling rivalry, others recall harmonious relationships. When growing up, many will mention how their parents encouraged them, supported their activities, and expressed confidence in their ability to achieve things, and how their families were actively engaged in their early development. Some leaders, such as Douglas MacArthur, had mothers who had the most influence on their development, others point to fathers. Others, including Andy Grove, credit both parents as being equally important. Many leaders tell us of heroes and role models in their lives. Usually, these came in the form of a family member in their formative years and later, as their careers progressed, in the form of mentors. There is some empirical evidence suggesting that traditional family environments favorably influence leadership development, yet leaders come from different backgrounds. Other leaders emphasize life partners who have supported them and helped them to contend with the pressures of leadership. As Barry Patmore, a retired partner of Andersen Consulting, noted, "Life partners make leading possible."

THE FIVE ESSENTIAL QUALITIES OF HIGH-PERFORMANCE LEADERSHIP

For many years, a considerable debate has been taking place as to whether leadership is a learned quality or whether there is a genetic component that suggests that some people are predisposed towards leadership through their DNA. The reality is that leadership is a combination of lifelong development *and* genetics. Most people have the basic genetic ingredients for leadership. The difference—and it is significant—is that high-performance leaders are conscious of these qualities and constantly work to develop them as they move through their lives. For the most part, leadership must be developed, but in the absence of certain fundamental qualities and certain DNA qualities that are inherent in the genetic makeup of a person, leadership qualities cannot be fully evolved or elevated to their highest form.

"Leaders do not have to fit a particular mold," commented Barry Patmore. That is an accurate and interesting observation coming from a career partner of a firm known for its high command and control style of personnel development, and referred to as "Arthur Androids" by *The Economist*. Applying a single model or construct for leadership can be a problem for any organization. Organizations that use a narrowly scripted definition of leadership, a prescriptive set of quantitative measures, or highly subjective criteria for identifying leaders run the risk of precluding emerging and creative leaders who do not fit an immediate need or a historical model. Such leaders who are "different" might be indispensable to the organization in the future, where conditions and circumstances may be radically different and increasingly unpredictable.

High-performance leadership is the standard that virtually all leaders must aspire to, must attain, be measured against, and be guided by in their personal journeys and professional performance. High-performance leaders lead from deep within their souls with beliefs and processes that extend outward and touch others. The source for their

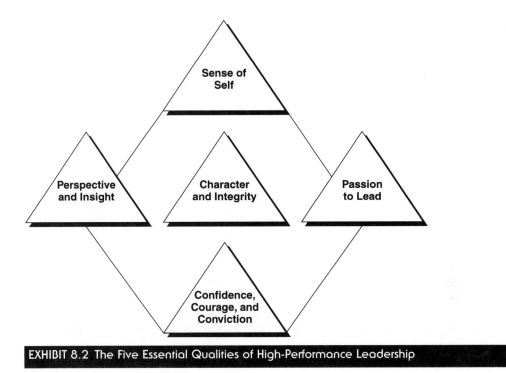

EXHIBIT 8.2 The Five Essential Qualities of High-Performance Leadership

leadership is founded in their values, beliefs, moral and spiritual centerings, personal ethics, and life experiences—in a sense, their *character.*

To fully appreciate what makes a high-performance leader and how to develop next-generation high-performance leaders who are capable of sustaining high performance, we must look past the obvious traits of charisma, social status, organizational financial performance, and popularity and look deep into what it means to be a leader. High-performance leaders share five essential qualities, which are illustrated in Exhibit 8.2.

1. Character and integrity.
2. Sense of self.
3. A passion to lead.
4. Perspective and insight.
5. Confidence, courage, and conviction.

Character and Integrity

"Employees with integrity are the ones who build a company's reputation," noted the late Robert Goizueta, CEO of Coca-Cola. Character is the nucleus and ultimate source of leadership. In its most essential form, leadership is all about character. Character is the single most important quality that a leader must have. Without character, there is no authenticity to leadership, no sincerity, no sense of credibility, and no moral basis for leading. Character defines who we are as human beings; it is our soul. Character is what distinguishes us as unique and different individuals and reflects our beliefs and outlooks.

Perhaps we are born with some of the elements of character, but developing it is a life-long journey of learning, adapting, value assessment, and decision making. Character embodies and personifies trust, sincerity, honesty, and integrity. Those qualities can be cultivated, but only to the point of knowing the consequences; in its truest form, *a person either has character or does not.*

As Southwest Airlines CEO Herb Kelleher noted, "You also have to have a clear set of values that you implant in the company. It's up to the CEO to set an inspirational example of how workers should behave." Character in the leader establishes the standard of behavior in the organization that others must emulate. Ultimately, character in leadership creates the trust and confidence that are the core elements of leadership, influencing the behaviors of others. This trust is often demonstrated through actions such as empowerment, confidence, and allowing people to use their discretion in problem solving and decision making. Character in leadership creates more open and honest communication and the knowledge sharing essential for collaboration and building effective coalitions. Richard Sennett, a sociologist at New York University, concludes that "Character is expressed by loyalty and mutual commitment, or through the pursuit of long-term goals." Character allows the leader to lead. In the absence of character, an individual might be a good manager and technician, but he or she cannot be a high-performance leader. Without character, one may be able to lead in the short run, but one cannot sustain effectiveness as a leader for any appreciable period of time. History is full of short-term leaders.

In understanding leadership, we must separate character from behavior, styles, and persona. How a leader chooses to manifest her or his character is reflected in his/her behavior. Depending on the situation and the moment, leaders portray many different behaviors, but their character is always the single most enduring and defining constant of being a leader. From one moment to the next, high-performance leaders may display qualities of the "democratic leader," "consensus leader," "autocratic leader," "charismatic leader," "tyrant," and a variety of other styles and popular leadership types. The key is to understand that high-performance leader behavior is how the leader chooses to act and express one's self in any one situation, with a group of people or in one-to-one personal interactions. The behavior may be problematic, but the character is constant.

The ability to understand the sources of one's behavior is important not only to leaders, but to all humans because it tells us much about how we interpret situations, make decisions, and interact with others. Behaviors influence all of our lives and have a profound effect on how we listen, learn, and are viewed by others. One of the keys to understanding high-performance leaders is noting that they have a deep understanding of their own behavior and personal styles. That is, high-performance leaders understand the sources of their behaviors, what motivates them, what stimulates them into action, what makes them happy, and what makes them sad. They understand who they are and how their education, life experiences, ethics, and morals guide them. This level of personal understanding and self-awareness contributes to the self-confidence and personal integrity of the leader. They have a profound sense of self.

Endemic to character are the morals and ethics of the leader. Leaders cannot lead effectively without moral authority. In the absence of moral authority, the leader is merely a manager or actor. Commenting about morals, Mark Twain noted, "Morals are an acquirement, like music, like a foreign language, like piety, poker, paralysis—no man is born with them." There are no direct or easy answers when it comes to morals and ethics, but it is apparent that high-performance leaders center their morals and ethics on "what is the right thing to do and doing the right things", as noted by Warren Bennis. For leaders, what is morally correct is a complex equation involving the best interests of the organization, what is legal, what is in the best interest of society, and what represents the greatest value to those involved. More fundamentally, high-performance leaders place the "morally right" interests of the organization ahead of their own self-interests and require exceptionally high levels of ethical behavior of themselves and of their organizations.

The moral and ethical centering that high-performance leaders rely on is central to their *being* a leader. It's part of their inner basis that helps to form the lens and filters through which they view the world and the construct in which they make decisions. The basis for this centering comes from many different sources, including religious convictions, philosophy of living, role models, legal doctrine and theory, lifelong learning and personal development, education, and career experience. With these convictions comes the recognition that the objectives and interests of the organization come before any personal goals or agenda. High-performance leaders understand that they have a profound *moral* obligation to grow and advance their organizations. High-performance leaders work to ensure that the values of the organization and its strategies are reflected and aligned with its behaviors. They recognize that any discontinuities and fractures between organizational goals and organizational behavior, especially at the leadership levels, can erode employee confidence and will adversely impact employee morale and individual and organizational performance.

Sense of Self

An essential aspect of character and high-performance leadership is having a sense of self, of who we are and what we stand for as human beings. The American journalist Marya Mannes noted (that) "Until we know what motivates the hearts and minds of men we can understand nothing outside ourselves, nor will we ever reach fulfillment as that greatest miracle of all, the human being." High-performance leaders have a great sense of who they are, they understand the basis of their values, and they possess a sincere understanding of the sources of their aspirations and the causes of their failures. High-performance leaders genuinely believe that they can be extraordinarily effective. They are supremely confident that they are capable of helping the organization and its people to achieve great things.

American poet and editor James Russell Lowell noted, "No man can produce great things who is not thoroughly sincere in dealing with himself." Mastering a sense of self is *essential* to being a leader and requires leaders to develop many qualities, among which the most important are:

- Cultivating a deep understanding of their personal strengths and weakness. As the twentieth century philosopher Andre Gide noted, "Each of us really understands in others only those feelings he is capable of producing himself."
- Not being threatened by the qualifications and capabilities of others and surrounding themselves with talented and energetic people. As former CEO Max DePree notes, high-performance leaders are exemplary leaders who "abandon their ego to the talents of others."
- Understanding the forces that shaped their character and influence their behavior patterns.

- Acknowledging their fears and sources of insecurities.
- Being self-assured in their knowledge of their value systems, standards of morality, and ethics.
- Cultivating self-confidence and empowerment in others.

To be effective, especially in the rapidly changing technological and societal landscape, leaders have to know how they feel, how they respond, what makes them act and react, and who they are as individuals. They must be centered and focused on the moment. They understand when they should manage their emotions, rely on their intuition, and reach out to others, and they judge correctly when to delay and when to make decisions. High-performance leaders work diligently to know themselves so that when they are learning new things, assimilating information, listening to others, making decisions, and interacting with others, they do so from the perspective of knowing how they feel at the time, what they stand for, and who they are. As one leader commented, "When I feel like I am off center or in less than an optimal mood, I'll try to defer making major decisions or interacting with people I don't necessarily enjoy being around or interacting with. It's not that I am avoiding them, rather I am avoiding making a bad decision or impression." In the process, they express their values, beliefs, and knowledge while respecting the views and needs of others. Significantly, this type of behavior may signal high-performance leaders are more reflective in their decision-making processes than their behaviors may indicate.

It is clear that a key aspect of high-performance leadership is the ability to "be in the moment." Individuals who have ever been actors, played sports, were members of a precision drill team, or were members of a musical group will recognize that being in the moment is sometimes referred to as being "in the zone." Being in the zone is like no other state of consciousness or behavior, and those who experience it recognize it as a unique status. When one is "in the zone," time seems to stand still, the environment and the individual meld into one, and a person is in tune and in touch with her or his thoughts, surroundings, body, and emotions. Everything that a person does seems to work at higher levels, with greater precision, integration, and stamina. Those who are able to perform "in the zone" liken it to a "transcendental state," where they are only cognizant of the very moment they are in, and they have only limited recollection of the past. High-performance leaders are "in the moment" when they:

- Are conscious of their emotions and state of mind at the moment.
- Draw on a combination of intuition, inner feelings, education, and formal training to process information, interpret communications, interact with others, and center themselves for the moment.
- Neutralize their emotions in an attempt to perform at higher levels.

Formal education is becoming increasingly important for leading but, as noted, education has not been a prerequisite for high-performance leadership. Intelligence is essential to the leader because the overall educational and socioeconomic awareness and knowledge of the general population and labor force is higher. This does not imply that leaders must be smarter or have higher IQs than those who follow. Such a conclusion would not only be erroneous but also ridiculous. Intelligence on behalf of the leader contributes to a certain level of respect between leaders and followers. Intelligence provides the leader with the basic material for further learning and more effective interpersonal dialogues.

In the dynamics of this new competitive environment, it is the combination of knowledge, emotional intelligence, and social skills that are the key indicators of leader potential and effectiveness, not status or age. In his study of over 180 companies, researcher Daniel Goleman concludes that it is the emotional intelligence (EI) of individuals that determines their effectiveness as a leader and also their status in the leadership development hierarchy. EI extends well beyond formal academic training into social skills, interpersonal interactions, and personal networking and working relationships. High-performance leaders understand that these social interactions are essential to leadership. The broader and more diverse the social acquaintances are, the greater are the possibilities for collaboration, networking, intelligence gathering, forging stronger personal ties, and self-improvement as a leader. High-performance leaders have the ability to develop and maintain many different social and professional relationships.

Finally, having a sense of self and respect for one's self are prerequisites for developing and expressing genuine appreciation and civility for others. In contrast to the traditional models of leadership that suggest a certain aloofness to others, high-performance leaders are appreciative of other people and their perspectives. This appreciation is expressed in a number of ways, including accepting views and opinions that are contradictory to those of the leader and sincerely acknowledging the efforts and contributions of others.

In contrast to the vision of the leader who is lonely and distant, high-performance leaders, such as David Coulter, Jack Welch, and the late H. J. Heinz and Milton S. Hershey, take a personal interest in others. This interest helps them not only to keep in touch with others, but it also allows them to build a stronger sense of personal and institutional trust and loyalty. Leaders of high-performance organizations set a broad agenda, provide the tools for their people to succeed, and then stand back and cheer. It is the personal trust and confidence that allows them to do this so effectively. In the process, they are active, engaging, and constructively challenging. They are, as demonstrated by Jack Welch and Andy Grove, constantly extolling their people to consider different perspectives and variations and the ramifications of their decisions and actions on all aspects of their businesses and stakeholders.

Civility and respect in leadership are indicative of character and are absolutely fundamental to high-performance leadership. Leaders set the standard for how people interact within and outside of the organization. High-performance leaders understand that real power in leadership comes from the ability to influence others and that respect and civility are essential to influence. Civility in leadership expresses appreciation and authenticity, both of which are fundamental to the perceptions, expectations, and realities of leading. When Larry Horner retired as the managing partner of KPMG in 1990, it was not too long before a partner commented that "You know, we really lost our style and stature when Larry retired. He was so gallant and always a gentleman. The firm had a lot of class then." In demonstrating civility, high-performance leaders exhibit a personal style and demeanor that sets them apart from others but at the same time does not alienate them from others. It is the style and grace that is both differentiating and inviting.

"When all is said and done, when you strip away the organizational chart, take away the titles and slogans and discount the bravado, you are left with the people. Always remember, organizations are all about people and only people," noted Abraham Gitlow, former dean of New York University's Stern School of Business. What this great teacher was telling his students was that in its most fundamental form, leadership is all about people, irrespective of the corporate trappings, salary, technology, or location. Leaders understand that their behavior signals appreciation and respect and creates higher empathy, and thus, stronger relationships. Stronger relationships build, in effect, greater levels of credibility, trust, and loyalty that further bind leaders to followers. Leaders who have developed these qualities are better equipped to express themselves, better able to exhibit a sincere personal interest in others and, most importantly, better positioned to develop the personal connectivity with others that is necessary to establish trust and successfully navigate strategic change and renewal.

Leaders who have a highly developed sense of self and who are intimate with their emotions are better able to forge more meaningful and synergistic relationships with others. The basis of this self-knowledge extends deeply into the human experience. This knowledge and awareness, in turn, creates higher levels of trust and more effective communications and collaboration between people. More importantly, having a sense of self allows leaders to *calibrate* their emotions and behaviors in a manner that best aligns them with those who they must lead and with the strategic intentions of their organizations.

Passion to Lead

High-performance leaders have "a driving and burning belief that they can lead. They live to lead, but more importantly, are willing to except any level of leadership," according to Susan Greenbaum, managing director of the Maloney Group. High-performance leaders are driven by a passion to lead and the visions and missions that they form for their organization. Having passion and a sense of purpose are essential for leaders. Displaying passion and a personal commitment to purpose and mission is essential if the leader is to generate trust and credibility and motivate and inspire others. Leaders who have a passion to lead and demonstrate it through their actions and energy stimulate the organization into action. The passions and actions of the leader set the tone and provide the context for overall organizational behavior and activities. Leaders who exhibit high levels of personal dedication and energy ultimately inspire the organization to higher performance levels.

Central to leading is having a well-defined vision and mission for the organization. In business, it is tres vogue to boldly display vision and mission statements in corridors, on banners, and in paperweights. Visions are wonderful things; virtually every company claims to have at least one. But just because leaders and their organizations have something that they think is a vision does not mean that they actually have one, or more importantly, that it is the appropriate one. In many organizations, there are significant disconnects and contradictions between what leaders have espoused as the vision and how the organization actually interprets it and behaves. The majority of vision statements seem to fall in the realm of rhetoric. That is, they offer us the common platitudes about "being number one to our customers" or "quality is our passion," or "delighting customers." Those are laudable goals of any company, but they are not very meaningful visions. In business, *all* companies should want to delight their customers.

The statistics support the lack of agreement as to what constitutes a vision or what represents a well-constructed and articulated vision. According to a survey performed by Gemini Consulting, 70 percent of U.S. companies say they have a mission statement, but only 41 percent of their employees report that they know what it is. Indeed it is hard to execute a vision and successfully compete when less than 50 percent of those who are responsible for giving it life apparently fail in their understanding of it.

High-performance leaders are driven by a vision for their organization. The word *driven* is important because it has a distinct meaning connoting the qualities of motivation, urgency, and passion. Robert Sanborn, CEO of Oakmark Fund, said of visions that "Most of the time, vision is just a speech. The great CEO makes decisions that realize the vision." Warren Bennis has defined *vision* as something that " ... always refers to a future state, a condition that does not presently exist and never existed before." To be effective, high-performance leaders understand that a vision must be a *guiding force* and must present either implicitly or explicitly a compelling *value proposition* for others to follow. Barry Patmore corroborates that notion by describing vision as "Something an organization needs to aspire to which is different from where it is today ... it's a destination that it may never fully reach, but it must always focus on it." Vision, for purposes of high-performance, is defined as:

> A representation of the purpose and desired future state that guides and motivates the organization to higher levels of performance.

The great social and business leaders, such as Dr. Martin Luther King, Barbara Jordan, Henry Ford, Mahatma Gandhi, Betty Friedan, Gordon Moore, and Bill Gates, all had great passions for their visions of the future and in their abilities to articulate those visions. Consequently, they used every opportunity and means provided to them to express it, to reach out to people and deliver it. Their personal passions helped express the vision in meaningful and personal terms that others could easily interpret, relate to, and embrace.

Thus, high-performance leaders are visionaries, and they translate those visions into tangible and action-oriented strategies that present a clear economic, societal, and competitive value proposition to the stakeholders. The most effective visions share six essential qualities. The vision:

1. Communicates a sense of *direction*. All organizations need a sense of direction, a goal and guide to a future state of existence. This sense of direction is necessary for the organization to develop and deploy its resources in the most productive and responsive manner. Direction is essential to articulating goals, aspirations, and objectives. Finally, a sense of direction is fundamental to effective communications.
2. Establishes a *context* for operating the enterprise. Context helps to define and clarify the environment in which the leader and the organization operate. High-performance leaders work to understand and interpret their environments and to calibrate their visions as influenced by the realities and opportunities presented by the environment and the competencies and resources of their organizations. The vision may coexist in the environment or, as David Coulter notes, an organization may try to redefine the environment through a radically new vision.
3. Describes a *future condition*. Effective visions provide a future-state and condition that represents a "better" state than the ones of the past and that exists in the present. The future condition is linked to, or provides the basis for, a compelling value proposition that can serve as a keystone for individual and organizational change. Great visions, such as those given to us by Dr. Martin

Luther King, John F. Kennedy, Henry Ford, and Golda Meir, have an enduring quality that transcends time and circumstances to unite people behind a common cause and to a common purpose.

4. *Motivates* people. Leaders understand that effective and meaningful visions provide a high value proposition to others. Those visions that appeal to the instincts, needs, and intelligence of people and touch their "soul" serve as a basis for systemic acceptance and motivation. With this energy comes personal commitment and higher levels of urgency and cooperation among followers and leaders to accomplish things that support the vision.

5. *Inspires* people to work toward a common state and a set of goals. By *inspiring,* I do not mean elevating behavior in some nationalistic or militaristic way. Those types of highly charged emotional states can certainly reflect a type of inspiration, but there are many other ways in which inspiration is created and demonstrated. *Inspiration* means providing the motivations, value propositions, and compelling arguments that will help people to voluntarily channel and focus their energies, emotions, and personal capital towards the realization of the vision. Leaders understand that inspiration "touches" people in different ways and appeals to their sense of belonging, commitment, sense of accomplishment, and ability to contribute to something greater and bigger than they themselves could achieve on their own.

6. Serves as a *centering point* for organizational behavior and performance. Visions provide a central point for focusing the resources of the organization, developing strategy, and measuring progress towards the vision. High-performance leaders understand that centering points also help to calibrate behaviors and actions. Centering points help leaders and followers to communicate and reference their behaviors to the needs of the organization.

Understanding the impact of a vision and how visions inspire and influence people is fundamental to any study of high-performance leadership. One needs only to replay Dr. King's famous "I Have a Dream" speech of August 28, 1963 to appreciate the importance of the above attributes. His words "I have a dream that one day this nation will rise up and live out the true meaning of this creed: that all men are created equal . . ." will forever resonate in the minds and hearts of tens of millions of people. They are words that transcend time and are a credo to live by each and every day. They provide a value proposition for a better society and more constructive human interactions. The words create a portrait of democracy that is as fresh, relevant, and compelling today as it was in 1963. In developing his vision, Dr. King exhibited a deep and accurate understanding of the environment, together with his own interpretation of the visions of democracy developed by Thomas Jefferson, Plato, and others. In this vision, Dr. King presents us with hope, a challenge, direction, inspiration, and a real sense of purpose. Visions, as Dr. King told us, are calls to action and codes to live by.

Having a vision and the ability to articulate that vision is absolutely essential to the effectiveness of the leader. Leaders use visions to rally their organizations, motivate others, and establish a context and basic lexicon for communicating throughout the organization. Visions can be established at all levels of the organization and by all different types of leaders, but they must be linked and aligned with the overall pervasive vision of the leader. The necessary prerequisite for success is that the individual visions must demonstrate an alignment to the overall and overarching enterprisewide vision established by the most senior leaders of the organization. Leaders ensure this alignment through the direct measures of cause and effect, congruency with strategy, financial proposition, as well as through monitoring individual behaviors for consistency.

A critical question with regard to leadership is "What is the mission of the leader?" Most often the common and superficial answer is "to lead." However, the reality is that there are significant disparities among researchers, authorities, leaders, and aspiring leaders as to what the "essential" mission of the leader is or ought to be. Some authors and leaders have advanced the obvious notion that the mission of the leader is to "develop others." No doubt that is an essential part of leadership, but it is not the primary mission of the leader. A different perspective on the mission of the leader is to be a "director of resources." That is also true, but it also misses the point. Another interpretation of mission is that the leader functions as an "arbitrator among many different factions." Finally, a popular description of the leader's mission is to "create wealth for others." All of those responses are the "things" that leaders usually do, but they are not the essential mission of the leader.

Tom Watson, Sr., founder of IBM, once said that "It's harder to keep a business great than it is to build it." Thus, the primary mission of the leader occupies itself with sustaining and advancing the status of the organization. An organization is most vulnerable when it is doing its best, when it is sitting high in the saddle feeling good about itself. Any competitor with an idea and minimum resources has the capacity to capture marketshare from the leader and ultimately displace it as the dominant player. Thinking about the mission of leaders, Barry Patmore summarized, "I think one of the primary missions of the leader is to create an organization that has, above all, sustainability." Ensuring that the organization can sustain and advance itself in a constantly changing environment is the central mission of the leader. Finally, perhaps the ultimate test of leadership comes after the leader has departed. As Barry Patmore notes, the "true" measure of the leader is "Whether the organization is in better shape after I've done something than before it was done." The betterment of the organization is a relatively straightforward and valid measurement for assessing the effectiveness of the leader. Walter Lippmann, commenting about the death of President Franklin Roosevelt in 1945, summarized what may very well be the ultimate test of leader: "The final test of a leader is that he leaves behind him in men the conviction and will to carry on."

Perspective and Insight

Insight, in the context of high-performance leadership, involves the ability to identify, analyze, interpret, and simplify technically complex or politically charged issues and solutions using a multidisciplined approach. Insight includes the ability to assess and interpret issues and develop solutions from a different perspective, to form and apply innovative standards and criteria to them, and to offer a unique personal interpretation regarding them. This perspective brings new and different meanings to the issues and, with them, new and innovative answers. In a sense, it is the individual tacit knowledge discussed earlier that makes the leader's perspective unique and meaningful.

"An effective leader is an individual who can see through the fog of reality to interpret events and be able to make sense of the blurring and ambiguous complexity," notes Warren Bennis. Insight and perspective requires that leaders have a great sense and awareness of reality. High-performance leaders have a highly developed understanding and appreciation of the situations, dynamics, opportunities, and threats that confront them and those in their charge. Max DePree summed up a major element of leadership when he said, "The first task of a leader is to help define reality." The high-performance organizations are reality-based companies that are guided by leaders who have an honest and realistic appreciation of operating environments, the status of their organizations, and themselves as leaders. They instinctively sense things and have an uncanny ability to see things differently and to bring clarity to ambiguity, priority to conflicting issues, and order to chaos.

One of the more important aspects of perspective is the life experience of the leader. High-performance leaders typically have a broad range of life experiences as a result of working and living in a variety of locations, developing competencies in several areas and experiencing a number of life issues and challenges. The high-performance leaders have life stories to tell and a portfolio of experiences of working in different locations with progressively greater responsibilities and very broad and highly diversified people. High-performance leaders share some common life experiences and qualities:

- They have developed sensitivity and appreciation for life by having lived and/or worked in many places, interacted with many different cultures, and developed relationships with many different types of people.
- Their personal growth and development usually includes parenting, care giving, volunteering, and/or teaching.
- They have overcome significant personal adversities, failures, and challenges, such as sickness, personal loss, the death of a close family member or loved one, divorce or domestic fragmentation, and/or career derailment.
- They have successfully transitioned between multiple employers, job changes, and/or geographical locations, or, like Bill Gates, Michael Dell, and Henry Ford, they are driven by entrepreneurial fervor.
- They have many varied outside interests that broaden their network of friends and acquaintances who personally challenge them to learn more and test themselves in new situations.

Perhaps nowhere is the mantel of leadership forged and tested more completely than in the leader's ability to recover from devastating personal losses or professional setbacks, such as career derailment. Adversity brings out character, and the ability to learn from adversity and turn failure or setbacks into opportunities are the trademarks of high-performance leaders. Leaders who have successfully transitioned out of adversity tend to:

- Be more empathetic and appreciative of life and the diversity of others.
- Be better at issue and problem "triage" because they have a greater referential base of experiences to draw upon in prioritizing needs, issues, and problems.
- Openly acknowledge their faults and deficiencies and readily acknowledge that they do not have all the answers.
- Be better positioned to lead their organizations through adverse times. They have the perspective and personal knowledge necessary to help motivate and sustain the organization and employees during extreme uncertainty, hardships, and competitive pressures.

Fundamental to sharing this perspective and leveraging personal insights is the ability to effectively communicate. Leaders cannot lead effectively unless they have the ability to communicate and make a "personal connection" with those who follow. Communication, in some form or another, occurs virtually every second that a person is awake, and it includes a wide range of activities such as listening, talking, reading, writing, voice tone and volume, writing style and use of vocabulary, body gestures, wardrobe, and role playing. The high-performance leaders demonstrate a unique propensity for communicating with a wide and varied constituency, in a way that creates a direct linkage between themselves and others. They use vocabulary that helps to foster commonality and open and honest dialogues, invites valid dissention, and ensures inclusiveness. Most importantly, they make those with whom they are communicating feel as if they are the center of attention and, as a wise mother once said, "the most important people in the world." To this point, there is a common story about William Ewart Gladstone, a prime minister of Great Britain in the nineteenth century, that recounts that if you were dining with him, you felt as though you were in the presence of greatness, *his* greatness. In contrast, when dining with Disraeli, arguably one of the greatest statesmen of all time, he made you feel as though *you* were the greatness. High-performance leaders help to elevate the sense of self, the sense of self-worth, and the self-confidence of others.

Communication is an enormously complex and highly specialized subject. It is multilevel and multidimensional. Factors such as the social architecture, the specific context in which the interchange occurs, and the mental and social disposition of those involved in the communication process must be considered. For purposes of strategic change and strategy formulation, high-performance leaders communicate using a variety of forums and methods. Specifically:

- To *teach* others. In teaching others, leaders communicate information, ideas, tacit knowledge, facts, techniques, and methods to do certain things or to think differently. High-performance leaders have exceptionally high levels of personal commitment to teaching others as it requires significant personal and sometimes financial investment. Teaching provides leaders with a forum to test ideas, refine their presentation and communication skills, and develop a more meaningful and rewarding personal rapport with their constituents, employees, and followers. More importantly, when teaching, the best leaders are also learning new things and developing new insights that contribute to and further extend their knowledge.

  High-performance leaders understand that although the investment of their time and direct financial and opportunity costs are often high, teaching is one of the best methods for achieving the leader's primary mission: the perpetuation and continuous advancement of the organization. That is because teaching others is one of the most effective means of mentoring and developing future leaders. Teaching transfers both explicit and tacit knowledge to next-generation leaders and provides the context for leaders to better interpret and anticipate the changes in the environment that all organizations face.

  Clearly, high-performance leaders are intelligent and display a working knowledge in several competencies. However, it is their ability to *learn* and draw upon many different experiences that makes them unique. They demonstrate a high propensity to learn from others and adapt, create, and apply new knowledge to the situations that they face. In doing so, they develop relationships and correlations between many different events and facts. They extrapolate and *extend* their learnings to anticipate trends and patterns, to form hypotheses and solutions to situations, to create more effective interactions with others, and to improve the decision-making processes.

High-performance leaders use a direct "Socratic" style of teaching that stresses not only "what" but also "why," "how," and "what for." They use many methods to get their messages and images across such as storytelling, metaphors, and informal conversations. The form and tone of expression that are used in conveying their knowledge and life experiences are critically important to how well the knowledge is interpreted and applied by others. The most effective means of communicating is direct personal contact and trying to stay "in tune" with the pulse of their organizations. To this end, there is an important *social* aspect to the transfer of tacit knowledge. The social aspect of knowledge and knowledge interaction gives it a very personal dimension and more meaningful texture. We are beginning to see the importance of the social aspect of communicating knowledge in the use of electronic messaging and extended enterprise concepts of organization.

- To *inform* others. Leaders also communicate to inform others of events, decisions, facts, and requirements. In the process, they use a variety of formal and informal tools, forums, and direct and indirect techniques. In particular, high-performance leaders use IT to leverage their ability to inform others, extend the physical boundaries of the organization, move knowledge, and create bilateral communications. The Internet, Intranet, and broadband communication technologies make this form of "personal leverage" possible and necessary, but they are not without their drawbacks.
- To *solicit* input from others. Leaders communicate in many ways to solicit information, data, reactions, input, and commitments from others to complement and fulfill their ideas, directions, and visions. The ability to successfully solicit input is important to creating and sustaining inclusiveness, openness, and honesty in the communication process.
- To *direct* the activities of others. Leaders communicate to influence, direct, command, and guide the actions of others. This form of communication is the one with which most people are familiar. Directing others requires special skills to be effective as a leader.

Exhibit 8.3 summarizes how leadership communications influence organizational performance.

In communicating, high-performance leaders are highly visible and accessible to their organizations. As AFL-CIO Executive Vice President Ms. Linda Chevez-Thompson commented, "We're not running the union from 815 16th Street. We are running the union from [places like] Cincinnati; I was in New Jersey; I was in Brookings, South Dakota; I went to Pocatello, Idaho; I have been to Kokomo, Indiana. I go to where I need to, to make sure that the labor movement, the real body of the labor movement, has a real feel for their leadership and what we stand for." High-performance leaders, such as Chevez-Thompson, use direct techniques such as personal visits and accessibility as well as others like IT to extend their presence and increase their accessibility and visibility.

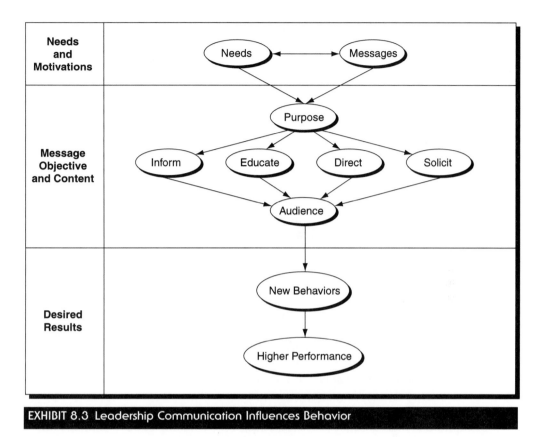

EXHIBIT 8.3 Leadership Communication Influences Behavior

Confidence, Courage, and Conviction

The great Roman philosopher Seneca commented, "There's one blessing only, the source and cornerstone of beatitude . . . confidence in self." Almost every study of leadership touches on the issue and importance of confidence as an attribute of leadership. Confidence is an elusive and fragile human quality. It can be won or lost in an instant. High-performance leaders have tremendous self-confidence along with a healthy dose of insecurity. That may present a bit of a dichotomy to some, but it is insecurity that drives leaders to higher levels of performance and, in turn, their confidence level.

Confidence in leadership is best expressed through dedication to the visions, dedication to their organizations, and personal commitments and loyalties. Confidence provides leaders with a sense of personal strength that allows them to persevere in the face of obstacles, instill hope during times of adversity, gain the trust of others during times of great uncertainty and change, and make decisions. Confidence manifests itself in many different ways and in various "doses" or degrees of influence. Some leaders express their confidence using much emotion and highly articulated and passionate behaviors. Some are quiet and calculating in their use and display of confidence. Irrespective of style, virtually all high-performing leaders express their confidence through their personal convictions, beliefs, and actions.

Confidence on the part of the leader and in others inspires people to assume personal responsibility for changing, taking action, accepting new challenges, making decisions, and succeeding. Confidence is essential for leaders if they are to forge trust and commitment on the part of their teams, and ensure cultural diversity, constructive contention, and the inclusiveness necessary to build long-term synergistic personal and professional relationships. In contrast, some of the most dangerous leaders are those who either lack confidence or have a false sense of confidence. Leaders who are inherently weak and not genuine in their sense of self are compromised in their ability to lead. The combination of these two characteristics can be fatal to any organization or society. Confidence must be developed and nurtured from the earliest years. It can be developed, lost, regained, embellished, and modified as we move through life. One of the greatest moments for parents is seeing that "glow" of confidence in the eyes of their child as they are learning and mastering new skills. High-performance leaders have natural sources of confidence; others must work hard to find their sources and build on them.

"If you want to lead, you must have confidence in yourself, but more importantly, you must learn to have the same level of confidence in others." My father, who was a career soldier and served in two wars, said that to me 35 years ago when I was playing youth league basketball. High-performance leaders work to build confidence in others by extending their confidence to others. Through this extension, they strengthen personal relationships, exhibit trust, and, most importantly, allow others the opportunity to develop as next-generation leaders. In the process, they can release enormous amounts of passion and creative energy in their organization, which can then be channeled to successfully achieve change and realize the overall vision, mission, and purpose of the organization. Confidence, accountability, and personal conviction are essential for leadership, and in their absence there is no basis for sustaining or advancing the interests of the organization.

With confidence comes credibility and belief in the decisions that one makes. "It's different finding yourself in a role where you are really charged with running the organization. You're charged with setting the tone. You're charged with leading," said David Coulter, formerly of Bank of America. An essential quality of leading is the ability to make decisions in a timely and effective manner. Make no mistake—high-performance leaders make decisions. Although they may strive for inclusiveness in soliciting input, accept ideas from others, provide encouragement, and extol empowerment, in the end, they must make the decisions and they alone are accountable. Unfortunately, not all leaders believe or practice that most obvious axiom of leadership. Those types of leaders always seem to find an excuse or characterize themselves as victims of something or someone. They have a unique ability to deflect responsibility and accountability onto others or towards other issues. One exceedingly clear characteristic of high-performance leaders is that they take *complete* ownership and responsibility for their actions and decisions. This accountability is unfiltered and unmitigated. One of the best examples of ownership and accountability comes from Dwight Eisenhower, who as Supreme Allied Commander wrote a letter exonerating his commanders and staff by taking complete personal responsibility for any failure related to the invasion of Normandy, *before* the actual landings began.

When leaders make decisions, they either directly or indirectly *allocate* and *deploy* the financial, human, operational, and intellectual resources of the organization and change it. High-performance leaders make decisions using the best knowledge available and fully utilize input from selective sources. Some of the distinguishing trademarks of high-performance leaders as decision makers include:

- Leaders move with speed and urgency. Leaders understand that if they procrastinate on a decision, the competition can beat them.
- Leaders recognize that if they show timidity or ignorance in the marketplace, the customer will find their competitors.
- Leaders acknowledge that if they are not innovative, they will not only lose hard-earned strategic position but also their most talented employees.
- Leaders make decisions that resolve conflicts and contention in their organizations and cultures.
- Leaders explain the rationale for the decisions made and actions taken, but they do not defend them. Decision making is both a prerogative and a necessity of leadership.
- Leaders are inclusive in their deliberations. They invite and encourage diverse opinions and ideas and dynamic dialogue. Ultimately, however, they make the decisions.
- Leaders delay making major decisions when under severe personal or political duress or emotional stress, which may cloud their judgment. They defer or delay making decisions until they better understand the implications of their state of mind and emotional state on their decisions.
- Leaders define and/or compartmentalize stress and pressure in a manner that allows them to constructively address their sources rationally and pragmatically.
- Leaders are honest with themselves and others about their feelings, preferences, and personal biases.
- They demonstrate discipline in their approach to leading, which includes consistency of behavior, high energy and stamina, and personal conviction.
- Finally, high-performance leaders understand that they have both an explicit and intrinsic impact on others, who interpret the verbal, behavioral, and visual gestures that they emit in many different ways.

There is some current rhetoric in leadership that espouses the notion of "communities of leaders" and consensus building as two fundamental themes of high-performance leadership in contemporary times. These are interesting ideas, but they do not reflect the realities of competing at Internet time. Clearly, everyone in a high-performance organization, irrespective of her or his level or status, how large the organization is, or how sophisticated it may be, is a leader in his or her own unique way. Leaders at all levels make decisions and influence others in their daily interactions with a wide spectrum of people. But they are not responsible for the overall conduct and performance of the organization, nor are they directly accountable to the shareholders, regulatory authorities, and law enforcement agencies for the actions of their organization. The senior executives, officers, and directors of the organization are legally, morally, and ethically responsible for the organization in the eyes of society, the legal institutions, and the investment community. Individual employees, managers, supervisors, and support staffs are responsible for their portion of the organization, no matter how small or large it might be, but they are not the ones who make the "big" decisions. Consensus building, together with the opinions of others in decision-making processes, is important, but not all people can or should be included in decision processes. Some people simply are not qualified to be involved. As Margaret Thatcher noted, "Consensus is the absence of leadership." Thus, in the end, high-performance leaders are the decision makers and they alone are accountable for the behavior of the organization.

LEADING FOR HIGH-PERFORMANCE RESULTS

Having discussed the essential qualities of leadership, we now turn to the issue of how high-performance leaders actually lead. There are countless theories and models for leading others, and no single model can present itself as the defacto standard. Each organization and each leader is different. How one might lead an organization in the very stable and predictable insurance business is entirely different than how one leads an Internet start-up company. There are, as we have discussed in previous chapters, very distinct patterns and trends that are influencing new leadership practices and dynamics. Leadership, as has been mentioned, concerns itself with influencing others to achieve higher levels of personal performance, greater levels of accountability, greater levels of contribution, and, ultimately, growth and development of the person. From this perspective, leadership in the highly dynamic world must, by definition, be very different than any of the models forged in the industrial era of well-defined industry structures, narrowly prescribed organizational roles, and geographical borders. Those styles of leadership simply will not work in today's highly fluid environment or that of the future marked with increasing uncertainty, worker mobility, and inter-networking.

High-performance leaders function in a wide variety of capacities. At times they may be subject-matter experts who possess the deep explicit knowledge as well as extensive experience and the formal education to analyze and solve a specific set of problems or issues. We commonly see this type of leadership in law, business, health care, technology, and other fields that require extensive technical expertise and working knowledge. These leaders can be inclined to be subtle in their leadership of professionals and, as Henry Mintzberg comments, can be "covert" in their demonstration of power, exertion of influence, and exercise of power.

High-performance leaders understand that although they have formal power, the real basis of their power and the most effective measure of their leadership is generated by, and flows from, those who follow. Thus, they are masters at building *coalitions* and collaborations, especially those that are cross-cultural and cross-competency. Rather than relying on command and control, high-performance leaders understand that their source of leadership comes from getting people to work together, rally to a common purpose, and personally commit to achieve superior results through collaboration and coalitions.

Let's summarize four important ways in which high-performance leaders actually lead.

Conductor/Choreographer

Andy Grove calls it "stage managing." Jack Welch likens the leadership process to that of an orchestral conductor. EVP Tom Sidlik of DaimlerChrysler calls it "creative guidance." The high-performance leaders are influencers, guides, catalysts, choreographers, and *conductors,* who understand and appreciate the capabilities, training, and perspective of others. As such, they have an ability to figure out how to best utilize and deploy their resources in a manner that is challenging and rewarding to the person and in the best interests of the organization. Some of the distinguishing characteristics of leaders as conductors include:

1. They have an appreciation for multiple competencies and highly diversified professional and personal experiences. They are able to constructively "coach" others and generally have a higher level of sensitivity and appreciation for the issues and challenges that confront others.
2. As conductors and choreographers, they extol their charges to experiment, learn, and optimize their talents.
3. They exhibit patience and understanding when coaching and teaching.

Leaders who effectively serve as conductors are cognizant of the capabilities and contributions of those around them. They function as intermediaries between the performers, the strategies, and the environment.

Coalition and Collaboration Builder

High-performance leaders recognize that the great organizations excel at innovation, are agile, have excellent operations, and use knowledge as a source of competitive advantage and differentiation. They readily acknowledge that breakthrough thinking and results are supported, indeed created, by collaborative groups of people who are motivated and unified by a single purpose or vision and have diverse life experiences as well as various racial, geographical, and ethnic backgrounds. The importance and role of the leader in collaboration was discussed in chapter 7.

Coalition and building collaborative relationships also extends into outsourcing with partners and selected vendors. The objectives and issues with respect to outsourcing are discussed in greater detail in chapter 9.

Change Agent/Catalyst

High-performance leaders recognize that the most competitive organizational designs are those that are agile, adaptable, and capable of redeploying themselves in a manner that best optimizes the resources of their firms. Most importantly, they understand that formal structures are only representations of the organization at any one point in time. High-performance leaders work to eliminate the boundaries that are created between competencies, functions, and structures and work to liberate employee energy and creativity. They accomplish those activities in many ways, including rotating employees through a series of assignments and defragmenting the organization by moving to more knowledge-based, competency-based, and process-centric designs.

In developing agile organizations, leaders work to design structures that provide both a business and social architecture. The business architecture represents the plan and arrangement of the organization and its resources. However, it is the social architecture that personifies and typifies how the organization communicates, defines its values, and actually functions. Leaders who create both open and adaptable social architectures provide an organizational climate that allows individuals to grow, to become increasingly engaged, and to become more fulfilled and satisfied as human beings. This sense of fulfillment allows those organizations to compete in many different ways using a variety of venues.

Champion of Operational Excellence

High-performance leaders are committed to operational excellence. They understand that operational excellence is a source of competitive advantage and employee satisfaction. They recognize that operational excellence is made possible through the effective utilization of knowledge, importing "best" ideas and practices from other organizations, and expressing confidence in others to learn and adapt. Leaders who champion operational excellence demonstrate several common characteristics:

1. They are constantly challenging their organizations and followers to critically assess their capabilities and realistically confront their limitations.
2. They and their organizations are in a constant state of learning and discovery.
3. They are driven by, and aligned with, the overarching vision of the organization.
4. They hold themselves to extraordinary performance levels and have measurements and reward and recognition systems that reflect that commitment.
5. They are committed to continuous quality improvement.

Chapter 9 provides a comprehensive discussion of operational excellence as a pillar of high-performance strategy and as a catalyst for strategic change and revitalization.

HIGH-PERFORMANCE LEADERSHIP: MEASURING CONTRIBUTION AND EFFECTIVENESS

Finally, we come to the critical issue of how to best measure leader effectiveness. Financial performance and strategic positioning are important to understanding how effective and valuable a leader has been, but as evaluative criteria they fail to provide a complete representation of the leader. Leaders, as discussed, must have character and the ability to make decisions, communicate, and support their organizations. Thus, to accurately and completely depict the performance of the leader, we must consider dimensions of style, character, and personal substance.

Realistically, there is no single measurement or set of measurements and processes for assessing leaders and no easy way to apply a simple set of criteria for evaluating the value, effectiveness, or contribution of leaders. The process of leading is far too complex and serious a subject to lend itself to easy measurements and simple multiple-choice and "how do you feel about" answers. But measuring any type of performance requires some set of guidelines, standards, or referential points. For the most part, measurements for leaders, at least in the United States, tend to concentrate on the short term at the expense of longer time horizons. They usually stress financial results. Although appropriate, financial measures alone are incomplete measurements of leader effectiveness.

Because leadership has so many complex interactions and exists in a rapidly changing environment, it makes sense that the evaluation of leadership must be performed using more measurements that include a wide range of attributes. The criteria should span the spectrum of leader activities that we have discussed throughout this work, recognize the hyper-dynamics of the operating environment, and address the immediate, near, and long terms. Most important, it should concentrate on aspects of creating and sustaining a high-performance organization and being a high-performance leader. In measuring sustainability, we must consider several different aspects. First, we must consider the ability of the leader to develop personnel and a management team capable of advancing and perpetuating the organization. As Chrysler CEO Robert Eaton noted, a "test" is whether the leader has developed "A team that knows where it wants to go and why it wants to go there and it's empowered to make it all happen. No individual or two or three people leaving will affect that." The second involves strategic positioning and whether the leader is positioning the organization for the long term. This requires developing an understanding of the organization's strategic intentions and goals, as well as the alignment of the leader to those goals. Finally, as Walter Lippmann noted in his 1945 editorial, *Roosevelt Has Gone,* "The final test of a leader is that he leaves behind him in other men the conviction and the will to carry on." The ultimate test is whether the organization is materially better off after the leader has completed her or his tenure at the helm.

The assessment of leaders should be premised on a multifactoral approach that links and integrates essential concepts such as time horizons with qualitative and quantitative criteria to provide a more comprehensive and accurate representation of leader performance. The use of a multifactoral approach provides flexibility and can be applied to a wide range of leadership levels, roles, and industries. Specifically, the multifactoral criteria presented are composed of three performance-measurement categories:

- Financial performance measures.
- Strategic positioning measures.
- Individual leadership measures.

Financial performance measurements are designed to assess the leader's performance and contribution to the fiscal well-being of the organization. These measurements include sales and profitability, as well as the market value of the organization. In the public sector, they can be adjusted and emphasis redirected to things like budget surpluses, tax collections, revenue enhancement through economic development, and privatization for cost reduction and service improvement. Strategic positioning measurements are designed to assess the effectiveness of the leader in creating competitive advantage for the organization. This measurement includes a broad range of strategic, visioning, and resource deployment considerations that, when taken as a whole, provide some degree of assessment as to whether or not the leader is positioning the organization to advance, grow, and become more competitive. In the public sector, financial-measurement criteria can be adjusted to reflect such items as economic development, education, IT, government downsizing, and consolidated/collaborative organizations for government. Finally, individual leadership measures are specific to being a leader. These measurements concentrate on multiple quality aspects of leadership, including communications, learning, and developing a sense of self.

SUMMARY

In this chapter, we have discussed the elements of high-performance leadership as it relates to strategic renewal and strategy formulation. High-performance leaders are professionally and personally committed to the ideals, the visions, and the purpose of the cause that they set forth for their organizations. They are morally committed to those who follow them, and they recognize that their primary mission is to advance the organization and not their own personal legacies or interests.

Let's summarize some of the top ideas and conclusions:

1. High-performance leaders know themselves and develop their character. High-performance leaders stand for something higher and more valuable than just profits and marketshare.
2. High-performance leaders understand their impact on others. Leaders recognize that their source of leadership includes the relationships, coalitions, and effective collaborations that they are able to generate.
3. High-performance leaders demonstrate personal commitment and convictions. Leaders are personally committed to the development of themselves and others. They provide opportunities for advancement, mentor others, resolve conflicts, and create cultures. They also demonstrate a commitment to the strategies and visions of their organizations through demonstrating consistency in behaviors, communications, and decision making.
4. High-performance leaders make the tough calls. Leaders are paid to make the tough decisions. High-performance leaders use an inclusive approach, encourage debate and discussion, then make the decision.
5. High-performance leaders practice civility and good manners. They respect others and treat them as equals.

Critical Thoughts and Discussion Questions

1. What special initiatives, programs, or projects demonstrate that the leader is a catalyst and proponent of innovation as a source of competitive advantage?
2. What actions and behaviors of the leader demonstrate the ability to craft strategies and visions that will enable the organization to compete more effectively?
3. What insights, perspectives, and analyses performed by the leader indicate that she or he has a deep understanding and appreciation of the changes in the operating environment?
4. What strategic programs, processes, and tactics has the leader developed that demonstrate her or his ability to help advance and perpetuate the organization and sustain growth and performance?
5. What strategic activities and behaviors demonstrate the leader has implemented a process designed to ensure that an adequate strategy and a vision are created for the organization?
6. What projects, initiatives, or results indicate that the leader is effective in global environments?

CHAPTER 9

OPERATIONAL EXCELLENCE AND ORGANIZATIONAL AGILITY: SUSTAINING CONTINUOUS RENEWAL AND HIGH PERFORMANCE

"Five years from now, we will be a different company, and five years from there we'll be another different company."

—JACQUES NASSER, PRESIDENT AND CEO, FORD MOTOR COMPANY
IN *FAST COMPANY* MAGAZINE

INTRODUCTION

"In the 21st century, sustainable competitive advantage will come much more of new process technologies and much less of new product technologies," predicts Lester Thurow in *Head to Head*. This chapter discusses the fifth pillar of strategic high performance: operational excellence and its complement, organizational agility. High-performance companies strive to develop and sustain competitive advantage from flawless operations and agile and adaptable organizational structures. They recognize that they can create or gain marketspace, reduce their structural and variable costs, and improve customer interactions through operational excellence.

Companies are not born with operational excellence. Rather, this high-value competency is developed. Organizations may have the necessary innate talents and genetic material to do extraordinary things, but like a gifted performer, athlete, or student, an organization must continuously practice and exhort itself to fully develop and optimize its talents. One of the distinguishing trademarks of high-performance organizations is that they have a relentless quest for flawless execution in their essential business processes (core) and customer interactions. In this chapter, we discuss some important issues and challenges regarding operational excellence. Specifically:

1. What is the definition of *operational excellence* relative to high-performance organizations?
2. Why is operational excellence important as a strategic pillar?
3. What are the characteristics and qualities of operational excellence?
4. How does an organization create operational excellence?
5. What is the role of organizational agility in operational excellence?

Supporting operational excellence are the technologies, structures, and competencies of an organization and its ability to rapidly change and rearrange these elements for optimal performance. Thus, creating and sustaining the ability to rapidly and efficiently switch among different technologies, processes, and outsourcing relationships are central to operational excellence. This chapter discusses the role and importance of creating agile and fast organizational competencies and explores the influence of such capabilities on developing and leveraging operational excellence for strategic advantage.

THE IMPORTANCE OF OPERATIONAL EXCELLENCE

The late Dr. Deming elevated operational excellence to the forefront of management attention through his work with Japanese companies and emphasis on quality as a differentiating source of competitive advantage. Although the concept of operational excellence is well established, it assumes new and higher levels of importance in the context of strategic change and renewal. Management and academic literature have given considerable attention to operational excellence. Some researchers address it in the form of supplier value chains, others point to a manufacturing or customer orientation, and oftentimes it is viewed from a quality perspective. For purposes of high performance and strategic renewal, *operational excellence* is defined as:

> The design and performance of integrated systems and processes that create superior strategic, competitive, and operational value through speed, flexibility, and cross-purpose adaptability.

Central to this definition are the terms *systems* and *processes*. A system is a set of integrated activities supported by related organizations and technologies that are designed to achieve desired outcomes based on predetermined measures. *Scribner's Dictionary* defines *process* as an "operation or succession of operations leading to some result." According to authors Vikram Sethi and William King, a process is a "set of interrelated work activities characterized by specific inputs and value-added tasks that produce specific customer-focused outputs." Others have defined it as activities, outputs, and events. Operational excellence is influenced by a number of factors, including the design of the process, the execution (performance) of the process, the technologies that enable the performance of the process, the knowledge required, the organizational and operational context in which the process performs, and the human beings responsible for the process. Any modification or disruption of these factors will affect the overall performance of the process as well as its outcomes, value generated, and *total* transaction costs. Operational excellence involves virtually all aspects of the organization, and it extends to include relationships with customers and business partners. Operational excellence starts with the challenge and objective of not only performing the process quantumly better than the competition but also in a very different manner. The more differentiated the process design is and the higher its knowledge content, the more difficult it is to imitate and, hence, the greater its possible strategic value is to the organization.

To achieve operational excellence, the high performers develop an overall business architecture that leverages IT, knowledge, human performance, and technology. This architecture allows the high performers to execute their operations and make decisions with great speed, tremendous quality, and as little unnecessary human intervention as possible. Operational excellence usually (but not always) leads to significant cost reductions and positions the company for greater revenue growth and better performance. Thus, one of the fundamental axioms for achieving operational excellence is the minimization of total transaction costs while maximizing the value created.

There are many examples demonstrating the importance of operational excellence. Known for its advanced product designs, Chrysler Corporation invested $240 million in development costs for its Sebring model. In comparison, Ford's costs to develop the Mustang were about $700 million, a threefold difference. Chrysler's commitment to operational excellence has also enabled it to accelerate its delivery time of finished product (i.e., the time it takes to deliver a car from its factories to dealers) by 46 percent, from 68 days to 37 days. At an average of $1,226 per vehicle, Chrysler also enjoys an almost 2 to 1 profit advantage per vehicle over GM.

Despite persistent quality problems, Chrysler has achieved high levels of operational excellence through process integration with internal functions and external suppliers and outsourcers. Cars are designed and managed through "platform teams," which integrate various functional and technical experts and provide for a single point of responsibility and accountability for the car from concept through production to market delivery. Chrysler has also reduced the time required to design and bring to market vehicles from around 55 months in 1990 to 38 months in 1993 to 24 months in 1998. The 1998 Chrysler Concord and Dodge Intrepid required only 31 months to develop, seven months less than the original LH versions in 1990/91. Those cars were developed at least 40 percent faster than prior models. In contrast, Ford's Taurus required 36 months and $3 billion dollars to be produced. Chrysler's ability to manufacture cars quickly combined with arguably the most progressive designs, the most innovative management team in Detroit, its outsourcing relationships, and $7 billion in cash made it a highly desirable acquisition candidate.

With its cross-platform integration initiatives that allow the same components and subsystems to be used across a variety of models, Chrysler has redefined the way cars are designed and built. For the near term, it has created a distinct competitive advantage over virtually *all* of its competitors. Central to Chrysler's design successes and manufacturing processes is the outsourcing of subassembly and subsystems to specialized suppliers and partners. These practices have their historical antecedents in the late 1980s, when Chrysler once again found itself on the business ropes confronting declining sales and diminishing financial capabilities. To reduce its costs, Chrysler aggressively de-massed and disaggregated its vertically integrated process and organizational designs and engaged its suppliers in the design and supplying of key components and complete subassemblies such as dashboards, electronics, environmental systems, drive trains, suspensions, and interior parts. When building these collaborative relationships, suppliers were given physical and performance specifications and were left to their own expertise to design and manufacture complete assemblies or subassemblies for Chrysler. In the process, Chrysler off-loaded internal costs and, through its SCORE program, lowered total costs by $1 billion with another $1.4 billion set as an objective resulting from the acquisition by Daimler-Benz. In addition to the obvious financial benefits, operational excellence also enables Chrysler to have higher levels of flexibility and responsiveness while reacting to customer needs and allowing an accelerated introduction of improvements and innovations as compared to its competitors. More importantly, it provides Chrysler with a unique opportunity to be *in closer tune with its customers because it is faster* than the competition. This means that Chrysler can better understand and create or react to its environments. Command the environment and a company will command the competition.

Chrysler's operational excellence is supported, in part, by the use of the CATIA software product that allows it to test thousands of engines, suspensions, drive trains, and seat designs without incurring the expense and time of building physical models. This capability provides Chrysler with the ability to virtually simulate an infinite number of permutations and combinations while reducing development time by at least six months and cost by millions of dollars. Co-CEO Robert Eaton noted, "In the past, time would only allow five designs of an engine intake manifold. CATIA has made possible 1,500 designs in six month's less time. It can also tell us what an engine is going to sound like, even before we build a single part. When prototype tooling is required by government regulations, we use processes like stereolithography to create the physical model directly from the computer data." Prior to CATIA, prototype development required four to six weeks. CATIA reduces the time to just a few days. Once a design is approved, Chrysler is also able to quickly generate the part specifications and part-numbering sequences, two activities that traditionally require a significant amount of time and effort. CATIA also contributes to manufacturing improvements and cost efficiencies that link Chrysler with its external suppliers for skilled pattern makers and supplies. The results are quantum, reducing a historical five-day cycle time to under eight hours.

Dell Computer, a company that is highly regarded and extensively studied for its use of e-commerce, provides another example of how operational excellence creates competitive advantage and fuels growth in the marketplace. Dell has adopted and successfully implemented an Internet-based business model that integrates customers, suppliers, internal competencies, and outsourcing partners into an overall business architecture that supports $40 million a day in revenues. The process, which includes the selective outsourcing of parts and subassemblies and certain operational functions, enables Dell to convert a customer order to shipment within 24 hours. Dell's performance compares to the one-time leader Compaq that requires as much as 35 days, as well as rival Gateway, that can meet demand within 12 days. As a result, Dell's cash flows are accelerated. Most importantly, Dell estimates that its raw material inventory is about 60 days "fresher" than its competitors. This "freshness" creates a significant source of differentiation in the minds of the consumers because they perceive extra value in buying the latest and "freshest" technology available.

In Erie, Pennsylvania GE's Transportation Systems Division (GETS) provides another example of operational excellence leading to competitive advantage and high performance. GETS designs and manufactures diesel and electric freight and passenger locomotives, motorized wheel systems for mining trucks, electric propulsion and auxiliary power units for transit vehicles, and many other products related to the heavy transportation industry. For over 30 years, from the 1950s to the 1980s, GM dominated the heavy locomotive industry, and "GE was an also-ran," according to Charles M. Vincent, a railroad industry analyst for PNC Asset Management Group in Philadelphia. "It was commonly regarded that GE produced inferior locomotives."

True to Jack Welch's mandate of being number 1 or 2 in their markets, GETS borrowed lessons learned from throughout GE and from the collaboration with customers and suppliers to reinvent its design and operational processes. The new processes have enabled it to grow its business faster than any of its competitors, including GM. According to *Transportation News,* GE has "... consistently beat General Motors, its only competitor for the U.S. locomotive market, the past five years." It has reduced manufacturing time per locomotive from 90 to 26 days and, as Mike Iden, director of technical services for Union Pacific Railroad in Omaha, Nebraska, observed, "GE has a manufacturing capacity that is lacking at GM." Rich Fleming, a spokesman for GM's Electro-Motive Division, countered, saying, "We have the means to manufacture as many locomotives as we get orders for," but he wasn't specific about why GM was not landing more orders and why or how GM was ceding marketspace to a competitor.

For Wal-Mart, it is product movement information at the individual SKU (item) level and communication between its stores, distribution centers, and suppliers that are central to its ability to create and sustain operational excellence. The results are lower prices, higher in-store product availability for customers, and one of the highest sales and profits per square foot of retail space in the mass merchandiser industry. To achieve operational excellence, Wal-Mart achieves superior performance and competitive advantage through the integration of human performance with in-store processes and IT. Wal-Mart's Retail Link provides direct information on sales, customer counts, transaction volumes, product movement, and customer preferences from Wal-Mart to its vendor-partners and buyers. The rapid exchange of this data enables vendor-partners to review product demand and item movement, build a history for specific products, profile future sales, determine the best mix for each store, and automatically restock items on a real-time, fast-time basis.

United Airlines (UA) provides another example of operational excellence that is the result of an overall architecture integrating technology with process design, human performance, and appropriate measures. UA spokesperson Manny Ventura notes that commercial airlines get thousands of maintenance bulletins, alerts, and notices, plus an unpredictable number of Airworthiness Directives yearly from the FAA and airline manufacturers. All this communication must be managed and acted upon to insure the safety of passengers and airworthiness of the UA fleet. Ventura notes "Our entire system was paper-based—we would physically move documents from in-box to in-box. This made things difficult during the FAA's random audits—they would call looking for status on a specific directive and we'd have to scramble to locate it." Using a combination of process design, organizational responsibilities, and LiveLink, an IT-based system, UA reinvented its operations to successfully route bulletins and directives to the appropriate maintenance personnel. The process ensures that all bulletins and directives are delivered to the correct person and areas of responsibility and that an audit trail is provided. The system, which supports the entire UA fleet and more than 300 engineers, helps UA to track the status of all bulletins and directives at any time, eliminates FAA citations, and increases the safety and efficiency of UA's airplanes.

The list of cases and examples for operational excellence is extensive and well studied. The point has been made: Operational excellence creates strategic advantage and is a catalyst for strategic renewal.

THE IMPACT OF QUALITY

In the 1990's, the concepts of TQM and CQI went a long way in helping many companies to become more competitive and profitable. However, much like the old sailor's adage that a rising tide in a harbor raises all of the ships at anchor, as the quality of one company improved, so did the quality of others as well as that of an entire industry. Soon the competitive advantages of quality enjoyed by the quality leaders were neutralized, or lessened, as industry rivals improved their products and services. Ultimately, quality as a source of sustainable differentiation among competitors loses its significance because it becomes a given, a consumer-expected imperative.

Today, quality is an absolute prerequisite for high performance. A company must have quality if it is to be a high performer, yet quality alone does not assure high performance. For example, Motorola, a quality leader, has aggressively pursued seven-sigma initiatives for its manufacturing and parts processes. That means that for every 10 million products or parts produced, only one part has a defective variance. That is an interesting and sometimes a laudable goal for a manufacturer, but from a typical consumer's perspective it is not very exciting or differentiating. Retail customers probably will not rush out to buy cellular telephones and pagers knowing that Motorola moved their quality standards from six-sigma standards to a seven-sigma standard. The economic value proposition (EVP) is not strong enough to motivate consumers to assume different behaviors, unless, of course, they are buying medical devices or some other high-precision product where safety, security, and health are involved. However, what may be strategic and more important to operational excellence is Motorola's commitment to becoming better. What they learn from their foray into seven-sigma quality could be of significant value if it can be effectively assimilated into a KMP and used elsewhere in the company as well as by its business partners, especially in the areas of new product design and launch. Ultimately, Motorola may become more competitive, but it will be a significant challenge for the company to regain the market prominence and influence that it has forfeited to competitors Nokia, Qualcom, and Ericsson, based on quality alone. A relentless commitment to new products and innovation are required.

It would be naive to conclude that quality alone can lead to high performance and dominant competitive position. For example, the Wallace Company, several winners of the Baldrige Award have filed for bankruptcy, and a few others, including Eastman Chemical, have demonstrated less than spectacular financial performance. Motorola, once a high performer, has experienced a steady decline in earnings and market luster since winning the Baldrige in 1988. Despite winning the Baldrige Award in 1990, sales of GM's luxury Cadillac have fallen from a high of 300,000 cars sold in 1985 to slightly over 180,000 sold in 1998. For the first time in over 40 years, retail sales of Ford's Lincoln luxury car line to consumers (not rental fleets) were higher than Cadillac's sales in 1998.

Notwithstanding the above, an analysis performed by the NIST of the Baldrige and Deming winners indicates that their stock performances have outpaced the S&P 500 by a 4 to 1 margin for the 1988 through 1995 period, achieving a return of 248 percent.

While the S&P gained 58.5 percent for the study period, the quality winners gained 248.7 percent. Even for those companies that did not win the award but made it into the finals, the NIST reports they bested the S&P 500 by a margin of 2 to 1. For the 1988 to 1997 period, *Business Week* reports that the 16 winners outperformed the S&P 500 index by a 3 to 1 margin for ROI. The 48 companies that competed but did not win bested the S&P 500 index by a 2 to 1 margin.

The importance of quality is explicit: A company cannot become or sustain high performance without having significant quality and a culture that has a passion for quality in everything that it does. Quality is an absolute prerequisite for high performance but quality alone cannot guarantee sustainable competitive advantage.

THE ROLE OF BENCHMARKING IN OPERATIONAL EXCELLENCE

"Benchmarking has become part of this new culture of ours. We're not too proud to ask for help when we see somebody doing it better...." noted CEO Robert Eaton of Chrysler Corporation in 1993. In the 1980s and through most of the 1990s significant discussion has been directed to the use of benchmarking as a means of creating and/or measuring operational performance. Author James Martin defines *benchmarking* as "A process of hunting for the best practice and comparing one's own operation with it." In contrast, another researcher states, "Benchmarking is the process of continually comparing a company's performance on critical customer requirements against the best in the industry." Although each of these definitions relates to what benchmarking is, they are deficient in defining and in describing what benchmarking actually involves and what it can provide an organization. For example, benchmarking is not exclusively the domain of "best practices." Second, there are no clear-cut criteria or universally accepted definitions of what is or is not a best practice. A more appropriate definition of *benchmarking* is:

> The process of using consistent tools and practices to identify, analyze, measure, and contrast the behavior and performance of comparable processes and activities within an organization, within a specific industry, or across various industries.

Benchmarks are useful in a variety of situations, especially to stimulate knowledge sharing, as targets for setting operational excellence goals or as corroborative evidence to address barriers and organizational objections. Benchmarks can communicate three important items: (1) what is possible, (2) what other companies have accomplished, and (3) what others are doing. Essentially, there are three approaches to benchmarking:

1. Intracompany benchmarks.
2. Intraindustry benchmarks.
3. Cross-industry benchmarks.

Intracompany benchmarks are usually the easiest and least costly to perform. These benchmarks, which are performed within a specific company on its operations, processes, organization performance, and a variety of other functions, compare performance and costs among similar and sometimes different functions. The major drawback of this approach is that it can be and often is biased by internal politics, usually is restricted in design and scope, and can be incomplete in its rationalization of processes. In contrast,

	Internal	Intraindustry (External)	Cross-Industry (External)
Definition	Benchmark is performed within the organization. Benchmark can be interdivisional, intradivisional, or within a department.	Benchmark is performed among a select group of competitors within an industry.	Benchmark is performed across industries using different companies.
Characteristics	▲ Easy to perform ▲ Inexpensive ▲ Confined area of interest, limited insights	▲ More complex process ▲ Higher investment ▲ Provides broader perspective and insight ▲ Can be difficult to perform	▲ Extremely complex, requires careful design and execution ▲ Significant investment ▲ Provides more comprehensive perspectives and greater insights ▲ Very difficult and expensive to perform

Approach to Benchmarking

Step 1: Determine what to benchmark
Step 2: Define benchmarking standards
Step 3: Determine benchmarking strategy
Step 4: Develop work and staffing plans
Step 5: Perform the benchmark
Step 6: Analyze results
Step 7: Formulate insights

EXHIBIT 9.1 Approaches to Benchmarking

intraindustry benchmarks are derived from several different companies competing in the same industry. These benchmarks are more diversified and representative than intracompany benchmarks. They are more expensive to perform and require greater effort to rationalize data to ensure meaningful and accurate comparisons. Finally, cross-industry benchmarks are those that include many different companies from different industries. These tend to be broader, more sophisticated, and can be more insightful. Correspondingly, they are also more complex and expensive. Exhibit 9.1 summarizes the three approaches to benchmarking and some of their important characteristics.

To benchmark with any confidence and accuracy requires careful preparation and the design of a work plan that ensures comparability and consistency in the collection, adaptation, definition, and analysis of data. In general, there are seven basic steps to performing a benchmark:

1. Determining what to benchmark
2. Defining the standards and attributes for benchmarking
3. Determining the benchmarking strategy:
   a. Intracompany

    b. Intraindustry
    c. Cross-industry
 4. Developing the benchmarking work and staffing plan:
    a. Approach
    b. Sources
    c. Staffing
    d. Methods
 5. Executing the benchmarking strategy and work plan
 6. Performing the analysis on benchmarking results
 7. Formulating insights and conclusions

Benchmarking is valuable, but it also has many inherent limitations which can often lead to erroneous conclusions and, more alarmingly, a false sense of security. At the very best, imitating a benchmark can get a company even with the competition, but that is unlikely in a rapidly changing environment. Rarely, however, can emulating a benchmark lead to significant competitive advantage. That is because the high-performing companies that set the standards are always moving them higher. Any competitor using a benchmark to "get even" or "level the playing field" is following an imitation strategy. By the time they understand and implement the necessary practices to import and successfully use the benchmark in their own organization, the leaders have continued to innovate and ultimately elevate their performance to higher levels beyond the original benchmark. This is the position that one of the largest food companies in the U.S. found itself in during the 1990s. It was behind the competition, especially Nestle. Unfortunately, such results are all too common and almost never position a company ahead of its leading competitors or industry upstarts.

For example, when Ford Motor set about to redesign its Taurus, which was the best selling car in its line, it used the Honda Accord and the Toyota Camry as its primary benchmarks. Ford went so far as to post big signs in the development center with the words "Beat Camry" and included it in the Taurus project mission statement. According to author Mary Walton, for 3 years, while the development team was locked away in the basement of a building, it was obsessed with beating Camry. It bought Camrys, drove Camrys, took apart Camrys, analyzed Camrys and even crashed a few Camrys, all in pursuit of bettering the Camry. Camry was Ford's fixation and preoccupation.

But while Ford was building its Taurus based on the existing Camry, Toyota was busy designing and building an entirely new Camry and creating a new benchmark. Using cross-platform features that it would share with part of the Lexus luxury line, the new Camry offered less optional equipment, had less standard features, was offered at a lower price, achieved higher quality, and presented a new emphasis on driver and passenger ergonomics and ownership value. It had what much of the consumer market wanted. When Ford finally released its Taurus, it launched a car that was larger, heavier, noisier, and higher priced than the Camry. For Ford, their benchmark had radically changed, and Ford had failed to anticipate that Toyota would change its formula for success. According to Mary Walton, despite all of its efforts and fixation on Camry, Ford still did not surpass its target benchmark. Toyota's Camry outperformed the new Taurus in price, quality, and customer acceptance and was the best-selling car in the United States for 1997 and 1998.

Many companies have fallen into the trap of spending tens, sometimes hundreds, of thousands of dollars on benchmarking and in pursuit of the elusive, and often ill and undefined, "best practice." The inherent difficulties with relying on such initiatives supposedly leading to operational excellence are many. For example, what criteria support the claim or conclusion that a practice is, in fact, a best practice? What processes were used to ensure that comparable activities and measurements were rationalized correctly, and what evaluative criteria were used to distinguish it as a best practice? Therein lies the twofold challenge: defining what is a best practice and justifying *why* it is touted and presented as the best.

Another consideration with respect to relying on a best practice is that it can be limiting, especially if a company is under the impression that the benchmark is actually *the* best practice. Mandating the use of a best practice can place unnecessary and unwarranted restrictions on institutional creativity and inhibit individual initiative. Ultimately, such mandates can compromise the innovation process. Companies that implement or rely on external sources providing vast databases that purportedly include best practices can supplant innovation and inadvertently compromise the generation and application of new knowledge in their organizations by forcing conformity and compliance to an arbitrary or outdated standard.

Given the rate of change occurring in the environment, the longevity and appropriateness of the best practice is always in question, because the performance leaders are always advancing the notion of operational excellence and setting higher and higher levels of performance. By the time the best practice has been identified, studied, described, legally approved for public disclosure, and sold by the consulting firms in the marketplace as a best practice, as much as 2 or 3 years could go by. By the time it is adopted and implemented by an organization, another year or two will have transpired. At that point, it is no longer a best practice, it is an "old practice." Perhaps a superior approach would be to create a "worst practices" database that codifies the problems, limitations, and lessons learned from making mistakes and describes what will *not* work.

CREATING OPERATIONAL EXCELLENCE

Organizations are not born with flawless processes and exceptional agility. Rather, they develop these qualities over a period of time through trial and error, learning, adaptation, and innovation. Although each organization is uniquely different, the high-performance organizations achieve operational excellence through a combination of activities and processes that are explicit in their behaviors and beliefs. In particular, there are five objectives that drive operational excellence at the process level:

1. Designing for economic and strategic value.
2. Designing for multiple domains.
3. Designing for flawless execution.
4. Designing for adaptability.
5. Designing for sustainability.

Designing for Economic and Strategic Value

Value is a relative term: What is of unique or high value to one organization may be commonplace or valueless to another. Optimizing the institutional value of a process and its contribution is what should drive the overall design of the process and organization. Thus, a starting point is to define *value* in meaningful terms. *Value,* in the context of high performance, is defined as:

> The creation of tangible economic and operational benefits through:
> (1) improved customer attraction and loyalty, (2) increased revenues and profitability, (3) reduced total transaction costs, and (4) increased competitive advantage.

Designing for operational excellence demands that a value proposition be developed. A value proposition is a representation or statement as to what a certain program, project, objective, or action is worth to the consumer, organization, and/or employee. Designing for value requires that the design of the process reflect several important characteristics. Specifically, the design of the process:

- Must be clearly aligned and ideally congruent with the strategies and operational objectives of the organization.
- Should demonstrate a distinct cause-and-effect relationship between what is expected, what is needed, and what is produced or what the outcomes are.
- Should optimize the competencies and resources of the enterprise and its capabilities, especially its human resources, IT, and knowledge.
- Should create synergy of purpose and leverage the performance of people and technologies.
- Should reflect an appropriate integration of technology.
- Must be *outcome*-driven (that is, it creates the desired outcomes, products, results, and buyer values).

Designing for Multiple Domains

Designing for operational excellence is a major challenge for even the highest-performing companies because it requires that many different aspects of the overall internal and external environment be considered. Moreover, it requires consideration of the four other pillars of strategy: IT, innovation, knowledge, and leadership. Because operational excellence is so pervasive and unifying, all aspects of the organization, its competencies, its technologies, its competitors, and its strategies must be addressed. To ensure that the process has achieved excellence, the design must be functional and adaptable to the environment in which the organization will operate. A key for this capability is to create processes that are adaptable, scaleable, and transportable across the enterprise and pliable to other uses. Underlying the concept of designing in multiple domains are three fundamental tenets:

1. The design or operation of the process can be singular, modular, vertically integrated, or externally extended through outsourcing and supplier relationships.
2. The design or operation of the process should provide for the efficient *switching* between these multiple forms of process and organizational designs in a cost-effective and time sensitive manner.
3. The design or operation of the process should consider the unique aspects and requirements of customers, manufacturing capabilities, and collaborative suppliers.

The concepts of singular, modular, vertically integrated, and extended enterprise (outsourcing) designs are important. Singular process designs and operations are those that exist for a very specialized purpose. Typically, these designs and operations are relatively independent of other processes and under different organizational competencies. Therefore, they are usually not included in a process module or subassembly that is used in a larger, more complex architecture or system. Examples of a singular design include processes such as the testing of products to satisfy legal requirements, complying with regulatory agencies such as the FAA, FDA, or EPA, financial auditing and external reporting to satisfy SEC and GAAP requirements, and tax compliance. In general, the design and operation of the singular processes can be performed by internal resources, external resources, or outsourcing partners. Typically, singular process designs and operations involve very little end-customer interactions. Although they are necessary for operating the organization, they are relatively low value-generating activities with respect to creating superior financial performance and competitive advantage or generating revenues.

Modular process designs and operations are those that represent a major subsystem, subassembly, or significant percentage of an overall process architecture or system. Modular designs are typically integrated into an overall process architecture that includes many processes and functions. Modular processes can be represented by complete subsystems that are ready to be "plugged into" or readily adapted to an overall larger product or operation. Typically, modular designs are the result of internal competencies and *collaborative* agreements with outsourcing partners, subject matter experts, or specialty providers. In general, modular process designs and operations provide high customer and competitive value propositions to their organization.

Examples of modular design are very common and can be found in a number of industries such as computers, automotive manufacturing, and the entertainment business. For example, Intel supplies about 80 percent of all microprocessors used in PCs, and Microsoft supplies close to 85 percent of the primary software in the form of Windows. Other companies supply the disk drives, communication software, cabinets and cases, modems, and monitors. PC makers Dell, Gateway, and Compaq merely assemble the various subsystems into a finished product based on customizable configurations. In the automotive industry, companies such as Johnson Controls, Allied Signal, and TRW provide major systems for electrical, braking, and steering, and Magna Torrero provides sophisticated body parts for the BMW Z3 roadster. On average, over 70 percent of the parts and systems used in Chrysler cars are provided through external suppliers. Recognizing that suppliers and collaborators possess the core competencies, knowledge, and processes required to manufacture their products, Chrysler relies on its suppliers to design the parts that it will use. As a result, it can be argued that Chrysler has become more of a designer, assembler, financier, and marketer of automobiles, rather than a manufacturer. It has de-massed its vertical operations and replaced it with a modular network of suppliers and outsourcers. Saddled with archaic processes and strapped for cash in the early 1990s, Volvo (now a division of Ford) adopted a similar strategy and is now in a position to produce highly configurable cars that match individual customer preferences.

Vertically integrated process designs have their historical roots in the industrial designs of twentieth century organizational theory. Vertically integrated process designs provide essentially for the entire process, whereby related human and physical and natural resources are owned and operated by the company executing the process. This form of process design and operation is best represented by the highly vertical designs that were used by America's industrial giants throughout the majority of the twentieth century. GM, in particular, still maintains this form of organization, which may explain, in part, why GM's costs per unit are higher and its quality seemingly lower than those of rivals Ford and Chrysler. However, GM's 1999 spin-off of Delphi Automotive Systems may be a precursor to a disintegration movement.

The foregoing leads to a natural question: Which process design is best: singular, modular, or vertically integrated? The answer is that it is problematic and situational to the organization. Many factors influence the selection of a process design including the number of partners available, quality requirements, complexity, total transaction costs, cycle times, proprietary nature of the intellectual capital involved, exclusivity of brand name, and the costs involved in switching back and forth among the various alternatives. The high performers stress three factors in their assessment and ultimately selection: flexibility, cost, and longevity of process design.

As discussed, many organizations utilize external service providers or outsourcing as a means of operational excellence, especially for highly specialized and noncore competency activities. Outsourcing is the

> Transferring of all or part of a function, resources, and personnel to a third
> party that provides specialized services that are contractually defined in
> scope, character, and cost for a specified period of time.

Originally, outsourcing was used to reduce costs and/or increase quality or services provided. However, more organizations are using outsourcing as a means to create collaborative partnerships. The decision to outsource is based on a variety of criteria including the strategic positioning of the firm, the growth trajectory of the firm, level and rate of technology change, functions to be outsourced, intellectual property rights involved, as well as many other business, social, and legal considerations. Organizations decide to outsource for many reasons, but the three most prevalent are to: (1) reduce costs, (2) improve service delivery capabilities, and (3) capitalize on external expertise and talent that are superior to what they have internally. Other reasons and factors include:

- Uncertainty about the future
- Refocus efforts and competencies of core processes
- Better alignment with business strategies and goals
- Improve organizational efficiency and effectiveness
- "Leapfrog" into new technologies and processes
- Generate cash infusions or lower debt
- Improve return on investment and economic value added by reducing nonearning or low earning asset base
- Off-load essential but nonstrategic work
- Increase "corporate mobility" for sale or divestiture
- Management is simply frustrated.

Outsourcing requires that an organization develop a realistic set of objectives and options based on existing and future needs of the company. It also mandates that it critically address tough questions such as, can outsourcing:

- Support the business direction?
- Represent a good "fit"?

- Reduce costs at sustainable annual target rates?
- Maintain required management controls?
- Retain functional/technical infrastructure flexibility for changing business needs?
- Improve technical competencies and capabilities?
- Mitigate risk and costs?
- Transfer or cloud ownership of certain intellectual properties?

Finally, outsourcing requires that the organization use a responsive set of processes and procedures, including:

1. Developing a realistic set of outsourcing objectives and options based on existing and future needs of the company.
2. Using specialized legal services that are experienced in contracting.
3. Assessing intellectual property laws and copyrights.
4. Understanding its exit options and costs.
5. Determining specific performance measures and evaluate performance against those.
6. Striving for a collaborative partnership with the outsourcer.

Outsourcing can be an important component to creating operational excellence and organizational agility. However, a poorly arranged outsourcing relationship can be debilitating to the organization and have a crippling effect on its ability to be agile. Exhibit 9.2 provides a summary of the approaches and considerations of outsourcing.

Designing for Flawless Execution

Albert Einstein said, "Everything should be made as simple as possible, but not simpler." Einstein's statement points to the heart of operational excellence. Simplicity in design, accountability, organizational structure, operation, and measurement leads to optimal performance and adaptability. Simple designs are elegant, flexible, and best positioned for use and switching among multiple domains.

The objective of operational excellence is *flawless execution.* Designing for flawless execution requires that the design for processes be made as "efficient" as possible. Efficient designs are those that are seamless, harmonious, eliminate extraneous work and unnecessary tasks, and minimize low-value activities. Efficient designs allow the flow of work and decision making to proceed at an accelerated speed, without subjective or unnecessary managerial interdictions. There are many qualities that facilitate or signal flawless execution. For example, the operation or execution of the process or operation:

- Occurs at an accelerated velocity relative to its previous state.
- Incorporates the best and most appropriate knowledge available.
- Supports speed and accuracy in execution and adaptability.
- Is not arbitrarily demarcated or bounded by organizational or functional departments.
- Provides for accountability to clearly reside with an individual or a team.
- Is designed around *desired outcomes,* results, or products, with quality engineered into the operation flow, not as an afterthought.
- Represents an "end-to-end" continuum of activities.

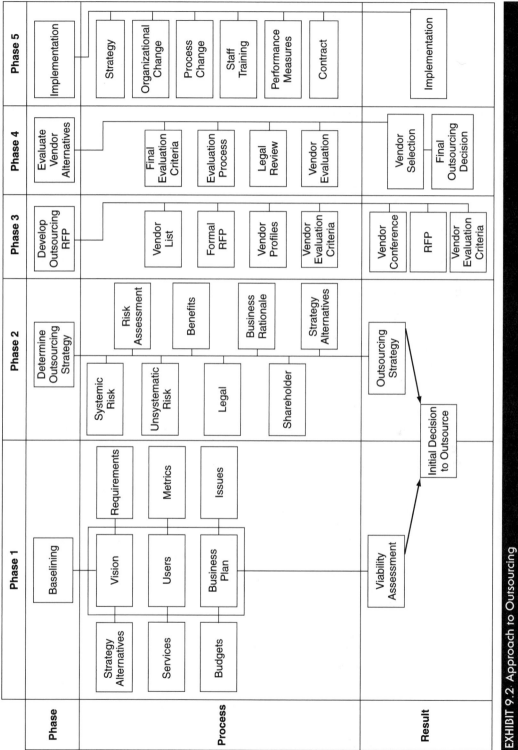

EXHIBIT 9.2. Approach to Outsourcing

233

- Provides that each task within a process has a unique purpose and role; there are no redundancies, no duplicate efforts or unnecessary human interventions or audits.
- The design of the process includes tangible performance targets and measures that are aligned with the strategies and value propositions of the enterprise.

Designing for Adaptability

Designing for process adaptability involves several considerations. First, the design of the process should reflect the organization's immediate needs as well as longer-term objectives. This requires the evaluation of the environment, an assessment of its volatility, and an understanding of the long-term direction and goals of the organization. Second, designing for adaptability requires that the organization recognize and address its capabilities and limitations. Third, the design must provide for transferability. That is, the fundamental construct, tools, and techniques of the process should be arranged in a way that they can be shared or adapted for use by other processes in other parts of the organization. Fourth, the design should incorporate the use of appropriate knowledge and realistic technologies and innovations. Fifth, the various organizational components responsible for the process must be capable of changing to meet the demands of the environment and new technologies.

Designing for Sustainability

Designing sustainable processes requires that the process be in a constant state of measurement and be capable of supporting continuous adjustments and improvement. Several characteristics demonstrate sustainability. First, sustainable designs provide for the transfer of knowledge. They have no mysteries and are supported by an abundance of documentation and information, and they reflect the unique tacit knowledge that is captured. Second, sustainable designs have heuristics associated with, or embedded in, them that interrogate the process, measure performance, influence the behavioral aspects of the process, and communicate its effectiveness. Third, sustainability requires continuous improvement and innovation. Frederick Smith, CEO of Federal Express, describes how his company ensures the sustainability of operational excellence by using 10 quality measures (benchmarks) for every package it handles. He notes that Federal Express "...measures operational performance most broadly through Service Quality Indicators (SQI) which assign points to various types of service problems. The fewer the points in the SQI, the better we are doing." The result is the ability to move and deliver over 3.3 million packages a day with over 99 percent accuracy for on-time and correct delivery. Federal Express' approach to operational excellence uses the measures to improve services and set higher levels of performance. When problems are encountered at Federal Express, they are attacked by select groups of knowledge workers who are not only chartered to "fix the problem" but also to understand why the problem happened, find and fix the cause of the problem, and share the knowledge throughout the company.

ORGANIZATIONAL AGILITY: ENABLING OPERATIONAL EXCELLENCE

"To grow, our companies have to become much more flexible, much lighter on their feet. You can't be light on your feet if you're carrying a lot of baggage," states Christian Koffmann, worldwide chairman of the Consumer & Personal Care Group, Johnson &

Johnson. Operational excellence and organizational agility are intertwined. Organizational agility is needed to respond to the changes in the environment and to support new process designs and organizational structures necessary for operational excellence. It is difficult, if not impossible, for an organization to sustain operational excellence in the absence of organizational agility.

If organizational agility is essential to operational excellence, then a question arises, What is organizational agility? *Webster's Dictionary* defines *agility* as "having the power of quick motion; nimble." Flexibility is another important attribute of agility and is defined by *Scribner's* as "easily bent or persuaded without breaking." Yet, does flexibility necessarily make an organization agile? Absolutely not. Can an organization be a high performer without speed? Absolutely not, because speed is the most important dimension of agility. Then, if an organization has great speed, is it an agile company? Not necessarily. Being fast simply reflects the rate of velocity at which a company is traveling; it does not guarantee that it is traveling in the right direction or that it can quickly stop or change direction. However, *speed is essential* to agility, and an organization cannot be agile without speed.

Organizational agility is:

> The capacity to quickly and efficiently create, redeploy, reconstitute, and reallocate the resources of the organization in a manner that optimizes their use in an environment or allows them to create new environments.

Many organizations mistake agility for reorganization. Agility and reorganization are both complimentary and contradictory. Some organizations suffer from reorganizing on an annual basis, usually without producing any meaningful financial or competitive results. Unfortunately, restructuring is an all too common tactic for CEOs who find themselves in career trouble and/or are uncertain and indecisive about what their future actions should be. Perhaps they are recycling mediocre talent or failing at making the tough and right decisions regarding products, processes, and people. Possibly, they are overly reliant on IT to cure systemic ills, or it could be that they just do not have the capacity to think strategically. As a consequence, they reorganize, often to keep their critics at bay; after all, it gives the appearance that they are trying to do something. U.S. accounting practices provide an economic basis for reorganizing and restructuring. For example, by taking advantage of one-time restructuring costs, organizations can inflate earnings and performance in later years. Lucent Technologies, for instance, took a one-time $2.8 billion charge to cover the expenses of a restructuring and employee severance expenses. This had the affect of recognizing several years of expenses all at once, rather than when they were actually incurred. Thus, Lucent's earnings and stock price benefited in subsequent years. Because Lucent was "conservative" and overestimated its expenses, it was able to "recover" almost $400 million in pretax income. Eastman Kodak, an underperforming company that seems to restructure itself annually, is another beneficiary of accounting provisions. From 1991 through 1998, while its marketshare for film was falling and competitor Fuji was gaining ground, Kodak incurred almost $4.5 billion in write-offs representing six "extraordinary" events. Collectively, the total write-offs exceeded the company's last 9 years of profits. However, its stock price benefited somewhat, at least in the short term. An underlying issue remains as to the quality of the company's earnings given its questionable strategies and experience in digital photography.

The ability of organizations such as Kodak to be agile is greatly compromised by their lack of purpose and consistency in their direction and priorities. Kodak, Unisys, and Sears are prime examples of companies that have reorganized themselves only to find that they have many of the same old issues and problems. Restructuring can lead to agility and is often mistaken for agility, but in the absence of developing the appropriate business strategies and complementary competencies and behaviors, restructuring alone will not create agility.

Developing agility is an extraordinarily challenging task because it involves human behavior and institutional culture. There is not a simple template or mathematical formula that stands as a defacto test or model for organizational agility. Instead, we have many examples of agility in practice, which when considered in a broader context yield a number of common characteristics. First, agility is a *state* in which the organization exists. Second, the *degree* or level of agility is unique for each organization. Third, the *need* for agility is different for each organization. The agility that Intel needs varies considerably from what Frederick Smith needs at Federal Express, or what Charles Schwab requires as a financial services firm. Fourth, the *ability* to be agile is directly related to human performance and the processes and technologies of the organization. Fifth, *sustaining* agility can be more difficult than creating it.

When considering organizational agility, it is easy to be drawn into discussions about what the physical structure of the organization should be and how it should be formally constructed and represented. The academic and consulting communities have presented many opinions on organizational structures and have offered many theories as to which organizational shape is superior in enabling organizational agility. Some consultants and management gurus are espousing easy answers to enormously difficult problems with catchy slogans such as "Flatter is better," "Bomb the bureaucracy," "Leaner is cleaner," and "Less is more." Some of the contemporary management literature present entertaining dilemmas, such as, Are diamond-shaped structures more effective than spider-web structures? Or is the hub-and-spoke structure better than the diamond-shaped organization for creating competitive advantage? Is the shamrock form of organization superior to the donut form? And do people really work better in "social camps" and "tribes" versus teams and hierarchies? By the way, "What are the differences between teams and tribes?" These are all interesting questions, but it is suspect whether their answers can create agility or lead to higher performance. Indeed, being flatter and leaner may be appropriate for some companies but may not be the cure to all organizational performance problems. Then again, it might be a starting point. The key strategic challenge is to determine what works and, most importantly, what works *best*.

For many high performers, not being locked into the dogma of a formal organizational structure is itself a source of agility. As Dee Hock, founder of Visa, noted in *Fast Company*, "The better the organization is, the less obvious it is." The truth and realities are that the type of organizational structure assumed by a company should be a direct reflection of its vision, competencies, processes, and, most importantly, its *strategies*. The components and structure of an organization should be a *source* of competitive advantage, not a sentimental legacy and certainly not an inhibitor to operational excellence and its ability to be agile.

It is obvious that some organizational designs will work better than others, but as Warren Bennis notes "Almost any design will work, if people want it to work." The most important factor in creating organizational agility is not the formal design of the organization; it is the people and leadership. Speaking of Disney, Michael Eisner noted in his 1996 Annual Report that "... I am aware that nothing stays the same. I knew that we would have to change the company, take some chances. ... I also knew we would have to continue to nurture and protect the Disney brand." The high-performance companies modify their structural designs and change and deploy their resources, especially people, to create and sustain organizational agility. In the process, they create and sustain operational excellence; the two concepts are interrelated and inseparable.

The impact of human behavior, institutional and individual competencies, and the design of the organizational structure on organizational agility can be appreciated by taking the best elements of the physical organizational design of any high-performance company such as Dell or Federal Express and superimposing it on, say, a traditional typical public utility or the IRS. Would the superimposition of Dell's or Federal Express' organizational structures create organizational agility and support operational excellence in the IRS? No way! The personnel competencies, performance measures, environmental influences, and staffing compositions are too different and the cultures too dissimilar. The high performers accept uncertainty and fluidity of the open marketplace as the great arbiter. In contrast, long protected by legislation, public utilities are only now learning what it means to be agile and competitive in the age of deregulation and consumer choice. The IRS and other governmental agencies which are statutorily endowed, and have no competition and have only limited incentives for meeting changing customer demands. Thus, the strategic starting point and prerequisite is that human performance is fundamental to organizational agility. Many companies attempting to become agile find themselves bound by their legacy management practices, antiquated competencies, dated organizational structures, and deeply rooted cultural inertia. Their long-learned management habits and traditional competencies, which are perpetuated by their organizational structures, compensation practices, and people, do not allow them to move with great speed or passion, or with extraordinary conviction and confidence. These companies cannot be agile, simply because their organizational structures and personnel, on which they depend, are not agile and in all probability do not have the capacity to become agile.

CREATING ORGANIZATIONAL AGILITY

Achieving organizational agility involves many aspects of behavior and a dedication to designing processes and structures for: (1) the redeployment and reallocation of resources and (2) the selective integration of organizations and processes. The high-performance companies do these either as a direct result of strategic mandate and goal setting, or because they have been doing them so well for so long that they are now part of their basic cultural fiber.

Designing for Redeployment and Reallocation

Redeployment and reallocation of resources and assets include the introduction of new technologies and processes and, most importantly, the addition of new personnel and the retraining of existing personnel. An organization cannot be agile unless its human capital has a high propensity for:

- Reading the environment
- Anticipating changes in the environment

- Functioning under uncertainty
- Reacting to changes
- Personal flexibility
- Learning and adapting

The speed at which any organization can change and how successfully it can change is directly correlated to its human resource competencies and their ability to assimilate the change. The high performers have leaderships and energized workforces that constantly scan the environment for changes. Phil Knight, CEO of Nike, exemplifies this by stating "We're constantly reviewing how the world has changed and how we are reacting to it." The high-performance organizations use information about the environment and the knowledge of themselves to craft new strategies for competing. However, as researchers Nandini Rajagopalan and Gretchen Spreitzer note, "When managers do not sense environmental changes, they neglect to monitor the organization/environment . . . [and] these actions can affect the likelihood, the direction, and magnitude of the actual changes in the content of strategy." The high-performance organizations hire individuals who have a high propensity to learn and adapt their learnings to new situations. Implicit in this is the ability of the individual to function under uncertainty.

Designing for Selective Integration

The high-performance companies explicitly organize their resources and actions around certain core processes and competencies. High-performance companies *selectively* integrate their organizations through the internal consolidation of common infrastructure functions and the selective use of key suppliers, alliance partners, and outsourcing specialists. One of the more effective ways of accomplishing this is to use the concept of the shared service organization (SSO) to provide for extraordinary leverage of resources and common services.

The SSO allows enterprisewide functions and common services to be consolidated across the company, thereby eliminating replication, duplication, and, of course, unnecessary cost. A SSO operates much like a separate business entity and without corporate subsidies. In its purest form, the SSO must compete with external service providers based on its performance and costs.

A significant consequence of shared services is their potential to reduce overhead costs while improving services. According to Lee Frost of the Amherst Group, the adoption of SSO has resulted in "Lexus-like customer satisfaction ratings of greater than 70 percent and 20-40 percent in sustained cost savings for companies such as Monsanto, Allied Signal, Amoco (preacquisition) and Rhone Poulene. Tenneco has saved several hundred million dollars by adopting shared service concepts for key financial, administrative, and IT activities. In creating its shared services, Tenneco concentrated its best resources at a single point and used a uniform set of standards and reporting measures to ensure superior results. Tenneco Business Services (TBS), an arm of conglomerate Tenneco Corp., saved millions annually simply by consolidating telecommunications services. Tenneco also closed four mainframe computer centers and consolidated all IT work in its TBS data center.

At one time, Johnson & Johnson had one of the most expensive accounting departments relative to its overall revenues, value produced and benchmarks. Although the company was enjoying superior financial performance and is a high-performing company, Johnson & Johnson has consolidated many aspects of its payroll operations and reduced the number of administrative personnel in the process from 120 to 26. The high-performance companies understand that shared service concepts for core administrative processes provide enormous leverage, reduce costs, and provide for operational excellence that would be more difficult to achieve under a fragmented and disparate organization structure.

Before its acquisition by U.K.-based BP, Amoco applied the shared services concept to 17 business groups, bringing them together under a single organization. In addition to human resources, Amoco consolidated legal, auditing, public and governmental affairs, purchasing and materials management, environmental health and safety, and information systems. By achieving economies of scale, reducing duplication, and selectively outsourcing some tasks, Amoco estimated that it saved $400 million annually by 1997. AlliedSignal reduced its IT costs through the redeployment of 130 IT staff members, and Monsanto redeployed 10 percent of its staff in creating Monsanto IT Shared Services. Finally, through their consolidation of the traditional accounting functions and creation of the Financial Services Organization, GE has saved tens of millions of dollars through standardizing the financial reporting practices of multiple operating units. In doing so, GE has set a world-class standard for shared services in the financial accounting function.

High-performance companies use shared services not only to eliminate redundant functions and reduce overhead costs but also to improve the quality of work performed and services provided. Shared service centers, if organized and deployed properly, can leverage exemplary practices and provide special expertise and cutting-edge technology to achieve optimum results and value. As illustrated in Exhibit 9.3, essentially there are five core processes that provide a basis for the selective integration of certain functions and ultimately shared services:

Creating demand. This process includes creating new markets and customers, extending relationships, penetrating new markets, and developing customer

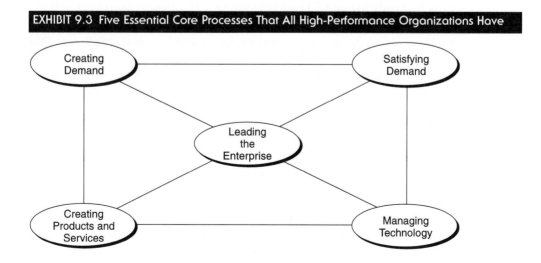

EXHIBIT 9.3 Five Essential Core Processes That All High-Performance Organizations Have

loyalty and excitement. It includes marketing research and consumer intelligence, sales, channel integration, advertising and promotion, demand forecasting, sales support, competitor information, and new-product/service introductions.

Satisfying demand. This process involves all of the activities, relationships, and processes necessary to meet and exceed customer demand expectations, including:

- Manufacturing and assembly
- Supply-chain management and integration
- Customer-relationship management
- Outsourcing and supplier collaboration

Leading the enterprise. This process provides for the coordinated management of the organization to assure optimal shareholder value and a competitive advantage. As discussed in chapter 8, leading the enterprise involves the careful choreography of many activities and includes: strategic visioning, managing shareholder relations, allocating, directing, and deploying the resources of the firm, making tough decisions, being accountable for organizational performance, and developing next-generation leaders.

Creating products and services. This process focuses on the creation of new products and services, new-product development, research, and innovation. Chapter 6 discussed the methods and techniques for innovation and developing new products and processes in high-performance organizations.

Managing technology. As discussed in chapter 5, IT is absolutely essential to creating a high-performance company and superior competitive capabilities. IT provides the enabling infrastructure and delivery mechanisms necessary for supporting flawless processes and organizational agility. In creating operational excellence, the concepts of logical consolidation and physical distribution are employed. Under logical consolidation, IT is managed as a "single" resource for policy and performance purposes. Under the concept of physical distribution, the IT resource and its applications, communication networks, technology, data, and human support are located at the point of the operation and process and are effectively managed. High-performance IT organizations have certain distinguishing trademarks. Specifically, they are:

- *Aligned* with the organizational strategies and financial objectives of the enterprise.
- Driven to provide selective *integrated processing solutions* for the design of new business processes, organizations, and collaborative work environments.
- Managed as an *enterprisewide resource* around the concepts of logical consolidation and physical distribution.
- Managed for *shared responsibilities* and *accountabilities* to ensure the success of IT-enabling projects and the effective application of IT resources.
- Managed to *formal performance levels* and *market-based service* principles.
- Managed to *enterprisewide standards* for development, integration, and management of systems.
- Responsible for optimizing best-of-breed technologies and software products.
- On an *organizational parity* with respect to recognition and reporting relationships with that of the CFO and leaders of line business units.

SUMMARY

High-performance organizations recognize that operational excellence is central to creating strategic advantage and can be a catalyst for strategic renewal. They create and sustain operational excellence through a number of methods. Specifically, high-performance organizations exhibit operational excellence and organizational agility in a number of ways:

- Operational excellence is a state in which the organization exists; it is not situational or a one-time event. It is a continuous process.
- They seek to extend operational excellence to all relevant functions, processes, and interactions, including those that are external to their organization and especially to those that involve customer interactions, key suppliers, and product/service design and delivery or manufacturing.
- They use operational excellence as a rallying mantra and catalyst for strategic renewal and change.
- They make it a strategic imperative to *selectively* integrate portions of their business designs, technologies, and outsourcing partners for greater leverage and economies of scale.

Operational excellence is central to creating and sustaining strategic advantage and change. Those organizations that establish operational excellence and its compliment, organizational agility, as a strategic pillar will generate significant advantages and financial results over those that do not.

Critical Thoughts and Discussion Questions

1. Considering the need for flawless execution, how can an organization use supplier relationships and outsourcers to help it achieve both operational excellence and organizational agility? In discussing this issue, consider the legal implications of outsourcing and also the implications of long-term vendor relations. What are some of the critical success factors involved in these relationships?
2. Discuss the importance of process design in achieving operational excellence. What types of designs are possible, and what types of the benefits and weaknesses do they represent?
3. To what extent can operational excellence and organizational agility be facilitated or inhibited by IT? Under what conditions could IT be a catalyst for operational excellence and organizational agility?
4. Discuss the meaning and merits of the term *value proposition,* and why it is an important concept in organizational transformation?
5. What programs and initiatives can an organization design to influence operational excellence in the following areas?

   - Customer satisfaction and loyalty
   - Cycle times for problem resolution, order fulfillment, and manufacturing/service delivery
   - Service and/or product quality
   - Vendor and supplier relations
   - Employee relations and morale
   - Employee morale, understanding, and commitment to the vision and strategy of the organization

10

BUSINESS INTEGRATION: ARCHITECTING THE ORGANIZATION FOR HIGH PERFORMANCE

". . . the successful modern corporation is a Lego set whose parts can be readily reconfigured as circumstances change."

—Warren Bennis in "An Invented Life"

INTRODUCTION

This chapter presents a framework for integrating the five pillars of strategy to create a high-performance organization. In doing so, this chapter addresses a number of important questions:

- How does an organization become a high-performance company?
- What critical thoughts, concepts, and practices drive the design and implementation for high performance?
- What does a typical transformation journey to high performance entail?

It is important to note that the intention of this chapter is not to be *prescriptive*. There is no uniform, boilerplate, or "canned" approach that fits all sizes of organizations and needs. And do not let anyone fool you into thinking otherwise. What works at Disney and Intel may not work at Chrysler and Citicorp, however, the basic components and the conceptual principles are common, and that is the important lesson. Like human beings who share the same genetic foundations for life but are uniquely individual and different, each high-performance organization is unique and different. Therefore, no "one-size" work plan or prescriptive approach can satisfy all needs. Nonetheless, there are certain commonalities and processes that are important and uniformly shared.

BUSINESS ARCHITECTURE: THE BLUEPRINT FOR HIGH PERFORMANCE

Take just a few minutes and think about where you are and the environment that you are in. Are you in an office building? Are you in a classroom? Are you in a hotel room?

Are you at home sitting by the fireside? Maybe you are on an airplane moving at 520 knots 35,000 feet above the Pacific? Exactly where you are does not really matter, because you are part of your surroundings and you are in and part of some type of environment, an ecology that has an intricate and interrelated architecture. To be successful in that environment, you must adapt to it or change it. The point is that you are part of an ecological framework, an architecture.

To understand how to operationalize the organization for high performance, it is first necessary to appreciate the concept of architecture. Architecture is the unifying construct of nature and society. In nature, architecture is represented by an ecology and the constant adaptation and evolution of life forms to their environments. Human beings architect their lives and habitats; other life forms adapt to their environments. Live in a cold climate, and your home is built for long cold winters. Live in Florida, and your home is built for the heat, high humidity, and an occasional hurricane. Nature provides the landscape and the environment from which to design and live. In designing a new home, the architect's challenge is to design within those parameters while optimizing functionality, financial constraints, space, and the host environment by using the best tools and materials.

The same is true for any organization. The most successful organizations will be those that have optimized the five pillars of strategy and strategic renewal for their current or anticipated environments. They will be the ones that are the most agile, best able to read their environments, most effective at anticipating changes, and best positioned to abandon their strategies almost spontaneously for another. Those organizations that cannot do these things or have not developed the five pillars of strategy will scavenge for the scraps and wonder if they will survive. The lesson learned from the leaders is that for a company to be great, it must have a strong sense of self-determinism and either harmonize and optimize with the environment or create a new one. The high-performance companies understand this and architect themselves to do one or the other and most oftentimes, both! As in nature, a species is driven by some innate force to perpetuate itself; the great companies strive for survival and self-perpetuation.

In *Organizational Architecture,* David Nadler and his coauthors define *architecture* as "the formal structures, the design of work practices, the nature of the informal organization or operating style and processes for selection, socialization and development of people." This is a good initial definition and representation of what an organizational architecture is. It goes beyond the conventional business mind-set of boxes and lines and process flow diagrams. High-performance companies take the concept and practice of architecture several levels farther.

Based on the lessons learned from the high performers, *business architecture* is defined as:

> A comprehensive plan for the realization of high performance through the integration of the organization's resources and competencies in a manner that optimizes and leverages their use, deployment, and interactions to an existing or intended environment.

The architecture of a high-performance organization demonstrates how the *major* components of the organization interact with one another to create synergy of purpose and high performance. There are five critical aspects that must be considered:

1. The architecture of a high-performing company, like that of a building, car, aircraft, or ship, is the result of deliberate *design* for *selective integration.*
2. The architecture must show a clear *congruency* to the purpose, strategy, and economic goals of the organization.
3. The architecture must be built to either harmonize with, *optimize,* or *redefine* its operational environment.
4. Architectures are linked to and supported by plans. These plans are both tactical and strategic.
5. The architecture utilizes the five pillars of strategy and strategic renewal as a basis for integration.

The integration of the five pillars of strategy and strategic renewal provides the starting point for developing high-performance qualities. The process of developing high-performance capabilities does not lend itself to being prescriptive. High-performance architecture is not the product of a single project or work plan; rather, it is a continuous journey that has guideposts and mile markers but no set end point.

The framework presented below is predicated on the notions of architecting for integration and competitive leverage. As the unifying construct, all high performance begins and flows from the business architecture. A well-designed business architecture ensures that business initiatives are convergent with the strategies and value targets of the enterprise and that operational, organizational, and knowledge integration is achieved. The framework discussed recognizes that organizations are either *undertaking* a journey to become higher-performing enterprises or are already *in* the journey or state of renewal to remain high-performing organizations. Thus, the ultimate product of the framework is the creation of integrated conceptual operating designs and blueprints (models) and a series of action plans for the development of high-performance capabilities or their renewal.

In designing a high-performance architecture for the organization, several "design rules" should be followed:

- High-performance organizations are living entities. Like all living things, they are driven by the need and desire to survive, to beat death and perpetuate themselves in some form. They have a driving life force. For an organization to be a high performer, it must have a strong life force, and the architecture must somehow capture and embody this. Some may call it values, others culture, but irrespective of the name it is given, it is similar to the innate life force that is in all living things . . . the will to survive and prosper.
- High-performing organizations are guided—indeed, driven—by a distinct economic and stakeholder value proposition, an overall business vision and strategy and a strong sense of self-determinism. The value proposition stipulates the societal and economic goals of the organization. Great visions lend themselves to the perpetuation of the organization; they feed the life force and vice versa. The vision establishes the direction, intent, and business philosophy of the organization, and the strategy sets the context to which it will perform. Any design for high performance requires that the value proposition be directly aligned with and supportive of the overall vision and strategic intentions of the organization.
- High-performance organizations create the convergent integration of strategy, purpose, operational processes, technology, knowledge, and human performance

to achieve extraordinary leverage. They cross-utilize resources and go beyond their immediate organizational boundaries and industries in search of synergistic relationships, collaborative powers, best practices, and new ideas. The design for any high-performance company must provide for the convergent integration of knowledge, process, technology, and human performance.

- High-performance organizations cultivate a set of core behaviors and values that transcend time and situations. These sustain the company through bad times and excite and propel the company in good times. Any design for high performance must not only embody these behaviors and beliefs but advance them to new levels.
- High-performance organizations dedicate themselves to operational excellence in all major activities and processes. The design for operational excellence allows an organization to set standards that others must equal and exceed. It also enables an organization to become more agile in its application of processes across functions and organizational domains. Any design for high performance must have operational excellence and the flawless execution of essential processes as objectives.
- High-performance organizations are knowledge-creating companies. They are extremely adept at learning, institutionalizing tacit knowledge, leveraging knowledge, and adapting that knowledge to existing or new environments. Any design for high performance must provide for the creation, adaptation, dissemination, and management of knowledge.
- High-performance organizations understand that human competencies are essential and either develop, adapt, or acquire the necessary competencies to support the design for operations and the organization. Any design for high-performance processes and organizational structures must demonstrate a calibration to the existing competencies or an acknowledgment that new competencies are required.

These rules are relatively universal and form the basic building code or genetic material for architecting the business for high performance. The cardinal rule for architecting for high performance is to provide for the integration of the five pillars of strategy and strategic renewal. That is, we *architect* for high performance through the integration of IT, organizational agility, and operational excellence, innovation, knowledge, and leadership. The important design concepts and tenets for each of the genetic components have been addressed in chapters 4 through 9.

ARCHITECTING FOR HIGH-PERFORMANCE

The high-performance companies view their architectures as the method that will allow the enterprise to create competitive advantage and sustain strategic renewal. As illustrated in Exhibit 10.1, the framework for architecting for high performance is composed of five segments:

1. Business baselining and evaluative assessment.
2. Enterprise visioning and strategy setting.
3. Organizational integration.

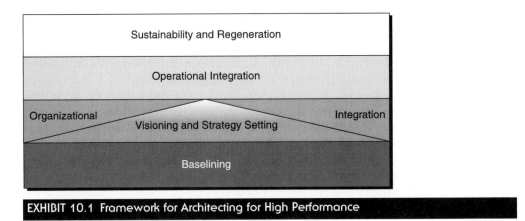

EXHIBIT 10.1 Framework for Architecting for High Performance

4. Operational integration.

5. Sustainability and regeneration.

Note that the term *segments* is used as compared to *phases* or *stages*. Those terms have a linear connotation and tend to bring to mind images of sequencing and a prodding, prescriptive steplike approach. Segments are simply a convenient way of defining activities that an organization must navigate in order to develop high-performance capabilities. The development of the business architecture is both progressive and *iterative,* because it reflects new knowledge and new strategies. The iterative approach allows for learning, experimentation, adaptation, and calibration of the designs to the environment. Let's discuss each segment.

Business Baselining and Evaluative Assessment

The development of the business architecture begins with a baseline assessment of the organization. As a starting point, any organization trying to become a high-performance company or sustain its high-performance must realistically assess itself, its processes, its environment, and its competencies. It must have a commanding comprehension of what its genetic code looks like, its strengths and weaknesses, and how it compares with the other high-performance leaders. It must understand the issues and factors that it confronts in the marketplace and how fast those factors change.

Creating the baseline requires the identification and formulation of business issues, an examination of values and competencies, an assessment of the technologies that the organization has in place or is planning to acquire, the identification of problems and opportunities, and the validation of strategic visions and plans for the organization. The business architecting process culminates in the creation of integrated designs and models for the organization that provide the "to-be" image and target for change and the desired performance. Typically, the business architecture results in new process designs for operational excellence, human performance and operational measurements for higher performance, organizational designs for agility, technology designs and integration, and knowledge embodiment.

A first step in architecting for high performance is determining whether the organization can achieve high performance, where the organization is in its evolution as an entity, what operational and organizational problems it may be experiencing, and most importantly, what its capability for change and performance are. Some companies may desperately try to be high performers but lack the necessary genetic matter in the form of competencies, technologies, finances, and leadership to do so. Others may have all of the ingredients but lack the will or leadership to succeed. These companies are usually complacent and highly risk averse. Still other companies may simply have product and market issues that inhibit their realization of high performance. These companies have to get their fundamentals straightened out before they can support any significant effort to build high-performance capabilities.

A company cannot move forward with any degree of confidence unless it knows where it is and what its capabilities are. The enterprise baselining segment is both context driven and context setting. It works within the known relationships and patterns of the organization and its environment. It also establishes the scope and defines the parameters for which high performance-integrated business solutions and architectures will be developed by baselining certain essential components of the company's processes, competencies, technologies, and management practices using independent and objective measures.

In performing the business baseline and assessment, major operational, competitive, knowledge, competency, and organizational issues are identified, and opportunities to create value and competitive position are explored and/or developed. Baselining and assessing a business are complex processes. They require skilled and mature professionals who have an appreciation for the intricacies of business operations, knowledge of competitive dynamics, and the ability to think broadly across industries and beyond the traditional solutions. Baselining requires the development and use of meaningful data to document and analyze the current business environment and key business practices of the enterprise. This "as-is" analysis provides the context for understanding current conditions and competencies and establishes the foundation for developing the new business architecture of the enterprise. It provides insights into the rationale for why a process exists, what value is produced, and how the process is performed. Most importantly, it provides a context and basis for identifying and prioritizing business integration opportunities and the level of complexity related to them.

During this portion of the architecting process, it is best to use an iterative process to search for, define, and formalize tangible economic and intrinsic value opportunities for the enterprise. This probing, learning, adapting process involves extensive testing, refining, and reformulating the hypotheses and the creation of alternative strategies and solutions designed to capture those value potentials. In performing the baseline and assessment, there are a number of critical issues and thoughts that must be considered. These include issues such as:

- What are the core competencies of the company, and how do these competencies compare with high-performance leaders in terms of depth, costs, value created, and ability to change?
- Given the performance profiles of the company's major processes, how is operational excellence expressed, and how does the performance of those operations compare with the high-performance leaders in terms of costs, cycle times, customer retention and satisfaction, revenue per employee, economic value added (EVA) created, and leverage of knowledge, human performance, and technology?

- Relative to the S&P 500 or other appropriate index measure, its industry, and other high value-creating companies (EVA-oriented), what has been the 5-year annual financial performance of the organization as described by:

  Annual sales growth.

  Rate of earnings growth and net operating margin percentages.

  Earnings per share (EPS) growth.

  Rate of market capitalization.

  Dividend payout.

  Investment in new property, plant, and equipment.

  Acquisitions and divestitures.

  Liquidity and long-term obligations as a percentage of assets.

  Stock price performance.

  IT expenditures as a percent of revenues and per employee.

  Training and development expenses per employee.

  Revenues per employee.

  Profitability per employee.

  Percentage of revenue and profit derived from new products and major product extensions.

  Quality of earnings.

- Given the overall financial performance of the organization, what external events have had the most profound influence on it, and what is the level of organizational and operational sensitivity to these influences?
- Relative to leadership and the demonstrated behavioral qualities of the leaders, do the behavioral qualities align themselves with the required competency mix for the organization to achieve high performance? What level of alignment is achieved? What qualities and characteristics do the leaders demonstrate that show an appreciation for and commitment to high performance?
- What indicators are present that demonstrate the impact of competitor strategies on the performance of the company? What makes these so unique and influential?
- What aspects of the strategy present and support a unique EVP to the organization, and how is consistency of this proposition to the strategies and business of the organization demonstrated?
- What aspects of the strategy represent breakthrough thinking and the potential to create new rules for others to compete by? Why are these aspects unique, and what types of competitive reactions can be anticipated that may neutralize them?

The baselining phase culminates in an assessment of the organization and a prioritized list of issues, competitive threats, problems, opportunities and initiatives, an alignment of those to the strategies and objectives of the organization, and the development of initial value propositions. The value propositions help the company prioritize its initiatives, objectives, and investments.

Enterprise Visioning and Strategy Setting

The great strategies focus on either changing the environment, creating a new environment, or changing the resources and methods of competing to harmonize or optimize performance within the existing environment. This segment of the architecting process is designed to provide for the creation or confirmation of a comprehensive vision and strategy or, more appropriately, set of strategies, for the enterprise. In designing an integrated business architecture, strategy can drive the design, or the design of the enterprise and its ability to integrate its operations can drive the strategy. To a large extent the environment or intended environment and organizational resources dictate the terms and approach.

In architecting for high performance, vision and strategy setting include the development of specific targets and broad measurements for aspirations such as: market-space, earnings growth, revenue enhancement, economic value creation, cost-performance improvements, and cycle-time improvements. Some of the key considerations in assessing and developing a strategy for high performance include:

- Given the strategies and operational profile of the organization, what and where are the opportunities for greatest competitive advantage and economic improvement? What is the potential magnitude of the competitive advantage created? What is the potential of the economic advantage created? What are the timing considerations related to these opportunities? What is the estimated level of risk, effort, and investment associated with the realization of these opportunities? What preconditions must be met for realizing the opportunities?
- Does the strategy provide for breakthrough opportunities and results that clearly define new rules by which others must compete?
- What is the sensitivity of the strategy to the actions of competitors, and how will competitors react to the strategy and affect it?
- What form of competitive advantage will the strategy create, and what is the longevity of the advantage? Can the advantage be neutralized?
- Given the competencies and capabilities of the organization, can the strategy be executed with existing resources and leadership practices, or does the organization have to acquire them?
- Relative to the competition, what form of business will competitors take, and what advantages do competitors have that have the potential to neutralize aspects of the strategy? Can competitors be neutralized and, if so, how, what cost, and what timing are involved?

Once strategies have been created, individual goals are developed to support the strategies. During this segment, the strategy is linked or driven by the vision for strategic renewal and high performance. Once the strategy has been developed, it is communicated throughout the organization and becomes the rallying point for much of what the organization does and how it acts.

As discussed in chapter 2, high-performance companies develop strategies at multiple levels in several different domains. Typically, the major domains include: the entire corporation, a business unit, human capital, operations, and IT. Individual strategies are developed for each of these domains, offering distinct value propositions and achieving a close alignment with the overall vision and corporate strategy of the organization. Not surprisingly, the level of detail becomes greater, and the content more specific and comprehensive, as one crafts strategies at the individual domain level. For example, an IT strategy may include an assessment of the organization's current use and deployment of technology as well as a forward vision and architecture for the use of technology in the future. An operations strategy may involve plans for the outsourcing of certain functions, the relocation of facilities to more economically desirable areas, and the use of complementary suppliers. Finally, a human capital strategy may contain plans for organizational learning and transfer of knowledge.

During this stage of strategy development and planning, an organization assesses individual products, services, market segments, etc. and develops appropriate unique strategies. These strategies are linked to, and fall within, one or several of the six strategic choices discussed earlier; specifically, an organization can choose to *innovate, substitute, imitate, complement, collaborate,* or *withdraw.* High-performers use a combination of these strategic choices to create a portfolio of strategies with an emphasis on innovation. For example, a company may choose to be an innovator in several products and/or markets, a complementor in others, and a collaborator in selected situations. The selection of choice is, as discussed, contingent upon a number of factors, including the financial situation of the organization, the competitive pressures that it is confronting, customer demands, internal competencies and capabilities, and its ability to forge external relationships. A good understanding of the strategic choices and an effective use of the concept present a powerful and relatively easy approach to understanding and developing strategies for successful competing and for achieving a sustained high-performance.

Organizational Integration

The third segment of the business integration and architecting process involves assessing and designing new organizational practices and adding or upgrading internal competencies. This part of the integration process can be performed simultaneously with the design of new business processes and concepts related to operational excellence and organizational agility discussed in chapter 9.

The creation of the integrated business architecture takes the organization from where it has been and where it is to where it should and needs to be by creating the *blueprint* and plan of the new "to-be" enterprise. The "to-be" blueprint represents the future state for the organization and should be directly aligned with the strategies and visions established earlier during enterprise visioning and strategy setting.

Organizational integration involves designing and testing innovative designs for processes and related organizational structures that support the strategies, value propositions, and aspirations of the enterprise identified earlier. The design of the new "to-be" operating model involves five important dimensions of the architecting process (human performance, processes, technologies, strategies, and management practices), which result in the development of conceptual models for:

- New "to-be" organizational designs.
- New "to-be" IT designs.
- Designs for the integration of "to-be" processes, organizations, and technology.
- New "to-be" designs for the integration of technology, knowledge, and human performance.

Architecting for organizational integration is perhaps the most challenging and complex process related to the high performance process. Often there are many internal barriers and long-standing behavioral patterns that must be overcome. There may be significant resistance to new standards and measures, and there may be a less than enthusiastic response to necessary changes. Major considerations with respect to crafting new organizational structures are managing the rate of change and the ability of the organization to assimilate new doctrines and performance measures. Thus, the process of change must be approached more as a continuous *journey* rather than as a single event or project.

Some of the key considerations and questions that require addressing include, but are not limited to:

- Given the strategic objectives and mandates for renewal, what is the organization's capacity to change, and at what velocity of change can it most likely sustain?
- What are the major factors that are influencing the organization's capacity and propensity for change? Why are these factors influential and determining?
- What behaviors and actions best demonstrate that personnel have an understanding and appreciation for the strategies and objectives of the organization?
- Given the strategies and business objectives of the organization, what aspects best demonstrate that its structure and operating construct can support the realization of the objectives?
- What aspects of the organizational construct and its operations present and support a unique EVP to the organization, and how consistent is of this proposition to the strategies and business of the organization?
- Relative to high-performance practices and costs, what types of SSOs are deployed for the performance of common overhead functions, and what operational properties best support their effectiveness?
- Given the organizational construct of the company, how are resources deployed, and what are the composition and competencies of these resources? What aspects of this deployment and composition demonstrate alignment of the organization to the strategies and objectives of the organization?
- Relative to the core processes of the organization, how are personnel distributed, and is this distribution of personnel consistent with the performance and operational priorities of the company?
- Relative to the design of the organization, has it demonstrated a propensity to facilitate or resist change? What aspects of the design of the organization demonstrate that it is conducive to change and adaptation?
- Given the strategic direction and business objectives of the organization, do the proper competencies exist in sufficient quantities to support the organization?
- Given the design for new process and organizational structures, what competencies are necessary for supporting their operation and execution?
- What are the major competency-related training and developmental needs of the organization, given its strategies and design for operational processes?
- Relative to compensation and performance recognition, what programs and initiatives demonstrate alignment and support to the competency needs and competency-development practices of the organization?

- Relative to the strategic and business objectives of the organization, what leadership and team member skills and behaviors are necessary for supporting their realization?
- What factors must be considered to determine the need for cross-competency teaming and cross-competency training?
- What management and organizational practices demonstrate that the proper balance and quantities are deployed to best achieve the strategic and business objectives of the organization?
- Relative to new process designs, changing strategies, and new business needs, what decisions and actions best demonstrate that emerging competency needs are identified and addressed in a timely manner?
- What programs, initiatives, and practices best demonstrate a commitment to cross-competency teaming and development of cross-competency skills?
- To what extent does competency influence the realization of the organization's strategic and business goals?
- Given the strategies and business aspirations of the organization, what economic and "emotional" value propositions are given to personnel to foster a sense of loyalty and commitment? How are these propositions consistent with the financial and business objectives of the organization?

The activities of this segment result in new organizational designs and requirements for new competencies, new performance measures, and new structural alignments.

Operational Integration

Designing for operational excellence requires the creation of new business process designs that integrate innovation, technology, performance measures, and organizational capabilities. The process of architecting for operational excellence is one of continuous development, testing, refinement, further development, and successful deployment. Operational integration is achieved by using a variety of methods including: conceptualization, iterative designing, prototyping and training, and recognition and reward systems. The design process usually includes a proof of concept stage that validates the operation of the design.

Some of the key issues and considerations that should be addressed in architecting for operational integration include:

- Given the design of the process, what is its capacity to change?
- What are the major factors that are influencing the organization capacity and propensity for change of the process design? Why are these factors influential and determining?
- Given the strategies and business objectives of the organization, what aspects of the process design best demonstrate that its structure and operating construct can support the realization of the objectives?
- What aspects of the process design and its operations present and support a unique EVP to the organization, and how is consistency of this proposition to the strategies and business of the organization demonstrated?
- Relative to the core processes of the organization, how are personnel distributed, and is this distribution of personnel consistent with the performance and operational priorities of the company? What demonstrates consistency of practice to need?

- Relative to the design of the organization, has it demonstrated a propensity to facilitate or resist change? What aspect of the design best demonstrates that it is conducive to change and adaptation?

This segment results in a set of blueprints and related documentation that describe how essential business processes will be structured and operate in the future. These conceptual renderings provide the foundation from which actual development and implementation can occur.

Sustainability and Regeneration

The nature of high performance is one of constant renewal and regeneration. The high performers recognize this and are in a constant state of change and experimentation. This segment of architecting for high performance focuses the organization on a continuous process designed to help keep the organization functioning as a high performer.

The process of continuous renewal involves the replication of core values, knowledge, and concepts related to optimizing the genetic code for high performance. Some of the techniques that the high-performance companies do to accomplish this include:

- Developing a series of organizational briefing sessions and seminars related to strategic renewal.
- Establishing continuous renewal as a performance standard for all business units and those responsible for their performance.
- Conducting a series of executive briefings specifically dedicated to the results and processes used to achieve quantum gains.
- Establishing a "High-Performance University" where selected executives, managers, and employees attend to learn more about the process and methods involved, exchange ideas, and collaborate.
- Providing a compensation incentive program for high-performance employees who constantly challenge the standards and set new ones.

The result of this segment is continuous attention and organizational focus directed to high performance. It results in the perpetuation of a culture that is high performance and that is dedicated to creating competitive and economic advantage for its stakeholders.

SUMMARY

There are many approaches to trying to develop and maintain high performance. This chapter provided a brief overview of one such approach. The key concept is not so much what or which approach to use, but to concentrate on three big concepts:

- Using the five pillars of strategy and strategic renewal as centering themes for developing a high-performance business architecture.
- Using the five-segment approach to achieve organizational and operational integration.
- Striving to develop and/or acquire competencies that are, by definition, high-performing.

Critical Thoughts and Discussion Questions

1. What are the relative positions and rankings of the organization's products within specific market segments relative to its key competitors? Do the organization's products hold:
   - Leadership position (#1 or 2 in the market)?
   - Follower position (#3–5 in the market)?
   - Laggard position (#6 or higher in the market)?

   Are these positions relatively permanent or is there fluidity? If fluid, what is the rate or velocity of change?

2. What technologies and products does the organization have that can potentially:
   - Create new markets
   - Significantly change the dynamics of a market

3. What are the sources of competitive advantage in those markets?
   - First-mover advantage
   - Technological leadership
   - Customer relationships
   - Least-cost provider
   - Price leadership
   - Highest service provider
   - Superior product performance
   - Patents
   - Collaboration and contracts

4. What is the threat of technological substitution in each market?

5. What factors are driving changes in these markets and to what extent can these be:
   - Anticipated
   - Controlled or managed
   - Used to create new markets and opportunities
   - Used to obsolete existing practices and products

6. What and where are the opportunities for external collaboration to more quickly and effectively identify and address emerging market trends and opportunities?
   - In what markets and market segments should the organization concentrate its efforts and why?
   - Financial rationale
   - Product rationale
   - Patient rationale
   - Competitive rationale
   - Technological rationale

7. What is the estimated longevity (life span) of the market? That is, are the growth rates sustainable at an ascending trajectory, or will they slow down?

8. What are the relative positions of the major competitors in each market as represented by:
   - Annual revenues within market
   - Number of units/devices sold or used in procedures

9. Relative to the major competitors in each market, what are the sources of their competing and do they have a sustainable competitive advantage?
   - Price
   - Economies of scale and least cost
   - Product quality and service
   - Product/technological innovation
   - Product design and ease of use in procedure or across disease states
   - Patient/physician brand awareness
   - Business relationship and customer loyalty
   - First mover advantage
   - Intellectual property rights and patents

References

For this work, much effort and care was directed to ensure that all sources of data, research, quotes, ideas, and concepts were accurately depicted and acknowledged. If for some reason a work, source, or author was inadvertently overlooked or omitted, it is an innocent error and not an attempt to diminish anyone or their work.

Chapter 1: Competing at the Speed of Life

Warren Bennis and Michael Mische, *The 21st Century Organization: Reinventing Through Reengineering* (San Francisco: Jossey-Bass, 1996).

Peter Burrows, "Dangerous Limbo at Apple," *Business Week,* July 21, 1997.

Jim Carlton, *Apple: The Inside Story of Intrigue, Egomania, and Business Blunders* (New York: Time Business Books, 1997).

James C. Collins and Jerry I. Porras, *Built to Last* (New York: HarperCollins Publishers, Inc., 1994).

Arie de Geus, "The Living Company," *Harvard Business Review,* March–April, 1997.

Dwight L. Gertz and Joao P. A. Baptista, *Grow to Be Great* (New York: The Free Press, 1995).

Gary Hamel and C.K. Parhalad, *Competing for the Future* (Boston: Harvard Business School Press, 1994).

Lee Iacocca, with William Novak, *Iacocca: An Autobiography* (New York: Bantam Books, 1986).

Nichols Imparato and Oren Harari, *Jumping the Curve* (San Francisco: Jossey-Bass, 1996).

Regis McKenna, *Real: Preparing for the Age of the Never Satisfied Customer* (Boston: Harvard Business School Press, 1997).

C. Owen Paepke, *The Evolution of Progress* (New York: Random House, 1993).

Arno Penzias, *Harmony: Business, Technology and Life after Paperwork* (New York: HarperCollins, 1995).

Douglas K. Smith and Robert C. Alexander, *Fumbling the Future* (New York: William Morrow & Co., Inc., 1990).

Lester C. Thurow, *The Future of Capitalism* (New York: William Morris & Company, 1996).

Chapter 2: Defining High Performance and Strategic Renewal

Jay Barney, *Gaining and Sustaining Competitive Advantage* (New York: Addison-Wesley, 1997).

Editors, "How Real Is the New Economy," *The Economist,* July 24, 1999.

Robert M. Grant, *Contemporary Strategy Analysis,* 2nd ed. (Cambridge UK: Blackwell Publishers, 1995).

Donald C. Hambrick, David A. Nadler, and Michael Tushman, *Navigating Change: How CEO's, Teams and Boards Steer Transformation* (Boston: Harvard Business School Press, 1998).

Michael A. Hitt, R. Duane Ireland, and Robert E. Hoskisson, *Insights and Readings in Strategic Management,* 3rd ed. (Cincinnati, OH: South-Western College Publishing, 1999).

Constantinos C. Markides, "A Dynamic Value of Strategy," *The Sloan Management Review* 40(3) (Spring 1999).

Richard Melcher, "Slip Slidin' Away at General Motors," *Business Week,* March 23, 1998.

Henry Mintzberg and Joseph Lampel, "Reflecting on the Strategy Process," *The Sloan Management Review* 40(3) (Spring 1999).

Michael Moeller, Steve Hamm, and Timothy J. Mullaney, "Remaking Microsoft," *Business Week,* May 17, 1999.

Nina Munk, "How Levi's Trashed a Great American Brand," *Fortune,* April 12, 1999.

Norman Pearlstine, "Big Wheels Turning," *Time,* December 7, 1998.

Vikram Sethi and William R. King, *Organizational Transformation through Business Process Reengineering* (Upper Saddle River, NJ: Prentice Hall, 1998).

Adrian J. Slywotzky, *Value Migration: How to Think Several Moves ahead of the Competition* (Boston: Harvard Business School Press, 1996).

Debra Sparks, "How Formica Got Burned Out by Buyouts," *Business Week,* March 22, 1999.

Ron Stodghill, II, "The Trouble with GM," *Time.* New York; July 27, 1998; p. 38, 2.

David Woodruff and Kathleen Kerwin, "Can GM Make a U-Turn in Europe?" *Business Week,* March 16, 1998.

Chapter 3: Globalization and Megamergers: Competing in a Transnational World

Nancy Adler, "Global Leaders: Women Leaders," *Management International Review* 37(1) (special issue, 1997).

Andersen Consulting, "The Evolving Role of Executive Leadership," *Andersen Consulting Institute for Strategic Leadership,* 1999.

Edmund L. Andrews, "11 Countries Tie Europe Together in One Currency," *The New York Times,* January 1, 1999.

Association for the Monetary Union of Europe, "Euro Preparation Guide for Companies: Managing the Changeover to the Euro," http://amue.lf.net/business/guidindx.htm.

H. S. Astin and C. Leland, *Women of Influence, Women of Vision: A Cross Generational Study of Leaders and Social Change* (San Francisco: Jossey-Bass, 1991).

Christopher Bartlett and Sumantra Ghoshal, *Managing across Borders: The Transnational Solution* (Cambridge, MA: Harvard Business School Press, 1989).

Guy Billoud, "Implications for International Business of European Economic and Monetary Unification," *Business Economics,* January 1998.

Geoffrey Colvin, "The Year of the Mega-Merger," *Fortune,* January 11, 1999.

Jonathan A. Davidson, Alison R. Ledger, and Giovanni Viani, "The Ugly Implications of EMU," *The McKinsey Quarterly* 1 (fall 1998).

P. W. Dorfman, "International and Cross-cultural Leadership." In B. J. Punnett, and O. Shenkar, *Handbook for International Management Research* (Cambridge, UK: Blackwell Publishers, 1996).

Editors, "A New Kind of Car Company," *The Economist,* May 9, 1998.

Editors, "Euro Brief: Unready for Blast-off," *The Economist,* November 7, 1998.

Editors, "Widening the European Union—But not too Fast," *The Economist,* November 7, 1998.

"Emerging Market Indicators," *The Economist,* August 15, 1998.

Jeffrey E. Garten, "Why the Global Economy Is Here to Stay," *Business Week,* September 7, 1998.

Robert Grant, *Contemporary Strategy Analysis* (Cambridge, UK: Blackwell Publishers, 1995).

Charles Hampden-Turner, "The Structure of Entrapment: Dilemmas Standing in the Way of Women Managers and Strategies to Resolve These." Paper presented at the Global Business Network Meeting, December 1993, New York.

IBM, "The Challenge—The Euro," www.europe.ibm.com/euro/challeng/index.html.

Jean-Pierre Jeannet and David H. Hennessey, *Global Marketing Strategies* (New York: Houghton Mifflin Company, 1995).

Michelle Krebs, "Behind the Scenes with Chrysler Corporation Chairman Robert Eaton," *Motor Trend,* November 1998.

Hal. B. Lancaster, "Managing Your Career," *The Wall Street Journal,* June 6, 1998.

David Leonhardt, "It Was a Hit in Buenos Aires—So Why not Boise?" *Business Week,* September 7, 1998.

Theodore Levitt, "The Globalization of Markets," *Harvard Business Review,* May–June 1983.

R.F.M. Lubbers, "The Globalization of Economy and Society Online." 3/7/98. Available at www.globalize.org/globview.htm.

Morgan McCall, G. Spreitzer, and J. Mahoney, *Identifying Leadership Potential in Future International Executives: A Learning Resource Guide* (Lexington, MA: International Consortium for Executive Development Research, 1994).

Allen Morrison, Hal B. Gregersen, Hal, B., and J. Stewart Black, "Developing Leaders for the Global Frontier," *Sloan Management Review,* fall 1998.

Kenichi Ohmae, *The Borderless World: Power and Strategy in the Interlinked Economy* (New York: Harper Perennial, 1991).

Kenichi Ohmae, "Managing in a Borderless World," *Harvard Business Review,* May–June 1989.

"On the Edge," *The Economist,* September 5, 1998.

Michael Parfit, "Human Migration," *National Geographic,* October 1998.

John Quelch and Edward Hoff, "Customizing Global Marketing," *Harvard Business Review,* May–June 1986.

Stanley Reed, "We Have Liftoff: The Strong Launch of the Euro Is Hailed Around the World," *Business Week,* January 18, 1999.

Judy W. Richard and Carol D'Amico, *Work Force 2020: Work and Workers in the 21st Century* (Indianapolis, IN: The Hudson Institute, 1997).

Joel L. Swerdlow, "Population," *National Geographic,* October 1998.

Noel M. Tichy, *The Transformational Leader: The Key to Global Competitiveness* (New York: John Wiley & Sons, 1997).

Sun Tzu, *The Art of War.* Translated by Samuel B. Griffith (Oxford, England: Oxford University Press, 1963).

Joan Warner, "The Euro: Are You Ready?" *Business Week,* December 14, 1998.

Michael L. Wheeler, "Global Diversity: Reality, Opportunity and Challenge," *Business Week,* December 1, 1997.

Chapter 4: Competing in the Changing Workplace: Strategy in an Age of Pluralism

Nancy Adler, "Global Leaders: Women Leaders," *Management International Review* 37(1) (special issue, 1997).

"America's Latinos: The Keenest Recruits to the Dream," *The Economist,* April 25, 1998.

Anonymous. "A Little Learning," *The Economist,* December 13, 1997.

Mahlon Apgar, IV, "The Alternative Workplace: Changing Where and How People Work," *Harvard Business Review,* May–June 1998.

Catherine Arnst, "Will the 21st Century Be a Woman's World?" *Business Week,* June 14, 1999.

Aaron Bernstein, "A Human Reason not to Raise Rates," *Business Week,* September 7, 1998.

"The Big Picture," *Business Week,* April 21, 1997.

"The Big Picture: CEOs Are on a White-Knuckle Ride, Too," *Business Week,* November 2, 1998.

Jeffrey H. Birnbaum, "Washington's Second Most Powerful Man," *Fortune,* May 12, 1997.

William Bridges, "The End of the Job," *Fortune,* September 19, 1994.

Peter Burrows, "Dangerous Limbo at Apple," *Business Week,* July 21, 1997.

Peter Burrows and Peter Elstrom, "The Boss," *Business Week,* August 2, 1999.

John A. Byrne, "How Al Dunlap Self-Destructed," *Business Week,* July 6, 1998.

Taylor Cox, Jr., and Stacy Blake, "Managing Cultural Diversity: Implications for Organizational Competitiveness," *The Executive: An Academy of Management Publication,* August 1991.

Laura D'Andrea Tyson, "Why the Wage Gap Just Keeps Getting Bigger," *Business Week,* December 14, 1998.

Kerry A. Dolan, "When Money Isn't Enough," *Forbes,* November 18, 1996.

"Economic Indicators," *The Economist,* September 26, 1998.

Editors, "How Much Is Enough?" *Fast Company,* July–August 1999.

Editors, "Little Things That Mean a Lot," *The Economist,* May 8, 1999.

"Emerging Market Indicators: Women in Politics," *The Economist,* September 26, 1998.

"Finance and Economics: Unproductive Comparison," *The Economist,* August 22, 1998.

Anne Fisher, "So You Lost Your Job? Be Worried—Be Very Worried," *Fortune,* April 28, 1998.

Charles Fishman, "The War for Talent," *Fast Company,* August 1998.

N. Fondas, "The Origins of Feminization," *Academy of Management Review* 22 (1997).

Judith J. Friedman and Nancy DiTomaso, "Myths about Diversity: What Managers Need to Know about Changes in the U.S. Labor Force," *California Management Review* 38(4) (summer 1996).

"Growing Gray Area: Where Blue Meets White Collar," *USA Today,* March 13, 1997.

Keith Hammonds, with Roy Furchgott, Steve Hamm, and Paul C. Judge, "Work and Family," *Business Week,* September 15, 1998.

Charles Hampden-Turner, "The Structure of Entrapment: Dilemmas Standing in the Way of Women Managers and Strategies to Resolve These." Paper presented at the Global Business Network Network Meeting, December 1993, New York.

Barbara Hetzer, "Find a Niche and Start Scratching," *Business Week,* September 14, 1998.

Roy S. Johnson, "The 50 Best Companies for Asians, Blacks & Hispanics," *Fortune,* August 3, 1998.

Daniel Kadlec, "How CEO Pay Got Away," *Time,* April 28, 1997.

Gene Koretz, "Big Spenders and Big Savers," *Business Week,* April 21, 1997.

Gene Koretz, "Economic Trends: Cycles of Death and Rebirth," *Business Week,* November 11, 1998.

Gene Koretz, "Economic Trends: Does Hiring Minorities Hurt?: Affirmative Action and Productivity," *Business Week,* September 14, 1998.

Gene Koretz, "Economic Trends: Job Mobility American Style," *Business Week,* January 27, 1997.

Gene Koretz, "Longer Life for American Men," *Business Week,* November 11, 1996.

Gene Koretz, "Savings' Death Is Exaggerated," *Business Week,* September 14, 1998.

Gene Koretz, "Solving the Savings Riddle," *Business Week,* November 11, 1996.

Gene Koretz, "Startups: Still a Job Engine," *Business Week,* March 24, 1997.

Gene Koretz, "Which Way Are Wages Headed?" *Business Week,* September 21, 1998.

Gene Koretz, "Wives with Fat Paychecks," *Business Week,* September 7, 1998.

David Leonhardt, "Two-Tier Marketing," *Business Week,* March 17, 1997.

Michael Mandel, "Nonstandard Jobs: A New Look," *Business Week,* September 15, 1997.

Michael J. Mandel, *The High Risk Society* (New York: Times Business Books, 1996.)

Mike McNamee, "First Hired, First Fired?" *Business Week,* August 17, 1998.

Robert McNatt, "Up Front: The Big Picture," *Business Week,* December 14, 1998.

Elaine McShulskis, "Child care: Helping the bottom line." *HR Magazine,* June 1996, 24–26.

Betsy Morris, "Is Your Family Wrecking Your Career?" *Fortune,* March 17, 1997.

Kathleen Morris, "You've Come a Long Way Baby," *Business Week,* November 23, 1998.

Ellen Newbourne and Kathleen Kerwin, "Generation Y," *Business Week,* February 15, 1999.

Daniel H. Pink, "Free Agent Nation," *Fast Company,* December–January 1998.

"Qualities MBAs Believe Are Offered by an Ideal Employer," *Fortune,* March 16, 1998.

Jennifer Reingold, "Executive Pay: Special Report," *Business Week,* April 21, 1997.

Edward Robinson and Jonathan Hickman, "The Diversity Elite," *Fortune,* July 19, 1999.

Judy Rosener, *America's Competitive Secret: Utilizing Women* (New York: Oxford University Press, 1995).

Judy Rosener, *America's Competitive Secret: Women Managers* (New York: Oxford University Press, 1997).

Judy Rosener, "The Ways Women Lead," *Harvard Business Review* (November/December 1990).

Richard Sennett, *The Corrosion of Character* (New York: W.W. Norton Co., 1998).

Rod Stodghill, III, "The Coming Bottleneck," *Business Week,* March 24, 1997.

Alex Taylor, III, "Consultants Have a Big People Problem," *Fortune,* April 13, 1998.

"Trend Spotter," *Worth,* May 1997.

"Up Front: The Big Picture," *Business Week,* April 14, 1997.

"Up Front: The Big Picture," *Business Week,* November 10, 1997.

Lixandra Urresta and Jonathan Hickman, "The Diversity Elite," *Fortune,* August 3, 1998.

U.S. Bureau of the Census, *Statistical Abstract of the United States* (Washington, DC: U.S. Government Printing Office, 1997).

U.S. Department of Health and Human Services, "Vital Statistics of the United States, 1992," United States Bureau of the Census; Washington D.C.

Murray Weidenbaum, "The Chinese Family Business Enterprise," *California Management Review* 38(4) (summer 1996).

Michael L. Wheeler, "Global Diversity: Reality, Opportunity, and Challenge," *Business Week,* December 1, 1997.

"Who's Top?" *The Economist,* March 29, 1997.

Clint Willis, "Super Chiefs," *Worth,* September 1997.

Bart Ziegler, "Stop the Presses," *The Wall Street Journal,* April 26, 1995.

Chapter 5: Information Technology: Competing in a Real-Time World

Stephen Baker, Joan Warner, and Heidi Dawley, "Finally Europeans Are Storming the Net," *Business Week,* May 11, 1998.

"The Big Picture," *Business Week,* June 3, 1996.

Jeffrey H. Birnbaum, "Unbelievable! The Mess at the IRS Is Worse than You Think," *Fortune,* April 13, 1998.

Mark Bove, "Advertising and Marketing on the Internet: Rapidly Changing Times." Thesis, University of Southern California, May 1999.

Eryn Brown, "9 Ways to Win on the Web," *Fortune,* May 24, 1999.

Erik Brynjolfsson and Lorin Hitt, "Information Technology as a Factor of Production: The Role of Differences among Firms," *Economic Innovation and New Technology* 3 (1995).

Peter Burrows with Gary McWilliams and Robert D. Hof, "Cheap PCs," *Business Week,* March 23, 1998.

Nanette Byrnes and Paul C. Judge, "Internet Anxiety," *Business Week,* June 28, 1999.

Lisa Chaddron, "How Dell Sells on the Web," *Fast Company,* September 1998.

Alfred D. Chandler, Jr., "The Computer Industry: The First Half-Century." In David B. Yoffie, *Competing in the Age of Digital Convergence* (Boston: Harvard Business School Press, 1997).

"CIO Chooses the 12 CIOs for Their Hall of Fame," *CIO Magazine.* September 15, 1997.

Peter Clemente, *The State of the Net: The New Frontier"* (New York: McGraw-Hill, 1998).

Amy Cortese, "A Census in Cyberspace," *Business Week,* May 5, 1997, 84.

Peter Coy, "You Ain't Seen Nothing Yet," *Business Week,* June 22, 1998.

Mary Cronin, "Ford's Internet Success," *Fortune,* March 30, 1998.

Paul David, "The Dynamo and the Computer: An Historical Perspective on the Modern Productivity Paradox," *American Economic Review,* May 1990.

Deloitte Consulting Group, *1998 Global Survey of Chief Information Executives* (New York: Deloitte Consulting Group, 1998).

Deloitte Consulting Group, *Leading Trends in Information Services: Ninth Annual Survey of North American Chief Information Executives—1997* (New York: Deloitte Consulting Group, 1998).

Robert E. Dvorak, Endre Holen, David Mark, and William F. Meehan, III, "Six Principles of High-Performance IT," *McKinsey Quarterly* 3 (1997).

Editors, "41% of US Online by 2002," *Women's Wear Daily,* February 12, 1999.

Editors, "Information Technology Annual Report," *Business Week,* June 21, 1999.

Editors, "The Net Imperative," *The Economist,* June 26, 1999.

"Emerging Market Trends: Personal Computers," *The Economist,* August 8, 1998.

Ernst & Young, LLP, "The Second Annual Ernst & Young Internet Shopping Study," *Ernst & Young* (1999), www.ey.com.

Peter Fabris, "CIO Hall of Fame: John Cross, Strategic Refiner," *CIO Magazine,* September 15, 1997.

Peter Fabris, "CIO Hall of Fame: Ron J. Ponder, Customer Caretaker," *CIO Magazine,* September 15,1997.

"The Future of Computing: After the PC," *The Economist,* September 13, 1998.

Heather Green and Seanna Browder, "Cyberspace Winners: How They Did It," *Business Week,* June 22, 1998. Shawn Tulley, "How Cisco Mastered the Net," *Fortune,* August 17, 1998, 207.

Heather Green, Gail DeGeorge, and Amy Barrett, "The Virtual Mall Gets Real," *Business Week,* January 26, 1998.

Neil Gross and Ira Sager, "Caution Signs along the Road," *Business Week,* June 22, 1998.

Ronald Henkoff, "A Year of Extraordinary Gains," *Fortune,* April 28, 1998.

Lorin Hitt and Erik Brynjolfsson, "Information Technology and Internal Firm Organization: An Exploratory Analysis," *Journal of Information Management Systems* 14(2) (fall 1997).

Stephen L. Hodgkinson, "IT Structures for the 1990's: Organization of IT Functions in Large Companies," *Information & Management,* 22 (1992).

Robert D. Hof, "Now It's Your Web," *Business Week,* October 5, 1998.

Robert D. Hof with Ellen Neuborne and Heather Green, "Amazon.com: The World of E-commerce," *Business Week,* December 14, 1998.

Robert D. Hof, Gary McWilliams, and Gabrielle Saveri, "The Click Here Economy," *Business Week,* June 22, 1998, 122.

"Is Silicon Valley Happy Valley?" *Business Week,* May 5, 1998, 30.

Paul C. Judge, "Surviving the Age of the Internet," *Business Week,* June 3, 1996.

Daniel Kadlec, "Lunch-Pile Wizards," *Time Digital,* March 23, 1998.

Robert Kuttner, "The U.S. Could Use a Dose of Europe's Privacy Medicine," *Business Week,* November 16, 1998.

Gary McWilliams, "Whirlwind on the Web," *Business Week,* April 7, 1997.

Michael Mische, "Defining Systems Integration." In John Wyzalek, ed., *Systems Integration Success* (New York: Auerbach, 1999).

Michael A. Mische, "The High Performance Information Technology Organization." In Michael A. Mische, ed., *Reengineering Systems Integration Success* (New York: Auerbach, 1998).

Michael A. Mische, ed. *Reengineering Systems Integration Success: Volumes 1 and 2* (New York: Auerabach, 1997 and 1998).

Jeff Moad, "R/3: Little Material Gain for Applied Material," *PC Week,* May 20, 1996.

A. H. Molina, "Current Trends, Issues and Strategies in the Development of the Microprocessor." Working paper no. 42, Programme on Information and Communication Technologies, University of Edinburgh, UK.

"O.K.—But Who Has the Coffee," *Time Digital,* October 5, 1998.

"Paradox Lost," *The Economist,* September 28, 1996.

Robert Ruttmer, "The U.S. Could Use a Dose of Europe's Privacy Medicine," *Business Week,* November 16, 1998.

Ira Sager, with Heather Green, "So Where Are All the Bargains?" *Business Week,* June 22, 1998.

Jude Shiver, Jr., "The New Marketplace," *Los Angeles Times,* September 14, (1997).

Matt Siegel, "Do Computers Slow Us Down?" *Fortune,* March 30, 1998.

Adrian J. Slywotzky, *Value Migration: How to Think Several Moves ahead of the Competition* (Boston: Harvard Business School Press, 1996).

Marcia Stepanek, "Rebirth of a Salesman," *Business Week,* June 22, 1998, 146.

Len Strazewski, "Under Surveillance: Extensive Public Files Spark Privacy Debate," *Government Manager,* April 6, 1992.

Randall E. Stross, "Why Barnes & Noble May Crush Amazon," *Fortune,* September 29, 1997.

"Survey the Millennium Bug," *The Economist,* September 19, 1998, 11.

Wendy Tanaka, "Companies are Learning to Clean Up and Simplify Their On-Line Sites," *San Francisco Chronicle/Examiner,* July 12, 1998.

Don Tapscott, *The Digital Economy* (New York: McGraw-Hill, 1996).

Doug Tsuruoka, "Law, MBA Students Enter Net for Classes," *Investors Business Daily,* September 30, 1998.

Shawn Tulley, "How Cisco Mastered the Net," *Fortune,* August 17, 1998, 207.

"Up Front: The Big Picture," *Business Week,* September 7, 1998.

"Virtual M.B.A," *Information Week,* November 14, 1994.

Tom Wailgum, "CIO Hall of Fame: Donald R. Lasher, General Partner," *CIO Magazine,* September 15, 1997.

"Weighting the Case for the Network Computer," *The Economist,* January 18, 1997.

Ron Winslow and George Anders, "How New Technology Was Oxford's Nemesis," *The Wall Street Journal,* December 11, 1997.

David B. Yoffie, *Competing in the Age of Digital Convergence* (Boston: Harvard Business School Press, 1997).

Chapter 6: Innovation: The Engine of Continuous Renewal

William J. Abernathy, *The Productivity Dilemma: Roadblock to Innovation in the Automobile Industry* (Baltimore: Johns Hopkins University Press, 1978).

Allan N. Afuah and Nik Bahram, "The Hypercube of Innovation," *Research Policy* 24 (1995): 51–76.

Teresa M. Amabile, "Motivating Creativity in Organizations: On Doing What You Love and Loving What You Do," *California Management Review* (fall 1997).

Susan Athey and Armin Schmutzler, "Product and Process Flexibility in an Innovative Environment," *Rand Journal of Economics,* Vol. 26, No. 4 (Winter 1995).

Michael Barrier, "Innovation as a Way of Life," *Nation's Business,* July 1994.

Frederick D. Buggie, "Expert Innovation Teams: A New Way to Increase Productivity Dramatically," *Harvard Business Review,* July–August 1995.

Clayton M. Christensen, *Innovation and the General Manager* (New York: Irwin and McGraw-Hill, 1999).

Clayton M. Christensen, *The Innovator's Dilemma* (New York: Irwin and McGraw-Hill, 1997).

Kim B. Clark and Steven C. Wheelwright, *The Product Development Challenge* (Boston: Harvard Business Books, 1994).

Mihaly Csikszentmihalyi, "Happiness and Creativity," *The Futurist,* September–October 1997.

Anne Cummings and Greg R. Oldham, "Enhancing Creativity: Managing Work Context for the High Potential Employee," *California Management Review,* fall 1997.

Thomas H. Davenport, *Process Innovation: Reengineering Work through Information Technology*

(Boston: Harvard Business School Press, 1993).

George S. Day, Bela Gold, and Thomas D. Kuezmarski, "Significant Issues for the Future of Product Innovation," *Journal of Production and Innovation Management,* 1994.

Peter F. Drucker, *Managing for the Future: The 1990s and Beyond* (New York: Dutton, 1992).

Editors, "100 Years of Innovation," *Time,* summer 1999.

Edward de Bono, *Lateral Thinking* (New York: Harper & Row, 1970).

"The E-volution of Big Business," *Fortune,* November 8, 1999.

Richard N. Foster, *Innovation: The Attacker's Advantage* (Summit Books, Oklahoma City, OK, 1986).

Gerald E. Fryxell, William Q. Judge, and Robert S. Dooley, "The New Task of R&D Management: Creating Goal Directed Communities for Innovation," *California Management Review,* spring 1997.

Janet Ginsburg and Kathleen Morris, "Xtreme Retailing," *Business Week,* December 20, 1999.

Peter C. Grindley and David Teece, "Managing Intellectual Capital: Licensing and Cross-Licensing in Semiconductors and Electronics," *California Management Review,* winter 1997.

Lisa K. Gundry, Jill R. Kickul and Charles W. Prather, "Building the Creative Organization," *Organizational Dynamics* 22 (4), 22–37, (1994).

Gary Hamel and C.K. Prahalad, *Competing for the Future* (Boston: Harvard Business School Press, 1994).

Rebecca Henderson, "Managing Innovation in the Information Age," *Harvard Business Review,* January–February 1994.

James M. Higgins, *Innovate or Evaporate* (Winter Park, FL: The New Management Publishing Company, 1995).

Jerry Hirshberg, *The Creative Priority: Driving Innovative Business in the Real World* (New York: HarperCollins, 1998).

Robert D. Hof, "A New Era of Bright Hopes and Terrible Fears," *Business Week,* October 4, 1999.

Robert J. Holder and Ned Hamson, "Requisite for Future Success . . . Discontinuous Innovation," *Journal for Quality and Participation,* September 1995.

G. David Hughes and Don C. Chafin, "Turning New Product Development into a Continuous Learning Process," address correspondence to G. David Hughes, Kenan-Flagler School of Business, University of North Carolina, 1996.

Rajan R. Kamathe and Jeffrey K. Liker, "A Second Look at Japanese Product Development," *Harvard Business Review,* November–December 1994.

John Kao, "The Heart of Creativity," *Across the Board* (New York: 1996).

M.J. Kirton, *Adaptors and Innovators: Styles of Creativity and Problem Solving* (Routledge, New York, NY: 1989).

Arthur Koestler, *Act of Creation* (New York: Viking Penguin, 1990).

Dorothy Leonard-Barton, *The Wellsprings of Knowledge* (Cambridge, MA: Harvard Business School Press, 1995).

Gary S. Lynn, *Organizational Team Learning for Really New Product Development* (Cambridge, MA: MSI, 1997).

Gary S. Lynn, Joseph G. Morone, and Albert S. Paulson, "Marketing and Discontinuous Innovation: The Probe and Learn Process," *California Management Review,* spring 1996.

Michael J. Mandel, "The Internet Economy: The World's Next Growth Engine," *Business Week,* October 4, 1999.

Charlan Jeanne Nemeth, "Managing Innovation: When Less is More," *California Management Review,* fall 1997.

William Pullen, "Strategic Shocks: Managing Discontinuous Change," *International Journal of Public Sector Management* 6(1) (1993).

Nathan Rosenberg, *Paths of Innovation* (New York: Cambridge University Press, 1998).

Richard S. Rosenbloom and William J. Spencer, eds., *Engines of Innovation* (Boston: Harvard University Press, 1996).

Joseph Schumpeter, *Business Cycles: A Theoretical, Historical, and Statistical Analysis of the Capitalist Process* (New York: McGraw-Hill, 1939).

Joseph A. Schumpeter, *Essays: On Entrepreneurs, Innovation, Business Cycles, and the Evolution of Capitalism* (New Brunswick, NJ: Transaction Publishers, 1989).

Carol Steiner, "A Philosophy for Innovation: The Role of Unconventional Individuals in Innovation Success," *Journal of Production and Innovation Management,* 1995.

Robert J. Sternberg and Janet Davidson, *Nature of Insight* (Cambridge, MA: MIT Press, 1996).

Robert J. Sternberg and Todd I. Lubart, "Creating Creative Minds," *Phi Delta Kappa* (Bloomington: 1991).

Stefan Thomke and Donald Reinertsen, "Agile Product Development: Managing Development Flexibility in Uncertain Environments," *California Management Review,* fall 1998.

Michael L. Tushman and Johann Peter Murmann, "Dominant Designs, Technology Cycles and Organizational Outcomes," *Research in Organizational Behavior* 20 (1998).

Michael L. Tushman and Charles A. O'Reilly, "The Ambidextrous Organization: Managing Evolutionary and Revolutionary Change," *California Management Review,* summer 1998.

James M. Utterback, *Mastering the Dynamics of Innovation: How Companies Can Seize Opportunities in the Face of Technological Change* (Boston: Harvard Business School Press, 1994).

James M. Utterback and William Abernathy, "A Dynamic Model of Process and Product Innovation," *International Journal of Management Science* 3(6) (1975): 639–656.

James M. Utterback and Fernando F. Suarez, "Innovation, Competition and Industry Structure," *Research Policy* 22 (1993):1–21.

Mary Walton, *Car: A Drama of the American Workplace* (W.W. Norton & Co., 1999).

Chapter 7: Knowledge: The Essence of Competitive Advantage

"Andersen's Androids," *The Economist,* May 5, 1996.

Warren Bennis and Patricia Ward Biederman, *Organizing Genius: The Secrets of Creative Collaboration* (Reading, MA: Addison-Wesley, 1997).

Sarah Cliffe, "Briefings from the Editors: Knowledge Management—The Well Connected Business," *Harvard Business Review,* July–August 1998.

Stan Crock, "They Snoop to Conquer," *Business Week,* October 28, 1996.

Tom Cummings and William Snyder, "Organization Learning Disorders: Conceptual Model and Intervention Hypotheses," *Journal of Human Relation,* 51(7) (1998).

Thomas Davenport and Larry Prusak, *Working Knowledge: How Organizations Manage What They Know* (Boston: Harvard Business School Press, 1998).

Max DePree, *Leadership Is an Art* (New York: Dell, 1989).

Peter Drucker, "The Age of Social Transformation," *The Atlantic Monthly,* November 1994.

Peter Drucker, "The Network Society," *The Wall Street Journal,* March 29, 1995.

Bob Guns, *Faster Learning Organizations* (San Francisco: Jossey-Bass, 1995).

Gary Hamel and C.K. Parhalad, *Competing for the Future* (Boston: Harvard Business School Press, 1994).

Morten T. Hansen, Nitin Nohria, and Thomas Tierney, "What's Your Strategy for Managing Knowledge?" *Harvard Business Review,* March–April 1999.

Justin Hibbard, "Knowing What We Know," *Information Week,* October 20, 1997.

Justin Hibbard and Karen M. Carrillo, "Knowledge Revolution," *Information Week,* January 5, 1998.

Gina Imperato, "Intelligence–Get Smart," *Fast Company,* April–May 1998.

Andrew C. Inkpen, "Creating Knowledge through Collaboration," *California Management Review,* fall 1996.

"In the 90's, Knowledge is Power," *Miami Herald,* May 20, 1996.

Larry Kahaner, *Competitive Intelligence: From Black Ops to Boardrooms— How Businesses Gather, Analyze and Use Information to Succeed in the Global Marketplace* (New York: Simon & Schuster, 1996).

Peter H. Kim, "When What You Know Can Hurt You: A Study of Experiential Effects on Group Discussion and Performance," *Academic Press,* 1997.

Hal Lancaster, "Managing Your Career," *The Wall Street Journal,* December 1997.

Dorothy Leonard-Barton, *The Wellsprings of Knowledge"* (Cambridge, MA: Harvard Business School Press, 1995).

Gary S. Lynn, "New Product Team Learning: Developing and Profiting from Your Knowledge Capital," *California Management Review* 40(4) (summer 1998).

"Management Consultancy: The Advice Business," *The Economist,* March 22, 1997.

Brook Manville, "What's the 'Management' in Knowledge Management?" Paper presented at the *Knowledge Management Conference,* June, 1998, Boston, MA.

J. G. March and J. P. Olson, "The Uncertainty of the Past: Organizational Learning under Ambiguity," *European Journal of Political Research,* 1975.

Jenny C. McCune, "Thirst for Knowledge," *Management Review,* April 1999.

M. E. McGill and J. W. Slocum, *The Smarter Organization* (New York: John Wiley, 1994).

Katherine Mieszkowski, "Report from the Future: Opposites Attract," *Fast Company,* December–January, 1998.

Henry Mintzberg, "Reply to Michael Goold," *Harvard Business Review* 38(4) (summer 1996).

Henry Mintzberg, Bruce Ahlstrand, and Joseph Lampel, *Strategy Safari: A Guided Tour through the Wilds of Strategic Thinking* (New York: The Free Press, 1998).

Henry Mintzberg and J. A. Waters, "Of Strategies, Deliberate and Emergent," *Strategic Management Journal* 1985.

Ikujiro Nonaka and Hiro Takeuchi, *The Knowledge-Creating Company: How Japanese Companies Create the Dynamics of Innovation* (New York: Oxford University Press, 1995).

Tom Peters, "Sharing Knowledge," *Executive Excellence,* December 1995.

Peter Senge, *The Fifth Discipline: The Art and Practice of the Learning Organization* (New York: Doubleday, 1990).

Thomas Stewart, "Brain Power: Who Owns It … How They Profit from It," *Fortune,* March 17, 1997.

Thomas Stewart, *Intellectual Capital* (New York: Doubleday/Currency, 1997).

Rhoda Thomas Tripp, *The International Thesaurus of Quotations* (New York: Harper & Row, 1970).

Dave Ulrich, "Intellectual Capital = Competency × Commitment," *Sloan Management Review* 39(2) (winter 1998).

"The Unlearning Organization," *Organizational Dynamics,* autumn 1997.

Lousia Wah, "Behind the Buzz," *Management Review,* April 1999.

Mark Wain and Gary Chau, "Corporate Scale Knowledge Valuation." Thesis, University of Southern California, May 1999.

Chapter 8: Strategic Leadership: The Core Competency for High Performance

Nancy Adler, "Global Leadership: Women Leaders," *Management International Review* 37(1) (special issue, 1997).

Warren Bennis, *On Becoming a Leader* (New York: Addison-Wesley, 1989).

Warren Bennis and Burt Nanus, *Leaders: The Strategies for Taking Charge* (New York: Harper & Row, 1985).

Warren Bennis and Patricia Ward Biederman, *Organizing Genius: The Secrets of Creative Collaboration* (Reading, MA: Addison-Wesley, 1997).

"The Best of Herb Kelleher," *Your Company,* August–September 1998.

"The Big Picture," *Business Week,* October 26, 1998.

"Blind Ambition," *Business Week,* October 23, 1995.

John MacGregor Burns, *Leadership* (New York: Knopf, 1991).

Nanette Byrnes, Richard Melcher, and Debra Sparks, "Earnings Hocus-Pocus: How Companies Come up with the Numbers They Want," *Business Week,* October 5, 1998.

Richard M. Cyert and James G. March, *A Behavioral Theory of the Firm* (Blackwell Publishing, Oxford, UK 1992).

Gail DeGeorge, "Al Dunlap Revs His Chain Saw," *Business Week,* November 25, 1996.

Howard Gardner, *Leading Minds: An Anatomy of Leadership* (New York: Basic Books, 1995).

Daniel Goleman, *Emotional Intelligence* (New York: Bantam, 1995).

Daniel Goleman, "What Makes a Leader?" *Harvard Business Review,* November–December 1998.

Daniel Goleman, *Working with Emotional Intelligence* (New York: Bantam, 1998).

R. Heifetz, *Leadership without Easy Answers* (Cambridge, MA: Harvard University Press, 1994).

Richard Hodgetts, "A Conversation with Warren Bennis in the Midst of Downsizing," *Organizational Dynamics,* summer 1996.

David Kirkpatrick, "Intel's Amazing Profit Machine," *Fortune,* February 17, 1997.

Michelle Krebs, "Behind the Scenes with Chrysler Corporation Chairman Robert Eaton," *Motor Trend,* November 1998.

Mark Maremont, "Judgment Day at Bausch & Lomb," *Business Week,* December 25, 1995.

Richard Melcher, "Where Are the Accountants?" *Business Week,* October 5, 1998.

Henry Minzberg, "Covert Leadership: Notes on Managing Professionals," *Harvard Business Review,* November–December, 1998.

James Brian Quinn, Philip Anderson, and Sydney Finkelstein, "Managing Professional Intellect: Making the Most of the Best," *Harvard Business Review,* March–April 1996.

Joshua Cooper Ramo, "Man of the Year: A Survivor's Tale," *Time,* December 27, 1997.

Robert B. Reich, "The New Meaning of Corporate Social Responsibility,"

California Management Review 40(2) (winter 1998).

Andy Reinhardt with Ira Ager and Peter Burrows, "Intel: Can Andy Grove Keep Profits Up in an Era of Cheap PCs?" *Business Week,* December 22, 1997.

Edward A. Robinson, "America's Most Admired Companies," *Fortune,* March 3, 1997.

Judy Rosener, *America's Competitive Secret: Women Managers* (New York: Oxford University Press, 1997).

Judy Rosener, *America's Competitive Secret: Utilizing Women* (New York: Oxford University Press, 1995).

Judy Rosener, "The Ways Women Lead," *Harvard Business Review,* 1990.

Richard Sennett, *The Corrision of Character* (New York: W.W. Norton, 1998).

Robert Simons and Antonio Davila, "How High Is Your Return on Management?" *Harvard Business Review,* January–February, 1998.

Thomas A. Stewart, "Why Value Statements Don't Work," *Fortune,* June 10, 1996.

James Waldrop and Timothy Butler, "The Executive as Coach," *Harvard Business Review,* November–December 1996.

Clint Willis, "Super Chiefs: Corporate Leaders Who Are Making Their Companies Great—and Shareholders Rich," *Worth,* September 1997.

John Wooden, with Steve Jamison, *Wooden: A Lifetime of Observations and Reflections on and off the Court* (Lincolnwood, IL: Contemporary Books, 1997).

Chapter 9: Operational Excellence and Organizational Agility: Sustaining Continuous Renewal and High Performance

Gene Bylinski, "The Digital Factory," Fortune, November 14, 1994

James Carbone, "Chrysler Expects $1 Billion in Cost Reduction from Suppliers," Automotive/OEM News, April 11, 1996.

Subrata N. Chakravarty, "A Tale of Two Companies," Forbes, May 27, 1991.

Claudia Coates, "Locomotive Industry Again Building Steam. DH: Transportation: Worldwide demand rises. Some nations are refurbishing old engines. In the U.S., railroads aim to better compete with trucks," Los Angeles Times, September 22, 1996.

Peter Coy, "Exploiting Uncertainty," *Business Week,* June 7, 1999.

Rick Dove, "Who Is the Agilest of Them All?" Automotive Production, August 1996.

Jeffrey Dyer, "How Chrysler Created an American Keiretsu," Harvard Business Review, July–August 1996.

Editors, "The Baldrige's Other Reward," *Business Week,* March 10, 1999.

Charles H. Fine, *Clockspeed* (New York: Perseus Books, 1999).

Warren Hersch, "The Transportation Industry: A Hotbed of Wireless Activity," Wireless, September 1996.

Sidney Hill, "Robots Are Back," Manufacturing Systems, March 1995.

Richard M. Hodgetts, "A Conversation with Warren Bennis on Leadership in the Midst of Downsizing," Organizational Dynamics, Summer 1996.

David Kirkpatrick, "Intel's Amazing Profit Machine," Fortune, February 17, 1997.

Christian Koffmann interview, worldwide chairman of the Consumer & Personal Care Group at Johnson & Johnson, "The Changing Concept of Power," Upfront, Spring 1996 (Volume 2, Number 1). [Internal J&J Newsletter].

"Locomotives Keep Lead on Competition, Erie Plant in Right Position to Meet Worldwide Demand," Transportation News, July 29, 1996.

Dyan Machan, "Blowing Bubbles," Forbes, April 21, 1997.

Jeremy Main, "Is the Baldrige Overblown?" *Fortune,* July 1, 1991.

Michael A. Mische, *"The Comprehensive Guide to Reengineering"* (San Francisco: Jossey-Bass, 1997).

David A. Nadler, Marc S. Gerstein, and Robert B. Shaw, *Organizational Architecture: Designs for Changing Organizations* (San Francisco: Jossey-Bass, 1992).

NIST, "Quality Stocks Yield Big Payoff," *National Institute of Standards and Technology,* Technology Administration, U.S. Department of Commerce (February, 1996).

On the Mark, "Ten Years of Excellence," http://www.miep.org/mqc/news/otm/firstquarter_98/tenyears.html.

Nandini Rajagopalan and Gretchen M. Spreitzer, "Towards a Theory of Strategic Change: A Multi-lens Perspective and Integrative Framework." Academy of Management Review, January 1997; 22 (1); 48–79.

Howard Rudnitsky, "One Hundred Sixty Companies for the Price of One," Forbes, March 1996.

Vikram Sethi and William R. King. Organizational Transformation through Business Process Reengineering. (Upper Saddle River, NJ: Prentice Hall, 1998).

Lester C. Thurow, Head to Head: The Coming Economic Battle among Japan, Europe, and America, Vol. 1 (Warner Books, Inc., May 1993).

Manny Ventura, system design analyst, United Airlines, Opetext Website.

M. Mitchell Waldrop, "The Trillion-Dollar Vision of Dee Hock," Fast Company, October 1996.

Dorine C. Andrews and Susan K. Stalick, *Business Reengineering: The Survival Guide* (Upper Saddle River, NJ: Prentice Hall, 1994).

Edward Bowman and Bruce Kogut, *Redesigning the Firm* (New York: Oxford University Press, 1995).

Adam M. Bradenburger and Barry J. Nalebuff, *Co-opetition* (New York: Currency Doubleday, 1996).

Sayan Chatterjee, "Delivering Outcomes Efficiently: The Creative Key to Competitive Strategy," *California Management Review,* winter 1998.

Ty Choi, "Conceptualizing Continuous Improvement: Implications for Organizational Change," *Journal of Management Science* 23(6) (1995).

Thomas H. Davenport, *Process Innovation: Reengineering Work through Information Technology* (Boston: Harvard Business School Press, 1993).

James Martin, *The Great Transition: Using the Disciplines of Enterprising to Align People, Technology and Strategy* (New York: Amacom, 1995).

Robert Miles, *Leading Corporate Transformation* (San Francisco: Jossey-Bass, 1997).

Daniel P. Petrozzo and John C. Stepper, *Successful Reengineering* (New York: Van Nostrand Reinhold, 1994).

James Brian Quinn, "Strategic Outsourcing: Leveraging Knowledge Capabilities," *Sloan Management Review,* summer 1999.

Robert M. Tomasko, *Rethinking the Corporation* (New York: Amacom, 1993).

Chapter 10: Business Integration: Architecting the Organization for High Performance

Index